*Class, Democracy,
and Labor in*

Contemporary Argentina

Class, Democracy,
and Labor in
*Contemporary
Argentina*

Peter Ranis

with a new introduction by the author

Transaction Publishers
New Brunswick (U.S.A.) and London (U.K.)

New material this edition copyright © 1995 by Transaction Publishers, New Brunswick, New Jersey 08903. Originally published in 1992 by University of Pittsburgh Press.

Library of Congress Catalog Number: 94-26252
ISBN: 1-56000-775-3
Printed in the United States of America

Library of Congress Cataloging-in-Publication Data

Ranis, Peter
    Class, democracy, and labor in contemporary Argentina / Peter Ranis ; with a new introduction by the author.
        p. cm.
    Rev. ed. of : Argentine workers. 1992.
    Includes bibliographical references and index.
    ISBN 1-56000-775-3
    1. Working class—Argentina—Attitudes. 2. Trade-unions—Argentina.
3. Peronism. I. Ranis, Peter, 1935–   Argentine workers. II. Title.
HD8266.5.R36 1994
322'.2'0982—dc20   94-26252
                                                                      CIP

To the Argentine workers
who give much more than they get

Contents

Introduction to the Transaction Edition

The New Menem Peronism: A Democratic Consolidation

A Historical Departure

Contemporary Argentina must be seen from the vantage point of a succession of governmental experiments each substantially flawed both institutionally and/or economically. This history included successive periods of "stürm und drang" of oligarchic rule of the 1930s followed by the populist personalist regime of Juan Perón and then weak civil governments hemmed in by corporate military and business interests and occasionally unyielding union leadership. Lastly, the increasingly authoritarian military governments provided a final backdrop to the initiation of a palpable and self-conscious democracy under Radical party (UCR) president Raúl Alfonsín in 1983. The orderly succession of another elected civilian president, Peronist party (PJ) leader Carlos Menem in 1989, gives pause for expressions of hope if not outright celebration.

The Alfonsín government has to be commended for pursuing democratic institutionalization, for defending civil government, and for maintaining a significant role for not only the nonexecutive branches of government but also for protecting basic civil liberties despite an increasingly desperate economic situation.

As Argentina enters its second decade of democracy, there is good reason to recall dictatorships, personalist regimes, military repressions and intrusions, disappearances of citizens, severe economic dislocations and a multitude of civic vices and individual shortcomings. And while it is too early to speak unequivocally of a promising democratic civility, it is evident that Argentina has achieved a level of economic and political stability in spite of years of false starts and multiple retreats.

My research on Argentine workers attempts to explain what organized workers, who earn a living daily, say about the specific time they are living in, the place in which they work, and the societal conditions they face and to which they react. It also aims to give support to an evaluation of the current Argentine democracy which sees that the Menem presidency, in all likelihood a two-term administration, promises to be the most dramatic and radical "sea change" in contemporary Argentine history.

As Perón, in 1946, made a significant qualitative change from the military junta's oligarchic antecedents by incorporating the working class into a newly expanded state role in the economy, then increasingly popular in postwar Europe and the United States, so Menem has engineered another equally profound historical shift from that earlier state-centered corporative-populist orientation to a neoliberal model, again in evidence throughout the world's economies. Menem's government provides a synthesis, a closure of sorts of previous conflictual, zero-sum approaches that preceded his economic stabilization and state privatization policies. The popular base of Peronism held its breath not knowing what to make of this dramatic turnaround, while the business sectors were more than astounded—and so a veritable ideological cease-fire sunk in and allowed for critical state, economic, and financial reforms to take hold. As a result, Menem's government has produced a symmetrical cultural orientation that has depoliticized, de-ideologized Argentine politics for a sufficient number of years for the Menem revolution to take hold and achieve undeniable results.

The personal popularity of Menem, consecutive Menemist/Peronist presidential and legislative victories in 1989, 1991, and 1993, the speed of the economic reforms via laws and decrees, coupled with the inability of the Argentine labor confederation (CGT) to respond collectively, provided the necessary breach and veritable armistice that allowed this new entrepreneurial, capitalist mentality to take hold, sink in, and actually mature. What has not been significantly emphasized, however, is that the Argentine working class, as analyzed in this study, has been predisposed to many of the Menem initiatives, certainly since the onset of democracy, and they have been clearly committed to a democratic capitalist culture, even though their union leaders were at first much more ambivalent.

Menem has seized the moment in clear terms and has been able to fill an economic, political, and ideological vacuum. There is no credible political party alternative in the Radicals, who, after all, attempted to move in the very same economic direction in the mid-1980s and were rewarded by the workers in their electoral support in 1983 and 1985. Thus, now they confront contemporary Menemism only on the edges of a necessary democratic critique. The military lacks any credibility in terms of undertaking economic reforms, not to speak of providing responsible democratic leadership. And the business community, both domestic and transnational, observes from a position of support and wonderment. In the past, presidents Perón and Alfonsín had chosen party stalwarts to develop their economic programs, while the military presidents, Ongania and Videla had chosen fellow Catholic and liberal advisors to generate their economic initiatives (Erro 1993, 199). The Menem government is the first administration in modern times to explicitly choose its economic direction from ideological/philosophical positions distinct from its own historical trajectory.

The Neoliberal Economic Revolution

The new neoliberal meaning for Argentina's society is little short of profound in its structural and policy implications. It represents, first and foremost, the stabilization of the Argentine fiscal and monetary system and the abrogation of decades-long uncertainty about the viability of the Argentine currency, the shrinkage of state responsibilities and functions, a demonopolization in theory and practice of the state's role in industrial development and the provision of utilities. It constitutes the liberalization of the costs of doing business through a dismantling of the scores of regulations, permits, and licenses that have inhibited and retarded economic operations. For example, there were stamp taxes covering all kinds of financial transactions such as credit agreements, letters of exchange, insurance and rental contracts, and mortgages that have been repealed. It will lead to the restructuring of labor-management relationships including a revision of social security and social welfare networks. And finally it marks an aggressive new attempt to insert Argentine exports into an increasingly competitive international economy.

The old system proved no longer capable of meeting the rigors and requirements not only of a democratic polity but also of a creative political economy. When Eric Hobsbawm, lecturing at the University of Budapest, discussed why Communism had come to an end, he could well have been speaking of a bygone Argentina. He said,

> The system broke down because economically the system became increasingly rigid and unworkable and especially because it proved virtually incapable of generating or making economic use of innovation, quite apart from stifling intellectual originality. Moreover, it became impossible to hide the fact from the local population that other countries had made far more material progress than the socialist ones. If you prefer putting it another way, it broke down because ordinary citizens were indifferent or hostile, and because the regimes themselves had lost faith in what they were pretending to do. (Hobsbawm 1993, 62)

As Perón originally appealed to workers as class collaborators with national capital, as Alfonsín appealed to workers as democratic citizens, so Menem appeals to workers as both autonomous and entrepreneurial. These appeals are historically driven and obey the cumulative experience of the Argentine working class as depicted in this study. However, distinct from the relationships between leader and the mass of the working class developed in the past, the reforms undertaken by Menem seem almost irreversible. The extent and depth of the economic changes cannot easily be altered, and it is this finality that makes the Menem revolution so powerful and fundamental. The changes have been so deepseated that Saúl Ubaldini, the ex-secretary general of the CGT and leader of a new militant splinter labor group within the CGT, the Movimiento de Trabajadores Argentinos (MTA), was quoted as saying, "The daily struggle is what we go out to defend each day. Revolution isn't shooting bullets but adapting oneself to evolution" (*La Capital*, February 7, 1994).

The Menem multiclass appeal rests easily within the ideological framework of early and mature Peronism, each obeying the pragmatic dictates of the time. But the Menem coalition is broader even than the Perón coalitions of 1945 and 1973, subsuming as it does almost every societal sector and interest. In 1945, Perón initiated an anti-oligarchic, national sectoral alliance, in 1973 an anti-military, multiclass alliance. In the 1990s Menem has mounted another multiclass alliance against public and private bureaucracies and a corporate-protectionist economy. The earlier Peronist coalitions produced opposition from various sectors of society including the agrarian, multinational business, church, and military and conservative and center-liberal party interests. None of these interests has had definable alternative programs to Menem's projects since 1990.

We have seen a new ideological coalition in formation after the failed Austral reform attempts of 1985 and through the Convertibility Law of 1991 and its implementation. The results of the elections of 1985, 1987, 1989, 1991, and 1993 all give credence to a new Argentine vital political center. The first election result showed voters in favor of Alfonist economic stabilization and the subsequent elections have shown them either against hyperinflation or for Menemist economic stabilization. Under both Alfonsín and Menem economic stabilization, price stability, export orientation, balance of payment controls, debt rescheduling, and higher savings index were on the policy agenda. However, what was sought in a preliminary way by the Alfonsín administration, faced as it was by an oppositionist Peronist leadership still convinced of the utility and viability of populism and corporatism, Menem was able to carry out in no uncertain terms due to significant changes in both the domestic and international conditions.

The old corporate nexus among business, the agrarian interests, the military, and the CGT has been undermined by a more pluralistic, autonomous bargaining type of political system with the government playing a critical leadership role but allowing the society to create its own space. Not only do we perceive a stimulus to venture capital, whether big or small, but a new arena for a postpopulist political dialogue that rejects no novel approaches to the political dialogue.

Critical for the essential restructuring of the Argentine economy was the hyperinflationary pressures that accompanied the election of Menem in 1989. Because of this there was overwhelming immediate support for the first two important pieces of legislation: the State Reform Law and the Law of Economic Emergency. These pieces of legislation were predicated on stabilizing the economy, radically reforming the monetary and fiscal policy, privatizing deficient and inefficient state enterprises, ending subsidies to the business sector and holding wages in line with productivity increases.

The fiscal reforms were solidified with the implementation of the Convertibility Law of April 1991, launched by economics minister Domingo Cavallo. This measure has been an astounding success. It has essentially allowed the peso to be freely converted to the dollar by committing the Central Bank to sell dollars whenever the dollar threatens to exceed the 1:1 value established in April 1991. No fixed term deposits of less than thirty days are allowed (weekly rates were the norm in inflationary times), savings accounts holders are no longer restricted to a fixed number of account withdrawals (they had been restricted to five a month), and there is no borrowing ceiling for small and medium-sized companies. The inflationary rate of 1990, which stood at 1,343 percent, was trimmed to 84 percent by 1991, and 18 percent by 1992. In August 1993, for the first time in twenty years, inflation stood at 0 percent (*Latin American Weekly Report [LAWR]* October 14, 1993). Since then there have even been monthly negative inflation rates so that the 1993 rate of inflation fell to an astounding, by Argentine standards, 6.8 percent while wholesale prices actually fell by 0.8 percent in 1993 (*Página/12*, February 1, 1994). Estimates are for an inflationary rate of only 4 percent for 1994 (*Ambito Financiero*, February 22, 1994).

At the same time state revenues have reached a historic high of 24 percent of GNP (*Argentina: From Insolvency to Growth* [hereafter World Bank], xiii). There has been a virtual upheaval in the government's tax collection abilities with dramatic increases in receipts from income, value added (IVA), and social security taxes (garnered by an army of new tax-collecting agents),[1] while export and import taxes have markedly decreased, transaction taxes on doing business have ended and the ubiquitous hidden tax of inflation has all but disappeared. These changes were coupled with the reduction of administrative expenditures due to the sale of state enterprises and the obvious reduction of state subsidies and the virtual abolition of deficit spending by the federal government. It is interesting to note as well that defense spending has fallen from 17.5 percent of the federal budget in 1988 to 10.2 percent in 1992 and from 6 percent of GNP to less than 2 percent of GNP (World Bank, xi, xix, 95; Fundación Mediterránea, December 1993, 6). Understandably tax revenues have increased from 15.7 percent of GNP in 1983 to 23.8 percent in 1992 and savings from –8.8 to 2.1 percent (World Bank, 7).[2]

The economic growth rate has also been very successful since 1991, increasing by 8.9 percent that year, 8.7 percent in 1992, and 7.6 percent in 1993. Estimates for 1994 are around 5 percent *(Economist Intelligence Unit Country Report: Argentina*

1994). Overall industrial production has increased by 40 percent since the Cavallo Convertibility plan was established in April 1991 (*La Prensa,* January 25, 1994).[3] The export sector has made modest gains despite the high value of the Argentine peso, a miracle in itself. GATT tariff reductions have helped Argentine exports, particularly strong have been traditional Argentine agricultural exports such as wheat, soy, meat, corn, vegetable oils, hides, cheese, and juices. More important for Argentina's insertion into not only Mercosur but the international markets generally is its 1993 22 percent growth over 1992 in industrial manufactured goods.

At the same time lower import tariffs and the relative strength of the peso have resulted in 1 billion more spent on imports in 1993 than in 1992. What is more encouraging is that $900,000 was spent on capital goods imports. The balance was spent on consumer imports, which have been made available to the average consumer as never before, including former luxuries such as automobiles, video cassette recorders, compact disk players, and microwaves. Meanwhile, privatization of utilities has noticeably expanded telephone, gas, water, electricity, and suburban travel services.

One of the most significant economic undertakings in Argentina has been the radical form that its privatization of state enterprises has taken. The Cavallo-Menem initiatives has sought to supersede the venerable Argentine contradiction of a state heavily into production, which at the same time has had little strength and ability to collect revenues and maintain fiscal stability and monetary controls. In the past inflationary spending and fiscal printing led to a series of uncontrollable hyperinflationary periods (not unique to Argentina, of course), which were certainly more devastating and disconcerting than in previous nondemocratic administrations and reached the highest absolute numbers in the late Alfonsín and early Menem administrations.

By the late 1980s therefore there was almost unanimity concerning the dereliction surrounding the provision of public services in the state enterprise sector. Much of the fault lay with the constant political changes that had forced personnel changes in both the directorships and administrators in almost all the public enterprises. As a result there was little policy continuity (Senén Gonzalez and Ximenez Sáez 1993, 2-3). Chronic crises occurred in the state companies' external indebtedness, budgetary insolvency, and general inefficiency. Specifically, the state companies were poor managers of resources and providing social and human services and generally neglected consumer preferences. The market did not act as a regulator and this often resulted in the state enterprises overinvesting in some areas and underinvesting in others (Bouzas 1993, Sguiglia and Delgado 1993).

The most successful privatizations have taken place in the state sector, including, most importantly, telephone, electricity, gas, water, petroleum. Major multinationals have associated themselves with powerful Argentine industrialists, complemented by international and domestic banking interests. Foreign interests have acted as technical specialists while Argentine industrialists contribute the administrative and institutional expertise. Since most of these utilities are traditional monopolies, access, commercialization, and generous profits are probably guaranteed, especially given the pent-up consumer demand evident in a postindustrial society such as Argentina.

One buyout of ENTEL (the previous state telephone company) is illustrative of the complex intermingling of multinationals and domestic enterprises. The company was divided into two regional companies with the shares distributed 50:50. One half of the new conglomerate called Telefónica has shares distributed among Citycorp (20 percent), Pérez Companc (15 percent), and the Spanish Telefónica (10 percent) and the rest are held by a series of local and international banking and industrial interests. The other half of the company is called Telecom and its shares are held by the French Cable et Radio (33 percent) and the Italian Stet (33 percent), Pérez Companc (25 percent), and J.P. Morgan Bank (10 percent) (Kosacoff and Bezchinsky 1993, 258–69). Among the domestic and foreign corporations who control newly privatized state assets, Argentine capital leads the way with 40 percent followed by Spain (15 percent), United States (12 percent), Italy (9 percent), France (7 percent), and Chile (6 percent) (Fundación Mediterránea, December 1993).

The prime negative outcomes of generally positive economic developments are the growth of unemployment and the increase of the poverty among the poorest strata of society, those who are least educated, or the youngest, or often pensioners. Unemployment until recently stood at over 9 percent and another 9 percent were estimated to be underemployed. Some of this increase from traditionally low levels of Argentine unemployment has come from the fact that government employment in a shrinking national administration has fallen from 670,000 in 1990 to 285,000 in 1992 while employment in the ex-state enterprises have diminished by 295,000 to less than 50,000. Most of these employees have taken early retirement, been retrenched, transferred to provincial administrations, or moved to private sector employment (World Bank, xvii). Though this is not very divergent from postindustrial rates throughout the world, it is historically very unusual for Argentina and implies major economic readjustments occurring via privatization, shrinkage of the state sector, and other market reorientations that put more and more premium on higher education and skill levels.

The proportion of those households living in poverty is estimated at 15 percent, down from 25 percent in 1988 (World Bank, 22). At the same time the restructuring of the Argentine economy, certainly up to 1990, had caused an exacerbation of income inequality and a greater variety and complexity of salaries based on uneven bargaining power among workers of different skill levels and among different varieties of firms. All these phenomenon are, of course, observable features of a post-privatized economy (Beccaria 1991, 323ff., and Beccaria in Kosacoff 1993, 330).

Distinct from previous periods of economic growth that focused either on import substitution or on agro-export policies, contemporary Argentine firms are investing abroad with new global strategies and initiating joint-ventures with local and foreign capital. In a word they are behaving like the multinationals of the industrial center. Apparently these shifts have been stimulated by Argentine privatizations, the end of tariffs and economic controls, the new interests of international capital in the Argentine economy, and the very strength of the Argentine stabilization plan (Bisang et al. 1992).

One of the most promising arenas of Argentine economic growth is the Southern Cone common market (Mercosur), which should, with several product exceptions, be a free trade zone by 1995. Mercosur by all accounts is making steady progress particularly in inter-Argentine-Brazilian trade. Previous Latin American free trade initiatives such as the ill-fated Latin American Free Trade Agreement (LAFTA) have been failures. However, today there is common commitment to end import substitution policies, a willingness to face international competition on a level playing field, a growing emphasis on specialization and other factors of production, a new aggressiveness in inserting oneself into world markets, and a broadly held view that economic inefficiency can no longer be subsidized.

The impact of a more efficient capitalist economy over a poorly managed corporatist system with few key players has several promising scenarios and a few dangerous possibilities. Capitalism in the central postindustrial nations shows positive signs of a growing decentralization of the market with a gradual increase in the numbers of employers' shares in contribution to national growth rate statistics. In the best tradition of Eduard Bernstein this holds out the possibility that democratic socialism is still on the agenda and not necessarily receding into a continuously unreachable future. If there is to be a democratic socialism, we must observe the growth of small scale capital enterprises within which there is working class collaboration. These authentic areas of cooperation and participation (already afoot in Western Europe, Canada, and the United States) must be continually coupled to the historical-cultural meaning of a society that presumes to make social justice a prime value.

Given Argentina's mobilized society, politicized unions, and high modernity and cultural indices, democracy appears as the optimal political choice because it is certainly more legitimate and historically less costly in terms of institutional disruptions and dislocations. But also it is the appropriate system because Argentine workers are very predisposed to democracy, as will be depicted in subsequent chapters.

Argentine workers made clear to me that they don't associate democracy with a state performing basic economic functions. Thus, they welcomed privatization during the Alfonsín years. They felt privatizing state economic sectors would allow the state to retain what it does best: in so many words to adjudicate, arbitrate, and regulate. Meanwhile, the private sector could focus on productivity, investment, and developing the society's assets. The Menem government's views on the state encapsulate that general worker perception. Argentina's Secretary for Economic Planning, Juan José Llach, epitomized this notion when he remarked,

> It is important to emphasize that the so-called welfare state that evolved after WWII and that fulfilled an important historical function has entered into a crisis. That happened, perhaps, because it pretended to be responsible for everything, to do everything, to replace the vital societal forces.... Now, we have to find a way to reconstruct not the old state but a new state stripped of a whole range of functions that the society can handle by itself. Instead the state will dedicate itself clearly, seriously and ethically to questions of justice, education, health, and the preservation of the environment— functions that are basically the responsibility of the state. Moreover, it is to perform these with clarity, responsibility and the capacity to respond to the necessities of its citizens and with their participation. This is the principle challenge we face as the end of the century approaches. (*La Prensa*, January 22, 1994)

The privatization reforms have had significant impacts on the general dynamism of the economically active Argentine community. One case study may exemplify some of these developments. In the short time that the former state telephone company (ENTEL) has been privatized there have occurred significant internal shifts in both the company and in the telephone union (FOETRA). The percentage of younger, better educated, and more technically prepared workers has increased significantly as has productivity as measured by employees per 1,000 telephone lines. The privatized telephone companies have based promotions not on seniority, but on when a worker decides to take an examination. Meanwhile Telefónica and Telecom companies and the FOETRA union offer preparatory seminars. Moreover, the examinations are based on testing initiative and multidimensional skills (Senén Gonzalez and Ximenez Sáez 1993, 4).

The impact of the arrest of inflation on a societal malaise cannot be overemphasized. It is the key transformatory breakthrough of the Menem administration. For the first time in a generation, Argentines can plan and predict their budgets. They remember well the time spent, which amounted to almost one working day a week, determining the best interest rates, continuously moving their money around, borrowing, purchasing over time, assiduously buying and selling dollars, and, in countless other ways, hedging against inflation. And so one can understand the inflexibility with which Cavallo has defended the Argentine peso. It appears that all else stems from the continual stabilization of the Argentine monetary system. Stabilization has allowed the administration for the first time in contemporary history to go beyond fiscal policy to entertain notions of economic restructuring and long-range planning. At the same time it is able to depoliticize the venerable questions of subsidies and multiple exchange rates, and avoid the tedium of daily responses to inflationary pressures. Economic stability also allows for an accumulation mentality that permits businesses to plan for new investments, exporters to judge new markets, retailers to chart future consumer demands, and labor unions to grapple with the countless issues beyond wages, such as job security, participation schemes, technology, and profit sharing. The Alfonsín preoccupation with runaway inflation and the subsequent policy retreats act as a profound warning to Menem.

Thus, from April 1991 and the initiation of the Convertibility Law to January 1994, Argentina has had an inflation rate of 53 percent, though the rate has clearly slowed down even more since the beginning of 1993. Further, in this period, general consumer purchasing power has increased by 8.2 percent (*Crónica*, February 23, 1994) even though wage rates have not kept up with rents (157 percent), doctor and lawyer services (137 percent), entertainment (92 percent), and restaurants (77 percent). Salaries have outpaced transportation costs (23 percent to 40 percent) and clothing costs (10 percent) (*Buenos Aires Herald*, January 4, 1994).

Reigning in inflation has allowed the government to undertake several profound social policy initiatives as profound as those undertaken during post-World War II early Peronism. In September 1993 the government legislated a new private pension fund system which would include the unions' own pension plans in an open, competitive market. These funds would be professionally managed and overseen by a superintendency made up of representatives of the state, employers, and unions (World Bank, 148). The pension fund managers (AFJP-Administradoras de Fondos de Jubilaciones y Pensiones) would oversee private and public pension funds and workers would have to choose, by October 1994, among one of the private funds or the state-sponsored fund (*Clarín*, February 19, 1994). The private funds would be run somewhat like mutual funds, that is, based on contributions and investment performance, while the state fund would be administered by the state Banco de la Nación. Employers and employees would contribute as they presently do but at slightly reduced rates. It is a kind of variable annuity but guarantees a minimum retirement income. The pension plans arise out of public discontent with existing pension plans which often pay less than minimum monthly incomes to retirees (*LAWR*, October 14, 1993).

In another critical area of health and social welfare policies (Obras Sociales), currently administered by the trade unions, a governmental decree in September 1993 abolished compulsory affiliation with one's union. Free competition among health insurance plans was to be encouraged. This was followed by another decree in December 1993, which reduced by half employers' contributions to the existing union welfare funds. The avowed purpose of this decree was to free those employer contributions for investments and the creation of new employment, and to force the union welfare funds to become more efficient and competitive. Thus, from early 1994, workers will be able to choose health plans from among many union providers. The prices will be set but the degree of service will obviously vary depending on facilities and efficiency levels. Thus, competition among the "Obras

Sociales" will be based on the quality of the health care and consumer satisfaction, and it appears obvious that the inefficient, smaller, poorly administered union plans may not survive the transition (World Bank, 80). While guaranteeing basic, universal coverage to the indigent, this change will also end governmental subsidies to deficient union welfare funds (many reputedly run haphazardly at best and as personal slush funds by union administrators at worst).

Since late 1992 the government has begun to enact labor reform legislation that have been the subject of intense debate since 1990 (see chapter 10). Governmental legislation has provided for flexible labor contracts of six months, eighteen months, and two years. This measure was further amended in mid-1993, allowing temporary contracts of up to three years with severance pay exclusion of up to ninety days.[4]

In a further attempt to rationalize social and labor policies, the government has introduced a Program to Support Productive Reconversion (PARP). This program, eventually targeted at 1.5 million young, low income workers without job experience and with low levels of education (early school dropouts for the most part), features a six-month training course to inculcate business skills and work habits. It is run by a newly formed training institute (ICAP-Instituciones de Capacitación Argentina de Producción) that eventually places the young people in private firms that invest in social or community projects and will hire program graduates for at least one year, with the Ministry of Labor picking up the salary for the first three months (*La Nación*, January 31, 1994).

In early 1994, the government also decreed a Program for Property Participation (Programa de Propiedad Participada) geared to worker participation in the privatized electrical and gas enterprises. The decree aims at allowing at least one or more employees to sit on the board of directors, establish the mechanisms by which the workers receive around 10 percent of the company shares and a 50 percent share of profits from the date of the privatization (*Clarín*, February 23, 1994).

Thus, the revolutionary public policy changes under the Menem administration are far deeper than even the import substitution departures of Perón in the post-World War II period, or President Arturo Frondizi's overtures to foreign capital in the late 1950s and early 1960s. In essence the coherence, complexity, and multidimensionality of the Cavallo stabilization program seems irreversible and will require at least an equally sophisticated countervailing position to critique what has transpired in Argentina since 1989.

Neoliberalism and Its Subjects

What has been the impact of these profound changes in the Argentine economy upon the society at-large and upon organized labor and working-class relationships and the political party system in particular?

The historical irony has not been lost on anyone in Argentina. The CGT had waited so long for an unfettered Peronism elected democratically and without military oversight. Then this very same Peronism turns out to be the government presiding over a neoliberal readjustment of the Argentine economy that conformed to the exigencies of the international market. This paradoxical situation has had a disorienting, disquieting, and soul-searching impact on Argentina with two major consequences. First, the intellectual interregnum in which social and political actors were searching for responses and reactions to the neoliberal thrust has provided the Menem government with a huge political opening in which to establish its intent and fulfill its programs with remarkable speed and self-confidence. Second, it has caused a slow, even tortured, reevaluation by labor unions and political parties as to their role as either critical allies or muted opponents.

There is obviously no easy anti-neoliberal strategy. The social democratic alternative is the only reasonable one, but it, too, is predicated on capitalist growth, democratic deepening, loyal party opposition, worker participatory schemes, and a civil and pluralist society—all of which are either being undertaken or, at least, considered by the new Menem Peronism.

Part of the confusion among the political sectors emanated from the fact that historically it would have been more appropriate for the democratic-liberal Radical party (UCR) to have undertaken this reformation, with Peronism remaining as the vigilant populist, though social democratic, opposition. Now, because the Radicals have not historically been a social democratic party in the economic arena and have often acted against working-class interests in the past, there is no mass party on the left-center of the political spectrum. Moreover, the socialist left in Argentina continues to be weak (for reasons to be depicted in this book). These sets of circumstances have forced Argentina's trade unions to seriously reevaluate their overall strategy.

Though effective as an oppositional force to military regimes and Radical civil governments, the CGT has been severely immobilized by the activist positioning of its historical party ally. The CGT has traditionally been a potent representative of working-class defense against inflation and unequal income distribution and workers have generally recognized this. However, it is also apparent that the lack of internal union democracy that rank and file unionists have decried (see chapters 5–7) has caused a sclerotic, inflexible labor leadership that has not mastered the new economic intricacies and challenges presented by the Menem epoch. This lack of participatory unionism has cost the CGT the ability to find and develop younger and more innovative leadership, capable of bargaining with skill and resourcefulness under the new neoliberal conditions.

With the end of inflation as the major arena of labor contestation, a new space emerges for an innovative union leadership that can grapple with the new postindustrial questions confronting the working class throughout the world. The debate is no longer simply salary but job security, fringe benefits, the length of the work week, technological unemployment, pension questions, work rotation, profit sharing and co-participation, a two-tier worker system, and so on.

The unions are *well placed* historically to play a major role but they are *poorly prepared* for such a venture. This book taps some of the obvious contradictions between CGT leadership and rank and file worker's values and attitudes. The CGT must understand the liberal-democratic predispositions of the Argentine working class if it is to properly evaluate the new capitalist cultural initiatives of the Menem administration. Indeed, since 1990, the so-called Menemist and independent unions have significantly moved to adapt themselves to positions more symmetrical with neoliberalism and the Argentine working class.

The majority of the larger unions comprising the CGT are making the painful adjustments to the new political economy and have managed to represent, since 1989 and the defeat of Saúl Ubaldini, the dominant faction. In March 1994 one of their leaders, Antonio Cassia, of the moderate Petroleum Workers Union, was elected the new secretary general of the workers' confederation (*Clarín*, March 14, 1994). There are, however, several unions (the most important being the state employees, teachers, and transport workers) that have formed substantial, if minority, labor schisms. One, the Movimiento de los Trabajadores Argentinos (MTA), is a faction within the labor confederation that includes Saúl Ubaldini as one of its leaders. The second, the Congreso de los Trabajadores Argentinos (CTA) led by Mary Sánchez of the teachers' union (CTERA), has created a rump association committed to a severe critique of privatization and the whole range of proposed labor legislation.

Argentine labor union administrators of "obras sociales" are well placed experientially to take advantage of privatization due in part to their historic responsibility at running clinics, hotels, sports facilities, and educational/training plans (see chapter 4). It is significant that the CGT decided not to take a collective frontal oppositional stance against privatization and left it to the individual unions to negotiate the new agreements. Victoria Murillo has written that some of the more powerful and influential labor unions (Commercial, Petroleum, Railway and Light, and Power Workers' Unions), faced with financial losses because of declining membership dues and welfare contributions (due to privatization and de-industrialization), have turned to ownership participation in privatized enterprises as a means to preserve employment and increase their financial resources. The example of the Light and Power Workers (Luz y Fuerza) is indicative of this kind of potential labor involvement with capital. This union, one with a long history of innovative strategies, has been a heavy investor in employee stock ownership plans (owning between 18 and 40 percent of the shares among fourteen electrical generator stations), real estate, a retirement fund, housing projects, and tourist services. Another union, Argentina's largest, the Commercial Workers

Union, already owns several hotels, housing projects, a sports complex, part of an insurance company, a retirement fund, and a credit card service, among other interests (Murillo 1994, 16–21).

It is clear that Argentine workers' views are not synonymous with a neoliberal outlook but they are far closer to this orientation than has generally been acknowledged. They generally support its economic reactivization mode while maintaining a more skeptical watchfulness regarding its social welfare and employment policies. Broadly speaking the neoliberal initiatives conform to worker outlooks, depicted in succeeding chapters, in several important respects. First, privatization of state enterprises had been welcomed by workers even before the Menem initiatives and certainly before the union leadership began to accept their viability. Second, based on worker attitudes tapped in this book, Menem proposals in the area of pensions and health insurance reforms should also be generally welcomed by the rank and file unionists, if not the union leadership itself. Third, the collective bargaining system that comprises negotiating by sector and industry under the auspices of the Ministry of Labor's supervision will no doubt be complemented by bargaining at enterprise or plant level based strictly on productivity and profit margins (this legislation should be in place by mid-1994). This, too, may have substantial support from the working class, while CGT leadership will most likely resist these changes. Fourth, it is in the area of labor flexibility measures and the concomitant unemployment caused by structural readjustments that the rank and file's and labor leadership's views seem to converge. But even here the differentiation of views among various strata of workers (educated versus uneducated, technically equipped versus unskilled, those in growth industries versus those in stagnant economic sectors) will be much more heterogeneous than the frontal opposition demonstrated so far by the CGT leadership.

The CGT and Peronism have been in what might be considered from labor's point of view a historical hug that has now the dangers of a "fatal embrace."[5] As a centralized union confederation, the CGT must continue to embrace a social democratic "left-of-center" position, though it does so alone since there is a political party vacuum here. The neoliberal qualitative shift in Argentine politics has moved the whole political society in a rightward direction. This does not obviate the need for the labor leadership to mount a critical orientation from a position of a historical ally. It is its only viable option. To form new alliances with its historical opponents would act as a grave disorientation to Argentine workers and serve mainly as a temporary reprisal filled with limited and short-run gratification. Rather, labor must make the long trudge with Menemism through the re-evaluation of historical Peronism and the creation of new institutions and policies in conformity with the new exigencies of the time.

Menem has broadened the traditional Peronist class coalitions even beyond Perón's efforts in 1973. Moreover, one can argue that the Perón coalition at that time was based on a broad political alliance mounted to avoid a potential leftist insurgency and a rightist military intervention whereas today, the Menem coalition can be attributed to the coincidence of economic positions among the major societal interests. And today, as opposed to the early Peronism of the 1940s, Menem is precluded from representing exclusively the overlapping interests of workers and consumers (Lamadrid 1993, 113).

The Menem government has been able to establish a large multiclass and multisectoral coalition as well as integrating conservative and other party affiliates to its government roster. It has preempted any possible alternative conservative UCD party program on the right and its relatively successful economic stabilization policies, along with other historical reasons, have kept the left in continual political purgatory. The most likely successful opposition coalition would have to develop out of existing political groupings all with a certain amount of public support, namely, the state sector unions, a dissident Peronist sector, plus elements of the left coalition known as the Frente Grande.

The Peronist legislative victory in October 1993 was a clear affirmation of the Menem policies, receiving as it did 42.3 percent of the vote in a multiparty system. This has been the fourth consecutive convincing Peronist victory since 1987 and has reaffirmed its place as the majoritarian political party in Argentina. It is also the first time in contemporary history that a civilian governing party has won the last legislative election before the end of its term![6] Cavallo's Convertibility Plan was clearly the important marker that determined the Peronist election victory. In a survey encompassing the capital city of Buenos Aires and the provinces of Buenos Aires and Córdoba the issue most broadly eliciting a pro-Peronist vote was the Cavallo economic plan, even more than purely party preference or loyalty or support for the government generally (*Clarín*, October 10, 1993).

Menem's legislative victory gave further impetus to his efforts to revise the constitution to allow himself a second four-year term as president and to pursue several other significant amendments to the 1853 constitution (Perón's 1949 Constitution had been revoked in 1956). As early as 1992, Menem had begun speaking of the possibility of serving two consecutive terms if the constitution that stipulated one six-year term was modified. He took his proposal for constitutional reform to the public and the general response was positive. He began speaking of a nonbinding public referendum in which it appeared, by public opinion polls, he would resoundingly win. Polls conducted in May 1993, for example, supported a referendum on the constitution by 85 percent and on allowing Menem to run for the presidency again by 58 percent (*LAWR*, June 3, 1993, 250). Threatened with a plebiscitary groundswell for a Menem reelection, the Radicals, under Alfonsín's leadership, endorsed a constitutional convention, obviating a Menem referendum that he had "threatened" to hold on November 21, 1993.

Radicals felt they could not effectively run against such a referendum for if they did, they would be unceremoniously defeated. Thus, by way of an agreement between Menem and Alfonsín on November 14, 1993, they threw in their lot with the Peronists and managed to receive scores of concessions on the content of constitutional reforms that would be voted on in the constitutional convention beginning in April of 1994. The so-called pact between the two party leaders was signed on December 13, 1993.

It was reported that the Menem government compromised on over sixty articles in order to obtain Radical support on the key articles that included the provision for presidential reelections. The Peronists and Radicals agreed in principle on various constitutional changes. Among the more important were: a "coordinating" cabinet chief, appointed by the president but answerable to both the president *and* congress, who could be removed by absolute majority vote of both legislative houses; severe restrictions on the use of executive decrees in lieu of legislative acts as well as limitations on federal intervention into the provinces; an agreement that draft bills rejected *en todo* by one of the legislative houses could not again be introduced during that congressional session; an agreement that legislative sessions were to be extended from six to nine months; the creation of a council of magistrates to regulate and oversee judicial appointments as well as judicial conduct; the institution of an ombudsman office with autonomy from the executive branch; and finally, direct election of, now, three senators per province who would serve four- instead of nine-year terms of office (*Noticias*, December 2, 1993).

There is little doubt that many of the agreed upon reform articles, initiated by the Radical opposition, have helped broaden the democratic dialogue and have acted as a limitation on the centralizing tendencies of the Menem executive. The constitutional dialogue, combined as it is with the continuing euphoria promoted by a stable currency, has given Argentina an atmosphere of political and economic normalcy rarely seen in contemporary history. The ascendancy of an institutionalized civil presidency more vulnerable to constitutional restrictions, combined with a successful economic model and an activist social policy designed to undercut corporate relationship and unleash societal initiatives, has combined to give Argentina an almost unrecognizable polity.

The ubiquitous success of Menem's anti-inflationary policy has outweighed the more selective impacts of unemployment and a declining income distribution for the unskilled and least educated sectors of society (Cortés 1993, 11-14).[7] Nevertheless, memories of hyperinflation have universally seared most social sectors. Past high inflation accentuated low capital investment, stagnant growth, policy strife and gridlock, and high intensity social sector conflict. All these areas have been substantially mitigated because of what one might call the "Cavallo factor." The old system is disappearing and the new system has been born though it is not yet fully mature. It seems to be predicated on attenuating ideological political conflicts, depoliticizing the economy to the rigors and requirements of domestic economic rationality, and global trade competitiveness.

Argentina Class and Society in Comparative Perspective

The extent to which the combination of basic civil liberties, democratic processes, state enterprise privatizations, and the entry of foreign capital have been supported by the Argentine working class at-large despite the insecurity marked by increases in unemployment and the pockets of poverty might surprise the investigator. The end of existing socialism in Eastern Europe has provided similar combinations of creative economic opportunities combined with a rise in personal insecurity (Wright 1993, 25). However, the Argentine organized workers have far more historical experience than their East European counterparts in having participated in the management of large union enterprises. However, this response demonstrates the problems with thinking of workers in monolithic class terms. Multiple dimensions and differences among laborers and employees, depending on a whole range of factors, defines a very complex working class. As we show below, workers have tended to be misrepresented by often economist notions of class that are unwarranted when workers are looked at as individuals and in detail.

The basis of class consciousness is not whether there is one class acting against another fraction or class interest but whether individual goals aim at anything more than gaining access to wealth and social justice; rarely do workers *qua* workers seek a recasting of capitalist culture or a sweeping overturning of all hierarchy and, in its place, the imposition of an overriding uniformity within society.

Karl Marx's depiction of worker alienation as it is addressed in this book has validity only in the most generic sense but it ceases to have meaning as it is specifically applied. Industrial and postindustrial job organization requires some alienation using Marxian terminology. One could speculate that even in the later Middle Ages, skilled craftsmen experienced long moments of alienation on the job—in repeating the same task with each Stradivarius violin produced—constrained, as they no doubt were, by time requirements, requests of middlemen, and individual contract stipulations.

One must recategorize Marx's germinal explanation of alienation more appropriately to apply it to contemporary working class lives. Objective alienation is no doubt inevitable if we apply the Marxian logic from his *Economic and Philosophical Manuscripts*. It is rather the *feelings* of alienation that we can attempt to mitigate. If we divide the concept into *general, specific,* and *overarching alienation* we can better get a handle on the dilemma. *General alienation* regarding the *feelings* that one is doing a competent job, bringing out a worthwhile product or service can be minimized. But *specific alienation,* that is, repetition, tedium, boredom on the job, cannot be totally addressed or revised nor can what I would call *overarching alienation*—that is, that we often work for someone else and often have to submit to disciplines of another's choosing. Probably *specific* and *overarching* forms of alienation have been present even before capitalism. The area of meaningful manipulation and where organized labor specifically and workers overall can make a difference remains *general* alienation.

To this end we need to think of the relation of capital to labor differently. As John Roemer has written,

> many could have played the role of capitalist, but someone had to. This is not to deny that the skills of capitalists may be somewhat scarce—it is just that they are not that scarce. Within the population of proletarians there are plenty of potential capitalists—that is, persons who are capable of performing that role but who do not, because of their lack of access to the means of production.... It does not matter who the capitalists are, but workers will be better off if someone is a capitalist. Capitalism is socially necessary; particular capitalists are dispensable. (Roemer 1982, 269)

In Argentina, as in the United States, the persistence of a petty bourgeois class (approximately 22 percent in Argentina) allows for that entrepreneurial mentality to penetrate the vast gamut that makes up the working class from laborers to "middle class workers" to the most credentialed professionals. It is this outlook that can often be harnessed on the factory floor and in the office. Under capitalism, a rigidly defined class system no longer carries the weight it might have had during early industrialization when such lines were more severely drawn. In the contemporary period, working-class perceptions, as we shall see in the Argentine case, are much more fluid and contradictory (Ranis 1994).

"Middle-class" workers hold the most contradictory positions in any capitalist class typology. Though many members of these strata, within the confines of the working class, hold relatively autonomous positions, often control the routines of other workers, and exercise all sorts of supervisory and controlling functions that separate them hierarchically from other elements of the working class, they are, nonetheless, members of the working class in the sense that they themselves are subject to subordination and are required to perform their functions in a particular time and place for a particular remuneration. Thus, they are not as Nicos Poulantzas described them, a "new middle class," but rather evolving, relatively privileged members of a new working class. As Eric Wright has written, one must accept these ambiguous social positions as symptomatic of the normally contradictory class relationships under capitalism (Wright 1985, 42).

More to the point, this development can lead to new, more productive ways of organizing the workplace. Often workers in Argentina control *how* but not *what* is produced. But this ability to understand fully how some product or some service is produced gives the worker a sense of control over the production process *per se*.

And so one of the first changes to reduce general alienation would be relatively simple, that is, to give workers more input and hence more sense of control. The basis for this change is already there. As Wright says,

> in many factory settings the actual operation of production continues to depend heavily on a wide range of accumulated knowledge on the shop floor, knowledge which must constantly be applied in non-routinized ways. Such autonomy, therefore, may not have a distinctly "petty bourgeois" character at all. The only thing which defines the petty bourgeois is ownership of the certain kinds of *assets*—land, tools, a few machines, perhaps in some cases "skills" or credentials—and self-employment, but not work autonomy. (Wright 1985, 53-54)

The important point Wright is making, reiterating the general orientation of Roemer on the subject of "capitalists," is that "petty bourgeois" characteristics and values are not limited to the petty bourgeois but are in plentiful supply among workers.

A degree of exploitation is inevitable in both capitalist and any conceivable postcapitalist societies in the foreseeable future, but what is containable and reformable is the degree to which workers will be able to apply, control, and even "sell" their skills and cultural assets.

Effective trade unions in the future must be able to appeal to and represent this more complicated nature of the working class and its role in production. In this regard, we might look back to look forward—look to Eduard Bernstein who perceptively understood the multiple working-class needs and wants encompassed by their aspirations to take on autonomous responsibilities, to achieve private property ownership, and to maximize their access to culture and commodities (Bernstein 1961). Others have repeated his observation. Richard Scase has written concerning the British case, "Appeals to class consciousness that emphasize the nature of subordination and exploitation in large-scale organizations are often rebutted by people who have personal knowledge of those who, through their *own* rather than *collective* efforts, have circumvented these class relations" (Scase 1992, 48). As this study shows, and that of, for example, David Halle in the American context and Peter Saunders in the British, people's evaluation of their class positions are often determined by personal consumption, life-styles, and home ownership (Halle 1984, Saunders 1989).

To increase production and enhance the possibility of distributive justice, working-class energy, interest, and imagination have to be harnessed. As Steven Vallas says in a study of AT&T workers, capitalist hegemony theorists (such as Edwards and Burawoy) make too much of capitalists' abilities to ideologically co-opt workers into the mechanisms of managerial control. Workers are aware of the actual challenges involving the introduction of new technology (Vallas 1993, 177ff.). Thus, though automation, far more than earlier industrial mechanization, has produced more highly skilled and knowledgeable workers, it has still subjected them to increasing managerial subordination. However, reading Vallas against the backdrop of my Argentine research, one senses that a conciliatory, variable-sum, optimization strategy, initially made between some capitalists and some workers, is highly feasible in the future, despite the advantages that capitalist managers have at present. (It is also interesting to note that managers themselves often hold ambivalent class positions, since they often control the production process of workers, but, at the same time, they do not own the means of production and they themselves often sell their expertise and labor to the owners [Wright 1993, 29].)

The key to the conundrum is to treat skilled workers as petty capitalists themselves who share not only in decisions (good and bad) but in remuneration (up and down). As Vallas explains, unions have hitherto only defended against technology as opposed to the right to help in shaping it. I would add here that the potential for workers to shape the technology will redound to the general increased productivity of the firm if the reward structure is complementary. Particularly the service union employees, we found, seem increasingly amenable to productivity incentives if "power sharing" is also placed on the agenda. The contradictions of class placement among credentialed "middle class workers" also stands them in good stead to increasingly challenge insulated capitalist ownership.

Selig Perlman once wrote that what distinguishes capitalists and workers is that the former have an "abundance consciousness" while the latter have a "scarcity consciousness." Thus, unions have focused on such defensive issues as job security, wages, and general working conditions (Perlman 1928). Increasing labor credentialism and intellectual autonomy make this increasingly challengeable, despite and possibly because of technology. Thus, the wage earner seeking to be a capitalist involved in a responsibility/incentive system may be the antidote to unproductive and irresponsible capitalism. After all we can argue, along with Marx, that it is only since the mid-nineteenth century that a clear distinction has developed between the artisan/craftsman/master and the transformation of some of them into middlemen/entrepreneur/financier/investor and the beginnings of modern capitalism. Possibly that breach can be closed once more in the twenty-first century.

As Frank Tannenbaum wrote more than forty years ago,

> The union, if it is to survive, must maintain the fealty of its members, and it can do that only by giving them a sense of dignity and standing, not only within the union, but also within the industry. Such a sense of dignity can only be had if the workers have a concern for all the issues and difficulties of the enterprise. (Tannenbaum 1951, 169)

This is echoed much more recently by a Japanese automobile union leader, Ichiro Shioji, who believes that this kind of respect for workers will only redound to the greater productivity of the firm. "Mere talk can never produce trust. What is needed are achievements. And what is required of the people concerned is sincerity...the relationship of trust between labor and management is the most important factor of productivity" (quoted in Marshall 1987, 120–21).

Argentine workers do not live by bread alone and, despite some of the hard economic times under the Alfonsín and Menem governments, they still solidly support a democratic political system. Laborers and employees, with certain differences that will be spelled out below, are predisposed to a host of cultural and political questions that complement and sometimes supersede purely material questions. As Lamont and Fourneir write, "Over the years we have increasingly come to conceptualize culture as institutionalized repertoires that have as powerful an effect on the structure of everyday life as do economic forces" (1992, 7). Thus, there is a dual sense of democratic liberalism slowly being consolidated in Argentina, one emphasizing the freedom to take initiative and feel unfettered by governmental intervention and restrictions into economic life and at the same time one expressing the expectation to be protected from the ravages of social and cultural inequities. These may often appear as contradictory demands but they describe the complicated nature of society/state relationships in the overlapping spheres of the economy, culture, and society.

As Sandra Wellman writes, "work is about social transformation as much as material production. Indeed its significance is more often seen to lie in the *quality of the relationship* involved in the allocation, production, or distribution of resources than in the bald facts of material survival" (Wellman 1979, 2). Although my study deals with the quality of existing democratic values espoused by the formal, unionized working class, two recent studies of the Argentine poor have demonstrated that these cultural considerations are not limited to the more economically secure classes. Nancy Powers found that the Argentine poor are able to separate out political from economic factors. Thus, values, ideology, and beliefs have a complexity that is important to people regardless of their economic position in society. Powers found, as I did among organized workers, that it was dangerous reductionism to attribute certain forms of consciousness based on economic class position alone. Apparently the poor share with the working class a complicated set of differentiated political concerns that mute class placement. Beyond economics, they have cultural, political, and historical identities (Powers 1994). Similarly Gabriela Ippolito found that democracy is fundamental to the Argentine poor even when it is often unaccompanied by economic improvements (Ippolito 1994).

A Concluding Word

The Menem government has been called to task by scholars, journalists, and by the Argentine Radical and left opposition for having hegemonic, if not authoritarian, tendencies.[8] Others have spoken of the government's centralizing tendencies and purely formalistic obeisance to minimalist democracy. The powers of the presidency and his economics minister are huge. The opposition is weak. Federalism is highly centralized. The legislature is essentially reactive and much legislation has been instituted by way of decrees. Possibly, the arrogance of the current administration, which seems to assert that it has most of the answers, may be its most dangerous attribute. Even economically there are some possible dangers in the overwhelming potential of cheaper Brazilian imports via the increasing Mercosur common market relationships and that reactivization and industrialization have not yet significantly impacted on the Argentine export position. Privatization has been essentially a remonopolization of basic utilities, even if they are much more efficient. Thus, this is certainly an administration that needs monitoring, and vigilance is the price for consolidating democracy in Argentina.

However, having said this, Argentina is far from being a society with room only for large capitalist enterprises and a single dominant one-party system. In fact, with a historical perspective in mind, one can reach certain tentative assessments about Argentine society and politics that are very positive, especially within the context of Latin American polities in general.

Let us look at what have been the concerns of observers about Argentina and try to respond from a larger, comparative context, using the cases of Germany and France in particular.

Argentina has been assessed as a weak, unconsolidated democracy. It is accepted, however, that Argentina has been a democratic society, if flawed, since 1983. It is now in its second decade of democratization after an undeniably vicious authoritarian interlude that followed other military and restricted democratic experiments. Germany itself went through a similar though much more extreme form of totalitarianism to emerge by 1949 as a consolidating democracy. France, too, under the fascist Vichy puppet government emulated these same totalitarian tendencies only to emerge in 1947 with a new democratic regime. If we look at either Germany or France in the late 1950s, or even early 1960s, at the end of their first decade of consolidation (*where Argentina is now*) we could see many still unresolved questions about the level of consolidation of their constitutional, political, and civil society.

The Menem government is attacked for attempting to institutionalize a party-hegemonic political system. It is true that Argentine political institutions are highly centralized and the legislature and judiciary quite weak. For many years Argentina, under civilian governments, was criticized as a weak state system, very susceptible to the demands and claims of historically powerful interest groups. This resulted in nonauthoritarian governments having great difficulty in undertaking consistent public policy directions. It is hard to expect redistribution of presidential powers to other Argentine political institutions while at the same time expecting historically powerful interest groups to accept deep concessions to a weak presidency. A strong, viable presidency seems to be a prerequisite to a political stability that will allow for de-escalating interest group warfare, eventually permitting a functioning institutionalized legislature and judiciary. The problem in Argentina has been its large and easily penetrable state rather than the centralized nature of its executive. It is difficult to take on both these challenges simultaneously without the danger of institutional and economic stalemate. Moreover, the routinization of the bureaucracy can come only after a period of a strong presidency. Certainly, privatization under Menem has overshadowed political institutionalization (despite 1994 constitutional reforms), but a weakened executive would hardly stimulate responsible interest group behavior.

Which is the model being forwarded? It is mostly the American case that seems to be in the minds of critics, replete with its own problems of interest group "colonization" of legislative committees, powerful legislators, and centrifugal federalism. Certainly the German and French cases offer us differing perspectives. The Germans went through a dominant one-party "hegemony" of sorts under the Christian Democratic party, led by chancellors Konrad Adenauer, Ludwig Erhard, and Kurt Kiesinger, lasting as it did for twenty years. This certainly did not in the least prevent the consolidation of a legitimate German democracy. The French went through an even more checkered deepening of democracy. Charles de Gaulle, wartime resistance leader and charismatic hero, singlehandedly as it were, founded several changing personalist movements (RPF, UDN, RPR), *not parties* in the traditional sense until De Gaulle's retirement and death. As premier, he sought special powers during the Fourth Republic, and later, as president of the Fifth Republic, he created a constitutional regime and governed through a very centralized political system, to say the least.

The power of the Menem presidency and that of his Minister of Economics, Domingo Cavallo, is clearly observable. But again, the powers of CDU German Chancellor Konrad Adenauer and his Economics Minister Ludwig Erhard in the late 1950s and early 1960s was at least the Argentine equal, coming as it did more than a decade *after* the establishment of a West German democratic system. It is also undeniable that in 1958 De Gaulle set up a centralized presidential system, under the auspices of the Fifth Republic's constitution, that severely inhibited legislative policy-making and law-making, and provided all kinds of built-in executive controls over the legislative process, agenda, and timetable. Clearly President de Gaulle, even as much as twenty-five years after the establishment of postwar French democracy, often governed and made fundamental legal changes by plebescite and referendum, *over the head* of the French National Assembly. One need only recall a few such special provisions as the president's lack of responsibility to the legislative branch, presidential emergency powers, the difficulty in censoring the president's hand-picked prime minister, the weakness of legislative committees, the brevity of legislative sessions, the long seven-year presidential term with allowable re-elections, the powerful Council of State and so on.

It is said that the Argentine military complex is still an apparent danger to democratic institutions. Germany was of course demilitarized by the allies and remained self-consciously opposed to a remilitarization for many years. France, however, ten years after the establishment of the democratic Fourth Republic, found itself engaged in a mortal struggle with a large faction of its military sector. This faction came perilously close to setting up a military regime but actually cleared the way for a virtual civil coup that forced a whole constitutional change over the heads of existing political institutions and created, basically by plebescite, a new constitution and an altered democratic political system.

We are appalled by the regime terror unleashed on Argentines, begun under the regime of Isabel Perón and maximized manyfold with the advent of the *Proceso* dictatorship between 1976–1983. Estimates of the disappeared range up to 30,000. This fact is horrendous and unforgivable. Here, too, one must give it an international and historical context. The German genocidal policy of murder and extermination against its own religious minorities and political opposition reached into the millions. The French Vichy government deported over 75,000 Jews to their certain deaths in German and Polish concentration camps. And certainly the anti-Semitism that reared its head under Isabel Perón's minister of social welfare, Lopez Rega and under the succeeding military junta was surpassed by the historically unique scourge against Jews in Nazi Germany and Vichy France. The historical role of the anti-liberal democratic Montoneros and the ERP on the Argentine left and the Triple A death squads on the right have their comparable history in Germany with the Bader Meinhoff groups and, the predecessor to the skin-heads, the neo-Nazis of the 1950s and 1960s. In France, on the other hand, one had the student uprisings as well as the OAS (Secret Army Society) and the ultra-nationalist Poujadists, who have their French successors to this day.

In summary, Argentina's political system is built on a healthy and viable societal fabric, dynamic economic interests and a sophisticated and educated working class. The traumas of past regime experiences are not so dissimilar from the post-World War II alleviation of fascist banal evils and the corruption of the civic community. As in the Germany and France of the late 1950s, democratic dispositions in Argentina are healthy and intellectual and cultural dissent is vigorous. It is simplistic to assume that present Peronist dominance (as German Christian Democracy or French Gaullism) is inevitable or forever. Much more likely Menemism is the product of the crisis of the democratic process working itself out in Argentina.

As I have indicated there is no 1:1 relationship between economic health and political democracy. But it is, I would submit, more than coincidence that control of fiscal and monetary instability and currency inflation have historically been the *sine qua non* of political institutionalization and civil democratization as the German and French cases, not to mention a similar Japanese example, indicate. Just as economic stability is the prerequisite for continuous good habits of investment and growth, so democracy also depends on predictability and repetition. They are mutually reinforcing facets of societal change.

Thus, it has not been my intention to excuse the excesses and limitations of Argentine democracy, nor to project simple randomized facile comparisons with consolidated democracies, but merely to advocate an analysis of Argentina politics from the vantage point of historical and comparative distance and perspective.

Notes

1.   Three thousand DGI [Argentina's IRS] agents made 490,000 visits and enlisted 164,000 new tax payers, while 136,000 individuals made "spontaneous" payments, 140,000 tax evaders were targeted, and 135,000 VAT "errors" were detected (World Bank, 63).

2.   Excise taxes on alcohol, cigarettes, and fuel continue as well as modest import taxes on non-Mercosur imports and some remaining exceptional taxes on automobiles from a Mercosur country—Brazil.

3.   Areas of positive growth have been seen in gas and petroleum production, trucks, automobiles, stoves, heaters, thermal tanks, refrigerators, air conditioners, clothes washers, various metals, pipes, hot and cold lamination, crude steel, cement, paints, tires, various forms of chemical products, sugar, wine, soft drinks, beer, and cigarettes (El Cronista Comercial, January 24, 1994, and Clarín, Supplemento Económico, March 13, 1994).

4.   Paid vacation is limited to twenty-two days. Daily flex-time work schedules have been instituted allowing up to ten-hour work days without overtime, compensated by certain days with less than eight-hour obligations with a 37 1/2 hour maximum per week (currently it is 48 hours). Moreover, the flex-time arrangement must be mutually agreed upon by employers and workers. Not all employers are eligible under this program. Those who have in the previous six months dismissed workers without cause cannot participate (LAWR, May 20, 1993).

5.   In a recent paper this relationship between Peronism and the Argentine unions has been appropriately labeled as a "captivating alliance." See Sarah Kelsey and Steve Levitsky, "Captivating Alliances: Unions, Labor-backed Parties and the Politics of Liberalization in Argentina and Mexico," paper presented at Latin American Studies Association meetings (Atlanta, Georgia, March 1994).

6.   Peronist Election Victories (%)

Year	PJ	UCR	PJ Margin	Total Non-PJ
1987	42.9	37.3	5.6	57.1
1989	46.4	33.1	13.3	53.6
1991	40.4	29.1	11.3	59.6
1993	42.3	30.0	12.3	57.7

PJ=Peronists; UCR=Radicals
Source: Latin American Weekly Report, October 14, 1993, p. 480.

7.   One of the more positive signs for neoliberalism in Latin America has been the Chilean experience. The earliest exponent of privatization and free market reforms, Chile's unemployment has plummeted from 17 percent in 1985 to only 4.7 percent in 1993.

8.   Ex-president Alfonsín has accused Menem of "systematically yielding to the temptation of hegemony" (*Latin American Weekly Report*, March 11, 1993, p. 2).

References

Argentina: From Insolvency to Growth. Washington, D.C.: The World Bank, 1993.

Beccaria, Luis A. "Distribución del ingreso en la Argentina: Explorando lo sucedido desde mediados de los setenta." *Desarrollo Económica* 31 (1991): 123.

——. "Reestructuración, empleos y salários en la Argentina." In *El desafío de la competitividad: La industria argentina en transformación*, ed. Bernardo Kosacoff. Buenos Aires: CEPAL-Alianza Editorial, 1993.

Bernstein, Eduard. *Evolutionary Socialism*. New York: Schocken Books, 1961.

Bisang, Roberto, Mariana Fuchs, and Bernardo Kosacoff. "Internacionalización de empresas industriales argentinas." *Desarrollo Económica* 32 (1992): 127.

Bouzas, Roberto. "Mas allá de la estabilización y la reforma? Un ensayo sobre la economía argentina a comienzos de los '90." *Desarrollo Económica* 33 (1993): 129.

Burawoy, Michael. *The Politics of Production*. London: New Left Books, 1979.

Cortés, Rosalía. "Regulación institucional y relación aslariada en el mercado Argentina, 1980–1990." *Realidad Económica* (February 1994).

Edwards, Richard. *Contested Terrain: Transformation of the Work Place in the Twentieth Century*. New York: Basic Books, 1979.

Erro, Davide G. *Resolving the Argentine Paradox*. Boulder: Lynne Rienner Publishers, 1993.

Fundación Mediterránea. Newsletters 8 and 9 (12 and 1), 1993, 1994.

Halle, David. *The American Blue-Collar Home Owner*. Chicago: University of Chicago Press, 1984.

Hobsbawm, Eric. "The New Threat to History." *New York Review of Books* (December 16, 1993).

Ippolito, Gabriela. "Political Orientations of Argentina's Urban Poor: Democracy, Capitalism and the State." Paper presented at XVIII International Congress of the Latin American Studies Association (Atlanta, Georgia, March 9-12, 1994).

Kelsey, Sarah, and Steve Levitsky. "Captivating Alliances: Unions, Labor-Backed parties, and the Politics of Economic Liberalization." Paper presented at XVIII International Congress of the Latin American Studies Association (Atlanta, Georgia, March 9-12, 1994).

Kosacoff, Bernardo, and Gabriel Bezchinsky. "Las empresas transnacionales en la industria argentina." In *El desafíos de la competitividad*, ed. Bernardo Kosacoff. Buenos Aires: CEPAL-Alianza Editorial, 1993.

Lamadrid, Alejandro. "Peronismo: Adios al proletariado." In *Desafíos para el sindicalismo en la Argentina*, ed. Omar Moreno. Buenos Aires: Editorial Legasa, 1993.

Lamont, Michèle, and Marcel Fournier. *Cultivating Differences: Symbolic Boundaries and the Making of Inequality*. Chicago: University of Chicago Press, 1992.

Marshall, Ray. *Unheard Vocies*. New York: Basic Books, 1987.

Marx, Karl. *Economic and Philosophical Manuscripts*, ed. Erich Fromm. New York: Frederick Unger, 1961.

Murillo, M. Victoria. "Union Response to Economic Reform in Argentina." Paper presented at XVIII International Congress of the Latin American Studies Association (Atlanta, Georgia, March 9-12, 1994).

Perlman, Selig. *A Threory of the Labor Movement*. New York: Macmillan Co., 1928.

Poulantzas, Nicos. *Classes in Contemporary Capitalism*. London: New Left Books, 1975.

Powers, Nancy. "Argentina: The Politics of Poverty." Paper presented at XVIII International Congress of the Latin American Studies Association (Atlanta, Georgia, March 9-12, 1994).

Ranis, Peter. "The New Working Class: Implications for Comparative Research Based on the Argentine Case." *Revista de Economía y Trabajo* 2, no. 3 (1994).

Roemer, John. *A General Theory of Exploitation and Class*. Cambridge: Harvard University Press, 1982.

Saunders, Peter R. *A Nation of Homeowners*. London: Unwin Hyman, 1989.

Scase, Richard. *Class*. Minneapolis: University of Minnesota Press, 1992.

Senén González, Cecilia, and Daniel Ximenez Sáez. "Caracterización de los cambios en el modelo de relaciones laborales en una empresa de servicias privatizada." Paper presented at 1st Latin American Congress on Sociology of Work (Mexico City, November 22-26, 1993).

Sguiglia, Eduardo, and Ricardo Delgado. "Desregulación y competitividad: Evaluación de la experiencia argentina." *Boletín Informativo Techint* (1993): 276.

Tannenbaum, Frank. *A Philosophy of Labor*. New York: Alfred A. Knopf, 1951.

Vallas, Steven Peter. *Power in the Workplace: The Politics of Production at AT&T*. Albany: SUNY Press, 1993.

Wellman, Sandra. *The Social Anthroplogy of Work*. London: Academic Press, 1979.

Wright, Erik Olin. *Classes*. London: Verso, 1985.

——. "Class Analysis, History and Emancipation." *New Left Review* 32 (1993): 127.

PERIODICALS AND NEWSPAPERS CONSULTED

Ambito Financiero (Buenas Aires)
Buenos Aires Herald (Buenos Aires)
La Capital (La Plata)
Clarín (Buenos Aires)
Crónica (Buenos Aires)
El Cronista Comercial (Buenos Aires)
Economist Intelligence Unit Country Report: Argentina 1994 (London)
Latin American Weekly Report (London)
La Nación (Buenos Aires)
Notícias (Buenos Aires)
Página/12 (Buenos Aires)
La Prensa (Buenos Aires)

Preface

This book, from its inception in the plan to speak to Argentine workers about the politics of everyday life through its final draft stage, took six years to complete. The interviews were undertaken over thirteen months, from mid-1985 through mid-1986. In the summer of 1987 I returned to Buenos Aires to develop the data book based on the structured, open-ended interviews, and I completed the initial manuscript in the summers of 1988 and 1989.

The events in Eastern Europe that symbolically culminated with the dismantlement of the Berlin Wall reinforced the overall view that the Argentine workers had communicated to me three years earlier. Further, the reactivization and the privatization of the state economy that Argentine workers welcomed in 1985–1986 had been implemented in no uncertain terms in Argentina by 1990. I returned to Argentina in mid-1990 to assess the current situation of the workers and to return to a number of interviewees to ask them about their current views. As they had been earlier, they were still hopeful that the government could carry off a privatization that protected their hard-won labor and social rights; however, at the same time they remained confident that the basic capacity of the Argentine worker would see them through the economic transition to a modicum of economic dynamism and stability. The beliefs were complemented by a recognition of the increasing viability and legitimacy of Argentine democracy and culture.

To recreate the many circumstances in which people were instrumental in helping me carry out this project would take up several pages of extended detail. But I cannot let this occasion go by without acknowledging a number of Argentine individuals who, through project assistance, institutional interventions, significant advice, or personal kindnesses, allowed my interviewing to move forward. First, I wish to thank my research assistant Olga Ventura for her important contribution to cataloguing the questionnaires into a data book, and my interviewer assistants, Licienadas Virginia Allende, Gisela

Caviglia, Maria Giraldes, and student Gloria Gascon. My deep appreciation also goes to Paco Risso of the Argentine Fulbright Commission for his friendly and upbeat support that now has spanned a quarter of a century during my various trips under Fulbright auspices or someone else's.

My heartfelt thanks also go to the following people, without whom the interview process would have been almost inconceivable: Jorge Caruso of SEGBA; Ramon Olivero of Ford; Daniel Botino, Marta Tridico, Lilia Cattani, and Santiago Lartatequi of the CTERA teachers; Armando Gini and Alberto Espina of the UDA teachers; Javier Nieva of ENTEL and CEFS; Romildo Ranu of SOIVA; Amoral Paz of the Banco Galícia y Buenos Aires; Carlos Moirequi of the Banco de Boston; José Badu, Miguel Arce, and Sandra Pérez of FOETRA; Baltazar Soto and Oscar Ortega of SMATA; Carlos Imbaud and Luís Roxas of Luz y Fuerza; Alberto Avella and Manuel Pedrera of AOT; Alberto Pirozzoli of Sudamtex; Victor Pizarro of Pravia, as well as Leandro Wolfson, Jorge Katz, Ricardo Gaudio, and Héctor Cordone. I also want to acknowledge the friendship and encouragement I received from Maria Cánepa, Nora Femenia, Aldo Fernandez, and Bertha Sperber.

I am very appreciative of the financial support given me by the Council on International Exchange of Scholars' Fulbright program — particularly the encouragement I received from Rosemary Lyons; and by the Research Foundation of the Professional Staff Congress and City University of New York. I would like also to express my thanks to Ernesto Steinbach for his many courtesies as director of IDES; to the Instituto Torcuato Di Tella and Natalio Botana; and to CISEA and Héctor Palomino, for their generous cooperation in the use of these two research institutes in 1987 and 1990. My appreciation also goes to Professor Anne Rothstein of Lehman College, CUNY, for her invaluable expertise and assistance in preparing the computer runs that provided the statistical associations. I am further indebted to my colleague at York College, Jo Carolyn Lewis, for her advice on presenting the tables. My thanks also to Jane Flanders of the University of Pittsburgh Press, whose editorial suggestions make this a much more readable book.

My appreciation to Bill Smith for his thoughtful reading of the study. In addition, many people read one or another paper and/or chapter while this manuscript was in progress. I thank the following colleagues and friends for their helpful comments: William Smith, Victor Treschan, Hobart Spalding, Sam Farber, José Havet, Héctor Palomino, Tom Kappner, Seamus O'Cleireacain, Daniel Kelly, Richard Boris, Robert Parmet, Edward Epstein, Daniel James, and Ronald Hellman.

Various sections and/or passages found in chapters 3, 5, 7, and 9 have previously appeared in the following publications: "The Argentine Working Class and Peronism under the New Democratic Regime: A Preliminary

Assessment," Working Paper Series No. 1 (New York: Bildner Center for Western Hemisphere Studies, CUNY, December 1987); "Argentine Rank and File Unionists and Their World," Occasional Papers No. 9 (New York: Center for Labor-Management Policy Studies, CUNY, June 1990); "The Contradictions of Class and Ideology Among Argentine Laborers and Employees," *Studies in Comparative International Development* 26 (Winter 1991–92); "Argentine Workers and the Nature of Democratic Values," Papers on Latin America No. 17 (New York: Institute of Latin American and Iberian Studies, Columbia University, June 1990).

The last, though most important, expression of my gratitude goes to Anne Humpherys, who gave me her love and support and who probably read every word of this book at least once and changed some in the process, and to my children, Maria and Paul, who indirectly coexisted with the manuscript in many unexpected ways. A big hug for my son, Paul, for yeoman work on the galleys. I wish also to thank Raúl and Luis Liendo and the many long-distance-running *muchachos* of the Costanera del Sur who kept my feet on the ground metaphorically and actually during a pressure-packed year in the intense atmosphere that is Greater Buenos Aires.

I

Introduction

1 *Putting Workers in Perspective*

I ASKED A young Argentine light and power worker: "What's your understanding of democracy?" He answered, "I walk where I want. I speak what I feel and I feel good about things, even though economically life is difficult. Compared to the repression, which is the only other system I really know, it is worlds apart."[1]

This book is about Argentina's working men and women from all walks of life, both in the factory and office and outside them. But when I speak about Argentine workers, it is not just to place them in the workplace as producers of Argentina's national wealth, but also to understand them as consumers of goods, pursuers of leisure and culture; as parents, students, homeowners, and voters; and as repositories of Argentine political culture.

This book is thus more and at the same time less than the study of Argentine trade unions, labor officialdom, and labor politics. My intention is, rather, to give space to the opinions of the contemporary Argentine working class. Workers were questioned as to their day-to-day personal and work experiences, their views as citizens and voters, their political values and commitments, as well as their general moral and ethical stance toward the leading issues in contemporary Argentina, and their beliefs regarding democracy and socialism. What follows is therefore more about workers themselves than about work or the work process itself.

Antonio Gramsci said over sixty years ago, "There exists in the totality of the working masses many distinct wills: There is the communist will, a maximalist will, a reformist will, a liberal democratic will. There is even a fascist will, in a certain sense and within certain limits."[2] Mirroring this

understanding, Wilhelm Reich wrote, "Class consciousness is not a knowledge of the historical or economic laws that govern the existence of the
human being, but it is: knowledge of one's own vital necessities in all spheres;
knowledge of ways and possibilities of satisfying them; and knowledge of the
obstacles that a social system based on private property puts in the way of
their satisfaction."[3]

Because of their multiple roles, it is difficult to wed the working class to
any ready-made concept of class consciousness or tie it to any objective
standard of class values and behavior. Contradictions within working-class
cultural and political orientations abound; to attempt to formalize an
expected pattern of values and behavior and to characterize other attitudes
as being, or implying, false consciousness is to simplify reality and blind us to
the nuances that can increase our understanding of workers.

Recognizing workers as citizens and consumers as well as producers,
then, makes us confront — painfully at times — the maddening contradictions presented by their needs and wants. We see that class consciousness
comes in many forms, under different guises — always partial, sometimes
instrumental, rarely if ever full-blown. Saúl Ubaldini, general secretary of
one of the Third World's most powerful labor organizations, the Confederación General de Trabajo (CGT), explained why he is a Peronist. He told a
reporter:

> He had seen Juan Perón only from afar, but that he had a special recollec-
> tion of Eva Perón whom he described as "practically the champion of the
> poor." As an 11-year-old studying at an industrial school in Buenos Aires he
> won a prize for best student and she came to make the presentations. The
> prize, he said, was 20 days in a first class hotel in the beach resort of Mar
> del Plata for him and his mother.[4]

This gives us a partial glimpse of the special combination of events and
circumstances in people's lives that only later become more coherently
identifiable as political values and ideology.

In light of these mixed elements, this book examines the values of
unionized laborers and employees expressed when they were asked to
evaluate Argentine historical developments of the 1970s and to interpret the
changing conditions of their personal, work, and political experiences in the
post-dictatorship period since 1983. I examine their views and opinions
against the backdrop of several generations of loyalty and commitment to a
Peronist sociopolitical orientation.[5]

But apart from placing contemporary Argentine workers within a
historic process, it is also important to listen to the voices of Argentine
workers for their own sake. There are only a few studies[6] on working-class

ideology, values, beliefs, and attitudes, and almost no attention has been paid to workers as individuals.[7] The typical analysis of Argentine workers concerns election results, when workers are included in voter surveys; or workers are mentioned in national income accounts, strike statistics, and statistical surveys of the Argentine economy and social structure — of which the working class is, of course, an essential ingredient. There are also analyses concerning questions of "labor and politics" which really focus mainly on the decisions taken by labor leaders and the CGT's relations with various types of government regimes as well as studies of trade union bureaucracies as they negotiate over collective bargaining issues.[8] As Peter Winn says of these works in general: "The workers — the presumed protagonists of labor history — only appear in these studies as institutional, theoretical, statistical abstractions; the concrete and complex realities of their experience are conspicuous by their absence."[9]

Reinterpreting Class and Democracy

Argentine workers' highest aspirations are to own a home and to give their children better educational opportunities. Can these largely personal aspirations for individual betterment form the bases for class consciousness? Since these two desires have not precluded a commitment to social and economic justice by the Argentine working class in the past, to answer this thorny question we must reexamine both the concept of class and the collective consciousness of that class and its potential for changing society.

Historical Marxists regard the working class as unique — objectively given the task of superseding capitalism not only because of their numbers but also because of the ethical nature of their collective consciousness. They become the first class in history to be capable of such an ethical collective consciousness.[10]

What is this "class" Marx was talking about? Those working in factories, mines, and construction work have always been in the minority, even during early capitalism, when Marx was writing. By and large, most workers apparently rebelled against injustice rather than capitalism per se. Even then, an explicitly revolutionary class consciousness was perhaps a pious aspiration to be found among only a minority of those who hoped to defeat capitalism through collective action. Thus Marx was inevitably drawn to the industrial laborer, because of his rebellious streak, as the historical agent for revolutionary change.[11]

The real question is: do workers struggle for purely class interests, or do these interests include a mixture of more immediate concerns, including the desire for property, access to culture, more equitable income distribution, freedom from oppression, and nationalism?

The existence of class is one thing, but — as Marx was fully aware — the pursuit of class consciousness is quite another. The search for this consciousness often leads observers to see phenomena that may indeed not be there. E. P. Thompson's view is insightful. "There is a cultural superstructure, through which this recognition dawns in inefficient ways. These cultural 'lags' and distortions are a nuisance, so it is easy to pass from this to some theory of substitution: The party, sect, or theorist, who disclose class-consciousness, not as it is, but as it ought to be."[12]

The majority of the working class — or, better said, the working *classes* — is comprised of a number of factions with a large variety of views and attitudes. At best, as Thompson has portrayed it, *class* is not a permanent structure or category; it is rather a relationship that emerges from time to time as people band together for one or another reason.[13] This phenomenon is compounded by the growth of the various sectors of the working class, thus adding to its heterogeneity and amorphousness. Marx himself saw that capitalism had "converted the physician, the lawyer, the priest, the poet, the man of science into paid wage labourers."[14]

In his social placement of people who work for a living, Marx was not so distant from Max Weber as is frequently supposed. He was aware of distinguishing characteristics of various forms of work and thus purposely laid his hopes on the military-type setting of the factory and the group camaraderie of its laborer as the seedbed for developing working-class consciousness.

But it took the concerted critique of Eduard Bernstein to fully comprehend and acknowledge the variations of working-class experience. As he wrote in *Evolutionary Socialism*, "It cannot be otherwise than that vital differences in manner of work and amount of income finally produce different conduct and demands of life. The highly skilled fine instrument maker and the collier, the skilled house decorator and the porter, the sculptor or modeler and the stoker, lead, as a rule, a very different kind of life and have very different kinds of wants."[15] Bernstein, like Marx a keen observer of the human condition, emphasized some of the more nonproductive sides of people's lives, and understood them as contributing factors to class definition and accepted their contradictory consequences.

The nature of work is only one criterion for making sociological comparisons. Differences of culture and education and leisure pursuits are equally important. Modern technology, organizational diversity, and the complexity of contemporary economies all contribute to variations among individual perceptions of one's life and work. Thompson accentuated this fact when he wrote:

If we stop history at a given point then there are no classes but simply a multitude of individuals with a multitude of experiences. But if we watch these men
over an adequate period of social change, we observe patterns in their relationships, their ideas, and their institutions. Class is defined by men as they live
their own history, and, in the end, this is its only definition.[16]

There are clear contradictions between the concept of class offered by
revolutionary socialists and communists, and workers' basic demands for
themselves and their families, that go to the heart of the human condition. It
is apparent that arguments for reform, rather than revolution, have struck a
strong responsive chord in Argentine workers because such arguments
better address their personal needs and goals. The relative autonomy of
human needs, whatever the political and economic system, appears universal. Some needs play a central role in the lives of all people—whether they
live in capitalist or socialist systems. Socialism as well as capitalism must
fulfill human needs that are probably precapitalist as well as presocialist. The
working class in Argentina is not unique in this respect, even considering the
Peronist phenomenon, which predisposes Argentine workers to a type of
"corporate democratic socialism."

The concept of class, in and of itself, has little power to persuade and
motivate people. It has been too often used merely as an abstraction in leftist
analyses of social structure. Though class as a concept helps to distinguish
social strata, it is only in conjunction with a host of other material and
ideological questions that it can account for antiregime or antiestablishment
behavior. Carlos Vilas, writing of class conflict in Nicaragua, adds to the issue
of class the equally important politically motivating phenomena of democracy, nationalism, and economic development.[17] Workers that I interviewed in
Argentina knew far more about what these three categories meant for their
happiness than the nature of class conflict—a subject on which they were
tellingly ambivalent and ambiguous. Clearly, people do not translate social
and economic injustice into political militancy as a result of rigidly defined
abstractions such as class, but must be directed by actual political concerns
to which class adds additional social reality.

Argentine unions have struggled relatively successfully for their interests
over the years by combining demands for social justice with a demand for
shared political influence. Through negotiations, manifestos, "battle plans,"
localized and general strikes, the unions have invariably pursued higher
wages and better working conditions. When Peronism is out of power, the
CGT tends to support more clearly a worker-type populism. When Peronism is
in power, this populism must necessarily lessen, since it must share access
with other factions of the governing coalition, including its bourgeois class
rivals. But the fight for workers' interests has continued in either case,

despite the fact that, as Hobsbawm writes about parallel struggles in Europe, the unions are always "an opposition that never becomes a government."[18] Playing that opposing role has historically been the labor unions' most credible and meaningful function.

In Eduard Bernstein's time, England was considered a country in which people sought equality in freedom, whereas in France people sought freedom in equality.[19] Argentina, it seems, is much closer to this French model. As my survey has indicated, Argentine workers demonstrate substantial support for democracy as a political system because it assures a modicum of autonomy in their way of life. My results tend to corroborate the findings of Booth and Seligson on contemporary Mexico, as well as those of Susan Taino on Chile and Argentina of the 1960s and David Halle on the United States.[20] At the same time, my findings raise questions about some of the past judgments concerning working-class authoritarianism.[21] For example, in Mexico, Booth and Seligson found that despite authoritarian political structures in the late 1970s, the Mexican political culture remained largely democratic.[22] Taino, applying classical measures of authoritarianism such as traditionalism, intolerance, submissiveness, and fatalism, found no substantial evidence for the existence of an authoritarian political culture in either Chile or Argentina. She found the Argentines just as democratic as the Chileans, despite the fact that the survey was conducted during periods of Argentine military intervention in the mid-1960s, when Chile was experiencing a constitutional democracy.[23]

Argentine workers' commitment to, and support for, democracy seemed to reach a new plane in the light of the contrast between the military *proceso* and the new democracy. While laborers occasionally expressed restiveness with liberty that bordered on license, in the main, workers supported the democratic principles institutionalized under Alfonsín, even when they voted against his Radical party for socioeconomic reasons. Previous assessments of the Argentine working class have underestimated its commitment to democracy as a political good, as something workers inherently appreciate and rank very high among their hierarchy of values. Democracy has become an integral demand among Argentine workers; we must absolve them of the "original sin" in earlier analyses that depicted an inherent working-class propensity toward authoritarianism of either the right or the left.

Why Argentina's Working Class?

A study of the working class thus offers a good opportunity to analyze basic questions about society-at-large and the role in society of its largest segment—wage and salary earners. Both in the Marxist and liberal/socio-logical tradition, the working class is crucial for the structure and direction of social change. But even to begin to understand how the working class might fulfill this role requires an analysis of real situations and within a manageable country context. Argentina, because of certain special features of its economic and political history, lends itself to further comparative exploration and speculation about the place of the working class in the theoretical literature that discusses class, values, and ideology.

First of all, Argentine workers have experienced in just one to two generations a gamut of political regimes—from civilian/populist through military/authoritarian to liberal/democratic governments. This distinguishes Argentine political culture from both the more stable liberal democratic and socialist systems of the industrialized world and the persistent authoritarian systems of the Third World. As a result, in Argentina, as in perhaps only a handful of other countries (possibly, though imperfectly, in Brazil, Uruguay, Portugal or Chile), one may study the various impacts of regime change on working-class values and attitudes. Argentina provides an interesting labora-tory for probing the values and beliefs of the working class in changing political contexts.

Second, Argentina is a developing capitalist country with a large number of salaried urban workers comparable to levels in developed Western European countries.[24] Further, within an ostensibly capitalist political culture, an extraordinarily high proportion of Argentina's *organized* workers are affiliated with unions.[25] These qualities are important to a study of class consciousness because, in the theoretical literature on social change and revolution, unions are not only evidence of forms of class consciousness but are also among the engines of political progress. The role of trade unions as representatives of the underprivileged masses and in socialist revolutions is the subject of heated historical debate.[26] Further, the power of Argentine unions in the councils of government has surpassed that of unions in most advanced capitalist and socialist countries. Thus the Argentine case, which provides us with an organized working-class structure that has a social influence and leverage far superior to most other trade unions throughout the world, can help clarify the questions about the role of unions in social change.

Third, Argentine trade unionism, in alliance with Peronism, gave the Argentine working class a major, legitimized, noncommunist political option—namely, a potentially militant populist alternative that dramatically improved living conditions under capitalism when it took over the reins of government. Moreover, the alliance between political Peronism and the trade unions, through uprisings, mobilizations, demonstrations, general strikes, and election victories, has managed to destabilize five apparently safely situated civil and military governments in just two generations (1962, 1965, 1969, 1975, 1982). Thus working-class political power in Argentina is a serious issue to be explored.

Fourth, the Argentine case provides striking proof of the results of the failure of traditional Marxist-Leninist approaches to address the nonproductivist side of workers' lives. In previous studies of the working class, too little attention has been paid to workers beyond their position in society as producers. Eric Hobsbawm writes: "It has been said: 'Inside every worker there is a human being trying to get out.'"[27] It is thus an incomplete Marxism that contends that workers' perceptions are all framed by the exploitative nature of their work experience, a reductivism that trivializes workers' considerable experience beyond the factory walls and office windows.

Fifth, Argentina, though a Third World country in terms of national income and industrial production, has a social structure comparable to that of advanced Western countries. Therefore, the results of this survey can be applied to other more technically advanced countries. As in these countries, the growth of the tertiary sector of the working class in Argentina — along with a proportional decline of the industrial laboring class and the stability of its self-employed sector — presents a complex, traditional as well as modern, variety of social strata.[28] Since the industrialization of the 1960s, the economic trend in Argentina has seen the lower ends of the working class move up in access to culture and education, while during the late 1970s through the 1980s, income among the "middle-class" workers, those who might be expected to share the outlook of intermediary social strata, has declined. This has had a leveling effect among the vast middle portions of the working class, from the ranks of unskilled and semiskilled laborers, through skilled laborers and employees, to technicians and professional employees.

More and more, the Argentine worker is a public service employee, a professional employee (such as teacher, court official, hospital and health clinic employee), or an employee in the private commercial sector (mainly in finance, sales, and services.)[29] Generally three out of every five employed workers today are from the tertiary sector, as opposed to the secondary sectors of manufacturing, transportation, and construction. The specifically industrial proletariat has been reduced to less than 15 percent of the economically active work force.[30] In 1973 one out of every eight voters was a factory worker, but by 1983, the number had dropped to one in fourteen.[31]

In one sense, Argentina has entered a postindustrial era. This has been partly the result of the deindustrialization policies of the military dictatorship of 1976–1983 (*el proceso*) and partly the result of Argentina's competitive disadvantage vis-à-vis Brazil as an industrial provider, combined with Argentina's advantages as a service, information-systems, and financial entrepôt.[32] These economic developments have helped increase the growth of Argentina's private service employees at the expense of its industrial labor force. When one adds to this melange a large organized civil service and nationalized enterprise sector, the result is a complex trade union structure that mirrors the nation's cosmopolitan, modern panoply of intellectual and cultural cross-currents.

The question remains, however: which experiences among Argentina's workers are unique, and which are general and thus can contribute to theory building about the working class as such? Let us approach the second part of the question by asking another that can be answered relatively easily. Who are the workers we are talking about?

The Argentine workers I interviewed reflect a radical change in the concept of *worker* from the days of Marx's concern with blue-collar proletarians. They are closer to his general definition: those who live by the sale of their labor power, who receive less than the value of the production and/or circulation of the goods and services in which they are involved, and who do not own the significant means of production. Today the working class in most capitalist countries can be subsumed under this category: people who by collective bargaining contracts or individual negotiations basically live on fixed wages and/or salaries. Some may spend most of their day in physical labor, while the work of others may demand very little physical exertion but require other forms of disciplined, routinized performance. Increasingly, both manual and nonmanual work under advanced capitalism are subjected to forms of organization that enhance production and profit for either the private sector or the state. I found Eric Wright's definition to be most appropriate in characterizing Argentine workers. For Wright, workers and their families are, first, excluded from control over money capital, physical capital, and labor power; second, they are basically excluded from the creation and execution of state policy and ideology.[33]

We have today in complex, technologically advanced capitalist societies a plethora of categories of work that replace an earlier industrial labor force. Workers may be subdivided into categories of skilled and unskilled, and (of course) unionized and nonunionized workers. Moreover, there are blue-collar laborers, white-collar commercial and service employees, public- and private-sector employees, employees in nationalized industry and professional, administrative and technical personnel in both the public and private sectors. Thus we have here a behemoth—a vast, complicated working class that comprises between 70 and 90 percent of economically active people in most nonpeasant societies.

This book attempts to tap these complex and changing dimensions of organized Argentine workers by focusing on that significant portion of the working class that is *organized*. Such a focus makes a difference not in the broad definition of who a worker is, but rather in certain social and legal forms that enhance a laborer's or employee's ability to contest particular political values and policy priorities. Alejandro Portes demonstrates that what gives unionized workers a basic commonality (beyond their lack of control over the means of production and a subordinate position in the places of employment) is their ability to use their collective organizations as an effective instrument against excessive exploitation and to defend their right to some form of coverage under a social security system.[34] For a study using this definition as its focus, perhaps no country provides a better laboratory than Argentina.

Surveying Argentine Workers

The survey on which this book is based attempted to tap the changing dimensions of the Argentine working class by emphasizing the period of redemocratization under the presidency of Raúl Alfonsín (1983–1989). The Argentine working class today, as represented by the General Confederation of Labor (CGT), displays a very heterogeneous class structure. Unionized workers are found in heavy and light industry, large and small factories, private and public sectors, industrial and service sectors, and manual and nonmanual trades. They range from the menial to "middle-class" trade union workers found largely in the service trades, government administration, and teaching. The salaried and wage sector comprises over 70 percent of the economically active portion of the population, with employers and the self-employed making up the rest. This gives the working class the overwhelming majority and makes it crucial for understanding Argentine culture and society.

Further, Argentine unions remain the principal organized nexus for one of the major political parties — the Peronist party. The huge rank-and-file membership of organized labor has allowed the CGT, in concert with the Peronists, to act as one member of a handful of powerful corporate interests.

Peronism, since its original removal from power in 1955, has survived illegal status, flawed elections, various forms of political proscription, and outright military repression to emerge again and again as Argentina's majoritarian political party. Its resilience was demonstrated by its dramatic gubernatorial, legislative, and presidential victories of September 1987 and May 1989. In fact, 1987–1989 was a watershed period; for the first time Peronism had recovered from successive presidential and legislative defeats within a system of genuine democratic political and cultural freedom. Its convincing victory over the governing Radical party of President Raúl Alfonsín signified a new level of Peronist authenticity under political normalcy. It marks the emergence of a more complicated and varied Peronism.[35]

The results of this survey of Argentina's unionized workers in all walks of life, combined with an investigation of their historic and contemporary relationship to Peronism, help to clarify many issues in the discussion of working-class consciousness. Workers are complex and contradictory. They are not as stultified and miserable as they are sometimes depicted, nor are they particularly virtuous or more capable of seeing the truth than anyone else. We can add to our knowledge of the working class and their ostensibly contradictory beliefs only by examining what workers think about their lives and work. But as we examine workers in a contemporary sociological context, it is important to place them in both a historical and institutional milieu to capture the relationships among the traditional forces in Argentina. Political Peronism and trade unionism have influenced workers' perceptions and attitudes toward the hard economic realities of their day-to-day struggles at work and at home.

This study is based on a stratified, random sample of 110 workers chosen from seven unions in Greater Buenos Aires (where the great preponderance of Argentine workers and employees are located). The quantified data was gathered from structured, open-ended interviews of organized laborers and employees conducted in 1985–1986. Since Argentina's political labor climate is largely dominated by the opinions of union leaders and delegates, my research attempts to take a different approach. To expand the picture of Argentine trade unionism, I tap the views of the working people for whom these union heads and district delegates claim to speak. Though it is clear that Greater Buenos Aires contains the majority of the nation's union leaders, delegates, and rank-and-file union members, union leaders with quite different political views have occasionally come from interior cities such as Córdoba and Rosario (particularly in the late 1960s and early 1970s). However, the results of this study suggest that critical social explosions such as the Cordobazo student-labor uprising of 1969 are not only atypical of recent Argentine labor history but also alien to the values of most Argentine workers.

Argentina has over 1,400 labor federations, unions, and associations. The seven unions represented in this study—three of which are among the nation's five largest—represent approximately 46 percent of Argentina's organized workers. The survey sample includes four industrial unions—textile workers (Asociación Obrera Textil, or AOT), autoworkers and mechanics (Sindicato de Mecánicos y Afines del Transporte Automotor, or

SMATA), metalworkers, including those in iron and steel (Unión Obrera
Metalúrgica de la República Argentina, or UOM), light and power workers
(Federación Argentina de Trabajadores de Luz y Fuerza, known simply as Luz
y Fuerza) and three service unions—those covering telephone employees
and technicians (Federación de Obreros y Empleados Telefónicos de la
República Argentina, or FOETRA), bank employees (Asociación Bancária),
and teachers (federated nationwide into the Confederación de Trabajadores
de la Educación de la República Argentina, or CTERA).

The study includes three of CTERA's most important unions—namely,
the secondary teachers from national public preparatory schools (Unión
Docentes Argentinos, or UDA), municipal primary school teachers (Unión
de Maestros de Primária, or UMP) and industrial arts teachers from the
national industrial preparatory schools (Asociación de Magistério de Enseñanza Técnica, or AMET). AOT, SMATA, and UOM workers interviewed
represent industrial textile workers, autoworkers, and metalworkers from
the foreign and domestic private sector,[36] whereas the great majority of Luz
y Fuerza light and power workers work for the state electrical enterprise of
Greater Buenos Aires known as SEGBA. Telephone employees that were
interviewed worked for the state telephone company, or ENTEL, and
teachers represent the public sector, while bank employees represent both
state and private-sector (foreign and domestic) banks. Thus the sample of
workers interviewed represents both the public and private sectors, national
and foreign capital, state and private enterprises.

The interviews were conducted between September 1985 and August
1986. Workers were drawn by lot using a random numbers table to ensure a
nonbiased sample in each workplace. At least fifteen workers were chosen
from each union. Supervisors, foremen, heads of departments, managerial
staff within the factory and office settings, and principals in the different
schools were explicitly excluded, as were custodial and caretaker personnel
at all sites. The survey included the middle strata in each work site comprising the semiskilled, skilled, and technician categories of laborers and employees.
These segments most fully represent the bulk of the working class.

Among textile workers (AOT), three factories were chosen randomly,
among hundreds of textile factories in Greater Buenos Aires, from the most
representative branches of the textile industry—namely, cotton, wool, and
stitching—one a large factory of more than 500 workers (Sudamtex), one of
medium size with approximately 200 workers (Ponieman) and one a smaller
factory of just over 100 workers (Pravia). Among Luz y Fuerza workers I
chose the large and prototypical electrical plant in Buenos Aires known as
Puerto Nuevo, employing approximately 800 workers. Among SMATA
workers I chose Ford Motors Argentina as a very large plant (over 3,000

workers), typical of all major automobile assembly plants in Argentina. Again, among metal workers (UOM) I selected Pirelli, a large representative, multinational plant of over 500 workers manufacturing cables and wires, and Koval y Blanck, a typical Argentine-owned smaller metallurgical plant producing auto horns.

Among service unions, I undertook interviews with FOETRA employees at one telephone exchange in the Belgrano district and one administrative complex in the Palermo district, both in the user-dense capital of Buenos Aires, ensuring a proportional mix of operators, technicians, linemen and splicers, and administrative staff. Within the Asociación Bancária I chose the largest banks from all sectors — that is, those with the most employees. The survey included the Central Bank (Banco Central de la República Argentina or BCRA), Banco de la Nación (the national bank), and two giant private banks, Banco de Boston and Banco de Galícia y Buenos Aires, each representative and dominant both in the foreign and domestic spheres. Among teachers, I chose three elementary and two secondary schools. I was careful to include a variety of residential settings and to include one academic high school (*colegio nacional*) and one industrial high school.

The structured, largely open-ended, in-depth questionnaire was administered by myself and four Argentine social science assistants. I conducted 53 percent of the interviews, while the balance were conducted by Argentine assistants[37] and taped for verification, accuracy, and a "feel" for the interviews themselves.[38] The average interview lasted approximately two hours and covered six major categories: (1) biographical data, (2) personal and family life aspirations and expressions, (3) labor union, work and job experiences and attitudes, (4) political experiences and attitudes, (5) judgments on current issues of import and opinions on key contemporary groups and institutions, and (6) the workers' overriding values and beliefs. There were 70 major questions and 33 follow-up questions, making a total of 103 queries.[39]

We sought permission from the enterprises and/or union shop stewards for all interviews. Their cooperation was essential, of course, and we had to make long and sometimes repeated explanations about the importance of interviewing workers in order to assure the success of the project. By and large, interviews were conducted in empty offices, conference rooms, and schoolrooms; at factories and offices we used rooms reserved for training, recreation, and medical attention. Very occasionally we had to conduct the interview in a *confitería* or pizzeria, which, though noisy, were nevertheless private.

The interviewees were given a one-page open letter detailing my credentials and project. I described my research project in a separate open letter addressed to the workers who were the subjects of my research.

Further, interviewers set aside five minutes before each interview to explain the reasons and sponsorship of the project. We made it clear that we did not represent either the United States or the Argentine governments, their union or any union, or their employer. After assuring subjects of their anonymity — that is, responses would appear only as part of a numerical sample or would be cited without direct attribution — we asked permission to tape record their responses. Not one worker objected to being tape recorded by me or my assistants.[40]

Only three people refused to be interviewed. The first was a textile worker who felt it too difficult and costly after a day's work to travel to and from the interview.[41] The second was a preparatory language teacher who said she didn't have time to be interviewed, and the third, who was contacted by one of my colleagues, was a metalworker who was apparently hesitant or timid about responding to an oral interview.

Obviously, one cannot trust absolutely the veracity of answers to an oral survey, but no outright lies or inconsistencies were discovered and no differences were perceived between my interviews and those of my Argentine colleagues. No doubt there are possible limitations to being a North American interviewing within an Argentine social setting, but I found the workers, after a few moments of reserve, seemingly oblivious to my origin and apparently also of the tape recording process itself. Typically, workers were very pleased, to say the least, that someone was willing to listen in such detail to their basic, deep-seated beliefs and opinions. The free-flowing nature of the interview questionnaire and the serious nature of the questions inevitably made the workers forget any misgivings they might have had and encouraged them to embark on what was in most cases a heartwarming, moving, and illuminating experience for me and — I believe — for my Argentine assistants.

A further limitation (and one that can only be surmised) is that we were largely tapping what workers said about their values, attitudes, and opinions, not how they had actually behaved in the past or would behave in the future. To compensate for this limitation, I have supplemented my survey results with many other sources, including government documents, labor laws, CGT position papers, individual trade union collective bargaining contracts, official economic surveys, vital census statistics, as well as book, journal, magazine, and newspaper accounts of the same issues on which the workers were asked to comment.

In retrospect, I have few reservations about using an open-ended (though structured) interview process. With infinite time and money, of course, we could have conducted more interviews; however, I think the sample is sufficiently large to be meaningful. The open-ended character of the interviews, on many occasions, resulted in moving stories, insights, and imaginative analyses that would have been impossible in a mail questionnaire or a questionnaire administered by a survey institute.

I often experienced a powerful sense of regret on completing a particularly interesting three-hour conversation with a laborer, employee, or teacher. I had learned so much and the workers had given so much of their intellect, personal values, and emotional involvement in the interview process. A year after the completion of my Argentine survey, I read Barbara Garson's book on American workers and her response reflects my own.

> And then as soon as a human being speaks, I hear things I never expected to hear, things I never could have invented. Yet they are things I know to be true, things that I somehow knew all along. . . .
>
> I have a soul meshing experience with someone and when it's over, it's over. I see them at the factory the next day, after they have revealed their doubts, and the intimate mechanism by which they cope, and if I've gotten a good interview, I don't want to talk to them again. My only consolation is that it has often been that kind of experience for them too. If it was really cathartic, they don't want to see me either.[42]

At first, the experiences gained from the many interviews were unsettling to me. Many of the findings contradicted some of my prior notions; they forced a reexamination of the literature about the working class and its social role in the West. But this challenge to my preconceptions was not only important intellectually; it has led me to a new perspective on workers. For John Madge, a powerful aspect of social science is "that the prospector . . . set[s] out in search of one thing and come[s] back with something entirely different, which he has learned to regard as far more significant and important."[43]

I begin by depicting the critical labor history before, during, and after Juan Perón's accession to power, his labor and social policy initiatives, and the continuing symmetrical relationship between Peronism and the Argentine labor movement through the many years of exile politics and internal labor opposition to a variety of civil and military regimes. (These are discussed in chapter 2.) I then examine the major institutionalized labor traditions that serve as a structural backdrop not only to the Argentine working class's stake in welfare capitalism but also to their relatively protected social position vis-à-vis other major corporate interests in Argentina. This is exemplified by some of the collective bargaining contracts won by Argentine labor into the 1970s (discussed in chapters 3 and 4).

After surveying the historical and structural antecedents of the Argentine labor movement, I assess their impact on the contemporary values of

Argentine workers not only as a labor force but also as political people and citizens (chapters 5–7). Last, the book evaluates the results of the survey. In chapters 8 and 9 I offer connections between my findings among Argentine laborers and employees and the theories about working-class consciousness and democracy that have been applied to them. Chapters 10 and 11 end with an assessment of how our findings help us to understand the Menem Peronist government and its relationship to the Argentine workers.

2 Labor and Peronism: The Historical Connection

> >

The Rise of Perón

TO FULLY UNDERSTAND the sociopolitical, cultural, and ideological context of contemporary Argentine workers, we must review the historical turning points that have shaped their interests and values. The development of early Peronism helps to illuminate the concerns of unions and workers in Argentine political culture today.

Since the nation's very inception as a centralized republic in 1880, reformism and corporatism have been the principal underpinnings of Argentine labor culture. At the turn of the century, there was little large-scale industrialization of the Western European or North American type; at the same time, there was massive immigration.[1] Argentina's urban "proletarians" (if one can use that term) were not overwhelmingly wage laborers but rather artisans — typically immigrants — employed in construction and small manufacturing establishments.[2]

Ruth Thompson has best explained the impact of this wave of immigration (*hacer la América*) on Argentine labor history: immigrants came to the New World to better themselves economically, and as long as they felt they could become part of the upper echelons of society, they did not lend themselves to a class struggle that sought to overthrow existing structures.[3]

Thus 40 percent of all strikes between 1907 and 1910 were centered on wage demands. Another 30 percent were initiated to defend trade union organization or were mounted against employers' reprisals.[4] Apparently, the

17

very success of the labor movement's economic struggles in Argentina blunted the political consciousness of the working class. Between 1910 and 1920, an era of deep revolutionary consciousness because of the dominance of an imported European anarchist tradition, strikes were largely concerned with wages and working conditions. Despite revolutionary rhetoric, union leaders were ready to negotiate and collaborate with both the state and private capital.[5]

A corporatist pattern was thus laid down in Argentina at least by the 1920s and consolidated in the 1930s. The development of light industry in the late 1930s resulted in a significant growth of the Argentine labor force.[6] Between 1934 and 1947 a potential industrial working class flowed into Greater Buenos Aires at a rate of 72,000 to 117,000 persons annually.[7] From 1935 to 1943, employment in the industrial labor sector grew by 81 percent, while real wages decreased by 10 percent.[8] These developments gave strong momentum to the trade union movement. Newly arrived workers from outside the capital were more concerned with immediate personal economic gain and tended to express their social consciousness in an awareness of being "poor" rather than membership in a class. For example, of the 113 strikes that took place in 1942, almost 90 percent were based purely upon salary claims and readjustments.[9]

Thus, by the 1940s the Argentine trade union movement had achieved institutional recognition and a certain coherent organizational structure, and was embarked on achieving material benefits for its affiliates.[10] It was at this stage that Juan Perón achieved political power. Not only did Perón give his support to the newer industrial unions (several of which are examined in this book, such as textiles [AOT], automobiles [SMATA], metals [UOM], and light and power [Luz y Fuerza]), but also this stimulus resulted in a phenomenal growth among the already established unions.[11] Under Perón's auspices and under the political hegemony of Peronism, trade union leaders responded to his inspired social and labor policies.

A major turning point for Argentine labor history was the meat packers' strike of 1943, in which the union demanded a salary increase, potential overtime of up to sixty hours a week, equal conditions for women, and the reinstatement of laid-off and fired workers. At the urging of the Communist party, the union leader, José Peter, asked workers to return to work with their demands unmet because the Anglo-American packinghouses were contributing to the Allied war effort against Nazism.[12] From the offices of the Ministry of War, under the aegis of the military junta of 1943, Perón intervened on the workers' behalf and forced a favorable settlement.

In essence, this intervention by Perón created a de facto coalition between elements of the military and a growing faction within the CGT based on the principle of the efficacy of state intervention into critical questions concerning labor policy and the economy.[13] Having won the workers' unfailing support, Perón moved quickly to consolidate the situation by recognizing an autonomous meat packers' union unaffiliated with the Socialist and Communist parties. Perón was to repeat these strategies with increased confidence and vigor throughout the years leading up to his landslide election in 1946. As one well-known Argentine writer put it, "Before Perón there were sindicalists, socialists, communists, anarquists and some Radicals but after they were essentially Peronists."[14]

Following the settlement of the 1943 meat packers' strike, Perón was named director of the Department of Labor and began his rapid ascent to power.[15] In a few short months Perón was able to enforce labor laws that had been legislated since the late 1930s but rarely implemented, such as laws mandating the eight-hour work day, coverage for job-related accidents, overtime pay, and sanitary conditions at the workplace. Most critical for the fate of Argentine working-class history was the promulgation (on October 2, 1943) of a decree-law, the so-called Law of Professional Associations, that officially recognized labor unions' representational rights under the law. Its most important provision stipulated that only one union could represent any particular industry or economic area.[16]

On the heels of that decree followed others that substantially improved the situation for Argentine workers in social security, retirement benefits, and equal treatment of women on the job. Some of the most important, in retrospect, were statutes that assured farm workers a minimum wage, decent food, housing, and hygiene, as well as a Sunday day of rest, vacation time, and indemnization for arbitrary firings. Further decrees mandated old-age pensions, a paid bonus month at the end of each year (*aguinaldo*), annual paid vacations, up to six months' sick leave, various pay increases, death benefits, survivors' insurance, and family assistance subsidies. Another crucial decree (law 32.347) established labor tribunals to try appeals brought by urban workers and farmworkers against companies or landowners regarding the above areas of social coverage.[17]

As a result of these and other interventions, Perón's rise was so rapid that by October 1945 the military command was sufficiently alarmed to make a belated attempt to curb Perón's growing power within the junta by placing him under house arrest and forcing his resignation. Perón's response was equivocal. He acceded to the military's demands on the one hand, but on the other gave the green light to his labor union supporters to mobilize on his behalf. Within a week of his astute and emotional farewell address over national radio,[18] a massive concentration of workers before the presidential palace (La Casa Rosada) obtained Perón's release from custody through a clear demonstration of his political power to the military government. Simultaneously, this demonstration provided the impetus for organizing the Labor party shortly thereafter, with Perón as its presidential candidate. When elections were held in February 1946, the Peronist coalition won the day with 55 percent of the vote.

It is instructive to examine Perón's thinking as it matured during this brief but critical interlude in Argentine history—the two years between his assumption of the labor post until his election in 1946. We will find that many of these early Peronist propositions are still among the political values of contemporary Argentine workers.

Perón's usage of Marxist terminology, but within a nonsocialist context, is striking. He spoke of the "proletarians," the "exploitation of man by his fellow man," the "dehumanization of capital." At the same time, Perón expressed fears of foreign ideological penetration[19] and continually reiterated the need to avoid class conflict between capital and labor.[20] His critique of Marxism was centered on what he called humanist and Christian attitudes—which, if applied, would render class struggle irrelevant.[21] Perón's corporatist scheme already was one of class collaboration under the auspices and direction of the state.[22] What Perón offered was not the individual consciousness of the unreconstructed liberal, nor the class consciousness that he identified with foreign and alien alternatives, but a unified, communitarian, social consciousness that would assuage class warfare, avoid the contamination of international socialism, and organize society to transcend the old liberal conceptions of the state.[23]

The state's relationship to the working class, according to Perón, had to be special since it provided a vindication for past wrongs. Though the social structure remains unaltered, the working class is given relief from its relatively impoverished position vis-à-vis the other classes. Meanwhile, Perón hoped for the continual growth of the middle class (that is, business and entrepreneurial groups), upon whom, he believed, any nation's greatness depends. And he would defend their interests at all costs against the oligarchy that had kept Argentina backward.[24]

Between the working class and middle class, Perón sought to establish an unbreakable bond of common interests and sentiments. The most significant speech of his early career was presented to the Buenos Aires Stock Exchange in August 1944. In it he attempted to assuage the suspicions of the business community as to his roles as vice-president, minister of war, and secretary of labor. Perón warned that the only dangerous working class is an unorganized and dissatisfied one. Only as an unorganized mass is it susceptible to foreign ideologies and subversive forces. With the state giving strong direction to the organization of workers' unions, communist and socialist trade unions could be subordinated to these new entities, which would be stronger and more active under government auspices.

Perón painted a specter of communist victories and influence in the world since 1917 and the loss of Russia by the capitalist world. He warned of the dangers of the Spanish Civil War. He went on to say:

> Better to give 30 percent on time than to lose everything later. . . . In order to avoid that the masses, once having received the necessary social justice, attempt to go beyond this, the first remedy is the organization of these masses. . . . That will be our insurance, the organization of the masses . . . because the state has the instruments that, if it is necessary, by force can put things in their proper place and not let them run amok.
>
> It has been said, gentlemen, that I am an enemy of capital, and if you observe what I have just finished saying you will not find a more determined defender than I, *because I know that the defense of businessmen, of industrialists, of merchants is the defense of the State itself* [my emphasis].[25]

Thus, Perón's reactions to the plight of Argentine laborers and employees were well within the capabilities of a modified welfare capitalist system, and his positions implied a considerable adherence to many of the standard liberal norms: the profit motive, material incentives, the work ethic, the potential for individual upward mobility, and the inherent positive features of owning private property.

Moving to the connected questions of social relations, social conflict, and the alliance of classes, Perón followed a similar course. Perón felt that without interclass agreement on the basic values of capitalism, the wealth of the middle and capitalist classes would never be secure. Perón's attitude toward the working class was highly paternalistic. In his same speech to the Stock Exchange, he said:

> If I were the owner of a factory, it wouldn't cost me anything to gain the affection of my workers with some social programs handled with intelligence. Many times it is achieved with a doctor who goes to the house of a worker whose son is sick, with a little gift on a particular day; the boss who passes by and slaps his workers on the shoulder and speaks to them once in a while, as we do with our soldiers. So that the workers are more efficient, one has to control them by the heart. Man is more receptive to commands when commands are directed at his heart, not his head. In the same way workers can be managed. It is only necessary that men who have workers at their disposal, reach them by these means, in order to dominate them, to make them true collaborators.[26]

Perón's major contribution in this phase of early Peronism was his ability to mobilize society from a unique vantage point. As the major figure in the administrative, economic, labor, and military hierarchies, he was able to shape the future of his country and affect its norms and values. His move to reorganize the role of the state in economic development, his efforts to have labor recognized, and his ability to encourage workers and owners to accept each other were instrumental in developing a national capitalist system of some consequence. The dual class system in which the working class had been virtually ignored was undermined.

Ideology, Politics, and Labor Under Peronism

Contemporary Argentine workers speak of the first Peronist governments as the golden age of Argentine history. They harken back to the institutions and policies of the late 1940s and early 1950s as a time when the working class had a secure place in society, a fair share of the wealth, and political representation. Such notions of the past, though somewhat romanticized, clearly recognize the benefits enjoyed by workers when Perón held political power.

The intellectual and ideological thrust of Perón's administrations between 1946 and 1955 can be understood in terms of an overall principle: a basic nationalist resistance to Marxist-Leninist views of society and human nature that has seemingly made most Argentines immune to the socialist message. But even though a hostility to socialism is clear in Perón's speeches and programs, it is far from the full story. For example, Peronist thinking produced a series of programs and policies that resisted unfettered capitalism while it interjected working-class needs into the political calculus.

Among many industrial sectors, Peronism has long been viewed as the only realistic alternative to the economic and political liberalism advocated by Argentina's wealthiest agrarian and industrial interests—those tied to foreign exports and/or investments. Whether in power or as a proscribed or legal opposition, Peronist leaders and cadres have demonstrated a generally coherent core of beliefs, despite some dramatic differences with dissident labor and youth groups. The appeal of Peronism based on these values continues to this day. That is why since 1989 the shift to an uncompromising liberal economic policy by Carlos Menem's Peronist government represents a significant departure from earlier Peronism. (This shift will be treated in the last two chapters.)

But rather than an organized set of interlocking principles, Peronism is better seen as a series of propositions adapted to developing Argentine interests just when the nation was buffeted by momentous international and domestic economic changes.[27] A resolution to free Argentina from British influence, suspicion of U.S. ascendancy, combined with an equally powerful fear of the growth of Soviet domination, led to the military coup of 1943 and Perón's own nationalist orientation within the GOU military lodge (Task Force for Unity).[28]

From this early visceral nationalism, the Peronist doctrine grew to encompass three leading principles for all sectors of Argentina struggling to transform the country from an economic colony of Great Britain as World War II was drawing to a close: economic independence, political sovereignty, and social justice.[29]

Perón's well-known "third position" (*tercera posición*) emerged at this time. He interpreted the fascist Italian experience, opposed to both Western capitalism and Soviet Communism, as a forerunner of a "Third World" position of apparent neutrality between the two dominant emerging postwar philosophies. Within this framework, *justicialismo*, as it came to be called, was created. Justicialism was described as a "third position" placed between the ideologically polar attractions of capitalism and communism.

Justicialism, from a rigorous intellectual standpoint, can hardly be called an integral political ideology. Nevertheless, it has resulted in an important historical movement with obvious cultural implications.[30] Though Perón misread the intrinsic capitalist nature of the economic systems of Mussolini's Italy and Hitler's Germany, he did follow a different method of asserting national over international interests. It is evident from most of what Perón wrote while in power that he saw this "third position" as a vehicle to channel anticapitalist reactions before they turned into an inevitable victory for communism — as fearful a specter for Perón as it had been for Mussolini and Hitler.[31] Thus as the Nazi shadow over Europe faded, Peronism became an ever more legitimate Third World force that obviated any kind of communist alternative in Argentina.[32] As Argentine president, Perón was very successful at undermining the potential legitimacy of communism just as the cold war was getting under way.

Argentina's Socialist and Communist parties were unable to curb this new and hearty form of populism and were forced into a vacillating and precarious opposition.[33] These parties mistook the nature of early Peronism and its appeal to the Argentine working class.[34] Marxists in Argentina have perceived Peronism as a kind of nationalist, chauvinist, petty-bourgeois tendency that was historically regressive because it was organized and led by a nonsocialist political party and union structure. Therefore, Marxists failed to assess its programs and policies on their individual merits but condemned them because of their flawed birth, as it were.

Moreover, one of socialism's major historical problems, which can be traced to its original inspiration in Marx's own comments on Louis Bonaparte's basis of support in the lumpenproletariat, was its ambiguous attitude toward the "uncultured" and uneducated elements such as made up a considerable percentage of the Peronist following.[35] Daniel James well describes the communist and socialist reactions to the mass uprising that brought Perón to power.[36]

This deprecation of the mass populist appeal of Peronism was manifested not only within the leftist political party structure but also among student and intellectual circles. An influential spokesman was Ezequiel Martínez Estrada, a well-known liberal author, who wrote to a colleague:

> The peculiar characteristics of the Peronist mass: shouting, good-for-nothings, disorder, disgust. The rallies are primitive sacrifices (*hecatombe*), and the beer they swiggle has been passed on to them by the savage Indians. . . . Peronism represents a vision of Argentine history like a repetitive cycle where everything is forever regressing.[37]

Julio Cortázar also expresses in various works the sensation of worry and fear of an "invasion" by hordes of *cabezitas negras* (darkies) that the Peronists evoked in sectors of the middle class.

Other familiar anti-Peronist epithets coined with the fall of Perón were the "deluge of animals" (Ernesto Sanmartino) and "books or sandals" (Americo Ghioldi),[38] while the vice-presidential candidate of the opposition Democratic Union in 1946 spoke of Perón's followers as "a drunken mob," "illiterate hordes," "instinctual savages," and "an indian alcoholic storm."[39]

The left failed to understand the great mass of Peronist supporters and voters. Considering the Peronist movement as some uncleansable sore, they lost the opportunity to build bridges between socialism and Peronism. By contrast, more than a decade later the Cuban Communist party dealt with and eventually allied itself with Fidel Castro, giving it a flexibility that the Argentine Communists did not have. The Communists thus lost the working class for generations to come.[40]

Ideologically, then, Peronism represented a political rejection of the traditional left as well as the right. In its bare essence it consisted of raising working-class consumption levels while strengthening the productive capacity of the industrial sector. The Peronist state interposed itself into the socioeconomic system in a Bonapartist fashion, consolidating a strong nexus between itself and the trade union movement. It played the role of arbiter in basic decisions involving income distribution, while it attempted to mitigate class conflict.[41]

Peronism, though it did not attempt to confront the capitalist mode of production, did initiate the first mass movement in Latin America with a majoritarian working-class support that confronted imperialist interests by supporting the development of a nationalist capitalist class in Argentina.[42]

However, as the limits of growth for light industry geared to the large Argentine domestic market (through import substitution policies) became apparent in the early 1950s, the capitalist class began to pressure for a slow reversal of the distributive gains made by workers under earlier Peronism.[43] As economic conditions forced restrictions on income distribution, the Peronist state adopted more traditional capitalist methods, and many of the workers' salary and wage gains were eroded, though politically labor remained a leading institutional force.[44]

Between 1943 and 1945, the Peronist state effected a political revolution, though it stopped far short of an economic or structural one. Perón consolidated the political potential and options of the organized working class while, at the same time, channeling and neutralizing their popular aspirations for confronting the capitalist system of values. He vindicated popular demands, as it were, in a way that neutralized class conflict. What he accomplished was significant. He expanded the domestic market and the workers' share in it; he weakened (at least temporarily) the agrarian sector's social dominance, and he spearheaded the first Argentine administration that seriously questioned foreign influence.

Further, Perón politically reorganized the Argentine public sector. The 1949 constitution provided for direct election and reelection of the president, established a central bank, nationalized foreign commerce, and made education free throughout the republic. Around the same time, the Peronist party was reorganized, with labor, political masculine, and feminine sectors. After Perón's victory in 1951 in which his party won 160 of 174 Chamber of Deputies seats and all 46 Senate seats, Perón became more and more an arbiter in all internal discussions of the Peronist Movement, as it now came to be called. In Perón's second term, the legislative branch lost most of its influence, and almost all key decisions came from the executive branch.[45]

Paradoxically, Perón democratized Argentina in the sense of bringing the working class more fully into the political process, though his administrations often placed cultural and political restrictions on the opposition that severely compromised that democracy. This combination of authoritarian and bureaucratic methods to increase political access and socioeconomic benefits for the masses still characterizes the present trilateral relationship among the Peronist political structure, the CGT apparatus, and the Argentine working class.

Social Structure, Economics, and Labor Under Peronism

While the economy grew in the late 1940s and early 1950s, the Peronist strategy of political and social integration without major economic structural reforms made good sense and defined a capitalist economy with a populist, distributionist orientation. While the economy expanded, a relatively high share of national income for the working class assured the consumption of the fruits of this developing economy, to the benefit of the industrial alliance between owners and workers. It was in the interest of both classes to restrict foreign capital during this period of rapid growth in light industries such as textiles and garments, furniture, housewares, utensils, food and beverage processing, and so on. Thus although the national capitalist sector was dominant, the working class was far better off than it had ever been.[46]

Principally, it was in social and cultural policy that the working class felt the change most tangibly. The Argentine constitution of 1949 promulgated several articles aimed at the rights of the working class, institutionalizing much that had already been applied for several years by specific de facto (1943–1945) and then de jure legislation (1946–1949). The unions are a good example. Though there is considerable dispute over the level of trade union autonomy under the Peronist regime, clearly the working class made tremendous headway in being acknowledged as a critical social sector that participated in and was seriously considered at the highest levels of socioeconomic policy making.[47]

Though Perón was clearly a dominant figure vis-à-vis the CGT Central Executive Committee, their views did not necessarily overlap. In fact, the Peronists' crucial decision to allow for the creation of factory and office shop committees and delegates helped to democratize the trade union structure and enabled organized labor to survive and even flourish despite the fall of their patron in 1955.[48]

Organized labor grew tremendously during the Perón years. In 1946 there were 877,000 affiliated workers in the CGT. After almost a decade of Peronism, the figure had grown to almost 2,300,000. Particularly impressive was the growth of organized labor in construction, chemicals, food and beverage, textile, metallurgical, leather, transportation, commerce and banking, communications, and public employees sectors. Overall, 43 percent of people on wages and salaries were unionized by 1954.[49] Though the number of union affiliates increased almost threefold, the number of national unions declined from 913 in 1946 to 83 in 1951.[50] This represented the centralizing tendencies of Perón's Law of Professional Association and greatly strengthened the labor unions' powers of collective bargaining. Though the number of strikes called by the trade unions dropped under Peronism, it is not at all clear that this was the result of cooptation and an absolute drop in militancy but rather because many of the workers' most dramatic demands had been met in the early years of Perón's first regime.[51]

Though in the early years of Peronism wages rose rapidly, exceeding productivity, in Perón's last years, because of inflation and sluggish rates of growth, real wages began to decline to World War II levels. However, rates for unskilled laborers remained substantially higher, bringing them to the levels of skilled workers.[52] Although there is substantial dispute about the figures, it is generally accepted that under Perón the workers' share of national income made major advances—approaching at times 50 percent—for the very first and only time in Argentine history.[53]

Thus, even though under Perón the trade unions lost a certain degree of their militancy and autonomy, they traded that organizational potential (which they had achieved only in the early Peronist years) for increased political access, social acceptability, and major wage improvements. Proof of their enhanced political power and economic advances could be seen even after the fall of Perón, when the CGT's sociopolitical cohesion was basically all that remained of the Peronist institutional legacy. Had the labor unions truly lost their legitimacy and autonomy under Perón, it is difficult to see how they could have managed to survive and recover their ability to confront subsequent post-Perón military and civilian regimes.

Perón was overthrown not because he was a deep-seated economic threat to the agrarian and industrial interests but because he had over time alienated the Catholic church, elements of the military, and some competing liberal cultural and political institutions and organizations that saw his regime as vulgar, pedestrian, personalist, and unpredictable.[54] One observer said, "Perón wanted to make the revolution a sociological displacement of political power while it simultaneously respected property. . . . He believed he could invert the classic imperial formula of 'subjugate without humiliation' with 'humiliate without subjugation.'"[55]

Finally, however, it was the opening of the national dialogue to the organized working class—perhaps Perón's greatest achievement—that won him the greatest enmity. As Hernández Arregui writes, because of Perón and since Perón almost any Argentine worker has a sense of what foreign domination means.[56] His several thousand speeches during his career sensitized the workers to the issues of social justice, economic independence, and political sovereignty. Though the total achievement of these goals was beyond Perón's commitment and ambition, his message was learned and taken to heart.

Though Perón was not a socialist, his ability to educate the working class politically encouraged workers to confidently and critically examine capitalism. This allowed the trade unions, from the perspective of interested working-class representatives, at least to think about institutions and processes that might alter and modify the nature of that same capitalism.

Labor in Opposition

The most powerful legacy of Perón's first administrations is the trade union movement. Over the three decades (1955–1985) preceding my study, labor continued to defend the socioeconomic and political gains achieved under Perón.[57] These decades are comparatively recent history for many of the workers in my survey sample. Though only a minority could remember Perón's decade in power, most workers remembered the years between the Arturo Frondizi administration (1958–1962) through the military dictatorship known as the *proceso* (1976–1983). For another minority of the workers — the youngest — their principal political memory is the brutality of the *proceso*. These changing political regimes, from limited democratic systems, through a revised Peronist populism after 1973, to a violently repressive military authoritarianism, have helped to form the political culture of the contemporary Argentine working class.

During this period, the potential power of Peronism forced political party reassessments, splits, realignments, and a dizzying series of strategic and tactical political shifts, as the organized working class continued to represent an unincorporated political interest. The issue became one of attempting to channel a CGT into the political process without its political champion — Peronism. All the significant political parties attempted to appeal to the trade union movement, and all failed. There were momentary tactical alliances between the CGT and one or another party (most notably, Perón's asking Peronists to support the candidacy of President Arturo Frondizi in 1958), but none weathered these short-run alignments. The CGT in opposition became the exiled Perón's dominant legitimate representative, acting as Peronism's political surrogate. Not until the late 1960s did elements of the Peronist revolutionary left, led by university students, force the Peronist movement to broaden its opposition to the military by including direct and violent confrontation. When Perón was reelected in 1973, the CGT regained its preeminence within Peronism.

Under successor regimes, the alliance of the domestic-oriented capitalist class and the working class, initiated and largely sustained under Perón, became harder to maintain under the increasing dominance of foreign capital and interests.[58] New economic factors, plus the inability of disparate political parties to absorb the working-class vote, caused a noticeable reversal of what had been Perón's success in assimilating the organized working class into a growing economy. Perón's ability, even from exile, to raise issues concerning Argentina's growing dependence on foreign capital gave the organized trade union movement an increasing oppositional role.[59]

Thus the organized Argentine working class constituted the major focus opposing (though certainly not unanimously) the capitalization project of the post-Perón administrations. This stance remained clear in every proscribed election from the constituent assembly election of 1957 under President Pedro Aramburu to the gubernatorial and legislative elections of 1965 under President Arturo Illía, which precipitated the military's return to power in 1966. The return of Perón in 1973 and his overwhelming majority victory capped this process.

Since the fall of Perón, the survival of Peronism through an organized and combative union structure had been possible largely because subsequent military and civilian governments have been unable to win the support of organized labor. The brunt of the new phase of capital accumulation had been borne by the working class, and income levels had been reversed, negating the achievements gained under Perón. To this essential factor were added varying forms of political neglect and, at times, overt military repression.[60]

The 1960s marked Argentina's most sustained period of industrialization. Income distribution was more equitable than at any other time except during Perón's three administrations. Salaries, however, still lagged behind general economic growth, while inflation was moderate and unemployment low. These conditions help to explain the impressive labor militancy of the late 1960s, the most embattled period since the aftermath of World War I. Moreover, Peronism was able to broaden its appeal to the middle strata of the working class, including sectors of the intelligentsia, university students, and independent professionals. Gerardo Duejo has described the changes of this period as representing a kind of Peronization of the middle strata of society.[61]

During the Frondizi years, massive foreign investment in automobiles, petroleum, and foreign credits from the international banking community demanded a more quiescent labor movement and invited policies of the carrot and stick, which in turn resulted in significant divisions within the trade union movement.[62] Simultaneously there was a weakening of the unions' rank-and-file shop committees, balanced by an increasing bureaucratization of the union leadership, as the CGT hierarchy solidified its position as the economic and political surrogate for outlawed Peronism. During this phase of the post-Perón period, labor established itself as a prime corporative actor in society, regardless of whatever civilian or military regime was in power and despite the proscription of political Peronism.

The capitalist accumulation process required minimal labor cooperation during this period of accelerated economic growth. Heavy industry received

a major impetus between 1960 and 1968. Extracting from UN data used by
Peralta Ramos, one finds that heavy industrial production stood at 35.1
percent of total production in 1950 under Perón, increased to 48.4 percent
under Frondizi in 1960, and to 53.9 percent in 1968 under President Juan
Carlos Onganía.[63] The 1960s was the most dynamic period of industrial
growth in Argentine history. Industrial expansion outpaced that of all other
economic sectors.[64] Despite this significant increase in industrial productivity, the industrial sector's share of total economic employment dropped
from 23.6 percent in 1953 under Perón to 18.7 percent in 1969 under
Onganía.

Within the highly capitalized industrial sector, there was a tendency
toward increasing concentration in the hands of fewer companies with larger
numbers of workers.[65] Foreign capital also made predictable inroads in the
economy, controlling almost 53 percent of the most highly monopolized
industries while dropping away to less than 2 percent of the smallest
manufacturing establishments. The largest and most dominant firms were
controlled by foreign capital. By the same token, of Argentina's 100 largest
firms (defined by total sales) by the end of the 1960s, foreign capital
constituted 60 percent of all industrial sales.[66]

These conditions help create an Argentina, on the eve of the Cordobazo
labor uprising of 1969, with a productive, streamlined, essentially fully
employed industrial laboring class with substantial bargaining power in
strategic manufacturing. Argentina seemed to bear out the Marxist predic-
tion that under advanced capitalism there would occur both centralization of
the productive process and concentration of the work force in fewer manufacturing units.[67] In addition, beginning in the post-Perón period, the distribution
of income for those on wages and salaries declined in Argentina. Instead of the
50 percent achieved under Perón, the workers' share fell to the low forties in the
early 1960s, but began to recover by the end of the decade.[68]

The 1969 Cordobazo uprising represents a major exception in Argentine
trade union history since World War I.[69] It was one of the few times that
Argentine workers, supported significantly and massively by university students
and intellectuals, undertook a wholesale confrontation against the monopoly of
foreign capital, a military government (that of General Onganía), and the
domination of Buenos Aires over the interior regional economy.

In Córdoba, Argentina's major interior industrial city, large metallurgical, automobile, and electrical plants, under foreign ownership and control,
employed large congregations of laborers within each unit.[70] Major capital
investment in Córdoba was especially concentrated and easily identifiable.
Vehicle and machine production in the city, concentrated especially in the
Renault and Fiat plants, grew from 10 percent of industrial sales in 1948 to 51

percent in 1968.[71] These facts help to explain the Cordobazo. For Juan Agulla, the Córdoba uprising of 1969 mainly involved a strategically placed and privileged working class.[72] Approximately 35 percent of university students were also workers, according to Francisco Delich.[73] This demonstrates an overlapping sense of identification between the two not found to that degree in Greater Buenos Aires. The students' willingness to participate in the uprising (though not to lead it) and to share its values no doubt fueled its confrontational and structural component.

Other labor manifestations in Argentina have focused on particular leaders and on policies of particular regimes but none challenged the validity of the capitalist marketplace itself. The Córdoba situation, on the other hand, subsumed regime and leadership questions and thus was a unique case with clearly revolutionary potential. The violent confrontations of May 1969 should be seen against the backdrop of stifled wage aspirations within a generally prospering economy, low unemployment, only modest inflation, and a moderately repressive military-authoritarian regime—an inflammatory set of conditions.

Agulla argues that the spark that led to the protests among the key strategic unions was the abolition by decree of the "English Saturday" that traditionally gave workers in Córdoba (and in several other interior provinces) a half day off on Saturdays.[74] That such an issue would provoke an uprising indicates a relatively sound economy, not one in which workers were desperate for work. In fact, according to Agulla, reformist and rising expectations in a booming consumer society fueled workers' resentment, frustrations, and pent-up aspirations.[75] But though the agenda was not explicitly revolutionary, most testimony makes it clear that it was perceived as threatening the regime.

Córdoba's industries overlapped, and workers understood each other's labor concerns. The homogeneity of a regional working-class community complemented by the radicalization of a major university community gave the uprising a unique antisocial ideological tone.[76] The social rebellion represented not only a challenge to the leadership of the military government but also to a "reformist" labor union leadership that had become accustomed to the norms of military-CGT collective bargaining since 1966.

The Cordobazo resulted in the gradual undermining of the military regime, symbolized immediately by the fall of the Córdoba provincial government and massive changes in General Onganía's national cabinet. Subsequently, from the fall of Onganía in mid-1970 to the Peronist electoral victory of March 1973, General Alejandro Lanusse attempted to reach a modus operandi with Perón in exile, implying the acceptance of Peronism at home as an inveterate working-class force with which to contend.[77]

Perón's Exile and Return

Perón's nexus to the Argentine working class remained fixed throughout the 1960s despite various regime attempts (and, in some cases, others from within the ranks of labor and political elements of Peronism) to form alternative *Peronismo sin Perón* groupings. By and large, however, the post-Cordobazo period saw the growth of an antiregime coalition that gradually looked to Perón as the aggregator of a multitude of sectoral and class interests. Moreover, the unleashing of student militancy gave Argentina its first experience with serious guerrilla violence and helped put the military regimes on the defensive.

Perón, writing from exile, had stimulated the youthful rebellion as a means of returning domestic Peronism to the Argentine political agenda.[78] In the late 1950s he attempted to distinguish the accomplishments of his regime from the Aramburu-led military junta that replaced him and emphasized the popular nature and formidable capacity of the Peronist opposition.[79] By 1963 Perón's opposition had hardened and radicalized noticeably, partially through the impact of his intellectual correspondence with John William Cooke, his personal delegate in Argentina.[80] His *La hora de los pueblos* (1968), fused Perón's early "third position" of the 1940s with the growing radicalization of Third World antidependency movements. We read the words of a leader confident of the demise of military rule and seeing the potential return of Peronist populism to Argentina.[81]

La hora de los pueblos contains an implicit call to arms. Perón legitimizes violence when arbitrary governments infringe on a people's basic civil rights. He also offered a strong argument attacking the military government's role as a surrogate for U.S. imperialist interests in Argentina, while simultaneously dominating its own people.

The radical Peronist youth organization, the Montoneros, as they examined Perón's exile writings, clearly took heart from many of his evolving ideological positions after 1955.[82] Perón had, in essence, fused an indigenous socialism with Argentine nationalism through Peronism, and the movement's youth were convinced of his sincerity. Their mistake was possibly in not taking Perón's often avowed anticommunism seriously enough, even while they absorbed his anti-imperialist message. Thus, in this relationship, the Montoneros probably misread Perón more than he misinterpreted their intentions.[83]

Once returned to Argentina, Perón represented a broader Peronist coalition than even that of 1945, including not only laborers and employees but also students, intellectuals, and even small business people.[84] This eventually forced the military government's hand and allowed the return of Perón and the mounting of a legalized Peronism through the candidacy of

Perón's representative in Argentina, Héctor Cámpora. Perón's "third position" became more viable in 1973 than it even had been in 1946, because it captured a popular ideology much more universal among Argentines of all walks of life than ever before. But, once in power, instead of the anti-establishment, populist, nationalist economic perspective of the 1944–1946 period, Peronism reemerged as a more reformist, establishment movement oriented to consolidating a moderate welfare-capitalist system with a guaranteed major role for the CGT in the councils of government.

Not more than six weeks after Cámpora's triumphant inauguration, Perón returned to Argentina on June 20, 1973, unleashing an intense intra-Peronist riot at Ezeiza airport that marked the beginning of a deadly internal struggle for control of the Peronist government. Shortly thereafter, Perón, with the overt support of key CGT labor leaders and politicians, engineered Cámpora's ouster, setting the stage for his astounding electoral triumph of September 1973.[85]

Restored to the rank of general, Perón appeared in his military epaulets on the balcony of the Casa Rosada, not as a *descamisado* as in 1945. He returned to persuade and accommodate, not to confront and isolate. This reality the Montoneros found hard to swallow, given Perón's socialist rhetoric during his years in exile.

The major initiative now shifted to the center of the Peronist movement, which had attracted a majority of Argentines from all generations and sectors. It was basically an antimilitary coalition spearheaded by the residue of the 1969 *Cordobazo*, which meant the Peronist militants, including the Montoneros and the combative sectors of the CGT. The coalition then turned upon itself when the struggle shifted to defining what that victory meant. The struggle raged between the Peronist student and mass "base" organizations and guerrilla factions against the Peronist government and labor organizations. Julio Godio makes a convincing case that the labor unions had been just as important to the restoration of democracy as the radical left and that the movement toward democratic socialism should have paused to consolidate the victory fully before moving slowly ahead with mass mobilization and involvement. He blames the Montoneros for the first breach in the popular coalition.[86]

To most workers, the *pátria socialista* was the *pátria peronista*. Young radicals seem to have needlessly isolated themselves by their implied, later explicit, criticism of Perón. The labor rank and file were seeking to decentralize the union power structure, democratize union elections, rotate union delegates more regularly, and establish better working conditions. Meanwhile, Peronist youth (led by the Montoneros and their strategic allies, the Trotskyite ERP guerrillas) were seeking to confront the right-wing

Peronist elements — labor union leaders, the business sector, the police, and finally the military — that were slowly surrounding Perón and cutting off access to him. Within the Peronist governing coalition, the CGT and Peronist politicians slowly forced the more leftist factions out of the government.[87] Instead of achieving a Peronist consolidation, the large pro-Peronist conglomeration disintegrated from within with all its terrible agony and sacrifice.[88]

Labor and Peronism in Power

With its return to power in 1973, Peronism largely repeated its experience of 1952–1955 but, because of the new outsized role of students and radical youth, it was now a regime that demobilized both militancy and popular political involvement. Peronism and the CGT leadership began to act as the military's surrogate in controlling the popular forces unleashed by Cámpora's election and Perón's return to power shortly thereafter.

A "social pact" signed in mid-1973 froze wage and price increases and suspended collective bargaining for up to two years. The business sector, of course, continued to make investment and production decisions, while the labor leadership was inhibited from confronting Perón — for whom they had been mobilizing since 1955.[89] Nevertheless, it is interesting to see that during the Cámpora and Perón governments labor militancy was more political, focusing on petitions to reincorporate workers fired under the military regime, demands for back pay from delinquent employers, and struggles over working conditions. Significantly, this occurred during a time when real wages made a major recovery and industrial employment grew by 10 percent in just one year of restored Peronism.[90] With the withdrawal of Cámpora and the death of Perón in July 1974 and the accession of Isabel Perón, workers were forced to refocus on salary and contractual questions.[91]

The major confrontations of June–July 1975 between the CGT (and its member unions) and the Isabel Perón government typified the kinds of battles the working class in Argentina had undertaken for several decades. They represented the values and attitudes of Argentine workers more accurately than the Cordobazo rebellion of 1969. The demonstrations of the mid-1970s were well organized with specific methods and specific goals, yet they were still within the limits of the political culture under representative government. They were led by the union leaders and organizers, yet captured the imagination of the rank and file and the general public at large.

The Isabel Perón government was apparently determined to break the "social pact" between labor and business, agreed to under Juan Perón, that collective bargaining could resume on June 1, 1975. It had become painfully clear in the two-year interim that prices had far outrun wages and that the workers' consumer power had withered away. When the sudden devaluation of the currency in June fueled 100 percent price increases in transportation, food, services, clothing and household goods, the labor sector saw collective bargaining as an absolute prerequisite for recovering their real wage base.

On July 7 and 8, 1975, Argentine workers mounted a complete general strike, the first of its kind against a Peronist government. It absolutely paralzyed the nation. The strike was a culmination of a ten-day intraparty debate over President Isabel Perón's decision to uphold her economic minister's policy of decreeing wage controls. On the second day of the strike, the government gave in and announced it would honor the wage hikes the unions had previously negotiated in collective bargaining agreements.

The general strike was a massive rebuttal to the economic policies of the Peronist government. For the first time in over thirty years of Peronist history, labor was pitted against Peronist political leadership. Labor received important moral and strategic support from several quarters, among them the majority of the Peronist bloc in Congress and most of the opposition parties. It made for an historically ironic confrontation as a traditionally labor-oriented Peronist government was strongly opposed by a coalition of its own labor unions alongside political parties generally to the right of the Peronist party.

The 1975 breakdown between labor and the Peronist administration resulted from several factors: raging working-class discontent with scarcities of consumer goods and a cost of living that rose by 350 percent in 1975; a large vacuum between the nation's political leadership and its own popular base; the misuse of public funds for state terrorism and political campaigning; the public's loss of confidence in the police (linked to the Argentine Anti-Communist Alliance [AAA], a secret terrorist death squad); and right-wing violence perpetrated with impunity. In this malignant atmosphere, the general strike managed to bring down the cabinet and forced the ouster of Minister José López Rega, reputed organizer of the AAA. This was, ironically, the beginning of the now rapid decomposition of the Peronist government, which in turn gave the military junta a pretext for intervention.

The Advent of Military Authoritarianism

The new political ingredient that acted as the visible catalyst for military intervention in March 1976 was the alliance between leftist Peronist youth, who tried to use Perón's leadership among the workers as a revolutionary prerequisite, and other segments of the population who had been persuaded by Perón's writings from exile to be more receptive to socialism. This uniquely Peronist threat to the dominant agrarian and industrialist classes precipitated Argentina's most devastating period of military authoritarianism.

The euphemistically named *el proceso* military dictatorship of 1976–1983 (*el proceso de reorganización nacional*) entailed monumental military intervention in and occupation of all facets of society. It massively affected all human affairs.[92] Though the military developed its Doctrine of National Security to legitimize the armed forces' involvement in an all-out war against subversion,[93] it was clear during the military's rule that even if war against guerrilla revolutionaries had been justified, they were not the main target. The regime was marked by thousands of crimes against civilians, abnegation of the Geneva accords in the treatment of prisoners, and an effort to annihilate rather than defeat the enemy.[94]

Society became largely militarized. The armed revolutionary groups failed to broaden their bases of support in the civilian sectors and were thus rapidly isolated and largely exterminated. But long after the ERP (People's Revolutionary Army) and the Montoneros ceased to be a military threat, the civilian population was still cowed by what can only be called state terrorism. The armed forces proceeded to purge the labor, educational, cultural and political communities of all opposition, the great majority of which was unarmed and unconnected with the guerrillas. The armed forces gradually broadened their "dirty war" to include the "naive," the "ambivalent," the "timid," and those still "neutral." As one observer recalled, "There were only the military and 28 million subversives." Of the "disappeared" (*desaparecidos*), 30 percent had been laborers, 21 percent students, 18 percent employees, 17 percent professionals and teachers. Thirty percent of the disappeared were women and 3 percent of those were pregnant. Sixty-two percent disappeared at night and 99 percent disappeared from homes, streets, factories, and schools.[95] Various estimates put the number of persons killed or vanished at between 20,000 and 30,000 during the seven-year "dirty war."

The military dictatorship of 1976–1983 resulted in very high inflation, reaching three-digit figures for one month. Extrapolating for certain months, if extended to annual figures, inflation reached 800 percent.[96] There was a tremendous expansion of speculation through the growth of the nonproductive financial sector, mixed with capital flight and plummeting material production. Argentina's debt when the military took over stood at $6.4 billion. By 1982 it had reached a staggering $38 billion.[97] Significantly, the mounting debt was accompanied by severe deindustrialization, one of the few cases in which a marked increase in the foreign debt was accompanied by declining economic growth. Industrial production fell by 10 percent. Business bankruptcies reached historic highs. Gross investment rates which had averaged close to 5 percent between 1960 and 1970 fell to a staggering − 16 percent between 1980 and 1983, while internal consumption rates dropped from 3.6 percent to − 3.6 percent.[98] Economic stagnation struck all sectors except for the very wealthiest groups who were tied to the multinational financial structure. The resulting situation caused a radical decline of the working-class share of national income from 49 percent in 1975 to 34 percent by 1980.[99] Unemployment, usually low in Argentina, reached 12 percent by 1981. According to Héctor Palomino, the industrial working class declined from 1,100,000 in 1974 to 800,000 by 1981.[100]

This powerful and regressive socioeconomic offensive against the working class resulted in the most devastating reversal of its position in the twentieth century. While the financial sector grew by 5 percent between 1975 to 1982, the industrial sector suffered a 3 percent decline.[101] The military's economic policies made tremendous inroads on workers' real wages and caused a major redistribution of income in favor of capital. In the first year of the dictatorship, the proportion of wages in Argentina's national income dropped from over 47 percent to under 31 percent.[102] In a UN study, Beccaria and Orsatti, using an index figure of 100 for 1970, calculated that basic wages and salaries had fallen to 48 by 1982.[103] Unit labor costs during the same period had dropped from a high of 109 under Perón in 1974 to 46 in 1982, and salaried participation (including employer contributions) fell from 42 percent of GNP in 1974 to 18 percent in 1982.[104]

Organized labor bore the brunt of the military's economic policies. By decrees the junta interfered with normal union affairs, collective bargaining procedures, and many of the traditional prerogatives of the CGT. In early 1976 the CGT was intervened; its funds were blocked, as were its bank accounts and real property. Most critical, the federation's vast social welfare budget was appropriated by the military. The dominant "62" Peronist leadership faction within the CGT executive committee was explicitly forbidden to participate in union affairs and public policy making, nor could labor unions participate directly or indirectly in political party politics.[105] The right to strike was abrogated, public employees could be fired without due process, and collective bargaining negotiations would no longer cover wages and salaries. Also critical was the military provision that eliminated the employers' contributions to workers' salaries and wages formally earmarked for retirement benefits and a 5 percent deduction set aside for a workers' housing plan. These funds were now to be transferred to a state agency and financed in equal proportions by both employers and workers.[106]

Two of the unions under study here were especially hurt by the military interventions just described. The light and power workers (Luz y Fuerza) lost their experiments in co-participation among other innovative measures introduced under Perón, and the bank employees (Asociación Bancária) lost an established tradition of seniority and step promotion procedures. Under a barrage of repressive measures, the trade unions were forced into a defensive posture. The antibureaucratic political struggles of the late 1960s through the early Perón years disappeared. This was particularly true in the beleaguered industrial sector whose militancy declined markedly before the repressive onslaught.[107]

By May 1976, however, the trade union movement began a very cautious counteroffensive that, by the time the details of the Malvinas War débacle became generally known in mid-1982, was culminating in major popular demonstrations. As early as mid-1976, the CGT demanded the release of labor union leaders being held as political prisoners and those who had not been tried. They also demanded an accounting of kidnapped labor leaders and rank-and-file workers who had disappeared. Further labor complaints centered on the interventionist policies of the military government, the inhibition of free collective bargaining over salaries and wages and the destruction of the Law of Professional Association that had guaranteed, since Perón, only one official union per industry sector. The last major grievance focused on the demand of the unions to recover control and administration over the vast sums of monies taken from union social welfare programs.[108]

With the orthodox Peronist "62" shorn of its political influence, by 1978 the CGT became increasingly divided between the more oppositional stance of the Committee of the 25 (the "25") and the more conciliatory Committee of Negotiation and Work (CNT). The division culminated in a major split concerning the one-day general strike protest organized in July 1981.[109] CNT leaders withdrew their support and advocated direct negotiations among industrialists, the military government, and labor representatives. Meanwhile, the "25" slowly evolved a more militant position on the eve of the Malvinas conflict. Argentina's invasion of the islands in April 1982 temporarily submerged growing labor discontent and dissent, as the working class joined in the massive display of popular support for the Argentine military.[110] However, after Argentina's humiliating defeat before British troops, who reoccupied the islands in June, labor's disenchantment and resulting mobilization grew rapidly. Both 1982 and 1983 saw a major resurgence in labor conflicts that by far superseded those of the previous five years of military rule.[111]

Oscar Oszlak summarizes the years of military dictatorship as displaying the worst features of liberal capitalism of the West, which combined a private economy with public politics, and the collectivist socialism of the East that supported a public economy with "privatized" forms of political domination. In his words, Argentina "eliminated all regulatory, coordinating and control mechanisms from accepted state and societal conduct. It chose an open and liberalized economy but provoked at the same time a disequilibrium among societal interests, via selective coercion and market discipline, that relegated an extensive social sector defenseless before what ended up as the law of the most powerful."[112] Near the end of this period of ferocious and single-minded fascism of the marketplace, the CGT sent an open letter to the retiring economics minister, José Martínez de Hoz:

> You have destroyed everything . . . because we Argentines depended on peace and you on war and the truth is that you have won. We didn't want you to go without listening to the voice of the majority of the people. . . . The wounds are great but you weren't able to kill us all, and those of us who have survived will never forget you. . . . The liquidation of our national industry and consequently the loss of jobs for thousands of Argentine workers is your greatest victory. . . . For all this we say to you: Mister Joe, mission accomplished: and we believe your friend Rockefeller and your friends from the international lending institutions (IMF and the Inter-American Development Bank) will recognize and reward you for it.[113]

II

The Structural Component

3   *The Contexts and Conditions of Labor Under Alfonsín*

> >

THE SURVEY OF Argentine workers was not conducted in a vacuum. To understand the responses of those interviewed, we need to consider several broader areas including the legal and contractual developments affecting organized labor, the social and economic contexts, and union structures. With this background, we can better understand the initiatives of the Alfonsín government and the CGT responses to these initiatives.

The Unions' Institutionalized Leverage

The Argentine labor movement, as labor movements go, has had a very successful history. It has been generally blessed with a propitious cultural, social and — at times — even political environment when compared to the typical conditions under which unions in developing nations are forced to operate. First of all, Argentina does not have a labor-surplus economy. There is a relatively small and skilled work force that is critical to modern capitalist development and, therefore, has enhanced labor's bargaining power in the nation. Second, urbanization in Argentina — unlike Brazil and Mexico, for example — is largely complete. Argentina's internal migrations have slowed, and the western and southern provinces have shown greater growth since the 1970s than the area around the capital. For example, most of the workers surveyed were born in large metropolitan areas and were thus socialized to urban values. Third, Argentina has a uniquely stable, self-employed (over-employed, if you will) work force in which large sectors of the working population hold more than one job, or work for others while working for themselves. It is quite common that a worker may spend part of the day in forms of self-employment.

Fourth, though there has been a major shift from an agrarian-based to an industrial economy, Argentina's foreign exports are still largely agricultural. This indicates the importance of the huge domestic consumer market in Argentina. The internal market remains the engine of industrial growth, and Argentine workers, as consumers, are a mainstay of the domestic economy. Fifth, a larger portion of the Argentine economy is geared to domestic food consumption than to nonedible exports. Much of the nation's bountiful agricultural harvest is consumed by Argentines. Especially important for the health of the populace is the fact that Argentina produces crops such as fruits, vegetables, beef, dairy products, and wheat and other grains, not traditional Third World products, raised chiefly for export, such as coffee, tobacco, and mineral ores. The working populace as a result has relatively high standard of nutrition, above-average world caloric intake and protein consumption, with the expectation that these standards will continue.

Moreover, because the working class is highly organized in Argentina, many public policies since World War II have been recognizably prolabor. The CGT has been supported at various times by government initiatives, especially under Peronism, that have transformed it into an essential corporate entity in politics. Compared to most Third World trade union organizations, the CGT is more powerful, unified, and centralized. It is an acknowledged interest group and power broker. Thus, a basically protec-tionist economy since early Peronism has continued to defend relatively high employment and to provide incentives for workers' continued political mobilization to protect their standard of living.[1]

Since 1945, there has been official recognition of labor unions' *exclusive* rights to organize workers, their rights to *collectively* bargain over wages and working conditions, their right to *represent* distinct economic sectors as sole bargaining agents, and the right to *act politically* on behalf of specific social programs and larger social goals. As mentioned earlier, these rights are contained in the Law of Professional Associations (decree-law 23.852, or LPA), designed under the first Perón administration to regulate the unions' role in socioeconomic matters, to determine union functions, and to order internal union procedures. In a word, the LPA legally permits unions to bargain collectively over all kinds of labor questions and therefore has been critical to the health of the trade union movement. It allows labor to negotiate as a social group on a par with the government and the private industrial sector (represented by the Unión Industrial Argentina [UIA]). The decree-law was promulgated during Perón's last days as minister of labor under the military junta on October 2, 1945—significantly, just two weeks before the massive street demonstrations that anointed Perón as political broker of the military regime and future candidate for president. The original decree was later submitted and passed by a Peronist-dominated legislature to become law after Perón's election victory in 1946.

The law has since been modified on four occasions, but it has not been significantly altered in several of its major provisions. The first significant changes came in 1958, under President Frondizi, with a Radical congressional majority that had been electorally beholden to an outlawed Peronist constituency. The next modifications came under Perón and a Peronist-controlled legislature in 1973, then under the military dictatorship in 1979, and, finally, under a compromise legislative package worked out between Radicals and Peronists under President Alfonsín in 1988.[2]

The major provisions of the LPA that have stood the test of time, though often challenged, are (1) Argentines' right of free association; (2) the right of unions to serve as representatives of the working class; (3) the basic provision of one union per industry; (4) the notion, though not originally spelled out, that employers must pay union delegates and shop committees while they are pursuing union matters during the workday, and (5) the guarantee that union delegates cannot be fired during their elective term. On the other hand, various key articles—such as the number and tenure of union delegates, the right to support specific political parties and become involved with political issues, employers' obligation to collect union dues in addition to contributing themselves to workers' retirement benefits—have been temporarily abolished, amended, and altered under subsequent civil and military regimes.

The various changes in the LPA reflect the strengths and weaknesses of organized labor and the kinds of coalitions it has been able to fashion with the civil and military regimes of the day. Peronist-sponsored governments tended to be most generous in their defense of trade unions' organizational and bargaining strength vis-à-vis employers. For example, the original LPA allowed union delegates four-year terms, with the right to run for reelection. Under the 1958 Frondizi-sponsored LPA, terms were reduced to two years; then under Perón in 1973 the four-year term was reinstituted. With the advent of the military government, the 1979 decree-law limited delegates to three-year terms, with only one reelection allowed. Finally, under Alfonsín in 1988, the LPA was returned to the original stipulation of four-year terms, with no restrictions on reelection of union delegates. The 1979 military decree regarding the LPA also stipulated that an election was valid only if 50 percent of union members voted and the winning candidate won at least

20 percent of the vote. Otherwise a runoff was necessary. Alfonsín's LPA restored the simple plurality system of previous LPAs, again strengthening the hands of Peronist union leaders.

The Perón-sponsored LPA of 1973 specifically enumerated the number of union delegates allowed per worker: one delegate for five to fifteen workers, two delegates for sixteen to forty, and three for seventy-one or more, with one more delegate for each fifty additional workers. The military LPA of 1979 stipulated that no more than 1 percent of workers could be union delegates. The Alfonsín revision of the LPA reached a compromise solution, giving unions one delegate for ten to fifty workers, two for fifty-one to one hundred, and an additional delegate for every hundred workers beyond that.

Under Frondizi's LPA, it was explicitly stipulated that 10 percent of the workers in a union could demand an extraordinary congress. Under Perón in 1973, in deference to the union hierarchy, the minimum was raised to 20 percent of the workers. The military decree of 1979 reduced the number to 5 percent, and Alfonsín's LPA of 1988 compromised on 15 percent of the workers.

Again, under Perón's 1945 law, employers were not required to contribute anything to union funds for whatever purpose. The law merely stated that unions had the right to build workers' vacation facilities, to have dining rooms at the workplace, to set up hospitals, clinics, pharmacies, and other agencies to enhance workers' health and education. But Frondizi's LPA (1958) mandated employer contributions earmarked for social welfare (*obras sociales*) and retirement purposes. Perón's LPA (1973) reaffirmed this article. Under the military, however, along with a separate decree-law (18.610), social welfare provisions were removed from union control and channeled into the military administration's department of social services. The Alfonsín LPA (1988) returned to the language of the 1973 LPA.

Regarding political activity, the 1945 LPA allowed union participation in politics as long as political decisions were decided by a union's general assembly or congress. Frondizi's LPA (1958) did not refer to this question at all. The Peronist LPA legislation of 1973 explicitly allowed unions to take political positions and to support political parties of their choice, but the military LPA decree of 1979 expressly prohibited political involvement by unions. Alfonsín's LPA (1988) made no allusion to political activity — the assumption being that it was again permitted because it was not explicitly forbidden, and this right comes under other constitutional protections of basic civil freedoms and rights.

Perón's LPA (1973) exempted unions from all types of taxes or public contributions, and successive LPAs maintained this exemption. Also, the right of union federations to intervene in affiliated local unions was not mentioned in the LPAs of 1945 and 1958. Perón's LPA allowed intervention in the affairs of union locals if a federation's statutes permitted it. The military's 1979 LPA abolished this right. The Alfonsín administration's LPA (1988) left the matter to the statutes of the individual unions, but required that the decision about intervention should be made at the highest delibera-tive level—specifically, the national congress of the union in question.

The 1945 Peronist LPA declared certain actions taken by employers against their workers to be illegal, with verdicts decided by a National Council of Professional Associations, made up of two employers' representa-tives, two workers' representatives, and three from the state. The Frondizi LPA added reasons for which an employer might fire workers—even active union delegates. The Frondizi legislation also guaranteed due process in disputes resolved by the council. The Perón LPA (1973) only mentioned explicitly illegal behavior by employers and reestablished the council by another name. The 1979 LPA, under the military government, added a reference to illegal behavior on the part of workers but did not provide for any particular jurisdiction. The Alfonsín LPA (1988) went back to the 1973 reading, but assigned judiciary competence without reconstituting a Nation-al Council of Professional Associations.

Finally, the Alfonsín LPA was the first to stipulate that a minimum of 20 percent of workers in any particular work setting must favor collective bargaining before a trade union can be formed and that a competitive list of delegates must be supported by at least 3 percent of a union's members.

As an important addendum, under Alfonsín a special piece of legislation (law 23.071) in 1984 revised the system of union elections to normalize union procedures after years of military intervention into union affairs.[3] Elections were to be organized by the unions' own by-laws, but observed by a national electoral board or the Ministry of Labor—elections being held during the normal working day. The law also specified that in the case of competing lists of candidates, for every 20,000 union affiliates, at least 4 percent of members' signatures (on petitions) were required in order to compete in the elections, plus 2 percent for affiliates beyond that number. (For example, a union with 30,000 members would need the support of 1,000 workers, or 3 percent, for a given list to be able to compete.) Most important, the unions maintained their plurality, winner-take-all, election system.

Perón's initial LPA of 1945 prepared for the right of unions to bargain collectively, a privilege ultimately sanctioned in 1953 by decree-law 14.250, a landmark piece of legislation in Argentine labor history.[4] Practically speak-ing, the LPA law further legitimized the process by which unions reached agreement with whole industries through negotiations linking organized labor, employers, and the government.

However, according to Javier Slodky, because of various military interventions, rarely has the collective bargaining law of 1953 been fully applied. Besides being rescinded during military dictatorships, it was superseded under Perón himself in 1973 by a consensual socioeconomic pact agreed to by both capital and labor.[5] In 1975 it was fully applied among all major unions (including six out of the seven unions under study here). These agreements were suspended in 1976, but collective bargaining negotiations were again resumed in 1988 by the passage of a new collective bargaining law (23.545).[6] Thus the momentous collective bargaining law of 1953 has been *fully* applied in only nine of the subsequent thirty-five years.[7] It will be remembered further that, because of Alfonsín's economic stabilization plan (Plan Austral) and its aftermath, unions were not allowed to bargain collectively on questions of wages and salaries during most of the Radical administration's tenure in office.

Collective bargaining under Alfonsín included for the first time workers in public administration. The law affects two major unions: state workers (ATE) and the more hierarchical civil service union (UPCN).[8] Also, the new collective bargaining law, once established for a particular industrial sector, applied to all employers whether or not they were party to the original negotiations in question.[9] With several minor modifications, the new collective bargaining law of 1988 returned to the basic law of 1953 which, for my purposes, was the point of departure in the last general round of negotiations applied to the unions in my survey.

Under Alfonsín, the CGT regained many of its formal powers lost during the military interludes. Critical in this regard is the CGT's right to administer its own social welfare programs, with an annual budget of nearly $1.7 billion. Estimates have it that the Argentine trade unions, plus other state and mixed collective agreements, have social welfare funds that cover 17 million Argentine laborers, employees, and professionals and their families—or approximately 60 percent of the entire population.[10] These funds come from a payroll deduction of 3 percent of workers' salaries plus another 4.5 percent contribution from employers; it is applied to expenditures for workers' medical services, hospitalization, tourism, recreational and sports facilities, and various educational and cultural programs sponsored by individual unions.[11]

Again, another crucial benefit that has stood the test of time since 1945 is the bonus of one month's wages, paid in two installments at the end of June and December. This applies to all workers, whether in the private sector, public administration, state enterprises, or mixed enterprises. Moreover, since 1946 all industrial laborers are included in a pension plan under social security. This was amplified in 1951 to include public-sector employees, and in 1954 it was again broadened to include professionals and independent workers, rural workers, retirees, and pensioners.[12]

Thus at the end of the Alfonsín administration, the CGT had maintained its monopoly of one union per industry, had won back its rights to collective bargaining by sectors and to negotiate cost-of-living adjustments (as the Austral Plan was superseded in 1987), and had regained control of its social welfare network.

The Sociological and Economic Context

Greater Buenos Aires, home of two-thirds of Argentina's trade unionists, is a huge, sprawling metropolis with overlapping and seemingly contradictory sociological and cultural features. Even more than most large cities, it has represented — certainly since the early days of Peronism — an amalgam of working-class, petty-bourgeois, and bourgeois life styles thriving side by side. Unlike Córdoba, which is more concentrated and industrialized, and which is a university city, Buenos Aires is highly commercial, a trading entrepôt, and a major port. Its population also includes a huge tertiary sector comprised of the federal government administration, employees in major multinational and domestic financial and banking enterprises, and others employed in various kinds of public and private social services.

Historically, Buenos Aires has gone through several phases of development, variously dominated by commerce and industry, finally producing a large cosmopolitan mass in which, though all classes are identifiable, the petty-bourgeois culture prevails.[13] Thus, although the working class (which includes both wage laborers and salaried employees) makes up the broad majority of the economically active population, the city's productive and cultural life is more visibly the world of the self-employed petty-bourgeoisie, and thus it is hard to distinguish between the needs and wants of the two classes.

Several factors contribute to this class fusion, as it were. Workers tend to identify themselves with neighborhood groups such as sports and soccer clubs that identify members as fans from Boca, River Plate, Independiente, Platense, Velez Sarfield, and so on, rather than by class. Wage and salary workers are scattered among many residential areas, often living in communities that include members of the petty bourgeoisie and professionals. Almost two-thirds (64 percent) of workers own their own homes (usually houses rather than apartments), although some of these may be only rudimentary. Home ownership absorbs a large part of their imagination and energy; after work, workers travel in all directions by mass transit, scarcely having the time to share a beer or a walk with a fellow worker. Such a high rate of home ownership distinguishes the workers' communities of Greater Buenos Aires from other more homogenous working-class neighborhoods such as the "red belt" encircling Paris, London's council apartment complexes, and the ethnic communities in U.S. cities.

Because racial, ethnic, and religious distinctions are relatively muted in Buenos Aires society, the city displays an almost blended social heterogeneity that cuts deeply into rigid class identifications—except of course for the Argentine upper class, who have always been imperially separate from the rest of society. In recent times, "tercerization" of the work force and deindustrialization have been magnified by the military regime's economic policies that forced some industries to move to the distant reaches of Buenos Aires Province, a dislocation that has resulted in heightened ambivalence about class relationships in Greater Buenos Aires.

Despite these changes, most Argentine workers belong to what Alejandro Portes calls the "formal proletariat," those covered by social security and other nonwage benefits, who are in the minority in most other Latin American countries.[14] For though the number of industrial laborers is declining, this loss is being compensated for by the influx of new unionized workers from the private service sector. The great majority of these "new workers" share the same wage and salary levels, educational opportunities, health and retirement benefits, and enjoy housing comparable to that of the industrial laborers.

For the first time in the history of Argentine state-labor relations, the Alfonsín administration was a majoritarian government that was neither Peronist—prolabor—nor military-dominated—antilabor. (Previous Radical civilian governments of Frondizi and Illía had depended on either Peronist support or military benediction.) Alfonsín's government was the most autonomous civil government since the Yriygoyen years of World War I.

After seven years of devastating military hegemony over the trade unions, the redemocratization brought by the Radical party's President Raúl Alfonsín presented organized workers and their representatives with new challenges and prospects. Alfonsín's victory in 1983 and the following plurality victory in the 1985 legislative elections placed the Radical party in competition with the Peronist party. For the first time in recent history, a competitive two-party system had a real chance. But while political democracy and the rule of law brought full civil rights and cultural pluralism much welcomed by the working class, severe economic hardship brought on by a soaring national debt victimized Argentine laborers and employees in all economic sectors. This uncommon convergence of political democracy and marketplace contraction gives the researcher an excellent opportunity to investigate the relative importance of democratic values and economic self-interest to the workers as individuals.

When Alfonsín became president, unemployment stood at only 4.2 percent, and a majority of those out of work had been so less than three months — in other words, most were not the hard-core unemployed.[15] Unemployment rose during the first half of the Radical administration, reaching about 6 percent by mid-1985.[16] In 1984 Argentina's population of 31 million was creating a gross domestic product of $58 billion. Growth rates were half those of the 1960s, as were gross rates of investment.[17] A 1986 World Bank mission to Argentina reported that between 1974 (the last year under Juan Perón) and 1985, average household income declined by about 20 percent. At the same time, income distribution in Greater Buenos Aires became more skewed in favor of the wealthiest 10 percent of the population, whose share went from 33 to 36 percent, while that of the poorest 40 percent of the population declined from 16 to 14 percent of the GNP.[18]

Not until 1986, when the economy grew by 7.1 percent and domestic investment stood at 18.5 percent of GNP, did growth rates begin to turn around. (Between 1980 and 1985 — three years under the military and two under Alfonsín — the GNP had dropped by 3.4 percent.) In 1986 the GNP grew in manufacturing and construction; state production of electricity, water, and gas; commerce and services; banking; and transportation and communication; whereas the GNP for almost all of these sectors had fallen in the previous year.[19]

The nature of the work force had changed. Data from the World Bank report indicates how much Argentina's economy since 1970 has been based on services, not industry. For example, the aggregate of government utilities, social and health services, commerce, transportation and communication, and banking continued to maintain a two-to-one advantage over manufacturing in the makeup of the gross national product.[20] Most threatening, however, was inflation — or hyperinflation. From an average rate of about 10 percent in the late 1960s (at the time of the Cordobazo), inflation rates since 1973–1974 have averaged between 150 and 650 percent — with the exception of 1980, 1986, and 1989, when hyperinflation led to the election of Carlos Menem to the presidency and Alfonsín's early resignation.[21]

Though the Argentine economy has increasingly come to resemble those of developing nations in Latin America and elsewhere — because of high inflation and an unstable currency, because of low levels of industrialization, and because of an inefficient public sector — Argentina's sociological statistical profile continues to read like that of a West European country. It would seem to provide good potential for long-run socioeconomic development: a birth rate just above 1 percent, high life expectancy; an extremely low population density (10 persons per square kilometer); a literacy rate of 94 percent, high caloric and nutritional levels, as well as one of the lowest ratios of inhabitants per doctor in the world.[22]

Moreover, 84 percent of the population is made up of working-age men and women. Among these, of the close to 10 million economically active workers who are officially earning incomes, 72 percent can be described as working class (those on wages and salaries), 19 percent are self-employed, and approximately 9 percent are landowners and employers.[23] Of the sample on which this study is based, within the manufacturing sector (or that sector to which AOT, SMATA, and UOM members belong) 81 percent are workers, 11 percent self-employed, and 8 percent employers.

The Luz y Fuerza workers represent the state industrial enterprise sector (along with gas and water workers) in which, understandably, those on wages and salaries make up 99 percent of economically active persons. Among FOETRA telephone employees (from the transport and communications sector), workers represent 78 percent, self-employed 18 percent, and employers 4 percent of economically active persons. Of the banking sector, from which our sample of unionized Asociación Bancária members were chosen, 77 percent are on wages and salaries, 18 percent self-employed, and 5 percent owners and employers. Last, teachers from CTERA represent both the public and private service sectors in which salaried personnel make up 87 percent of the economically active population, 11 percent are self-employed, and 2 percent are owners and employers.

Thus one can see that by 1980 the traditional manufacturing proletariat constituted just 23 percent of total workers; if we were to add workers in state industrial enterprises and construction, the figure would be 32 percent. On the other hand, according to the latest census figures, 56 percent of the wage and salary workers of Argentina are currently employed in the service sector, both public and private.[24]

Equally impressive is the stability among the self-employed during these years. Since the 1980 census, most surveys indicate a rise among the self-employed in the economically active population to approximately 20–22 percent, with a concomitant fall among industrial blue-collar workers to about 19 percent of wage earners, and to only about 13 percent of those economically active in the population. Self-employed persons, though not as numerous as elsewhere in Latin America, make up a stable, relatively prosperous, and socially integrated group quite unlike the typical "lumpen capitalist" profile found in much of Latin America; working for oneself is often preferred by many Argentines. Hector Palomino calls self-employment among Argentine workers not only "a refuge against unemployment but a stimulus for leaving their condition as workers."[25] The growth of the self-employed sector is another consequence of the military *proceso*, since that regime made fixed-wage employment much less secure, particularly in the private sector, than under previous civilian and military regimes. In fact, between 1970 and 1980, 35 percent of new jobs were classified as self-employment.[26]

Nonetheless, neither industrial laborers nor the self-employed make up the current majority of economically active people in Argentina. Most of the work force in the mid-1980s belonged to the tertiary sector of employees, both private and public. This sector continues to grow because of the increasing needs of an urbanized population that demands the services of federal agencies, particularly important state enterprises such as the railways, subways, and shipping; production of petroleum, electricity, gas, and water; telephone and postal services; hospital and health care; and education. Further, Argentina has a huge private service sector that includes commerce, banking, retailing, and the multitude of other private services that characterize a modern urban society.

As we have seen, Argentine workers had made considerable achievements under previous Peronist governments. Income distribution had measurably improved in their favor through 1975, but with the onset of the military *proceso* government, working-class incomes took a sharp downward turn from which they recuperated only in part during the Alfonsín years. For example (using 1970 as a base year with an index number of 100), wages and salaries had fallen to 48 by 1982, the last full year of military rule.[27] Not coincidentally (using the same base year and index), employment in industry had reached 119 in 1975 but dropped to 73 by 1982.[28]

At the same time, unit labor costs and income distribution fell meteorically; unit labor costs rose to 109 under Perón in 1974 but plunged to 46 by 1982, while (specifically in industry), salaries and wages as a portion of GNP declined from 42 percent in 1974 to 18 percent in 1982.[29] Under those conditions, of course, worker productivity in industry (again using the 1970 index of 100), increased from 99.7 in 1975 to 141 in 1983.[30]

Overall, the military period saw the loss of 425,000 industrial jobs.[31] Beccaria and Orsatti found that there were 10 percent fewer industrial workers by the end of the 1970s, a corresponding decrease in employment, an expansion of underemployment and enforced layoffs, a weakening of labor's bargaining power, and a loss of the rights of trade unions to bargain over productivity speedups.[32] This was very evident in the industrial unions I surveyed: textile, auto, metal, and light and power workers.

With the advent of democracy and the Alfonsín government, national income distribution was made more equitable through 1983 and 1984, only to have these changes reversed in 1985 and 1986. Using an index of 100 for mid-1983, real industrial salaries moved to 121 in mid-1984, dropped to 91 with the onset of the Austral reforms of mid-1985, and regained only slightly to 97 by mid-1986.[33] Having fallen to approximately 30 percent of national income, those on wages and salaries improved their position only slightly, reaching 33 percent in 1985. By 1987 workers' share of national income had again fallen to below 30 percent.[34] This represents a major reversal of historical patterns in which workers' wages and salaries tended to fluctuate between 40 and 50 percent of national income. Though not approaching U.S. and Western European income distribution, Argentina had always maintained a position midway between Third World and industrialized nations in this respect. The military intervention had reversed that standing, and the Radical government proved ineffectual in righting the situation. Argentine wages and salaries as a percentage of national income are now comparable to those of Mexico.[35]

There is little doubt that Argentina's welcome to power of the Radical party and President Raúl Alfonsín in 1983 was a dramatic repudiation of seven years of military rule. Alfonsín's honeymoon was the longest granted any administration since Perón's in 1946. Popular across a wide social spectrum, Alfonsín solidified and institutionalized Argentine political democracy and civic pluralism. Alfonsín's democratic consensus paralleled somewhat the support given to West German Chancellor Konrad Adenauer after the Nazi horror.

Clearly, the 1983 victory was a political watershed. It represented the first defeat of Peronism in an open, freely contested election and the first Radical party majority victory since the late 1920s. Alfonsín's success was due in part to his coherent critique of the military dictatorship, whereas the Peronist candidate, Italo Luder, supported amnesty for the military as part of his political campaign. (The Peronist leadership, it will be remembered, had opened the way for the military's entry into politics in late 1975, and some Peronist leaders in the CGT allegedly collaborated with the military government after 1976.) In addition, the suppression of the Peronist left had begun in earnest under Isabel Perón's government.

When Alfonsín's popularity inevitably began to wane, a turn of events not unusual in Argentina's volatile political climate, he embarked on two popular measures that gave him the time to undertake deeper and more substantial socioeconomic reforms.[36]

First, Alfonsín removed the prosecution of the previous military juntas from a military tribunal and transferred it to civilian jurisdiction. The trials precipitated a massive outpouring of support for the government and a severe condemnation of the military dictatorship. Surveys found that 67 percent of the population favored extending the trials to all those responsible for excesses independent of rank,[37] and 92 percent supported the trials of junta commanders from the three armed forces.[38]

Second, Alfonsín instituted a major currency reform, combined with a wage and price freeze. The 1984 inflation rate had reached 566 percent, and by the first two weeks of June 1985 (if projected yearly) had climbed to 1,200 percent. The Alfonsín government's economic reforms of June 14, which became widely and popularly known as the Austral Plan, was conceived as a draconian first step to counter runaway inflation, replace the worn-out peso, freeze prices and wages, control deficit government spending, and stimulate a resurgence of private investment in the economy. The reforms were approved by the IMF and international lending banks and were initially supported by Argentine business and labor groups. Nevertheless, despite the stability of the Austral for over a year and a negligible inflation rate, the reforms did not cause an upsurge in production. Instead, there was a perceptible slowing down in certain crucial economic areas and a recession in others. My survey confirms that Alfonsín's awaited industrial "reactivization" scheme was a major policy failure, spelling the beginning of a slow decline in the value of the Austral and with it confidence in the Alfonsín government.

Slowly working-class discontent became more visible. One factor was that labor unions were not permitted to bargain collectively for wage increases, and all pay hikes resulted from individual bonuses, overtime pay, and prizes for higher production, not basic wage rates. In addition, there were the slow, uneven beginnings of price increases for utilities, services, and finally some consumer goods. This squeeze provides the context for my examination of attitudes among Argentine workers at the onset of re-democratization.

The Union Structure

Despite the devastation suffered by the trade unions and the working class between 1976 and 1983, the redemocratization after the Radical victory offered new challenges. The CGT had survived military intervention and normalized its various functional prerogatives, choosing its leadership cadres through mandated elections, although top-down dominance of old-line leaders remained the rule.[39] The CGT leadership was able to resist a full-blown democratization sponsored by the Radical party because such a revision was defeated by a Peronist-dominated Senate. Also, for its part, the Alfonsín administration was not in a rush to reinstate the collective bargaining law and incorporate wage discussions after the institutionalization of the Austral Plan in mid-1985 — especially after the Austral Plan was reinvigorated by the Spring Plan in 1987, which postponed free union collective bargaining negotiations for several more months.

With their social role and political power intact, today the CGT contains 1,412 unions, of which 75 have come together as national-level federations. Two-thirds of these (comprising 50 unions) cover every province of Argentina. But the vast bulk of Argentine unions are small. For example, 914 of the total have fewer than 5,000 members each, and 638 of these fewer than 1,000. The jurisdiction of only one in seven unions extends beyond a single province, department, district, or city. It is estimated that 58 of the largest federations and unions make up two-thirds of the total rank and file.[40]

A large proportion of Argentine workers—over 50 percent, or 3,359,460—are unionized.[41] Within the industrial sector, encompassing the AOT, UOM, and SMATA, et al., 65 percent of all workers are unionized; among the state enterprises, such as the electrical company, SEGBA and the telephone company, ENTEL, 95 percent belong to unions. Within the financial service sector, including bank employees, 70 percent are unionized; and among service workers (including public employees and teachers, for example), 41 percent belong to unions.[42] Unionization in Argentina is the highest among Third World countries and compares favorably with figures for Great Britain and surpasses the figures for West Germany, Japan, France, and the United States. Affiliation in Argentina far exceeds levels of unionization in Mexico and Brazil.[43]

Argentina's top ten unions have close to 1,800,000 members, equivalent to about half of total union membership. Only three—metal, railway, and construction workers' unions—can be considered traditionally proletarian. The other seven are in the service sector: commercial employees, teachers, bank workers, state and civil service employees, and health and food service workers.[44] Three of the five largest unions are included in my survey—namely, the metalworkers (UOM), teachers (CTERA), and bank employees (AB).

The growth of services in the Argentine economy is seen specifically in the growth of the commercial, financial and social service (education, health) sectors. This "tercerization" has also given rise to a proportional feminization of the economy. It has been estimated that although women make up only 27 percent of the work force, 45 percent of newly employed workers are women and the great preponderance of them are employed in the tertiary sector.[45] This is particularly so among teachers and commercial, state, and bank employees.

This high index of unionization in Argentina reflects several factors in labor's development vis-à-vis the society and the economy. First, as a society constantly confronting inflation and hyperinflation in the last several decades, organization is one of the key means by which workers can defend themselves against this attack on their living standards. Second, because of the generous social welfare benefits provided by trade unions, enforced by law, joining unions has become a customary means of participating in social and cultural benefits otherwise too costly for most workers. Low levels of unemployment have enhanced union affiliation. Third, widespread union membership was encouraged by the power of the Peronists, who supported the union structure and, of course, encouraged membership. In turn, the unions' membership broadened the powers of the CGT, traditionally aligned with the Peronist party. Fourth, the CGT's successful role as a political force has spurred union affiliation in a corporately organized society. The centralized nature of collective bargaining in Argentina has given workers a unified voice in economic matters along with the government, the agrarian sector, the industrialists, the military, and the church.

Paradoxically, one of the strengths of the CGT—its ability to drive a hard bargain—has allowed it to defend its rather authoritarian structure and general lack of strong democratic roots as not alien to working-class interests. Under military regimes, particularly the most recent one, the CGT has been careful not to overstep its bounds, keeping its lines of authority in order so as to prevent an even greater intervention by the armed forces into the internal affairs of the union structure. Under Peronist regimes, the CGT was even more careful to regulate destabilizing grass-roots movements that could lead to wildcat strikes and embarrass the Peronist administration. On the other hand, the relatively few periods of civil democratic rule—the Radical governments of presidents Frondizi and Illia and particularly Alfonsín's—have meant the greatest growth of democratization within the CGT structure. But internal pressures for more rank-and-file participation in governance have been weak at best.

From the Aramburu caretaker military government of 1956 through the Frondizi administration in the early 1960s, some degree of pluralism was fostered among CGT leaders.[46] During Arturo Illia's Radical government in 1963, leadership cadres in the CGT formalized a distinct political tendency with the formation of the "62" faction, dedicated to a "Peronism without Perón," plus another section dominated by independents and Communists, El Movimiento de Unidad y Coordinación Síndical (MUCS).[47] Later this gave rise to El Movimiento Obrero Unificado (MOU) formed by Peronists, Communists, and some independents. By the advent of the Onganía military government of 1966, the CGT hierarchy was more pronouncedly Peronist. This tendency was consolidated by the second Peronist government of 1973-1975, in which the dominant Peronist grouping was the majority "62" faction against the rest of the leadership factions.[48]

With the advent of the military dictatorship in 1976, the split among CGT leaders followed a division between the more strategic unions that had been directly intervened by the armed forces and those that had not. By 1977 the two groups of union leaders formed a Comisión de los 25 (the "25"). Later that year the unions again split into the Comisión de Gestión y Trabajo (CGyT, later the Comisión Nacional de Trabajo, or CNT) and the "25." The former represented the more moderate, negotiating, conciliatory wing of the CGT, while the "25" was the more confrontational, oppositional faction — those that led the first general strike against the military in April 1979. Subsequently, the CNT and the "25" aligned to form the CUTA (Conducción Unica de los Trabajadores Argentinos) and to develop a common program vis-à-vis the military government. They called for improved wage levels, the return of social welfare programs to the unions, reestablished union autonomy, freedom for imprisoned union members and leaders, and information concerning union militants and leaders who had "disappeared."[49]

By 1980 the split had reasserted itself and CUTA was divided again into the more confrontational "25" and the more conciliatory CNT. The "25" faction (officially the Movimiento de Renovación Sindical Peronista, or MRSP) controlled the CGT, and they ultimately chose as their leader Saúl Ubaldini of the brewery workers. The CNT minority faction was led by Jorge Triaca of the plastics workers.[50] This split continued with the formation of the CGT-RA (República Argentina), later the CGT-Brazil, and the CGT-Azopardo factions (the groups took their names from the streets on which they were organized and held meetings). The former was an offshoot of the "25," the latter of the CNT. Under the CGT-RA majority faction, two further work stoppages were held in July 1981 and March 1982. Then came the Malvinas invasion and the military débacle. In the post-Malvinas era, the CGT unified again to organize three more general strikes against the military between December 1982 and October 1983.

From the return of democracy (1983) until mid-1985, the CGT leadership was divided into several visible factions.[51] However, by August of 1985, Saúl Ubaldini had consolidated his ascendancy by his election as CGT general secretary. During 1985 and until the "normalization congress" of November 1986, Ubaldini managed to unify the CGT as never before.[52] (Since then, there had arisen another split among leadership forces, reflecting various approaches to the deepening economic crisis.) By November 1986 the CGT political leadership structure had been "normalized" by the election of a national executive committee at its national congress. Bloc voting dominated by major unions resulted in the confirmation of Saúl Ubaldini as secretary-general. The makeup of the CGT Central Committee mirrored the factional divisions of the leadership. Of twenty-one members, the Ubaldini faction numbered seven; six were from the "62" group, under metallurgical labor leader Lorenzo Miguel; six were from the "25" faction, now tied to the "renovating" wing of the Peronist party; one was aligned to the Radical party (UCR); and one was "independent."

The Ubaldini leadership faction represented the more militant wing of the CGT, supporting the use of work stoppages (thirteen general strikes occurred under President Alfonsín), mass demonstrations, social protests, and advocated a continued focus on the primacy of the soaring foreign debt as a political issue. This faction, although it had powers of mobilization and a wide grass-roots following within the CGT generally, did less well in presenting lists of candidates or competing as a specific faction. In other words, it was dominant at the national executive level but often unorganized at the plant and office level. Nevertheless, it had the support of union leaders representing, among others, construction workers (UOCRA), transport workers (UTA), one of the two civil service unions (UPCN), textile workers (AOT), and sanitation workers, among others.

The Ubaldini group represented most clearly an assertive trade union movement outside the control of private enterprise, the state, or political parties. Though it used confrontational tactics against the Radical adminis-tration, it maintained amicable relationships with other corporate groups, particularly the Unión Industrial Argentina, the Catholic church, and the military command. High-level negotiations between the CGT elite under Ubaldini with major business leaders were commonplace, and Ubaldini was in the forefront of religious celebrations and marched in Catholic processio-nals. Vis-à-vis the armed forces, Ubaldini's CGT had not made a clear statement on the prosecution of military officers accused of crimes in the "dirty war" and of responsibility for the disappeared.

The "25," a group tied to the Renovating Peronist party wing, advocated a shift toward the more left-oriented Peronist youth factions and left-of-center, non-Marxist minority parties such as the Partido Intransigente (PI). They were also responsible for compiling multiparty delegate lists in several internal union elections. Important unions affected by such reforms were the automobile workers (SMATA), railway workers (Ferroviários), telephone employees (FOETRA), commercial workers, tobacco workers, and another public employee union (ATE). The "25" had the closest ties to the reformist party faction under the leadership of Antonio Cafiero, governor of the province of Buenos Aires. This labor-party alliance focused on a modest antibureaucratic labor agenda and called for greater internal democracy in both the CGT and the Peronist party.

The "62" faction represented old-line bureaucratic and paternalistic trade unionists dominated by the most powerful industrial union, the metalworkers (UOM). Their perspective was also corporatist, but with a strong negotiating orientation and an "economist" acceptance of basic liberal-capitalist ideology. In recent times the "62" has sought private negotiation and bargaining instead of publicly exposing hardened positions that could lead to confrontations with the state and the business community. The other major unions within this faction represented petroleum workers (SUPE), light and power workers (Luz y Fuerza), meat packers, and health workers.

Significantly, since March 1987 an insurgent group of fifteen unions (called the "15")—led by the "62" and UOM's Lorenzo Miguel, but including several leading unions of the "25"—began separate negotiations with Alfonsín's Radical government in the hopes of avoiding a continuing cycle of confrontations between a democratic government and the CGT. Dramatically, in March 1987, the government chose a new minister of labor from their midst—Carlos Alderete, national head of the light and power workers' union and a member of the "62." This move seemed an attempt to establish a West European–style "social pact" with built-in wage increases related to the cost of living in return for no-strike pledges. With the advent of the Carlos Menem Peronist government in 1989, new factional alignments eventually developed within the CGT. These will be discussed in chapter 10.

The Alfonsín Initiatives

Law 23.071 of July 1984 provided for internal reforms in union elections. It laid down rules for elections for union delegates and factory and office shop committees. It was a compromise measure providing for the greater possibility of competitive, multilist union elections without intervention by the national labor federations, and it made it easier to petition and achieve alternative leadership lists. It was directed at unions that had been intervened by the previous military regime.

After studying the returns from thirty-seven union elections held between 1983 and 1985, Ricardo Gaudio and Héctor Domeniconi found that the "62" and the "25" won eleven elections each, the CGyT (later the "15") six, and the Ubaldinistas (the "20") three. The other victorious slates were filled by nonaffiliated Peronists, independents, and others without an easily identifiable tendency. However, the "62," when not winning, were most often the runners-up and thus showed great organizational strength. But more important, the researchers found that since the return of political democracy and electoral reform legislation, there had been increased pluralism in CGT union elections.[53] This was particularly marked when compared to the "62" domination of elections held in previous decades.

Before 1983, opposition in most unions was seen as an "enemy more than as a circumstantial adversary."[54]

Defining union democracy as assuring representative leadership and the right of opposition groups to express their views, and to compete in and win elections, Gaudio and Domeniconi found a definite increase in democratization in Argentine unions since the mid-1960s.[55] Among the ten largest unions — those with membership of 50,000 or more — there was some kind of competition in eight (including six of the seven unions studied in my survey, but not the textiles workers, or AOT). On the other hand, during the last Peronist government (1973–1975) only three unions held competitive elections. Among the thirty-seven unions surveyed by Gaudio and Domeniconi, under Peronism 25 percent had elections among three or more competing lists of candidates. In the democratic period under Alfonsín, this figure had increased to 72.4 percent of the unions surveyed.[56] At the same time, under Peronism of the 1970s, in 67.4 percent of elections candidates ran unopposed, whereas since 1983 single-list elections had dropped to 21.6 percent.

Regarding voting competitiveness, Gaudio and Domeniconi found that minority candidates had received more votes since the ascendancy of Alfonsín. For example, in the 1973–1975 period votes for the losing slate averaged 49.1 percent of the vote of the winners, while after 1983 the figure improved to 65 percent.[57] Again, in the Peronist epoch, even when there was a substantial minority slate, the majority won in 100 percent of the contests. By 1984–1985 opposition slates won 45 percent of the elections in which more than one list was presented. Ironically, the more demonstrably pluralist elections occurred in unions that had been intervened by the military and then had to be "normalized" with the advent of political democracy.[58]

Although there was increased intraunion competition, the alternative lists were also headed by Peronists of one or another stripe, such as the "25" or a pluralist-party slate headed by "oppositional" Peronists, often also comprising the Radical, Intransigent (PI), and leftist candidates. Among Gaudio's and Domeniconi's sample of thirty-seven unions, some Peronist or Peronist-led slate won in thirty-six cases. Despite this, the authors, in a more detailed case study of union elections under Alfonsín, conclude that there has been an increase in democracy as marked by the proliferation of alternative lists, albeit the Peronists continued to dominate.[59] Overall, union elections since 1983 have been fairer than in the past, have followed correct timetables, usually have had competing candidates, have been marked by fewer irregularities, and have involved more open politicking among aspirants. Multiple, open-ended elections are a new and promising phenomenon stimulated by the general climate of democracy established during Alfonsín's tenure in office.

However, this is not to say that there is mass democracy in Argentine unions or that special worker-petitioned assemblies are the norm. It is one thing to observe multiple lists, closer elections, and the expression of minority viewpoints, but it is another to see direct rank-and-file involvement in nominating leadership cadres and running the unions. Under Alfonsín, the Radical administration attempted, through the failed Law of Union Restructuring—called the Mucci proposal after Alfonsín's minister of labor in 1984—to democratize union life by a thorough labor reform. It stipulated looser requirements for rank-and-file petitions for special union assemblies, thereby undercutting the formal nature of biennial delegate assemblies; proportional representation of losing minority lists in union delegations and shop committees; direct oversight of elections by the Labor Ministry; and an electoral process that starts with shop committees at the bottom and extends all the way to choosing union and CGT executive leaders.[60] Equally important, it advocated increased arbitration powers for the government and "crisis legislation" over certain socioeconomic questions. This affected the unions' right to strike and threatened the return to centralized collective bargaining that unions were pressing for. The Mucci proposal was defeated by a Peronist-controlled Senate as being far too intrusive into CGT internal prerogatives.

Alfonsín's legislative challenge to CGT bureaucratic traditions represented a major challenge to Peronist union leadership. The successful Radical offensive, exploiting the economic crisis surrounding the implementation of the Austral Plan, sought publicly to reverse the unions' "distributive" mentality to a focus on "production," reinforcing the loss of workers' wages as a percentage of national income. Moreover, they have created wage gaps, however, between the powerful and strategic unions as opposed to the less important and nonstrategic unions.[61] On the question of decentralizing collective bargaining, however, the Radicals were defeated.

The Alfonsín UCR had won two impressive presidential and legislative elections in 1983 and 1985 (before its setbacks of 1987 and 1989).[62] As a result, the CGT had for the first time to react to an aggressive, democratically legitimated, and popular civilian government with obvious grassroots support among union members with the potential to penetrate its future leadership echelons. The CGT therefore had to develop a new set of goals and principles. It had in the past thrived as the legitimate opposition to minority civilian governments (Presidents Frondizi and Illia, 1958–1966) in lieu of illegal or semilegal Peronist political organizations; or it had been an intervened or subjugated spokesman to generally unpopular and undemocratic military regimes (in 1966–1973 and 1976–1983). Under Perón's governments (1946–1955 and 1973–1975), the CGT served at least as an institutionalized interest group and at most as a fourth branch of the government. Its new role as oppositional spokesman for a huge sector of civil society confronting a sophisticated and aggressive administration required a critical self-evaluation of its future prospects.

Thus the Alfonsín administration's two major advantages in dealing with organized labor after 1983 — its early popular political mandate and the aura of economic reformism produced by the Austral Plan — led to a generally defensive labor position. Spurred by a worsening public debt, mounting inflation, and industrial stagnation, the Radical government was able to go on the ideological offensive by mid-1985. The Austral Plan had dire consequences for the working class. Firings as well as layoffs in the private sector became more commonplace; employment opportunities were largely frozen; the workday was often reduced, and there were many union complaints of irregular and late wage payments.

By the end of 1985, real wages had dropped by 37 percent when compared to the premilitary period of Peronism (1974), and unemployment reached over 7 percent by 1986.[63] Central government expenditures in vital social services also declined when compared with Peronist outlays (given in percent):[64]

	1974	1985
Overall expenditures for social services	14.7	8.2
Education	8.8	5.5
Health	3.9	2.3
Housing and urban services	1.9	0.3

Orsatti further shows that in 1974 the index between the minimum wage vis-à-vis the cost of the basic basket of consumer goods was 1.86, whereas it dropped to 0.78 in 1985. He charts a gradual deterioration of working-class purchasing power (measured by the relationship between the paid wage and value of the wage when spent) since 1974, falling by an average of 16 percent during the first three Alfonsín years.[65]

The CGT Response

The CGT reactions to the Radical government were expressed in thirteen general strikes, nine between September 1984 and January 1987. Further, most of the striking unions were in the tertiary sector, where workers had suffered the greatest inroads on their wages and buying power. In late 1986, for example, 85 percent of strikes during a two-month period were called by the service unions, including court, bank, telephone, and state employees, teachers, and hospital workers.[66] Inflation was the key concern during general strikes in the early Alfonsín years. CGT demands from mid- to late 1984 included: the 20 percent monthly price rises, deepening recession, rising unemployment, the nation's debt burden, the absence of domestic investment, the need to open the economy to productive foreign investments, demands for increased social expenditures, better income distribution, and reductions in tax evasion.[67] The constant pressure of inflation kept the CGT in a defensive mode; there was little time to develop alternative programs of its own. Constant general strikes allowed the UCR government at various times to label the labor confederation as "antipopular" and "reactionary."

However, despite the endless struggle to keep up with the cost of living, the CGT in the mid-1980s did take positions without developing concrete proposals concerning technology, investment strategies, and industrial renovations.

A typical position of Argentine unions, during a hiatus in the severe inflationary pressure, was expressed in the platform of the metalworkers' (UOM) congress of December 1985, six months after the implementation of the Austral Plan. The union demanded that it be consulted on major social decisions. Specific demands included: (1) that the UCR government abolish the military decrees still on the books regarding collective bargaining, professional association, social welfare, and so on; (2) that Argentina's relationship to the IMF be thrown open to public debate and not be the result of a fait accompli among government technocrats; (3) that the government consider forming a common front among Latin American debtor nations, that it coordinate a national plan like that forged by Perón in 1974—that is, developing a "third position" in international affairs; and (4) that the government stimulate a scientific, technological renovation in industry and retool the Argentine laborer to make him "master of the machine and not its slave or enemy."[68] The CGT under Alfonsín took the position that labor had to negotiate with the government and the business sector in a dozen areas, from wage and prices to public health to the environment.[69]

In August 1985, two months after the implementation of the Austral Plan, the CGT released its most comprehensive program, called the Twenty-Six Points, directed at the Argentine socioeconomic situation. Among other statements, the labor confederation called for a debt moratorium until authorities could determine which interest payments were legitimate, and an immediate halt to new borrowing. In addition, the CGT advocated legislation to stimulate economically productive areas of the economy instead of those geared to speculation; nationalization of bank deposits; a tax reform plan that rewarded productive investment, and construction of housing with accessible credit for the poor and working classes. Also the trade unions asked for a policy of stimulating industrial exports to avoid costly imports, workers' participation in managing state enterprises, and the promotion of private enterprise. Further, the CGT demanded the return of control over union social welfare programs, an increase of basic salaries and pensions, and increases in the federal education budget.[70]

Even after this plan, the CGT continued to speak out on economic issues. In early 1987, the "25" leadership of the trade union movement spoke of the devastating impact of the debt burden that had cost Argentina almost $16 billion since 1984. The interest on the debt in 1985 was worth 74 percent of total agricultural production, or 46 percent of the value of industrial production. In any recent year the amount required to service the debt could have paid for the creation of 300,000 industrial jobs, 600,000 homes, 2,600 hospitals, or 5,000 schools.[71]

Conclusion

The CGT, despite its internal differences, remained a major base of support for the Peronist movement's opposition to the Radical government, as proved in the elections of 1987 and 1989, which swept Peronism back into legislative and executive power. On the other hand, CGT leadership groups were still split between the confrontational and conciliatory factions— exhibiting a conflict that has often paralyzed it and given it little role in the Peronists' intraparty self-appraisal that occurred after 1985. Though a "renovating Peronism" lost the intraparty primaries for the control of the presidential candidacy in mid-1988, this element within the party, anxious to separate itself from its corporate-military nexus, no doubt will continue to play a role in restoring working-class rank-and-file enthusiasm for a more social democratic version of Peronism. The reformist wing of Peronism needs the CGT and its "62" and Ubaldinista factions for their social agenda, whereas the CGT leadership can use the additional inspiration of new democratic values and orientations. It is clear from my survey of workers that both sets of concerns, depicted in this chapter, are important to Argentine workers.

The social consciousness of the CGT, despite its authoritarian tendencies and gangster elements, is one of the few brakes on a total acceptance of liberal-bourgeois democracy in Argentina, and without the CGT the nation would take its place alongside Mexico and Brazil, with their paternalist-liberal structures. This has been dramatized once again by the Ubaldini-led opposition to some of the Menem-sponsored economic liberalization initiated in 1989. What indeed makes Argentina unique is the distributive, political, and economic potential of its organized working class.

Like all contemporary Argentine institutions, the labor confederation has its roots in corporatism and in certain authoritarian habits. In this it is like the Peronist movement itself and the Radical party's clubhouse bossism, as well as the clannish inner circles of powerful industrialists like the Unión Industrial Argentina (UIA) and more obvious authoritarian structures such as the military and the church. The CGT's internal democratic procedures leave something to be desired, but its leaders were correct in refusing to have the CGT singled out as the scapegoat of democratization under Alfonsín.[72]

Demographically and politically, the CGT emerged from the military *proceso* weakened by major losses of membership in the industrial unions and general stagnation or smaller losses in the tertiary sector. There are of course structural limits to the CGT's ability to organize in a poor economic climate—in particular, in the absence of Argentine industrial growth. Nevertheless, it might be possible for the trade union movement to work more closely with the social needs of the growing unemployed sector— the domestics, pensioners, retired persons, and other marginal elements of the society who have borne the brunt of fiscal reforms since the inception of the Austral Plan. My survey found ample recognition among workers of the powerlessness of the poor, for example.

There is one further question mark regarding future relations between the CGT and the Peronists. Ironically, were the CGT to become a more independent, autonomous trade union movement without explicitly merging itself with the Peronist party, it might force the Peronists to become a working class–oriented party rather than the more contradictory right-center-left conglomeration it now is. However, this contingency appears quite remote not only because of the attitudes of the Peronists' own rank and file, but also because of the CGT leadership's predisposition to maintain ties to other corporate sectors, such as the Catholic church, the military, and the Unión Industrial Argentina. There is also a real danger that an independent trade union movement would simply degenerate into one of pure "economism" undirected by any ideological foundations. The CGT during the Alfonsín years, through mobilizations and dialogue, seems to have tried to orchestrate the right mix of connections among the power structure, the various wings of the Peronist party, including the "62," and the needs of workers themselves.

On the other hand, in the unlikely event that the CGT opts for a more classic leftist oppositional stance, it might inadvertently be playing into the hands of landed interests and the military. Groups that have taken a strong confrontational stance in Argentina have traditionally been a factor in undermining democratic institutions. The workers' real choice seemed to be reduced to accepting bourgeois democracy or bourgeois authoritarianism. In other words, in the past when workers really made crucial demands on weak civil governments, these governments have been undermined and military intervention made plausible. Thus it appeared in the trade unions' interest to strengthen democracy without strengthening President Alfonsín and the Radicals. The CGT and the workers seemed to have understood this.

Certainly it is not fair to portray the CGT as a single-issue organization focusing on the redistribution of income, although that issue has and should maintain its priority. But the unions have also wanted to be involved in decisions concerning investment policies and the restructuring of the state, as is now clear under the Menem presidency. In lieu of a socialist model, the CGT focuses on a kind of militant reformism that pragmatically chooses confrontations as one of the weapons in its arsenal. The open dialogue of collective bargaining, when finally reinstituted by political democracy, offered promise as well as challenges — as did the social pact policies of past Peronist regimes. Both are far and away favored over military interventions by a widespread majority of union leaders and the unions' rank and file.

4 *A Portrait of Seven Union Contracts*

▶ ▶

NO UNION EXISTS in a vacuum. The seven unions in this study have developed and changed as the socioeconomic conditions have developed and changed. In order to understand the attitudes of union members at any given moment in time, one needs to understand both the socioeconomic history as well as the particulars of union structure and the critical issues facing them. The collective bargaining contracts of Argentine unions, moreover, are interesting documents in themselves, as they demonstrate in very clear terms both the gains of the workers and — to the degree to which these contracts were abrogated in the interim years of military rule — the costs of post-Perón authoritarian regimes.

Textile Laborers — AOT

My survey began with a representative, traditional industrial union. Through the personnel and administrative offices of the Asociación Obrera Textil on El Plata Street, I was able to get a computer printout of all textile factories in Greater Buenos Aires. Applying a stratified, random sample, I selected three factories of different size from the three principal branches of the textile industry — namely, cotton, wool, and textile stitching (the Sudamtex, Ponieman, and Pravia factories). Other branches manufactured such goods as stockings, bags, ribbons and elastics, mattresses, silks, dyes, and so on, but they were smaller installations, more on the level of shops, not factories.

I conducted a total of fifteen interviews, distributing my attention in proportion to the size of each factory: eight interviews were conducted at the Sudamtex cotton factory, four from the Ponieman wool factory, and three from the Pravia textile stitching plant. Interviews were randomly chosen: I numbered the payroll sheets, then applied the first three numbers of a random numbers table to select the textile laborers for in-depth questioning.

I originally thought it would be intimidating to interview workers in or near the plants in which they worked because of the proximity of their superiors. My experience in the textile factories, however, disabused me of that notion; I found the workers frank and direct in their answers with little noticeable timidity or reserve. I realized that Argentine workers' self-confidence about their role in society allows them to speak freely. Their belief that the CGT is a major social player translates into a sense of self-worth.

In the textile factories, as elsewhere, management and unions made work-site facilities available for my interviews. For example, at Sudamtex, I was offered the use of private facilities across the street from the factory in an office adjacent to the workers' recreational hall. At the smaller Pravia factory, I was given the clinic and first aid office in which to conduct my interviews without impediment and without interruption. Neither management nor union delegates tried to determine the findings. The management in one factory merely indicated that they were interested in the final published results of my survey. My experience at Sudamtex was a model for procedures that I was able to apply to other unions in other industries and institutions.

At the time of my interviews, membership in the Asociación Obrera Textil (AOT) was placed at 74,000, an astounding drop from its 1979 figure of 128,000, before the military dictatorship's deindustrialization policies had taken effect.[1] The general secretary of AOT was Pedro Goyeneche, elected in December 1984. He represented the Lista Azul of candidates, variously associated with the CGT's "62" and the "Ubaldinistas." No competitive slate of challengers emerged; a Lista Rosa tried to form, but was unable to get enough signatures to qualify. Somewhat above 54,000 members turned out to vote, out of a total of 74,000 eligible voters. Close to 49,000 (or over 90 percent of those voting) chose the single slate.

The AOT, founded in 1945, thrived in its early days as a result of Juan Perón's import substitution policies of the late 1940s (which concentrated on light industries such as textiles, food processing, and home utensils). It once had 175,000 members. By 1986, 20,000 members worked in the capital of Buenos Aires, and more than 50,000 (or 70 percent of AOT members) were located mostly in the province of Buenos Aires.

The unionized textile workers have 12 percent deducted from their paychecks for their retirement pension, another 3 percent for social welfare benefits (*obras sociales*) such as modest-priced, subsidized vacation hotels, health clinics, pharmacies, and other amenities such as sports clubs and weekend recreational facilities. Another 2 percent is deducted for union dues. Employers have to contribute an additional 4.5 percent for the laborers' social welfare benefits.

Argentina's textile industry is depressed, and its laborers are among the lowest-paid unionized workers. During the period of my interviews, average wages for textile workers were considered approximately 50 percent of what was needed to fill the basket of goods needed by a typical family.[2] When one counts overtime and the extra pay awarded for not being late or absent, textile laborers earned on the average slightly over $100 a month.[3]

The textile union's last industrywide collective bargaining agreement was negotiated in June 1975, in the last year of the Peronist government (under Isabel Perón), followed in 1976 by dictatorial wage decrees under the military *proceso*. Subsequently under Alfonsín's monetary stabilization policy (Austral Plan), wage negotiations continued to be prohibited in industrywide collective bargaining between 1985 and 1988. This prohibition existed for all the unions under consideration in this study.

The 1975 agreement negotiated by AOT and FITA (the Federation of Argentine Textile Industries) is representative of industrywide agreements signed under the last Peronist government, though it contains some features unique to textile manufacturing.[4] While many of its provisions were breached during the military dictatorship, the agreement is a good illustration — even in a union with a severely declining economic base — of the kinds of workers' rights in the workplace that were codified under Perónism.

For example, workers earn eight hours' pay for seven hours of work (considered the normal day schedule), as well as 7 percent extra remuneration for night shift work. Several other special indemnities were stipulated.[5] On the question of productivity, the contract includes several interesting clauses. The owners maintain the right to organize and direct the work process, materials, and labor for the purposes of increasing production, taking into consideration quality and cost factors. However, the AOT has negotiated for itself certain crucial prerogatives. Before introducing any new methods of production, the owners must communicate with the AOT to discuss the time they will be initiated and their possible impact on working conditions and wages. These plans must be relayed to the union ten days before new processes are to be implemented. The workers, through the union factory shop stewards' committee (hereafter called the factory shop committee or in Spanish, *la comisión interna*), have the right to study the plan, make suggestions as to its feasibility, and raise any questions regarding the impact of the production technology on workers' health and safety.

Moreover, if the new technology will displace workers, they have the right to their accustomed wage in another function as long as they attempt to learn a new job quickly and in good faith. Under no conditions can the new technology be used to lay off workers. Disputes that arise in this area are to be adjudicated at a Municipal Collective Bargaining Commission made up of ten members representing AOT and FITA equally, plus a representative of the Ministry of Labor. Bonuses under the new technology would be applied at such a time when 70 percent of the labor force in that section of the factory exceeds the production norm.

As one of the lowest-paid industries, textiles have built bonuses into the wage scales as a tool to increase worker productivity. Laborers receive a 25 percent bonus for perfect attendance every two weeks (or fifteen days). This is added to a typically low base pay of about $85 a month.[6] In addition, union delegates and members of the factory shop committee are counted present when performing authorized trade union functions. Nor can the company count a work stoppage initiated by the Executive Committee of the AOT as absenteeism on the part of the textile laborer.

The bonus for attendance can also easily be forfeited—a frequent complaint in my survey of textile laborers. For example, time lost through sickness, or the first thirty days following an accident (the latter covered by workmen's compensation), leaves of absence, permission to stay home or leave early—all are counted as disqualifications. Also, unauthorized or wildcat strikes or wage stoppages are counted against the laborer. Any worker with a single absence or two late arrivals (not exceeding a total of ten minutes) during any two-week period loses 50 percent of the bonus or receives only 12.5 percent over the base salary. Two absences or two late arrivals exceeding a total of ten minutes forfeits the entire bonus.

Autoworkers—SMATA

Ford Motor Argentina is the nation's largest and oldest automobile assembly plant, dating back to 1915. Along with Renault-Fiat, Mercedes Benz, Peugeot, and Volkswagen, it constitutes a sizable portion of the Argentine industrial sector. The automobile plants are essentially assembly plants in that the raw materials and parts are imported from the United States and Western Europe, and cars are assembled and finished in Argentina.

I chose Ford as a representative of a key automobile assembly plant. My initial contact was made at the public relations and press offices of the

SMATA union on Belgrano Street in the capital. The assistant press secretary introduced me to the metropolitan branch union delegate in whose jurisdiction Ford was located. Through him I met the factory shop committee at the Ford plant in General Pacheco, a town about twenty miles from the capital in the Province of Buenos Aires.

I met eight of the ten members of the union's factory shop committee who questioned me at length regarding my credentials, the purpose of my study, and the methodology involved. They said they would discuss my request and let me know of their decision in several days. After a week I received their approval, contingent on the Ford management's decision. (Management's approval was essential, since I planned to interview laborers during the normal workday routine, and Ford would have to replace them for the two hours or so duration of the interviews.) They placed my project on the agenda of their next meeting with Ford managers. Two weeks later, approval was granted.

At Ford, as elsewhere, I began with the personnel office. I was given the complete payroll list of laborers, and after numbering them I used a random draw. The sample that resulted drew from all sections of the Ford complex — namely, the assembly plant, metal stamping plant, motor mount section, and the truck assembly plant, as well as far-flung operations devoted to engineering, mechanics and maintenance, control and inspection, and road testing. Interviews were conducted in various plant sites within the sprawling Ford complex: some in the union rest areas, some in offices adjacent to the Ford automotive high school on the premises,[7] and still others in various laborers' recreational facilities.[8]

Ford Motors Argentina had been seriously affected by the recession of the last years of the *proceso* dictatorship which had continued unabated during the Alfonsín administration. By 1985, production had fallen even further: Argentina produced close to 300,000 units in 1973, whereas in 1985 production was less than half that figure, or below 150,000.[9] The Austral monetary and fiscal reforms instituted in June 1985, though stabilizing the currency for a full twelve months, had a recessionary impact on investment and consumption. This directly affected the auto industry.

At the time of my interviews at Ford, the company employed slightly over 3,000 laborers and approximately 1,500 employees. (Ford's percentage of the Argentine domestic market had fallen from close to 50 percent in the early 1970s to about 15 percent in 1985,[10] but still employed 40 percent more workers than its nearest competitor — Renault, located in the interior industrial city of Córdoba.) Ford was working at 30 percent of capacity, assembling about 150 vehicles each day or 3,000 units a month, including seventy Ford Sierras, thirty Ford Falcons, and fifty pickup trucks. In the early 1970s through 1980, however, Ford had occasionally reached 600 units per day or 12,000 units a month. The cost of a new car to the Argentine consumer was astronomical—reaching about $15,000 for a modest Falcon or pickup truck to $20,000–25,000 for a Sierra sedan.

SMATA (Sindicato de Mecánicos y Afines del Transporte Automotor) was founded in 1945 during Perón's ascendancy. Like the textile union, SMATA lost significant membership through the loss of jobs during the deindustrialization of the late 1970s and 1980s. Union affiliation dropped drastically from over 121,000 in 1973, to 72,000 in 1979, to 54,000 in 1984.[11] Its members are automobile workers in several very large assembly plants, but also include mechanics and repairmen at several thousand distributorships, garages, and gas stations throughout the country. Thus, the large SMATA sectionals of auto assembly workers are regularly underrepresented in direct elections because of this combination of thousands of small auto shops—and the outcome is an unchanging, national union leadership.

SMATA held union elections in April 1984, not long after Alfonsín's Radical (UCR) government came to power. However, because of irregularities cited by candidates for office and others under the LPA, or Law of Professional Association (decree-law 22.105), most recently amended and weakened under the military in 1979, the April elections were annulled and rescheduled for October 1984. Unlike the textile union elections, there was greater competitiveness among the autoworkers. Three lists of candidates competed for control of SMATA at the national level. With 78 percent of eligible members voting, the Lista Verde (a "25"-oriented leadership list) won with 21,077, making José Rodríguez the secretary-general of the union. The Lista Azul y Blanco received 18,634, with its candidate Jorge Costo; and the Lista Naranja, under Miguel Delfini's independent and "combative" leadership faction, received 2,614 votes. Combined votes for the two opposing lists outnumbered those for the victorious slate.[12]

As with AOT, SMATA's last industrywide collective bargaining agreement was reached with the automobile companies' association (FAATRA) in July 1975.[13] It is a more complex document than the textile contract and contains several unique features that illustrate worker-management relations in automobile plants such as Ford.

A new worker receives one paid vacation day for every twenty days of work. After six months in the factory, each worker receives a paid vacation equivalent to a hundred hours of work (based on an eight-hour workday). This comes to two and a half weeks' annual vacation, which then increases with years of service.

In case of accident or illness related to automobile factory work, laborers receive a normal wage until reintegrated into the work force. Workers with a lingering incapacity are given work that they are capable of doing until they are well enough to be returned to their former jobs. Management must maintain hygienic, healthy facilities, with rational use of natural daylight or artificial light appropriate to the nature of the work.[14]

The automobile plant also must provide on-the-premises medical facilities and free medical care, as well as first-aid cabinets distributed throughout the plant. Also, management has to take every precaution to keep dust, vapors, and other noxious fumes under control by ventilation. (At Ford, there were various laborer complaints — common in the industry — about tin dust and paint fumes.)

For workers whose job requirements take them outside the plant, the company must provide a $2 meal allowance; workers who travel more than thirty miles receive a 30 percent wage supplement for the days they travel.

If called to military service while employed with an automobile company, the laborer is entitled to $8 a month for a year, dispensed as $4 a month during his year's obligation, and the balance ($48) paid in one lump sum four months after returning to his original job at the company. On the death of a spouse or child, workers are given a subsidy of $40; and for the death of parents, parents-in-law, or siblings, workers are given a subsidy of $30.

Workers receive paid leaves of absence of ten days for marriage, as well as several days' leave for the birth of children (based on provisions of law no. 18.338).[15]

Unless an installation is too small to warrant it, the employer is required to provide cafeteria facilities on the premises. Ford had an excellent cafeteria for workers with an extraordinarily varied, abundant, and relatively economical menu — workers spend less than seventy-five cents for lunch. (It takes the average automobile laborer about twenty-five minutes to earn the cost of a meal.) Those auto factories with an uninterrupted workday — for example, from 6 A.M. to 2 P.M. — have to provide a twenty-minute break for refreshments during the shift. (This did not apply to Ford.)

On the other hand, automobile plant workers have many obligations. Once the company provides the appropriate equipment and tools, it expects laborers to produce nondefective and useful goods. Workers are expected to use materials economically and efficiently, as well as maintain, lubricate, and clean machinery and tools properly. Each worker is personally responsible for the equipment and tools under his or her jurisdiction. Any kind of malfunction, abnormality, or potential danger regarding the equipment or machinery is to be immediately reported to a superior.

Insubordination is not tolerated. Workers are forbidden to leave the assembly line without permission. Nor may workers initiate political discussions on the job, distribute propaganda of a political or ideological nature, sell chances or lottery tickets, or take up personal matters that have nothing to do with the work process. Workers are not permitted to smoke.

A particularly grave offense is to accept payment, tips, or other gratuities for removing materials or tools that are company property, even if these materials are deemed to be excess or without value. Parcels are subject to examination when workers enter or leave the factory. Any quarrels or scuffles on the factory floor result in severe disciplinary action.

Disciplinary procedures range from warnings to suspension without pay and finally to dismissal. All accusations include a presentation of charges in writing to not only the laborer involved, but also the factory shop committee. The SMATA factory shop committee has an opportunity to frame a rebuttal to the charges within seventy-two hours.

The factory shop committee has the following principal functions: to observe the fulfillment of the contract (which includes the provision of a union meeting hall and office); to perform its duties and tasks while avoiding attitudes that could provoke acts of insubordination; to notify their superiors when they are undertaking union business; and to bring before the factory's Conciliation Committee (a mixed owner-union committee) any outstanding or unresolved disputes with management.[16]

Last, any interpretations of the contract that cannot not be resolved between SMATA and FAATRA are brought before a national Mediation and Interpretation Committee made up of three representatives from labor and management and a Ministry of Labor representative.

The above contract came under considerable scrutiny in the winter of 1985. Ford and the factory union committee of SMATA had been involved in a bitter dispute which had resulted in a major setback for Ford workers. On June 25, 1985, Ford had fired thirty-three workers for "disciplinary reasons," later described as applying to workers who were "troublemakers" and repeatedly absent. The factory shop committee, headed by Miguel Delfini, cited Ford's violation of an agreement between the company and the factory workers which precluded any firings or layoffs until July 31, 1985. That agreement had been signed on May 17, when rumors of impending production layoffs were rife. On June 25, led by the factory shop committee, the workers locked in plant personnel and locked out incoming supplies. The national head of SMATA, José Rodríguez, called the Ford workers' seizure an "extemporaneous measure."

On June 27, the factory shop committee allowed the 1,500 office employees to leave, after two days' internment, while the union laborers and delegates continued their occupation of the Ford plant. On the same day, Ford made the following demands: (1) that the plant occupation be lifted before any kind of negotiation could take place; (2) that Ford be allowed to inspect its equipment and machinery; (3) that the plant be cleaned up; (4) that an inventory of equipment take place; (5) that the cars that had been used by strikers be inspected (rumors had it that workers were driving around the plant grounds with zero-mileage cars). Workers offered to negotiate directly with management. Ford rejected this offer, saying that it would negotiate indirectly with the factory shop committee and only in combination with representatives of the National Labor Relations Board. The workers voted to continue their occupation of the plant and agreed to meet with management under Ford's proviso. Late on June 27, Secretary of Labor Bigatti declared the Ford workers' takeover illegal.

Meanwhile, the Ford workers allowed a notary public to inspect the plant premises. He found that the cafeteria was dirty, that food had been dispensed without payment, that new cars had been used, stained, soiled, and often abandoned on the premises with windows left open; there were also a certain number of missing items from storage and one pilfered car radio.

At the meeting between Ford and the factory shop committee on June 28, the workers' delegates accused Ford of a lockout. The shop committee said that when workers had voted (in a workers' assembly at Ford) to return to work while negotiations took place, they were unable to do so because Ford had cut off the necessary materials, supplies and tools, had cut off electricity to the plant, and had informed the office and supervisory staff not to return to the Ford plant. The factory had in effect suspended operations until further notice. On June 29, with the situation deteriorating for the occupying workers, the shop committee held another workers' assembly in which they decided by majority vote to allow any laborers to leave who wished to do so. Reportedly, 1,000 left, leaving almost 2,800 workers still inside.

On June 30, Labor Secretary Bigatti reiterated that the seizure of the Ford plant was illegal and that it must be lifted immediately. On the same day the SMATA shop committee received public support from the Sanitary Workers' Union, The Mothers of the Plaza de Mayo, minority factions of the Peronist movement, the Intransigent party (PI), the left political party named the Movement Toward Socialism (MAS), and Adolfo Pérez Esquivel, a human rights activist. Negotiations broke down thereafter, and after nineteen days the workers ended the occupation on July 14, 1985. On July 21 Ford fired an additional 305 workers, including the entire factory shop committee. On July 22 a judge from the district in which Ford is located, San Isidro, charged the union with "illegal measures against peoples' rights, usurpation of property, illegitimate use and damage to automobiles." Further, he accused the shop committee of criminal intent.[17]

On July 24, the president of Ford Motors Argentina, Robert P. Sparvero, and José Rodríguez, general secretary of SMATA, signed an agreement before the minister of labor, Hugo Barrionuevo. Ford promised no more immediate layoffs other than those already ordered. Both sides promised to study the causes of the workers' occupation of the factory. Ford announced its plans to reopen operations on July 29, but stated that if the recession continued to shrink the domestic automobile market, the company might have to resort to encouraging voluntary early retirement of its labor force. The agreement committed Ford to order no new layoffs until November 30, 1985, and to reopen talks with SMATA at the Ministry of Labor beginning September 30, 1985. Ford's victory was total. After further study of the individual cases, Ford eventually rehired seventeen of the fired workers. Thus there was a net firing of 321 workers in 1985, reducing Ford employees by early 1986 to about 3,400 workers, a 10 percent decrease.

Indeed, by the time I began my interviews in May 1986, Ford had managed to reduce its work force by another 300 laborers or so, through its early retirement indemnization program—a topic of much discussion among many of the auto assembly workers. Ford, many workers seemed to think, targeted some of the remaining SMATA activists, older (more costly) workers, and those with a history of absenteeism for their early retirement program appeals. (Ford policy apparently involved a combination of the carrot and the stick—reducing their costs and getting rid of potential "troublemakers"—a kind of housecleaning.)

The early retirement indemnization program had worked quite well, particularly in a country where members of the working class seemed always to be on the lookout for opportunities to go into business for themselves and needed the seed capital for such a venture (more about that below). In essence, any worker seeking early retirement would receive three times a monthly minimum wage (at $80 a month) times the number of years employed at Ford (let's assume twenty years), plus two months of actual pay for early retirement (let's assume $300), plus a month's actual vacation pay and a month's actual bonus pay. The total, one-time retirement payment would come to $6,000. This appealed to many workers, particularly those who feared being fired in the future, although I heard quite a few horror stories of ex-laborers who by mid-1986 had not been successful "on the outside" and had seen their indemnity payment melting away rapidly without steady work.[18]

Metalworkers—UOM

The Unión Obrera Metalúrgica (UOM), founded in 1943 under Perón's aegis as minister of labor, is the largest and most powerful industrial labor union in

Argentina. Estimates of its membership have ranged from 130,000 to 267,000 to 312,000 affiliates.[19] According to most sources, its membership has declined only slightly since the early 1970s, though the metalworkers' union is notorious for inflating affiliation figures to attain greater representation at CGT congresses. Like most Argentine unions, it is federally structured, though its overwhelming power base lies in the industrial eastern seaboard, extending from the capital to the limits of Buenos Aires Province and the outskirts of the industrial city of Rosario in Santa Fe Province. The capital has close to 50,000 UOM members and Greater Buenos Aires at least another 65,000. The towns of Villa Constitución, San Nicolás, and Campana contain the huge iron and steel works of Acindar, the state iron and steel enterprise (SOMISA), and the metals firm of Techint. These three industrial towns contain another 9,000 UOM laborers.[20] The balance of workers are scattered throughout the country, with a growing minority of companies moving to the capital of the southernmost Patagonian region, Ushuaia.

My interviews were conducted at Pirelli, a large multinational company, and Koval y Blanck, a small, private Argentine metallurgical plant. The Pirelli firm is located in Mataderos, on the northwestern edge of the capital, on the very border of the Province of Buenos Aires, and Koval y Blanck is just over the provincial line in the San Martín district. I received permission from the company administrators and shop committees and drew up random sample lists. Interviews were conducted in either the nurses' office, an empty office, or UOM library facilities at the work site.

UOM union elections are held indirectly via a large national congress made up of representatives of the various metallurgical sectionals. Representation is based on a complicated formula that gives proportionally more weight to the medium-sized and less populated districts, those containing the smaller factories and metal shops. Thus UOM leadership, like SMATA's, has been dominated by conservatives for over a quarter of a century, despite the rise of heavy industrialization beginning in the late 1950s.

Delegates from each UOM section are elected in direct elections and then represent the membership in indirect elections at the national union congresses. Each section sends a minimum of three delegates plus a proportion of the total vote of the district. Thus such major districts as the federal capital of Buenos Aires send twenty-seven delegates, Avellaneda (a large industrial suburb of Buenos Aires), eighteen, and Vicente López, fifteen. On the other hand, each of the hundreds of small districts throughout the country send three delegates, regardless of their total membership. Certain populated zones with large industrial plants send one delegate for every 2,400 members; other far-flung districts send a delegate for every 340 affiliates. Thus the less conservatively oriented membership of the northeastern corridor, from the suburbs of Buenos Aires (for example, Avellaneda and Quilmes) to Rosario and Santa Fe, are generally underrepresented in UOM leadership cadres, internal affairs, and political policy making.

In the UOM elections of 1984, Palomino showed that the conservative leadership of the general secretary, Lorenzo Miguel, received the overwhelming majority of his votes from UOM election districts that featured noncompetitive single-list union elections.[21] Nevertheless, there are sectionals that oppose Miguel's control of the national UOM apparatus. Foremost in this regard is Alberto Piccinini's leadership over the UOM contingency at Acindar in Villa Constitución and the minority national slate under the control of Francisco Gutiérrez, who is particularly strong in Quilmes.

As among SMATA autoworkers, UOM laborers have fallen on difficult times. For example, in the six months preceding June 1985, over 6200 metallurgical workers had been fired and over 25,000 laid off from several days to several weeks.

The UOM collective bargaining contract resembles the AOT and SMATA agreements in many respects.[22] Nevertheless, there are several key features worth mentioning. For example, UOM laborers receive a 1 percent hourly wage increase automatically for each year of seniority apart from normal wage bargaining packages. For dangerous or unhealthy forms of work, laborers receive an additional compensation of 20 percent per hour. Specifically, dangerous tasks undertaken by laborers are also awarded a 20 percent hourly bonus. Unspecified extra pay is also granted to workers who receive a secondary school diploma or use a foreign language in their work. The UOM collective agreement also has a complicated scale of hourly wage increases depending upon changes in work categories.[23]

Light and Power Workers—Luz y Fuerza

Through the light and powers workers' national press secretary, I was brought into telephone contact with administrators at SEGBA (literally translated, the Electrical Services of Greater Buenos Aires), the national electrical company. Through them and the Luz y Fuerza press secretary, I gained access to the personnel director at Puerto Nuevo, employing 800 laborers, one of the two largest light and power installations in Argentina.

I was given the payroll list for all intermediary labor personnel. As elsewhere, after eliminating custodial and supervisor categories, using a random numbers table, I chose fifteen workers from the major functional categories at Puerto Nuevo. All interviews were conducted in a classroom where SEGBA often ran educational and technical seminars designed to help laborers move up through a multitude of job categories. (These classrooms were available because the light and power workers' interviews happened to fall in the months of mid-December to mid-February, Argentina's summer vacation time.)

The light and power workers in Argentina are typical of industrial workers in the tertiary service sector working for a nationalized electrical company. SEGBA produces, transmits, distributes, and commercializes electric energy. Its basic jurisdiction comprises the almost 13 million inhabitants of Greater Buenos Aires (or over 40 percent of all Argentine consumers of electricity) and counts close to 3 million paying customers. The company, by way of various privately owned ancestors, including German and French interests, dates back to the last decade of the nineteenth century. Not until 1958 did it become a mixed public-private enterprise, and in 1968 it was nationalized.

The light and power workers' union (Luz y Fuerza), also founded in 1943 during the early days of Peronism, has seen its Greater Buenos Aires membership remain relatively stable, going from 53,000 in 1973 to 58,000 in 1984.[24] Its reported national membership is 70,000.[25] Using my own compilation from the Ministry of Labor's comparative statistics for the various provincial and local union branches throughout Argentina, I calculated a net decline from 83,000 light and power workers in 1979 to 65,000 by 1983.[26]

Puerto Nuevo is the major power plant of Greater Buenos Aires. In addition to generating electricity and regulating its output, workers are employed in repairing and maintaining electrical equipment, producing combustibles, and maintaining buildings and grounds and the depository. Under the categories devoted to *operations*, workers are divided into semiskilled technical workers, assistant operators, operators, and section chiefs. The more skilled classifications for *maintenance* include maintenance assistants, maintenance technicians, and master technicians.

The light and power workers' last industrywide collective bargaining contract, as with other unions I surveyed, dates back to 1975. Unlike other union agreements, however, this is a truly massive document, filling a 252-page booklet.[27] I will only emphasize some of its more original articles and sections that best exemplify the guarantees to workers employed in the state sector. The agreement is also unique in its self-conscious language regarding the *comunidad organizada*, which is reminiscent of the rhetoric of Perón's presidential speeches. Perón's pronouncements constituted an eclectic series of philosophical statements that resemble twentieth-century papal encyclicals and positions espoused by early Western European Christian

Democracy, and complemented by some original propositions collectively known as *justicialismo* — as the Peronist ideology is still called today.[28] Each of the ten chapters of the light and power workers' agreement is introduced by one of the philosophical-ethical principles of *justicialismo*. Chapters are entitled: "The Right to Work," "The Right to a Fair Wage," "The Right to Improve Your Skills," "The Right to Dignified Work Conditions," "The Right to Good Health," "The Right to Social Welfare," "The Right to Social Security," "The Right to the Protection of the Family," "The Right to Economic Betterment," and "The Right to Defend Your Trade Union Interests." All these concepts were ensconced in much of the literature and policy perspectives of the early Peronist administrations immediately after World War II, and many are reaffirmed in the Peronist constitution of 1949.

The preamble to chapter 1 sets the ideological tone of the document:

> Work is considered the indispensable medium that satisfies the individual's and the community's spiritual and material needs, the cause of all the conquests of civilization and the foundation of general prosperity. From this it follows that the right to work must be protected by society, giving it the dignity it deserves and providing employment to those who need it.

As I found out during my interviews with light and power workers, many of them are sons of deceased, retired, or older light and power workers. This is due to provisions in the contract guaranteeing that children of light and power workers, especially those who graduate from SEGBA's own technical secondary schools, will have first priority when openings occur in the electrical industry. Ten percent of office job vacancies are to be filled by daughters of light and power workers. Also, SEGBA commits itself to fill 4 percent of the openings with those with partial physical impairment. Further, the company guarantees stable employment, a given wage level, and regular increments.

Wage deducations taken by the union, beyond the normal union deduction of 11 percent for retirement, include 2.75 percent for tourism and recreation, 1.5 percent for housing, 3 percent for a supplemental workers' retirement fund, and .25 percent for cultural and sports activities. (The light and power workers' union owns ten first-rate resort hotels, two of which I saw myself, and eight recreation and sports facilities for daily use.)[29] As a supplemental retirement fund, workers with at least five years of service receive seven months' pay in their last month's paycheck, augmented by 5 percent for each year of service beyond five years. (These benefits are limited to the equivalent of ten months' wages.) Married SEGBA laborers who are called to perform obligatory military service continue to receive 100 percent of their basic wage; unmarried men with dependents also receive a full wage, whereas bachelors without direct family obligations received 60 percent. Workers are guaranteed their old jobs upon their release from the military.

SEGBA established fifteen category steps for light and power employees. New workers move up one category every three months, with a wage increase of approximately 1 percent for each move. (This amounts to an approximately $2 monthly increase in the lower-rung categories.) The wage jumps become larger at category 6 and even larger at category 10. Each worker receives a further 2 percent for each year of service. Moreover, those with twenty-five years of service receive the pay of the next category above *without* a change in their job function and responsibilities. SEGBA also gives each worker who reaches twenty, thirty, and thirty-five years of service a month's bonus to mark the occasion.[30]

Light and power workers are entitled to construction loans to build a house, or they may borrow up to one month's wages for clothing or food, to be repaid in ten monthly installments. The contract also details a complex scale of bonuses of between 13 and 21 percent for various kinds of highly technical work. Those who work continuous or rotating shifts (such as morning to afternoon, evening to night) depending on their category, receive bonuses of 3–21 percent over their base wage.

SEGBA provides three competitive scholarships for every 1,000 workers to pursue diplomas in technical or preparatory secondary schools, or university degrees in appropriate fields, such as engineering, science, and architecture.[31] Workers who earn university degrees while employed automatically receive an 18 percent a month bonus; if the degree is applicable to their areas of specialization, they are entitled to a monthly bonus of 35 percent. Those in specialized functions who receive secondary school diplomas while employed receive a 12 percent monthly bonus.

The chapter of the contract that deals with working conditions begins with this justicialist credo that affirms the dignity of work and the rights of workers to self-improvement and recognition:

> Work constitutes at the same time a right and a duty to society and to social solidarity. By fulfilling their labor obligations, workers contribute their efforts to the community and become conscientious and responsible protagonists within the society. For that reason the workers and their families have the right to a life of dignity while they perform a useful task and receive a just compensation. They must have the right to improve themselves, to develop their creativity, to be informed, to further their education and skills, to be promoted according to their merits and dedication, to receive special protection from the risks of the workplace by the fulfillment of the norms of hygiene and security and to assure themselves social security and welfare to the end of their lives.[32]

Light and power workers cannot be penalized for their politics, union beliefs, religion, or race, as long as such factors do not lead to insubordination and interfere with the performance of their jobs. The contract also spells out in explicit detail causes for dismissal,[33] generous leaves of absence,[34] various paid leaves and sick leaves,[35] basic on-the-job hygienic standards,[36] and compensation for dangerous work.[37]

Light and power workers receive 150 percent of their hourly wage for normal overtime, 375 percent for Sunday work, and 500 percent for working on national holidays. All light and power workers receive a paid holiday each July 13, the Day of the Light and Power Worker. Light and power workers with five to ten years of service receive fifteen days' paid vacation a year; those with fifteen years, twenty days; those with twenty years, twenty-five days; and those with more than that, thirty days.

Workers injured on the job receive full pay until they can return to work. If an accident is so serious that a worker must retire from active work, the firm duplicates for six months the income the injured worker receives as a mandatory state accident insurance benefit for retirees.

Workers who marry receive a loan from the enterprise of twenty times the daily pay of a worker in category 7 (approximately $150), to be repaid in 100 consecutive monthly payments. For each child born of that marriage, the debt will be reduced by 25 percent.

This, then, suggests the interesting labyrinth of benefits and responsibilities spelled out in the state electrical workers' contract. It is not clear how these impressive provisions and relationships work out in daily practice, however; I will return to some explicit complaints regarding workers' jobs and benefits.

Telephone Employees—FOETRA

After discussions with staff members of FOETRA, the telephone workers' union, I was introduced to a union delegate from the capital who represented the key telephone exchange in Belgrano, one of Argentina's most densely populated zones in the heart of the capital, with an enormous number of telephone subscribers. Through him, I contacted Argentina's largest administrative telephone complex in nearby Palermo. The Belgrano telephone exchange building on La Pampa Street houses telephone operators, linemen, technicians, and repairmen, while the Palermo complex (called El Golf) includes administrative, engineering, and design units. As with my research into other unions, I drew a random sample of workers and my assistants and I conducted interviews.

The phone workers are employed by ENTEL, the state-owned telephone company officially founded in 1950. Once British-owned, the telephone network was reconstituted as a mixed enterprise in 1948, under Perón, and nationalized in 1952. ENTEL is divided in three roughly equal sectors. There are over 10,000 technicians and ancillary semiskilled personnel in such areas as cable splicing, internal equipment maintenance, telephone installation, equipment testing, and telephone line installation. There are also approximately 10,000 telephone operators and adjunct personnel and, finally, over 15,000 professional, nonprofessional, and skilled personnel divided among mechanical designers and drawers, equipment and cost analysts, and administrative and budget staff.

Total union membership is said to be 40,000, of which 20,000 employees work in Greater Buenos Aires; membership remained the same between 1973 and 1984.[38] In June 1985, Julio Guillán was elected FOETRA general secretary, winning over half of the 13,000 votes. His victory was one of the few cases in a major union (along with those of CTERA and Asociación Bancária) in which a multiparty delegate leadership slate won in a genuinely contested election.[39]

The most recent FOETRA-ENTEL labor agreement, a huge document of close to 100 pages of two-column print, dates to 1975, the same year the Luz y Fuerza–SEGBA contract (discussed above) was negotiated. Like the light and power workers' contract, its articles and provisions guarantee an overwhelming number of special rights and duties for state employees.[40]

Bank Employees—Asociación Bancária

The Asociación Bancária was one of the most difficult unions to deal with because of the great variety of banks as well as the general complexity of both the banking sector and the bank employees' union profile. The union, founded in 1924, is among the largest Argentine unions. Along with the Commercial Workers' Union—Unión Comercial—it has been one of the fastest growing unions in recent decades. National union membership was estimated at 186,000 as of 1984, compared to 84,000 a decade earlier.[41] There are 79,000 unionized bank employees in Greater Buenos Aires alone. Bank employees are divided among workers in national banks (approximately half of all union members), in private Argentine banks (about a third), and in foreign banks (representing another 20 percent or so).[42]

In elections held in December 1985, the Asociación Bancária proved to be one of the most pluralistic of the seven unions I studied, with many candidate lists. Elections were very competitive and the lists spanned most of the ideological political party spectrum. There were 77,000 votes cast out of a total of 186,000 affiliates. The Lista Morada, under José Tejerina, won with 13,131 votes. This list represented a truly broad-based coalition representing Radicals, Peronists, Argentine Communists, and Intransigents (PI). The Lista Granate, headed by Eloy Monzon, represented an equally broad-based list — including Peronists, Radicals, and two small parties, the Movement for Independence and Development (MID), and the Popular Socialist party; it received 12,800 votes. Third place, with 11,582 votes, went to the Lista Blanca headed by José Zanola, a major "62" leader of the CGT Central Committee who represented both that faction and the "25" Peronist faction.

The bank employees' contract recalls features of the other collective bargaining documents but stipulates several features special to the banking community.[43] It became clear during their interviews that bank employees are highly educated. Bank employees need above-average skills in organization, mathematics, and applied technology. Though salaries are extremely low for entry-level personnel, the union contract offers several articles that compensate, to a degree, for the low base wage scale. For example, bank personnel who perform technical functions receive a monthly add-on of between 35 and 105 percent over their base salary, depending upon professional background and bank category. This includes qualified employees who have worked as accountants, lawyers, architects, notaries, doctors, engineers, geologists, legal stenographers, bookkeepers, graphic designers, topographers, librarians, mechanics, teachers, and professors of all kinds. Many have university degrees or have completed more than half of their university studies.

Thus the banking sector hires from an eclectic group, and the interviews amply demonstrated this. Employees without professional degrees who nevertheless work at specialized, technical tasks receive an added increment to their monthly base wage of between 12 and 53 percent, depending on the importance of the task. Included in these categories are such banking jobs as publicity, translation, systems analysis, computer programming, accounting, mechanical design, specialized typing, library cataloguing, and a host of other skilled areas within the bank. In addition, employees whose prime responsibility places them in the categories of program analyst, computer programmer, and computer operator receive additional compensation of between 43 percent to 95 percent — again, depending on the nature of the responsibility and skill.

Last, given the nature of their staff, banks understand the special educational needs of their employees. For example, all employees who take secondary or university-level courses in private or public institutions, and who are studying for recognized diplomas or degrees, may enjoy leaves with pay for up to twenty-one days a year to prepare for and take examinations.

The Teachers' Union—CTERA

Another white-collar service union of great complexity is that covering the various teachers and allied educational employees who have banded together in a federation called the Confederación de Trabajadores de la Educación de la República Argentina (CTERA). In terms of membership, it is—along with the metalworkers' and bank employees' unions—among the five largest unions in Argentina. But because its members are widely dispersed, its organization decentralized, and because it is comprised of a handful of separate unions with overlapping yet distinct problems, it remains relatively weak within the CGT (although a month-long strike at the start of the Argentine fall school term in 1988 seemed to consolidate and politically strengthen the confederation).

CTERA is estimated to have approximately 189,000 members, out of a reported 600,000 primary and secondary public and private schoolteachers in Argentina—one of the nation's lowest percentage levels of union affiliation.[44] However, the teachers represent the kind of independent, white-collar, professional union needed to complete our picture of Argentine rank-and-file unionized workers.[45]

Although historically there were various teachers' unions, mostly local and mostly in the capital, none of them managed to sustain itself and develop as a national entity. In 1953, during the last years of early Perónism, the Union Docentes Argentinos (UDA) was organized with government support. Just before Perón's fall, the Peronist government recognized UDA as a legal organizational entity (*personalidad profesional*). UDA was intervened by the military government in late 1955 and dissolved in 1956. Under the military government of 1955, a commission was authorized to develop a professional teachers' code or statute, which would give teachers a jurisdictional basis as an economic and professional entity with legal rights and obligations.

Not until the civil government of Arturo Frondizi in 1958 was a teachers' statute made into law (14.473).[46] The law stipulates that teachers are to be paid in proportion to the cost of living and that retirement benefits after twenty-five years of service are to be pegged at 82 percent of base pay (one of the key sources of complaint, and a strike grievance mentioned in interviews). Other stipulations include the right to freely organize for their professional interests, and the rights to tenure and sabbaticals.

The 1960s saw a proliferation of many teachers' unions in both private and public schools, at the provincial and municipal levels, and among technical as well as liberal arts teachers. CTERA finally had its birth in 1973 as a confederation of many provincial and municipal unions. In 1974, under the second Perón era, UDA was legally restored and reorganized. There then commenced a long and involved jurisdictional struggle between CTERA and UDA. Because UDA is a Peronist-founded union, the CGT backed it in the dispute. The legal battle was short-circuited by the military coup of 1976 that suspended CTERA's activities and dissolved UDA. The teachers suffered grievously under the military *proceso*, with the assassination, disappearance, and kidnapping of hundreds of delegates and members from both unions. Finally, in 1984 with the reestablishment of democratic procedures under Alfonsín, CTERA was given official legal recognition as a labor organization (*personeria gremial*). UDA was also legally restored as a labor organization. In early 1985, CTERA gave UDA observer status at its national meetings and UDA subsequently recognized CTERA. In May 1985, UDA formally became a constituent union forming part of CTERA.

Within the capital and Greater Buenos Aires, two CTERA affiliates are important, although they are relatively small unions. First is the Asociación del Magistério de Enseñanza Técnica (AMET), a union of 5,000 secondary-level teachers employed in Argentina's many technical and industrial high schools. Second is the Union de Maestros de Primária (UMP), a municipal union of primary schoolteachers, with 3,000 members out of a total of about 12,000 municipal primary schoolteachers in the capital. UDA claims 5,000 union members in the capital out of 25,000 potential members. Thus though UDA claims approximately 20,000 secondary schoolteachers in Argentina, over half (11,000) are congregated in the capital, Greater Buenos Aires, and the Province of Buenos Aires.[47]

Largely because of the variety of groupings and regions covered by the teachers' federation, CTERA's national union leadership is possibly the most broadly based and pluralist of any major union in Argentina. The makeup in 1986 of its twenty-three-member executive committee included ten Peronists of the left, right, and center; eight from the Argentine Communist party, and five from the governing Radicals. Its constituent rank and file in the capital is even more mixed. In the CTERA elections of 1983, approximately 60 percent of its affiliates were Radicals, 30 percent were Peronist, and the other 10 percent were divided among leftist groupings such as the PI, MAS, the Argentine Communist party, and the Workers' party (Partido Obrero).[48]

During the Argentine autumn of 1986, CTERA was confronting the UCR government with varying work stoppages and all-out strikes to protest the admittedly poor salary levels, the lack of competitive hiring for full-time openings, and other denials of the 1958 statute that provided for 82 percent retirement levels. As of June 1986, for example, a beginning secondary schoolteacher earned an average of about $110 per month, and a preceptor (home room attendant and student advisor) as little as $62 a month. After long and arduous negotiations, the teachers finally received salary increases, though none of their other demands. For example, for those with an average of fifteen years' service, a full-time preceptor received $144 a month, a librarian $160, a typical teacher approximately $200 (depending upon his or her specialty), department heads $240, and principals $440 per month.

Conclusion

As one can see from the description of the seven union contracts that make up this survey, whatever the differences in their individual histories and agreements with management, workers all shared to one degree or another an inheritance of solid social benefits and protection dating from the Peronist era. Whether the majority of individual workers surveyed personally experienced the golden days under Perón or not, there remained a kind of class memory of the rights of labor that is a persistent undercurrent to the second half of this study. The responses of the 110 individual workers speaking of their lives, thoughts, and dreams in 1985–1986 largely attest to this collective experience.

III

The Human Response

5 *The Rank-and-File Worker*

►►►►►►►►►►►►►►►►►►►►►►►►►►►►►

THE SURVEY ON which this book is based includes seven of the most important industrial and service unions in Argentina, representing approximately 969,000 workers—that is, over 29 percent of total union rank-and-file membership and approximately 46 percent of the members of the nation's largest unions. Fifty-five percent of the sample are industrial (blue-collar) laborers, and 45 percent (white-collar) employees. Three of the unions are industrial: the textile workers' union (AOT), the automobile workers' union (SMATA), and the metalworkers (UOM); one other industrial union—representing light and power workers (Luz y Fuerza)—organizes workers at the state electrical enterprise (SEGBA). In the service sector, the telephone workers' union (FOETRA) represents employees of the state telephone enterprise (ENTEL), while the bank employees' association (Asociación Bancária) includes both public- and private-sector service employees. Last, the teachers' unions (CTERA) represent workers principally in the public sector. Thus my sample of unions is a varied mixture: private and public, industrywide, state enterprise, service, and professional unions. All have their national headquarters in the capital of Buenos Aires.[1]

It will be remembered that, except for bank employees, whose organization predates 1930, the other six unions were founded during Perón's first postwar administration.[2] Using Alvaro Abós's figures for union membership in 1973 and 1984, I found that unionized bank employees grew by 121 percent during 1973–1984, whereas during the same period the metalworkers' and light and power workers' unions saw only modest growth, estimated at 6 percent and 8 percent, respectively.[3] My calculations indicate that the

91

teachers' unions have grown by about 43 percent since the early 1970s—
including all the many teachers' unions within CTERA.[4] Telephone union
membership remained stable, while during this period autoworkers and
textile workers suffered losses of 55 and 33 percent of their membership,
respectively. Overall, Abós finds that among nineteen major service unions,
there has been a 17 percent growth rate since 1973, and among twenty-three
major industrial unions, there was a 23 percent decline in membership.[5]

Thus, using calculations for the mid-1980s presented in the Argentine
Ministry of Labor's compilation, *Estructura Sindical*, plus Abós's figures and
various newspaper accounts, we see that the seven unions in this survey are
all among the top twenty of Argentina's over 1,400 unions in membership. The
rankings are as follows: CTERA, second; UOM, third; Bancários, fifth; AOT,
sixth; Luz y Fuerza, twelfth; SMATA, fifteenth; and FOETRA, sixteenth.

The major statistical breakdown of this study distinguishes between
blue-collar *laborers* and white-collar *employees*. Both terms encompass those
who live on fixed wages and salaries set by collective bargaining. Following
the general Marxian definition of *working class*, they are people who basically
live by the sale of their labor power, who receive less than the value of the
production and/or circulation of the goods and services in which they are
involved, and who do not own the significant means of production associated
with their employment.

My study includes a conglomerate of labor vis-à-vis service unions
representing industries, utilities and communications, finance and education. Some are public, some private and domestic, and some multinational
enterprises.[6]

Workers: Demographic and Socioeconomic Background[7]

The Argentine work force is relatively young: 78.2 percent of workers
interviewed were not yet fifty and only 21.8 percent were older than fifty;
fewer than 2 percent were over sixty years of age. The largest single group—
22.7 percent of the total sample—were in their forties. Employees were
markedly younger than laborers: 30 percent of employees were under thirty,
and 70 percent under forty. (In fact, 95 percent of bank employees were
under forty, and 45 percent under twenty-five.) On the other side, only 18.3
percent of the blue-collar laborers were under thirty, and 56.7 percent were
over forty. Textile workers were the oldest, two-thirds of them being over
forty years of age. (See table 1.)

Males made up 73.6 percent of the sample and females 26.4 percent (see
table 2). Unionized blue-collar workers were virtually all male except in the

TABLE 1. Workers' Age (in percent)

Age	Laborers	Employees
Under 40	43.3	69.4
40 and over	56.7	30.6
Total	100.0	100.0
	(N = 60)	(N = 49)
X^2 = 6.384, 1 df, p < .01		

Note: The term "Laborers" covers blue-collar wage earners; "Employees" refers to salaried white-collar workers.

TABLE 2. Workers' Gender (in percent)

Gender	Male	Female
Laborers	65.4	25.0
Employees	34.6	75.0
Total	100.0	100.0
	(N = 81)	(N = 28)
X^2 = 12.161, 1 df, p < .001		

textile union, where women constituted 46.7 percent of the sample. Among employees, on the other hand, women made up 44 percent. The highest female contingent was in the bank workers' union, which was 50 percent female. Women constituted 40 percent of telephone employees and 40 percent of teachers.

Ninety percent of the workers were born in Argentina, with representative minorities born mainly in Italy and Spain. Among those born abroad, 54.5 percent were Italian by birth. Fifteen percent of laborers were foreign-born, whereas only 4 percent of employees were born abroad.[8]

Almost three-fourths of the employees and well over a third (36.7 percent) of laborers were born in the capital or in Greater Buenos Aires (GBA). A significant minority of laborers (38.3 percent) had come from other Argentine provinces to work in the capital or Greater Buenos Aires, and another 11.7 percent came from the interior portions of the Province of Buenos Aires. However, fully three out of every five workers were from the capital, from GBA, or from the Province of Buenos Aires. Among bank employees, 90 percent were from the capital or GBA. Atypically, two-thirds of textile laborers came from other provinces.

Overall, 80 percent of the workers in my survey were born in urban areas with 10,000 or more population, and 58.2 percent of the workers were born in metropolitan Argentina — defined as cities of 250,000 or greater. Overall, white-collar employees had significantly more urban roots than laborers,[9] a difference that affects the political values and attitudes of both groups, as we shall see. Among employees, 92 percent were urban-born, with 76 percent born in metropolitan areas. The most urbanized group in the sample (95 percent) were bank employees. Even most laborers were born in urban areas: a minority of 30 percent were born in the countryside, with the largest proportion of those (over 50 percent) found among textile workers. Therefore, textile unionists were the only organized workers in Argentina to replicate the rural-to-urban migration so common elsewhere in Latin America. Other workers in the sample were much more metropolitan by origin.

Among workers interviewed, most had migrated to the capital or to GBA at least a generation ago, when apparently it took less than a week to find stable work. Hence, their integration into urban life was a very rapid and positive experience, unlike the situation in so many other Latin American countries.[10] For example, 82 percent of employees had been residents of the capital or GBA for over twenty years; for laborers, the figure was 74.9 percent. As much as 44.5 percent of the total sample had lived in the capital or GBA for over thirty years.

Many Argentine workers are the children of immigrants. Among blue-collar laborers, 36.7 percent of their fathers were born outside Argentina, and 26.6 percent were born in Italy or Spain. Among white-collar employees, foreign-born fathers made up 22 percent of the total — again, with almost half immigrating from Italy. Textile laborers had the highest ratio of foreign-born fathers (53.3 percent) and bank employees the lowest (15 percent). Somewhat fewer workers' mothers (20 percent), were born outside of Argentina, with sizable minorities coming from Italy, Spain, contiguous Latin American countries (Uruguay, Chile, Paraguay, Bolivia), and Eastern Europe.

Parents of white-collar employees are clearly better educated than parents of blue-collar workers. (See table 3.) Overall, fathers are propor-

TABLE 3. Workers' Parents' Education (in percent)

Parents' Education	Laborers		Employees		Total	
	Father	Mother	Father	Mother	Father	Mother
Primary	53.3	56.7	84.0	78.0	69.0	66.3
Secondary	6.7	1.7	36.0	28.0	20.9	13.6
University	1.7	0.0	12.0	4.0	6.4	1.8
	(N = 60)		(N = 50)		(N = 110)	

tionally better educated than mothers. At the extremes of the educational spectrum, 50 percent of the fathers of unionized bank employees had completed secondary education, whereas among the metalworkers and autoworkers no fathers had completed secondary school. Again, 35 percent of bank employees' mothers had completed secondary school, whereas none of the mothers of textile and automobile laborers had done so. Overall, 25.5 percent of fathers and 28.2 percent of mothers had not completed primary education, but only 5.6 percent of fathers and 4.6 percent of mothers had no formal schooling at all.[11] Thus, workers' parents are relatively well educated in Argentina.

The occupations of workers' fathers are given in table 4. The entry of the children of the self-employed into the ranks of salaried workers gives ample proof of the porous boundaries (with movement both ways, both in good and bad times) between the class of wage and salaried workers and the petty-bourgeois sector of the economy. During periods of austerity and wide-spread unemployment, workers are forced to find self-employment — living by their wits, as it were. In good times, self-employment often beckons in the form of an informal second job which, if it succeeds, becomes the worker's primary employment. As I have shown in previous chapters, this explains in part the historical stabilizing influence of the self-employed sector on the Argentine economy; it acts as a kind of safety valve. It also bears out Marx's understanding that there is pressure exerted on small entrepreneurs in the later stages of centralizing capitalism.

The educational profile of the interview sample (given in table 5) shows that, although workers in Argentina have substantially more education than elsewhere in the Third World, white-collar employees are significantly more educated than blue-collar laborers. This is understandable, given their situation as "middle-class workers" or skilled employees in the state sector,

TABLE 4. Workers' Fathers' Occupations (in percent)

Fathers' Occupation	Laborers	Employees
Unskilled workers	58.4	24.0
Skilled workers and craftsmen	21.7	40.0
Small farmers	15.0	6.0
Self-employed persons	0.0	20.0
Other[a]	4.9	10.0
Total	100.0	100.0
	(N = 60)	(N = 49)

a. The category "other," as in subsequent tables, includes the miscellaneous answers "don't know" and "no answer." However, in cases when "don't know" and "no answer" are unusually large and statistically significant, they are reported separately.

TABLE 5. Workers' Educational Level (in percent)

Education	Laborers	Employees
Did not complete secondary school	88.3	24.5
Completed secondary school	10.0	20.4
Some university	1.7	55.1
Total	100.0	100.0
	(N = 60)	(N = 49)

$X^2 = 50.408$, 2 df, $p < .001$

finance, and education. As might be expected, employees are far more likely to have at least finished secondary school or attended a university than laborers.[12]

Over 8 million Argentines were attending school at some level in 1985. Over 94 percent of children from age seven through thirteen were in school.[13] My survey showed clearly that younger workers were associated with markedly higher levels of education than older ones.[14]

Among blue-collar families, especially from rural areas, secondary education was often more of a major sacrifice than for employees. One textile laborer, with rural origins, told me a typical story. For his family, despite the fact that public secondary education was free, the supplemental costs of books, uniforms (Argentine students must purchase two smocks or jackets to protect their clothing in school), families' expected social contribution to the school, and—especially for teenagers—the inability to help out the family economically by working made a five-year commitment to secondary school very problematic.[15] This example helps to explain the relationship between lower educational achievement and rural origin—both typical of blue-collar workers and less typical for longtime urban workers;[16] moreover, laborers are more likely to have rural roots in the first place and thus have experienced interrupted educations, typical of small towns and farm communities. (See table 6.)

TABLE 6. Workers' Place of Origin (in percent)

Place of Origin	Laborers	Employees
Urban	70.0	93.9
Rural	30.0	6.1
Total	100.0	100.0
	(N = 60)	(N = 49)

$X^2 = 8.411$, 1 df, $p < .004$

Among all workers, 67 percent were married, 24.8 percent single, and the rest divorced or widowed.[17] Most laborers (85 percent) were married, whereas 40 percent of employees (who tended to be younger) were single.[18] Most married workers had children — only 9.8 percent did not — and 59.8 percent of those with families usually had two or three children (only 18.3 percent had one child, and 12.2 percent had four or more). Again, this profile is more reminiscent of family conditions in Western Europe than in much of Latin America.

Workers' Perceptions, on the Job and Off

On work and income

When asked if they liked their work, 13.6 percent of the working-class sample said "very much," and 75.5 percent said "quite a bit" or "so-so," while 10.9 percent said "no."[19] Employees tended to be more negative about their jobs, 18 percent giving a "no" response. Only 5 percent of laborers said "no." Subdividing the sample by unions, CTERA teachers were the most enthusiastic about their jobs and FOETRA telephone employees the least. Generally, workers were content with their jobs, with a passive acceptance of its rigors. Argentine workers expect to work and want to work. Seemingly those with the greater variety of tasks had the most positive outlook. As in other worker studies, routine and repetition were major causes of dissatisfaction.[20]

When asked what they least liked about their jobs, 53.6 percent of the sample discussed overall working conditions; 14.3 percent spoke of disorganization and bureaucratic problems, but only 6 percent focused on low salaries. Employees tended to demonstrate greater frustration with their jobs, since only 8.7 percent saw no problems related to their work, whereas among laborers this figure rose to 31.6 percent.[21]

Each union sample seemed to have special work problems. For example, among textile workers and light and power workers, many were frustrated by continually changing schedules — from day shift, to swing shift, to graveyard shift — and they also cited certain dangerous and unhealthy work conditions.[22] Among telephone and bank employees, the main problem was the routine. One telephone technician told me, "My work as such — sketching telephone cables, already designed and constructed — is very boring, repetitious, and tedious."[23] A bank employee who computerizes bank statements said, "When I began to work here I wanted to progress and I believed that they would value my abilities, but I see that it isn't happening.

They have shunted me off doing something that doesn't interest me, and it is boring."[24] Another bank employee, who had to drop out of his first year as a university economics major to go to work, said: "The monotony, the routine of always doing the same thing. I would have liked to do research in social sciences."[25] Still another bank employee recounted,

> Accounting is my specialty. But I'm not doing that now because of the birth of my baby. [They had changed her section.] I'm receiving bill payments for gas, electricity, and phone service and then submitting them to Gas del Estado, SEGBA, and ENTEL. I rather enjoyed the math part of my former job in determining loan interest rates. Now the work is boring.[26]

The major complaint among teachers was a generalized malaise concerning bureaucracy and red tape.

As Barbara Garson found in the United States, Miklos Haraszti in Hungary, and Maria Celia Paoli in Brazil, the extent of communication among workers on the job is greatly exaggerated. The structure of the factory and office and the content of the work often makes it all but impossible. Workers have little time, and they lose even the inclination, to exchange thoughts and pleasantries on the job. In the Ford auto plant, and in the metallurgical, SEGBA, and textile factories, the noise and occasional necessity to wear earplugs give conversation a low priority versus accomplishing the job at hand. Service-sector work is safer, quieter, and cleaner, but employees are often just as closely supervised, routinized, and separated from their cohorts; as a result, mental fatigue occurs just as often as does the laborer's physical fatigue. ENTEL telephone operators particularly come to mind. While most employees are much less tied to a fixed place than laborers, and white-collar employees can in little ways manage to waste a bit of time — occasionally walking between jobs, running errands, or "schmoozing," to use Schrank's picturesque term — lunch and contracted work breaks are a solace in both contexts.[27]

When questioned about their salaries, 70 percent of the workers reported having difficulty managing on their income. (See table 7.) The comment of one textile worker was typical: "You have to adjust the bedcovers so that your feet don't stick out."[28] Some 20.9 percent said they got along more or less, and only 9.1 percent expressed satisfaction with their salaries. Only autoworkers were relatively satisfied with their wages.

Minimum wage in Argentina during 1985-1986 was $80 a month. The majority of employees were at the lower end of the economic scale, almost half making below $200 a month, whereas laborers' wages tended to range substantially over $200 a month. Blue- collar textile workers, however, were at the bottom of the pay scale, along with telephone and bank employees.[29]

TABLE 7. Workers' Monthly Wages, in U.S. Dollars, 1985–1986 (in percent)

Monthly Wages	Laborers	Employees	Total
$100–$149	14.0	28.0	20.6
$150–$199	17.5	18.0	17.8
$200–$249	31.6	16.0	24.3
$250–$299	15.8	10.0	13.1
Over–$300	21.1	22.0	21.5
Other	0.0	6.0	2.7
Total	100.0	100.0	100.0
	(N = 57)	(N = 50)	(N = 107)

Light and power workers and teachers (those with long service) were in the middle of the pay range, and metal and auto factory laborers were the best paid. (Three of the four industrial unions in the survey — UOM, SMATA, and Luz y Fuerza — had above-average wages compared to those of other Argentine workers.) In February 1986, it was estimated that a family had to pay $301 a month for a basic basket of foodstuffs.[30] Judging from this evidence, only slightly more than one-fifth of the working-class families could have managed well on one breadwinner alone.

Responding to the question, "How much do you think you should earn?" 27.9 percent of all workers replied that they needed between $300 and $500 a month, and 35.6 percent said they required over $500 a month. The majority of workers usually said that they needed about double what they were actually making at the time. Nationwide, teachers were surely one of the poorest paid unionized groups (although teachers in the capital and GBA were better paid). Because of the federal structure of provincial education and the substantially different budgetary and socioeconomic character of each province, varying collective bargaining arrangements have resulted in a very uneven picture among Argentina's primary and secondary school-teachers. This has proved to be one of the weaknesses of the CTERA federation's general wage structure.[31] It is also very clear that the lowest paid workers were those in unions with the highest proportion of female workers, such as textile workers, bank and phone employees, and of course teachers. For example, 64.3 percent of the women in the survey earned less than $200 a month, compared to only 30.4 percent of male workers.[32]

I asked the workers, "Of the things that your present salary doesn't permit you to do or have, what do you miss most?" To this query, the most frequent answer was the need to improve their housing. Overall, 41.8 percent gave this response (50 percent of laborers and 32 percent of employees). The inability to afford family outings and vacations were each cited by 13.6 percent of the sample. A typical answer came from a metalworker: "I can't finish my house; I want to give my kids what I didn't have. I'm working thirteen hours a day with overtime. Then I work at home doing body and fender repairs."[33] An unmarried bank employee recounted, "I'm not happy about not being able to go out to eat, take out a date, or make trips."[34] Another bank employee held down two jobs to make ends meet, earning $220 at the bank and working part-time in a real estate business for another $140 a month. This corroborates José Nun's observations about the high proportion of Argentines who work in the underground economy. He estimates that only 39 percent of Argentines in the work force earn their income in the formal, legal sector; the other 61 percent either work in both sectors, work totally in the informal sector, or are self-employed in the informal economy.[35]

On personal matters

In terms of workers' personal aspirations, 31.2 percent spoke of a desire to increase their knowledge and education; 22.9 percent spoke of getting a better job or a promotion in their current work; and 17.4 percent focused on improving their standard of living.[36] As Halle noticed in the North American context, workers often focus on education as the key to upward mobility and believe it is within their power to overcome adversity by study and hard work.[37] Overwhelmingly, this was the viewpoint of white-collar employees in this survey. Fifty-four percent wanted to study and increase their knowledge, whereas a considerably smaller number of laborers (11.7 percent) chose that alternative. This pattern is associated with youth—employees in my sample were substantially younger (and thus seemingly more aspiring) than laborers.

In response to the question concerning their aspirations for their children, almost two-thirds of workers who were parents hoped that their children would attain a better educational and/or professional level than they themselves had.[38] This was, understandably, an even more abiding passion among laborers (70.8 percent) than among employees (56 percent). One textile worker told me, "I can't give them an inheritance, but I hope to give them a start to a profession with which to confront life."[39] Working with one's hands, getting dirty, having to change into special overalls holds no particular romance for the Argentine laborer. I recall getting on the SEGBA bus with light and power workers, whom I had a previously interviewed in work clothes, and seeing them now changed into clothing indistinguishable from that of white-collar employees or professionals. The lunch pail and the hard hat are not flaunted emblems of the Argentine working class. Though they have *dignidad* and self-respect, laborers know that there are easier, more satisfying ways to earn a livelihood and, inevitably, they want their children to get sufficient education to avoid manual labor.[40] As a metalworker said, "I want them to keep on the path I've started; that they study and don't end up in the factory." (He was already thinking that his oldest child, an eleven-year-old daughter, might pursue a computer career.)[41]

To the question, "What's your favorite way of enjoying free time?" workers mentioned reading books or listening to music, enjoying sports, games, and hobbies, spending time with the family or taking them out, and fixing up the house. The last activity was a favorite pastime for 35 percent of the laborers. Among employees, the most popular response was reading books or listening to music (54 percent), enjoying sports, games, and hobbies (40 percent); only 2 percent chose fixing up their homes. The laborers' clear preference was for fixing up the house (as well as the family car—6.7 percent),[42] whereas employees focused more on reading, sports and hobbies. This relates not only to the different educational levels of the two worker categories, but also to the fact that laborers were more likely to be heads of households and thus responsible for home maintenance and upkeep.

Argentine culture is home-centered, and among Argentine laborers the home acts as a powerful anchor. I found that 73.6 percent spoke of owning their own house or apartment, or living with parents who owned their own home. Only 13.6 percent did not own their home; in 12.7 percent of the cases home ownership could not be determined.[43] Argentine census data show private home ownership in Argentina increasing from 17 percent in 1946 to 64 percent in 1986, although 8.8 percent of the housing in the capital and GBA is considered rudimentary.[44] Argentines, although hardly unique in this regard, value home life and associate it with family, friendships, leisure, security, and the good life. The home represents a basic center of gravity, something solid amid the seeming whirlwind of economic and political change.[45]

Unlike the workers depicted by Goldthorpe in Great Britain, the Argentine worker does not seem to have a particularly instrumental view of work—that is, a feeling that the absolute wage on the job is the orienting value in life and worth making sacrifices for in other areas.[46] Rather, Argentine workers more resemble French workers as described by André Gorz. Their attitude is that work is a necessary requisite to enjoying life outside the factory and the office.[47] Varying degrees of alienation continue to be a fact of life for Argentine workers. But they most often balance their frustrations on the job with satisfactions outside the workplace. Work experience becomes attenuated and modified by home, neighborhood, schools for their children, and culture in general. Workers are cognizant of the living wage mainly as a means to gain access to cultural, educational, and recreational pursuits for themselves and their families as well as the accumulation of consumer goods that make their lives outside the factory and office more comfortable and civilized. For the Argentine worker, consumption represents buying greater autonomy, freedom, and leisure, as it were.

Outside of work, as Haraszti discovered among Hungarian laborers (and Garson among their North American counterparts), "Football, beer, motor cycles, the house and T.V. programs regain their rightful places."[48] Family life, embodied in the stable home, represents a counterweight against the regimentation and discipline of the workplace. Paoli, writing of São Paulo laborers, depicts the home as the "public world of talk" as opposed to the silence of the factory world. She goes on to say,

> The house, with its windows looking out on the street activity; the neigh-borhood streets, the marked-off territories of groups of children; the small grocery stores and boteguins; the open fields on which soccer was played and courtship took place, the sidewalks where, at the end of the day, chairs were placed so that people could get some fresh air and chat—this was the symbolic world that established a positive time in common. Its day-to-day cycle of activities created meaning opposed to that of the factory world. In this space there was also a particular kind of hierarchy and order that of-fered much broader opportunities for circulation and discovery and, thus, for identifcation with the urban world . . . in which workers saw themselves differently—the negation of the massiveness of the factory building. . . . This negation seems to have arisen from the attempt to turn every place in the neighborhood into a place in which speech was free and constantly exer-cised.[49]

Daniel James, in a different setting, observes a similar pattern as he quotes from Rodolfo Walsh's book *Quién mató a Rosendo?* A brother of a jailed Peronist asks him,

> But tell me something . . . how old are you? He told me 40 odd. And tell me, what have you done with your life up to now? Because I don't see that you've done very much. You've always been in prison. . . . And when he said to me that he didn't have anything, I said, of course what would you have if you've always been in prison soaking up a beating, half dead of hunger, and you a mature man and you've got no family, you don't have anything.[50]

Karl Marx, in his early writings, also saw the home as being virtually the only place that allowed workers to affirm their human possibilities.

> The worker, therefore, feels himself at home only during his leisure time, whereas at work he feels homeless. His work is not voluntary but imposed,

forced labor. It is not the satisfaction of a need, but only a means for satisfying other needs. Its alien character is clearly shown by the fact that as soon as there is no physical or other compulsion it is avoided like the plague.[51]

Even in the *The German Ideology*, when Marx idealistically referred to nonalienated labor in the future communist society, I think he really was conjuring up what people would like to do in their leisure time and not what "work" could be like for the foreseeable future. Marx wrote:

> While in communist society, where nobody has one exclusive sphere of activity but each can become accomplished in any one branch he wishes, society regulates the general production and thus makes it possible for me to do one thing today and another tomorrow, to hunt in the morning, fish in the afternoon, rear cattle in the evening, criticize after dinner, just as I have in mind, without ever becoming hunter, fisherman, shepherd or critic.[52]

Finally, I believe that Eduard Bernstein—though perhaps he confused the notion of owning the means of production with ownership of property itself—perceptively understood working-class aspirations to private ownership and commodities.[53]

Questioned as to what concerned them most about their lives, workers focused on three principal concerns: personal health and fear that illness would deprive them of the capacity to care for their family and themselves; giving their children a good education; and developing their personal aspirations and talents. Among laborers, the principal anxiety was fear of illness (26 percent), an understandable concern in a contracting economy. Employees' main frustration was not being able to fulfill their aspirations and talents (28 percent). This was particularly true of telephone employees working for ENTEL, many of whom felt they were in dead-end jobs without the possibility of advancement. One telephone worker explained, "Staying with ENTEL concerns me. I don't want to be a telephone worker forever. That is closer to death than to life. The state enterprises are almost designed to destroy your capacity for invention and your personality generally."[54]

Asked to talk about the last time they went out and had a good time, most workers spoke of the traditional Argentine family outing with a barbecue (*asado*) (44 percent), others spoke of a special occasion or reunion among family or friends (19.3 percent), and some mentioned attending a cultural or sports event (16.5 percent).[55] Laborers were more prone to gather with family and friends, whereas employees spoke much more often of attending cultural or sports events. However, the *asado* stood out as a principal way of having a good time. The main ingredients of a good *asado*— steak, Italian bread, mixed green salad, good wine, and cheese and *flan* (custard)—are all available at relatively modest prices in Argentina.

Among the "most important events" of the workers' lives were the birth of children, a wedding, or some personal or professional achievement. Among laborers, 58.3 percent mentioned the birth of a child as the most important event of their lives, while employees—although 36 percent also focused on the birth of children—were far more likely to mention events that marked personal and professional achievement (30 percent for employees, compared to 6.7 percent among laborers).

When questioned as to whether they had a friend they admired and took as an example for their own lives, laborers were slightly more likely (55 percent) than employees (45 percent) to have identified role models in their lives. Of those who said yes, laborers were more likely than the employees to single out workmates—in their case, factory comrades—who were industrious and ambitious to get ahead in life. Laborers seemed less cynical than employees and still believed in the greater possibilities of the Horatio Alger saga, as it were.[56]

On exploitation

I asked the workers what they thought of the company, enterprise, or organization for which they worked. (See table 8.) Workers' positive assessments of employers had to do with being "treated like family"; working for a good, serious, or responsible enterprise; and receiving good wages and being paid on time. The major complaints among workers were management's bureaucratic treatment of workers; deteriorating infrastructure and equipment and poor maintenance; declining salaries; and poor working conditions in general.

The laborer portion of the sample had a more positive outlook toward their employers than did salaried employees. Particularly older workers tended to be "company men," loyal to the enterprise and less critical than younger workers.[57] Whereas a minority of blue-collar laborers took a negative position (31.7 percent), a 57.1 percent majority of white-collar

TABLE 8. Workers' Opinion of Employers (in percent)

Opinion	Laborers	Employees
Bad	31.7	57.1
Good	68.3	42.9
Total	100.0	100.0
	(N = 60)	(N = 49)
$X^2 = 6.137$, 1 df, $p < .02$		

employees had a low opinion of their employers. What stands out is the proportion of laborers who spoke of the company as treating them like family (20 percent) and paying good wages and paying on time (20 percent), while their major complaint was that of deteriorating infrastructure and equipment (18.3 percent). Employees chiefly appreciated working for a serious, responsible institution or enterprise (18 percent), while their chief complaint—and the single most repeated criticism among employees (36 percent)—was of poor management and bureaucratic treatment. This was a particularly strong sentiment among teachers.

Also it is interesting to note the importance of educational level in relation to worker satisfaction. (See table 9.) The more educated workers were more likely to have a low opinion of the enterprise or organization for which they worked.

A typical response came from an autoworker who told me, "I have a good opinion of Ford. I have to thank them for a lot. They kept me working when I was having my [drinking] problems—Ford has the first Alcoholics Anonymous branch in the country, with seventy members—and they pay well, too."[58] A metalworker at Pirelli recounted, "They are a very correct firm. When payday comes, they pay. But they expect you to work; they're not going to give you something for nothing."[59] On the other hand, an ENTEL telephone operator complained:

> The problems for the phone operators at ENTEL are very serious. It is unhealthy work and very stressful. One has to always be paying very strict attention, always sitting in the same position with the telephone receivers on the ears, working with seventy-year-old equipment, while being constantly controlled by the supervisors who stand behind one, watching whether the little light bulbs above the switchboard are on.[60]

Bank employees had complaints of a different tenor. One employee of the central bank lamented (typically), "They don't recognize individual effort,

TABLE 9. Workers' Opinion of Employers by Educational Level (in percent)

Opinion	Did Not Complete Secondary	Completed Secondary	Some University
Bad	32.3	52.9	60.7
Good	67.7	47.1	39.3
Total	100.0	100.0	100.0
	(N = 65)	(N = 17)	(N = 28)

$X^2 = 7.310$, 2 df, $p < .03$

and the more senior people keep you from progressing. In the private companies the young people have more access to learning and doing new things than in the state enterprises."[61] Among teachers, the problems caused by bureaucratic inadequacies were often singled out. One primary school-teacher told me, "Our principal's background is out of date and she is behind the times. The means of teaching are inadequate; there is no provision for slow children. The children are treated poorly. There is no close analysis of individual children's needs. It is a very cold environment."[62]

Overall, whereas all workers demonstrated a certain ambivalence and skepticism toward their employers, laborers in the private sector were tangibly more content than their public employee and labor counterparts. Public sector employers received lower marks for bureaucratic inefficiency and poor working conditions and pay scales, whereas employers in the private sector, often dominated by multinational corporations, tended to get better appraisals in these areas. There were two interesting cases that help highlight to these general sector differences: among public-sector SEGBA laborers, two-thirds of the light and power workers complained about the deteriorating conditions at Puerto Nuevo, citing worn-out turbines, cables, tools, and equipment of all kinds; and only a third of the schoolteachers spoke approvingly of their school as a responsible institution.

Overall, in both the public and private sectors, blue-collar laborers were more often satisfied with their employers than were white-collar employees. Answers to the question, "In whom do you have more confidence: in the government or in the company, enterprise, or establishment for which you work?" are presented in table 10.

Private industrial enterprises, especially those in foreign hands, received the highest marks among workers. Employees tended to be more associated with frustrated feelings vis-à-vis their employers (be it banks, ENTEL, or schools) than laborers.[63] Moreover, employees were two and a half times

TABLE 10. Workers' Confidence in Institutions (in percent)

Confidence	Laborers	Employees	Total
In company, enterprise, or establishment (not the government)	51.7	36.0	44.5
In the government	16.7	10.0	13.6
In both	18.3	30.0	23.6
In neither	10.0	24.0	16.4
Other	3.3	0.0	1.9
Total	100.0	100.0	100.0
	(N = 60)	(N = 50)	(N = 110)

more likely than laborers to have confidence in neither their employer nor in the Radical government of Alfonsín.[64] Of course, after the reinstitution of a democratic polity with a less paternalist role for government, workers were bound to look more to an employer for the resolution of their problems than was the case under military or civilian authoritarian regimes.[65]

Yet these quantifiable reservations about workers' job experiences apparently do not add up to an unequivocally high level of alienation in Argentina. Answers to the question, "As a worker do you feel exploited?" are given in table 11. Interestingly, 69.1 percent of all workers did not see themselves as being exploited, even though a minority spoke of low pay, long hours, and hard work.[66] At the same time, twice as many white-collar employees felt exploited as laborers. Equally significant is that women felt much more exploited than men (see table 12). Finally, as table 13 shows, the more educated the worker, the higher the index of alienation.

Overall, Argentine workers expected to work hard, but they also expected to be duly compensated. They made a clear association between the concept of exploitation and poor pay.[67] Workers with positive feelings about their employers also were much less likely to perceive themselves as exploited, despite having to work hard for their wage or salary. (See table 14.) The most satisfied segment among the workers was, for example, the highest paid portion of the work force—namely, autoworkers and metalworkers, who, in my sample, were all men. On the other hand, the lower-paid sectors of the work force—textile laborers, phone and bank employees, and teachers—reported the highest perceptions of exploitation. These sectors in my sample also had the highest proportion of females among the unions studied. Light and power workers fell into the intermediate strata in both wages and feelings of exploitation. Thus, although women and more educated employees reported higher degrees of alienation than was the norm, the great majority of laborers, almost four out of five, said that they did not feel exploited.

TABLE 11. Workers' Feelings of Exploitation (in percent)

"Do you feel exploited?"	Laborers	Employees	Total
Yes	21.7	42.0	30.9
No	46.7	32.0	40.0
No, but pay and working conditions are poor	31.7	26.0	29.1
Total	100.1	100.0	100.0
	(N = 60)	(N = 50)	(N = 110)

Note: Figures do not always total to 100.0 because of rounding.

TABLE 12. Workers' Feelings of Exploitation by Gender (in percent)

"Do you feel exploited?"	Male	Female
Yes	24.7	48.3
No	42.0	34.5
No, but pay and working conditions are poor	33.3	17.2
Total	100.0	100.0
	(N = 81)	(N = 29)

$X^2 = 6.043$, 2 df, $p < .05$

TABLE 13. Workers' Feelings of Exploitation by Educational Level (in percent)

"Do you feel exploited?"	Did Not Complete Secondary	Completed Secondary	Some University
Yes	20.0	35.3	53.6
No	49.2	35.3	21.4
No, but pay and working conditions are poor	30.8	29.4	25.0
Total	100.0	100.0	100.0
	(N = 65)	(N = 17)	(N = 28)

$X^2 = 11.379$, 4 df, $p < .03$

TABLE 14. Workers' Feelings or Exploitation by Opinion of Employers (in percent)

"Do you feel exploited?"	Opinion of Employer	
	Good	Bad
Yes	12.7	55.3
No	63.5	8.5
No, but pay and working conditions are poor	23.8	36.2
Total	100.0	100.0
	(N = 63)	(N = 47)

$X^2 = 37.577$, 2 df, $p < .001$

A textile laborer told me, in response to my question about exploitation, "No, here I am on my job as always, like a soldier."[68] An autoworker said, "No, I do what is expected per hour, per formula, and no more. There is a written worker/Ford contract. I laminate six doors per hour."[69] Similarly, another Ford autoworker recounted, "No, I feel comfortable here. If I felt exploited, I wouldn't stay. I've studied here and they pay well and *on time*."[70] A metalworker explained, in answer to the same question, "No, because to be exploited you have to feel it in your own flesh, and here we are all exploited but not by the company but by the international economy."[71] Another metalworker gave this response: "No, if I were exploited, I couldn't put up with the rhythm of twelve hours a day that I've been working over the last two months. [He was pleased with the overtime opportunity.] When you enter the factory, it's to work."[72] And again, another metalworker reported,

> Exploited by the firm, no. I do my job, if it wasn't here it would be some-where else. I feel exploited by the situation the country's in. But here too, no; because these are circumstances one has to pass through so that tomor-row will be a better day. In other countries they've passed through periods like this too and have then moved forward.[73]

A telephone employee responded, "No, it's my fault because I didn't study and have a career. You have to accept the rules of the game."[74]

On the other hand, a telephone employee told me, "Yes, [I feel exploited], because in my section [long distance operations] they don't take the human factor into consideration. They see us as an extension of the switchboard, a number on a listing."[75] Meanwhile, a teacher complained, "Yes, [I feel exploited] because of the extra hours of meetings during the teachers' rest period so that I can't do my lesson plans in school but have to take them home. We have silly staff meetings after 4 P.M. when teachers should be free to go home."[76]

On union and management matters

White-collar and blue-collar workers tended to have rather different relationships with their unions. In particular, as table 15 shows, laborers have

TABLE 15. Workers' Years as Union Members (in percent)

Years in Union	Laborers	Employees	Total
5 years or less	18.3	53.1	33.9
6–10 years	16.7	14.3	15.6
11–20 years	35.0	26.5	31.2
21–30 years	26.7	6.1	17.4
Other	3.3	0.0	1.8
Total	100.0	100.0	99.9
	(N = 60)	(N = 49)	(N = 109)

Note: Figures do not always total to 100.0 because of rounding.

been union members for much longer periods than employees. Thus, for example, whereas 65 percent of laborers had belonged to their industrial union for over ten years, and 30 percent of them for over twenty years, 53.1 percent of service-sector employees had been members of their union for less than five years. Laborers were more likely to have a longer union relationship partly because they were simply an older pool of workers.[77] A complementary factor was the high turnover among the very youthful bank employees and teachers before achieving tenure. Many left for other careers.

When workers were asked, "Of all the problems left to be resolved by your labor union, which is the most important?" most tended (as could be expected) to emphasize wages and salaries, although these issues were combined with many other concerns. One textile worker responded by saying, "Unions are very weak now because of unemployment. They are only strong during high employment, like in the late 1960s to early 1970s under Onganía and Lanusse. What good unions do, I have no idea; . . . it's like the military—one needs them every now and then."[78] And another textile worker complained about his plant, "Union delegates are out of touch with textile workers at Sudamtex. We have twice as much work with obsolete machinery; two-thirds of the workers have been fired since the early 1970s. . . . The noise level is so high [on the weaving floor] you don't know whether its raining outside or not."[79]

On the question of social benefits and working conditions, an auto-worker told about an accident he suffered on the job. An auto fender had crushed his finger. "A nurse at Ford treated my injured finger [there was no permanent staff doctor at the Ford site]; a month later I had to have an operation to implant a plastic tendon. The union did not push the matter."[80] He was suing privately for recovery of medical expenses, he said.

A light and power worker complained, "The union is paralyzed. They don't fight for a decent wage. Union leaders are coopted. It is unsafe and unhealthy here at Puerto Nuevo. There are problems with water leakages, coal dust, darkness, and dangers working at heights fixing cables."[81] Finally, a teacher offered this view: "The biggest problem is getting the 82 percent of salary stipulated for retirement. This would allow younger teachers to move up; maybe over 50 percent of the older staff would retire, including reactionary, old-fashioned principals."[82] Workers' opinions about their unions, especially complaints about their shortcomings, are given in table 16.

It is clear that workers saw low wages as the outstanding problem that unions have a prime responsibility to address. By focusing on union cooptation, workers questioned the unions' ability to bargain from a position of strength. On the question of deteriorating social benefits (such as health care and vacation facilities), blue-collar laborers' complaints surpassed those

TABLE 16. Workers' Identification of Unresolved Union Problems (in percent)

Unresolved Problem	Laborers	Employees	Total
Inadequate salaries and wages	36.7	56.0	45.5
Corrupt, coopted, demagogic union leadership	25.0	26.0	25.5
Deteriorating social welfare benefits	25.0	12.0	19.1
Inadequate protection of workers' jobs	3.3	16.0	9.1
Lack of members' participation and democracy	1.7	8.0	4.5
Absence of labor unity	1.7	4.0	2.7
—			
Satisfied with union	10.0	0.0	5.5
—			
Other	6.7	4.0	5.5
	(N = 60)	(N = 50)	(N = 110)

Note: Percentage responses do not add up to 100 because of multiple responses.

of employees, mainly because their unions (UOM, SMATA, AOT, and Luz y Fuerza) have historically offered much more generous social welfare programs than employee unions have. Thus laborers were demanding the return of benefits lost under the military dictatorship. Employees also worried more than laborers (by a 5:1 ratio) about the unions' defense of their jobs, especially in the public sector—knowing as they do the relative low productivity and inefficiency attributed to public-sector employment.[83]

Lack of internal union democracy was a concern among only a small minority of employees and an even smaller fraction of laborers, although over a quarter of all workers, whether in a state or private-sector industry, singled out some deficiency in union leadership, either corruption, demagoguery, or weakness vis-à-vis management. Only a fraction of workers focused on issues such as lack of union democracy, rank-and-file participation, and the absence of labor unity.[84]

When workers were asked to focus specifically on *union leadership*, there was evident dissatisfaction, though by no means to an overwhelming degree. Of the rank-and-file workers, 56.8 percent expressed some reservations concerning union leadership, whereas 37.6 percent were generally satisfied.[85] While 27.5 percent said their leaders were undemocratic, unrepresentative, and too bureaucratic, 18.3 percent thought their union's leadership was too political, corrupt, and dishonest.

How were the major complaints manifested? Answering the question, "Are you satisfied with your union leadership?" one autoworker said, "No way; union leaders are bought off with homes and cars by company owners to keep workers quiet. The owners give in to minor demands to avoid major demands. What occurs are private agreements between union leaders and individual owners."[86] A metalworker gave this response: "No, because they don't represent my feelings nor that of my fellow workers. We had elections recently, with one single list, the *Azul y Blanco* list that follows Lorenzo Miguel [UOM labor leader]."[87] Finally, a light and power worker told me, "No, they are not my choice. They're not involved in the needs of the workers. They lack humanity and caring for the workers." He explained how almost every Luz y Fuerza laborer had to use the courts to sue for several claims on back pay under the military governments.[88] Among white-collar workers, a bank employee said, "No, José Zanola [leader of the Buenos Aires bank employees' union] got a better deal for the private and foreign bank employees. The public-sector banks, which led the strike, were left out in the cold."[89] Finally, a teacher complained, "No, CTERA is a power structure, not a union that cares enough about the everyday conditions of the teacher."[90]

Nevertheless, following a pattern we have seen, laborers were generally more satisfied, with almost half (47.5 percent) expressing satisfaction with their union leaders, while only a quarter of employees (26 percent) were satisfied. Further, employees, twice as often as laborers (38 percent to 18.6 percent), focused on undemocratic union leadership as an issue. The blue-collar laborer was signficantly less concerned with democratic procedures and expression within the union structure than the white-collar employee.

On the whole, most of the general as well as localized strikes under Alfonsín were for better wages and working conditions.[91] When asked about labor militancy, 69.8 percent of laborers reported having participated in a strike against their company, enterprise, or organization, whereas among employees the figure was 46.9 percent. Clearly, the incidence of strikes among industrial laborers was significantly higher than among white-collar unionists.[92] Industrial laborers generally have had more strategic bargaining power than members of typical service unions, though with the increasing scrutiny of a large and inefficient state sector, this could lead to the growth of union militancy among service and state enterprise workers in defense of an embattled public sector. In any case, there seemed to be a relationship between the use of strikes and higher pay levels. Workers who participated most frequently in walkouts under Alfonsín tended to be laborers, and apparently by taking this action were able to alleviate some of these problems.

Just as the industrial unionists reported above-average wages, the level of rank-and-file militancy was also greater among the industrial unions. During the year I spent in Argentina, I consulted police and newspaper accounts of strike turnouts and levels of absenteeism from the job during general strikes of the CGT. Although my analysis was neither quantitative nor scientific, it seemed to me that the level of workers' involvement in strike protest was skewed heavily toward the industrial unions. For example, during 1985–1986, absenteeism during strikes among light and power workers was broadly averaged at about 90 percent; autoworkers' walkouts averaged about 85 percent; among textile workers it was 80 percent; and among metalworkers 75 percent. White-collar employees' strike absenteeism was significantly lower, with telephone employees reporting 60 percent. Teachers were absent from the classroom at a rate of 25–30 percent, and bank employees' absenteeism during strikes was generally less than 10 percent.

Despite their low pay, bank and telephone employees are increasingly vital to the running of Argentina's modern economy, and one might expect this to give them more future leverage at the bargaining table.[93] Laborers at Ford, SEGBA, various textile and metallurgical factories, and employees at ENTEL and state banks had all undergone various strikes in the mid-1980s. Fewer employees than laborers had participated in job actions because there had been no individual primary or secondary school strikes during this time. The CTERA federation calls strikes at the national or provincial level, and such job actions were not common among teachers until the 1987-1988 period. Another factor explaining why fewer employees were involved in strikes is the distinctly youthful profile of the bank employees. Many were simply too young to have participated in a walkout against their employer.

Rank-and-file workers, both laborers or employees, went out on strike more than half the time in one of the nine general strikes organized by the CGT under Alfonsín (between 1983 and 1986) or in an industrywide walkout called by their union. Employees tended to have participated in general or unionwide strikes, since their employment was subject to national grievance procedures; when they walked off the job, they were in essence striking against federal or provincial authorities. On the other hand, blue-collar laborers were much more likely to have individual disputes with a particular factory or enterprise. A significant minority of laborers (41.4 percent) had participated in a strike *solely* against their company or state enterprise (SEGBA). Finally, only 3.4 percent of laborers and 13.9 percent of employees said they had not participated in a labor strike because they had no confidence in the CGT and its reasons for calling the strike.

When workers were asked if they felt they ought to participate more in the decisions made between their union and their company, enterprise, or institution, responses were very divided, though similar in their trends. For example, a majority of the workers called for increasing assemblies and more open union procedures, especially with regard to grievances. However, many workers didn't see the need for greater participation in union affairs, feeling that they had an opportunity to be heard through existing delegates. Among laborers, the satisfaction level reached 46.7 percent, while among employees it was 36 percent. On the other hand, 54 percent of employees called for more assemblies, while among laborers the figure was 43.3 percent.[94] Only 9 percent of the total sample of workers (8.3 percent of laborers and 10 percent of employees) were indifferent to union affairs, expressing either passivity, cynicism, or outright repulsion.[95]

Regarding sharing more in decision making in the enterprise, company, or institution, most workers advocated better communication between management and themselves, as well as more worker involvement on matters touching on basic work procedures and decisions about working conditions.[96] On the other hand, only a minority felt they had sufficient input, or felt that it was not their role, or felt that they lacked the expertise to get so involved in management. The differences between blue-collar and white-collar workers were noteworthy. (See table 17.) Among laborers, 52.7 percent wanted greater involvement in the decisions of the employer, and 68 percent of employees were so inclined.[97] Significantly, 23.6 percent of the laborers felt that participation in management wasn't their responsibility and/or they lacked expertise, while only 4 percent of employees felt that way. Thus workers wanted to have more impact on management decisions than union decisions, although there was a strong association between those workers who wanted more participation in management and those who wanted more involvement in union affairs.[98] Workers having a negative opinion of their employer were most likely to demand a greater decisional

TABLE 17. Workers' Satisfaction with Participation in Union-Management Decisions (in percent)

	Laborers	Employees
Opinion of union		
Satisfied	46.7	36.0
Dissatisfied	43.3	54.0
Indifferent or		
other response	10.0	10.0
Total	100.0	100.0
Opinion of management		
Satisfied	47.2	32.0
Dissatisfied	52.7	68.0
Total	99.9	100.0
	(N = 60)	(N = 50)

Note: Figures do not always total to 100.0 because of rounding.

role in the union structure[99] and the enterprise itself.[100] However, on the big questions, workers seem to feel generally adequately represented by their respective unions.

There is a paradox here. Blue-collar laborers appeared to be more accepting of the rules of the game set up in the factory or enterprise, though their unions were more likely to take militant stands by way of strikes concerning wages and working conditions. On the other hand, white-collar employees individually expressed more militant attitudes and were more skeptical of hierarchy and authority than laborers appeared to be, but they belonged to unions with generally less clout and little propensity to take up such issues as the organization of the workplace and other traditionally managerial prerogatives. Moreover, employees—given the nature of their better education as "middle-class workers"—put more weight on non-economic features of an organization such as communication, participation, and involvement in democratic decision making and leadership selection.

Summary

The results of my survey indicate that the Argentine working class has, overall, a high degree of self-confidence and identify with the cultural values of urban bourgeois society regarding social mobility and personal aspirations. They share with other portions of the society—the self-employed, petty-bourgeois sectors—much of the same socioeconomic background and access to culture. They work hard in order to enjoy the cultural and social fruits of their labor. Their frustrations focus on feelings of being inadequately rewarded for their efforts, though for the most part they comprehend the difficult international and domestic structural causes that are partly responsible for their present malaise. Yet they are far from fatalistic about their situation and avoid extreme cynicism and nihilism.

By and large, the laborers and employees who make up the Argentine working class are long-term residents of the country and thoroughly integrated into the society of Greater Buenos Aires and the nation. The union structure, though neither pluralistic nor participatory, still offers workers a basic orienting institution in their struggle for better living and working conditions and equitable wages. Only moderately concerned with the lack of strong democratic procedures within the union structure, Argentine workers see the CGT more as a major power factor that represents a counterweight to the larger economic forces that confront them.

6 *Workers as Citizens*

On Political Parties: The Peronist Connection

THE WORKERS IN my survey espoused political positions that ranged from a right-of-center liberal-democratic orientation to a left-of-center democratic socialist orientation. (See table 18.) Their sympathies were evenly divided between the Radical party of President Alfonsín and the Peronist movement.

It is evident that the Radicals had a more evenly apportioned strength among laborers and employees than the Peronists, and that the latter was a more labor-based party; almost half of blue-collar laborers expressed sympathy for Peronism. The only exception to this breakdown was the strong support among autoworkers for the Radicals (60 percent). Also apparent was the greater propensity of white-collar employees in the service sector to back left-of-center parties (such as the PI) and leftist parties. Laborers as a bloc tended to be more politically centrist. By and large, employees showed a greater tendency to split their sympathy and votes between the left and the right in a much less predictable manner than did laborers, who seemed more solidly centrist and Peronist. Nevertheless, there was apparently strong bipolarization owing to the equally strong pull of the two major Argentine political groupings.[1]

Although Argentine workers clearly supported one or another party, they were, as in the trade union context, usually not active party members.[2] As shown in tables 19 and 20, only 7.4 percent of all workers reported being active in the affairs of a political party. However, employees were substantially more apt to be party activists (14 percent), compared to only 1.7

percent of laborers. Teachers were politically the most activist—possibly compensating for the historical weakness of CTERA within the CGT despite the numerical strength of the teachers' union. Employees also reported greater involvement in union activities (14 percent). A few more laborers were active in their trade unions than in political parties per se, but even then their participation (6.7 percent) was less than half that reported by employees. Comparing rank-and-file activism in unions and political parties, we see that employees were more active in both contexts.

In attempting to attain a historical profile of my sample, I assessed their voting patterns in the three most recent national elections through 1986.

TABLE 18. Workers' Political Party Preferences (in percent)

Party Preference	Laborers	Employees	Total
Peronists	45.0	22.0	34.5
Radicals	36.7	32.0	34.5
Intransigents (PI)	5.0	20.0	11.8
Left (MAS + PCA)	1.7	12.0	6.3
Right (UCD)	0.0	4.0	1.8
Other	6.7	10.0	8.2
None	5.0	0.0	2.7
Total	100.1	100.0	99.8
	(N = 60)	(N = 50)	(N = 110)

Note: Figures do not always add up to 100.0 because of rounding.

TABLE 19. Workers' Union Activism (in percent)

Union Activist	Laborers	Employees	Total
No	93.3	86.0	90.0
Yes	6.7	14.0	10.0
Total	100.0	100.0	100.0
	(N = 60)	(N = 50)	(N = 110)

TABLE 20. Workers' Political Party Activism (in percent)

Party Activist	Laborers	Employees	Total
No	94.8	86.0	90.7
Yes	1.7	14.0	7.4
Other	3.3	0.0	1.9
Total	99.8	100.0	100.0
	(N = 58)	(N = 50)	(N = 108)

Note: Figures do not always add up to 100.0 because of rounding.

The results, given in table 21, reflect the massive turnout for Perón in his 1973 landslide victory and show his major appeal among laborers and employees alike; Perón was favored by a 3:1 margin among laborers and by a 2:1 margin among employees over his nearest competitor—the UCR Radical candidate.

In 1983, with the reestablishment of democracy, Alfonsín was elected with a majority of the working-class sample. (See table 22.) This was as important a support base for Alfonsín as the workers' support for Perón had been a decade earlier. Among all workers, Alfonsín had twice the support of the Peronist candidate Italo Luder. It was particularly impressive that in this election Alfonsín approached Perón's level of popularity among all workers. Both laborers and employees—almost identical in their support for Alfonsín and the Radicals—gave him a solid vote of confidence. The estrangement between employees and Peronism was manifest in the first election following the military dictatorship. Also indicated in the 1983 figures (and reflected in workers' reported political party preferences), many employees supporte.' Oscar Alende of the Intransigent party (PI)—a party they perceived as more antiestablishment than either of the other two major parties, and the one most manifestly antimilitary in its platform. Employees left Peronism in droves in 1983, no doubt because of their perception of the unsavory connections among elements of the CGT, right-wing Peronism, and the military. But a solid minority of laborers maintained their steadfast support

TABLE 21. Workers' Vote in 1973 Presidential Election (in percent)

Candidate/Party	Laborers	Employees	Total
Perón (Peronists)	68.6	45.5	59.6
Balbín (Radicals)	20.0	22.7	21.1
Other	11.4	31.8	19.3
Total	100.0	100.0	100.0
	(N = 35)	(N = 22)	(N = 57)

Note: 44.1% of the sample were either too young in 1973, or in some cases were in the military service or were ineligible as foreigners.

TABLE 22. Workers' Vote in 1983 Presidential Election (in percent)

Candidate/Party	Laborers	Employees	Total
Alfonsín (Radical)	55.8	56.5	56.2
Luder (Peronist)	37.2	17.4	27.0
Alende (PI)	0.0	19.6	10.1
Other	7.0	6.5	6.7
Total	100.0	100.0	100.0
	(N = 43)	(N = 46)	(N = 89)

for Peronism and rejected the Intransigent party alternative. The election again powerfully affirmed a two-party system, with 83.2 percent of the workers voting for either the Radicals or the Peronists, compared to 80.7 percent in 1973.[3]

In the legislative elections of 1985, blue-collar laborers in large measure returned to the Peronist fold, indicating what would occur in the national elections of 1987 and 1989. (See table 23.) Laborers again were the major bulwark of the Peronist vote, while employees divided their loyalties among the Radicals, Intransigents, and Peronists.[4] (See table 24.) The historical two-party bifurcation was apparently only momentarily slowed, as the two major political parties shared just under two-thirds of the total vote cast, with a large minority of third-party voting scattered among groups from left to right.

Even more powerful was the clear evidence that Peronism and Radicalism predominantly attracted male affiliation (to varying degrees), while women were drawn in much greater numbers to parties further to the left and right on the political spectrum. (See table 25.) Further, those who identified with Peronism and Radicalism saw these two parties as having a center, center-right ideological orientation, whereas those supporting alternative parties had a clearly more leftist perception. (See table 26.)

TABLE 23. Workers' Vote in 1985 Legislative Election (in percent)

Party	Laborers	Employees	Total
Peronist	50.0	18.2	34.1
Radical	29.5	31.8	30.7
PI (Intransigent)	6.8	25.0	15.9
Conservative (UCD)	0.0	9.0	4.5
Left coalition (FREPU)	4.5	11.4	8.0
Other	9.2	4.5	6.8
Total	100.0	100.0	100.0
	(N = 44)	(N = 44)	(N = 88)

TABLE 24. Workers' Political Party Identification by Type of Worker (in percent)

Party Identification	Laborers	Employees
Peronist	45.0	22.4
Radical	36.7	32.7
Other	18.3	44.9
Total	100.0	100.0
	(N = 60)	(N = 49)

$X^2 = 10.346$, 2 df, $p < .01$

TABLE 25. Workers' Party Preference by Gender (in percent)

Party Preference	Male	Female
Peronist	39.5	20.7
Radical	38.3	24.1
Other	22.2	55.2
Total	100.0	100.0
	(N=81)	(N=29)

X² = 10.925, 2 df, p < .004

TABLE 26. Workers' Ideological Orientation by Party Preference (in percent)

	Peronist	Radical	Other
Right	29.4	33.3	26.7
Center	55.9	57.6	26.7
Left	14.7	9.1	46.7
Total	100.0	100.0	100.1
	(N=34)	(N=33)	(N=30)

X² = 15.444, 4 df, p < .004

Note: Figures do not always add up to 100.0 because of rounding.

The workers were asked, "With which political party/parties do your three closest friends sympathize?" From their answers it appeared that laborers in particular were estranged from both the left and the right. Employees were much more ecumenical in their choice of friends, who were scattered over the political map. However, even they avoided extremes. Laborers were more sectarian, with 30 percent having exclusively Peronist friends, though the majority had Radical friends. Employees had friends with loyalties all along the political continuum, although concentrated in the center and center-left—Peronists, Radicals, and Intransigents. They were much less likely than laborers to have friends from only their own political party, and interestingly 20 percent of the employees mentioned having a friend or two who supported the Intransigent party (PI). This was particularly true of CTERA teachers. Most significant was the apparent social ostracism of both left and right among workers. Only 5.5 percent of all workers had friends who claimed allegiance to the Conservative party (UCD), and 2.7 percent who had friends aligned with any of the left political parties. Laborers, most notably, had no friends from either left or right. Employees, on the other hand, mentioned having some friends on the right (12 percent) and on the left (6 percent).

The pattern of centrist political identification continues when we examine the response to the question, "Is there some other political party for which you feel some affinity (other than your own)?" Although 34.5 percent of all workers said "none," those who answered positively singled out the Intransigents, the most popular second choice (15.5 percent), Radicals (13.6 percent), and Peronists (11.8 percent). Again, the left and right were seemingly isolated. Only 6.4 percent mentioned the left and 1.8 percent the conservative right. Laborers mentioned the left (5 percent) but completely rejected the conservative right, while among employees, 8 percent mentioned the left and only 2 percent mentioned the right.

Workers were then asked, "Which political party do you consider furthest from your own?" Here the laborers' major distancing was from the left, with 36.7 percent mentioning a leftist political party or left coalition, and among employees the rightist conservative party was mentioned by 40 percent. A typical response came from a metalworker who said the political party furthest from his own was the Communist party. He said,

> The hammer and sickle. As far as I know they are always trying to leave their soil [the USSR], and, for example, their athletes run away. That's a clue that things are not going well. It's a closed circle here [referring to the Argentine Communist party] where one can't penetrate. They're activists, intelligent, but many of them are not laborers but people with professions and careers. Their type of life doesn't do much for the people themselves.[5]

The data also indicated that although the right and left were seen to be ideologically incompatible with working-class values, the right was slightly more socially acceptable in employee family circles, probably fallout from the psychological pressures of the "dirty war" of military repression, when leftist friendships were fraught with danger.

For many in the working class, particularly among laborers, leftism, inside or outside Peronism, was associated with "antiverticalism," a kind of disloyalty to Perón and his "third position" and to the golden years of reformism and welfare capitalism instituted under Perón. This helps to explain the internal Peronist party defeat of the governor of Buenos Aires, Antonio Cafiero, by Carlos Menem, governor of La Rioja Province, in the presidential primaries of May 1988. Menem represented traditional verticalism much better than Cafiero, who hoped to overwhelm labor officialdom with a more modern, pluralist party instead of the more paternalistic movement of Perón's days in which the CGT was a major actor.

For other workers, the Communist party was not to be trusted because of its longstanding opposition to Peronism and its insistent attempts to divide the working-class vote. The Argentine Communists' Sixteenth Party Congress in 1986 reiterated exactly this notion—that they were the appointed historical "vanguard" of the Argentine Peronist-leaning workers.[6] Again, some laborers in particular saw the Communists as manipulators looking for long strikes to destabilize the government, regardless of the sacrifices or consequences for the workers involved.[7]

In response to a question about their earliest political memories from childhood, 60 percent of all workers recalled the socioeconomic words and deeds of early Peronism (25.5 percent) and the struggles of the post-Perón period (34.5 percent). Responses that mentioned other issues not directly bearing on Perón amounted to a total of 22.7 percent among all workers, and 17.3 percent had no specific political recollections. Interestingly, there were no appreciable differences between the laborers' and employees' focus on the positive and negative aspects of Peronism as their earliest memories. In this regard a teacher recounted, "I remember the sayings of Perón—the pictures of Perón and Evita—the impact of Perón nationalizing the British railroads."[8] A metalworker remembered, "Evita gave me a pair of shoes and a pair of pants. I came from a very poor family. I had the luck of once receiving a bicycle from Eva and Juan Perón."[9] A light and power worker told me:

> We were extremely poor. There were six of us children. We ate one-day-old bread. There was one chicken for eight, and being the youngest I always got the rear end of the chicken. My mother bought used clothing. My brothers and I divided the suit's vest, jacket, and pants; none of us was dressed properly. Once Perón came, we could buy good shoes and we had three chickens for the family and I got one-third of a chicken for myself.[10]

The memories were not all positive, however. A bank employee recalled, "When I was a boy [in the early Perón years], I went to pick up a toy at the post office [gifts from Perón and Evita for Christmas] and when I returned to the house, my father scolded me, saying that he didn't need Perón giving us gifts and made me return it."[11] Another bank employee recounted, "When I was a child, I remember my father refused to sing the 'Peronist March' and had to hide in the attic for two days and my mother was thrown out of her job when she refused to join the Peronist party."[12] A teacher recalled, "Once in a car with my parents we ran into a Peronist street rally. The numbers and chanting of the people made me afraid."[13] And, finally, another teacher told me, "When Perón was ousted in 1955 [when she was nine years old], books by Perón and Evita and the Peronist party literature were burned; you couldn't even mention the name 'Peronism.'"[14]

Similarly, when asked to describe their first political ideas or sentiments as an adolescent or teenager, 49.1 percent recalled either the words and events of early Peronism (20.9 percent) or the issues and experiences in the battle between Peronists and anti-Peronists between 1955 and 1976 (28.2 percent). All the other memories (such as of previous Radical governments and policies and the *proceso* dictatorship) received 39 percent. (Some 9.1 percent couldn't recall their first political ideas or sentiments as adolescents.) Almost two-thirds of the laborers mentioned Peronism as their first orienting perspective, as opposed to slightly less than one-third of the employees. For example, a light and power worker, typifying many laborers, told me, "When I was eighteen years old, I felt a complete change with Perón's social benefits for the workers. It was a really extraordinary thing that changed my life."[15]

Some of the younger employees (among a generally more youthful group) had different experiences. A telephone employee said, "I learned habits of caution because friends and companions disappeared. I learned things couldn't be changed by revolutionary action overnight."[16] A bank employee said, "I never had any real political feelings because of the *proceso* experience. To think about and speak about politics was mostly prohibited."[17] Another bank employee told this story: "I pretty much avoided politics until 1983 [when she was nineteen]. My friends in secondary school formed a student center but weren't allowed any political activity [under the *proceso*], even though their goals were only a larger library and a better laboratory."[18]

Thus among employees, the most common first political memory as teenagers was the *proceso* military regime (mentioned by 26 percent). This was in large part due to the relative youth of the employee portion of the workers (particularly the rank-and-file bank employees who were the youngest group in the survey). That so many young employees' first political memories as adolescents were associated with passivity, timidity, and fear connected to their political awakening under the last military regime likely explains the massive support of this group for the Alfonsín candidacy, which confronted the military policies more frontally than the Peronist candidate, Italo Luder.

I asked workers to name the three Argentine public figures they had most admired in their adult life. Juan Perón and/or Eva Perón were mentioned by 79.1 percent of the entire sample. *All* of the laborers, and 54 percent of employees, named either Perón or Evita as among their three most esteemed public persons. Alfonsín was given third place overall, but second place among employees. (See table 27.)[19] Evidently, the historical power of Peronism over the minds and hearts of contemporary Argentine workers still had a major political impact in 1985–1986. Nostalgia for the Peronist past has been a continuing political phenomenon ever since Perón's ouster in 1955 and continues virtually unabated today.[20]

TABLE 27. Workers' Three Most Admired Public Figures (in percent)

Admired Public Figures	Laborers	Employees	Total
Juan Perón	56.7	34.0	46.4
Eva Perón	43.3	20.0	32.7
Raúl Alfonsín	26.7	30.0	28.2
Various sports figures	41.7	20.0	31.8
Various scientific figures	13.3	36.0	23.6
Various political figures	23.3	24.0	23.6
Various literary figures	11.7	30.0	20.0
	(N = 60)	(N = 50)	(N = 110)

Note: Percentage responses do not add up to 100 because of multiple responses.

This nostalgia is present, too, in the workers' response to historical Peronism vis-à-vis its contemporary manifestations and helps to account for the disparity between the overwhelmingly positive responses to Juan and Eva Perón and the more lukewarm response to the modern Peronist party. When the workers were asked, "Do you consider Peronism a political party effectively representative of the working class?" 50 percent replied "yes"; 2.7 percent said "more or less"; and 47.3 percent said "no."[21] A metal-worker said, "Peronism always seems to pull for the worker, but yet certain interests figure in it. But it's our fault that we've allowed that type of leader to rise up. Maybe the party is good, but those who represent us, no."[22] A light and power worker told me, "No, it is a party in disintegration. Perón in 1973 was a shadow of his former self. I've had a slow disenchantment with Peronism over the years."[23] On the other hand, a telephone employee explained, "Yes, because [the Peronist party] is the working class."[24] And a bank employee had this to say: "Yes, but at the moment [the Peronists] seem totally disoriented due to internal problems. Until they put their house in order they can't represent anybody. I can't understand how a Peronist deputy can have a mansion in San Isidro [a fashionable Buenos Aires suburb]. In no way does he represent the working class."[25]

A significant portion of all workers (19.1 percent) said that under Perón, yes, Peronism was representative, but that this was no longer so today. Therefore, 71.8 percent of the sample gave positive marks to historical Peronism. Among laborers, this support rose to 78.4 percent, but even 64 percent of employees supported historical Peronism. Excluding Perón's own regimes, contemporary Peronism claims the support of a bare majority among laborers and slightly less than a majority among the employees.[26] A strong association emerged between workers who were satisfied with their union leadership and those who saw contemporary Peronism as a viable representative of the working class. (See table 28.)

TABLE 28. Workers' Satisfaction with Union Leadership by Opinion of Peronism as Representative of the Working Class (in percent)

"Are you satisfied with union leadership?"	Peronism Is Representative	Peronism Is Unrepresentative
No	41.1	72.9
Yes	58.9	27.1
Total	100.0	100.0
	(N = 56)	(N = 48)

$X^2 = 9.374$, 1 df, $p < .002$

Despite a certain ambivalence toward contemporary Peronism, these attitudes did not, in most cases, translate into a desire to scuttle Peronism or to create an alternative working-class political party. The majority of workers did not see the need to start a "political party that exclusively counts on the support of the working class." Employees, in particular, were opposed to the idea (68 percent), while 51.7 percent of the laborers said no.

As one textile laborer said to me, "No, [a party] can't just represent workers; it would be too divisive; then doctors would have their own party and what would teachers and clerks do, for example?"[27] A fellow textile worker said, "No . . . just a working-class party doesn't mirror all the classes of the country. The party has to have the middle class and professionals to be effective and respected."[28] A light and power worker told me, "No, it needs other classes—like rich and poor, like pleasure and pain."[29] Another light and power worker said, "No, it would polarize society and social classes, because Peronists are working-class but we also need other classes, just as the UCD [Conservative party] is not only for the wealthy but some workers belong as well."[30] Similarly, a bank employee said, "No, it wouldn't work, because the working class is made up of people with middle to low education and you are going to need people who can guide them."[31] A teacher said, "It's not a good idea, because it would be based on a limited class reference. It wouldn't have a promising future. It really needs the support of elements of the middle class as well."[32]

The most common single answer among all workers (given by 32.7 percent) was that an exclusively workers' party would be too divisive for Argentina. Even among those who answered yes to the question, 14.5 percent thought that even though it was a good idea they were skeptical about its political success. This was particularly true among laborers (20 percent), who obviously saw themselves as a shrinking proportion of the social class structure. Thus a majority of the working class saw effective political parties as being multiclass, as did more than two-thirds of the

employees. Almost three-quarters of all workers were opposed to the
formation of a sectarian working-class party, while less than one-quarter
unambiguously supported such a venture.

There was additional evidence as well that those workers who believed in
forming a new working-class party were also from that minority of workers
who held what could be called "authoritarian" notions about society. This
was most manifest in that group of workers who supported the role of the
military during the *proceso* ($X^2 = 6.041$, 2 df, p $<$ .05), who accepted their
"dirty war" against subversion ($X^2 = 5.186$, 1 df, p $<$ .03), and who
believed their justification of the "disappeared" ($X^2 = 4.060$, 1 df, p $<$ .05).
Thus, it is clear that a democratic outlook was not connected with seeing the
necessity of a political party devoted exclusively to workers, and (inversely)
that the democratic majority among workers saw the essence of political
parties as necessarily multiclass. This they felt was more likely to preserve
democracy than forming a single-class party.

Nor did communism or the Argentine Communist party offer a good
alternative for Argentine workers. The question was framed, "Do you think
Communism offers any valid solutions for Argentina"? To this question, 78.2
percent of the workers said no, with only 9.1 percent saying yes, and 12.7
percent not answering or saying they didn't know. Eighty-eight percent
among employees and 70 percent of laborers said no. Workers' negative
opinions about Argentine Communism tended to focus on the Communists'
authoritarian reputation and lack of working-class connections. On the
other side, they had strong material and cultural reasons for supporting
Peronism.[33]

A metalworker answered the question about Communism by saying,
"Probably it would be good if everyone worked for the good of the country.
But I think liberty is more important. It's beautiful to be free, but one has to
work."[34] Another metalworker said, "No, because even though [the Communist party] can move you ahead, the people will end up being exploited by
them, and before I want that, I prefer the exploitation by Peronists or
imperialists."[35] A light and power worker told me this joke:

> Only in theory is communism good. For example, the story goes, "If you
> had two houses, the Communists come and give one to the poor, O.K.?
> "O.K.," says the worker. If you had two cars, the Communists come and
> give one to the poor, O.K.? "O.K.," says the worker. Now in fact you do
> have two pesos and the Communists will come and give one to the poor,
> O.K.? "Oh, no, no!" says the worker.[36]

Another light and power worker said, "No, [the Communists] are regimented like little tin soldiers. They are not synchronized into Argentine

idiosyncracies; they have too disciplined a view of the world for Argentines."[37]

A bank employee said, "I don't understand their proposals. It may be marvelous for the Russians and the Cubans but not for me. . . . I see where many of our protest singers have enriched themselves, drive around in a Mercedes-Benz and have homes in Europe. I wouldn't mind being a leftist like that!"[38] A teacher told me, "No, [the Argentine Communists] have always been on the side of the powerful, not on the side of the poor. It really is made up of well-off people. The average people have no faith in the Communist party."[39] And another teacher claimed, "No, just mention the party and there is an immediate rejection."[40]

The general view among the Argentine working class was that Communism was out of step with Argentina's cultural values and that it was simply too authoritarian in its makeup and outlook.[41] To the workers, the parties of the left appeared far more elitist than Peronism, under which workers had risen to positions in the legislature and the executive branch when Peronists held legislative or executive political power. Overall, Argentine workers saw Peronism as a working-class party that met the essential needs of the rank-and-file unionists, a political party that had stood the test of time.

On the Issues

The economy and privatization of the state

Among all Argentine workers, the major contemporary problems mentioned were the foreign debt, its general impact in slowing down the economy, and a concomitant rise in unemployment. These issues were mentioned by 89.9 percent of the workers (77.9 percent of laborers and 100 percent of employees). A telephone employee encapsulated the concern: "It is the external debt; all the other problems stem from this, such as poverty, unemployment, lack of possibilities for the future."[42] Specific social problems such as poverty, crime, and inadequate health care, housing, and education were also mentioned by 28.4 percent of the workers.

The Argentine workers felt (38.2 percent) that poor political and economic leadership was the cause of the debt crisis, while 30.9 percent singled out the *proceso* military dictatorship as being the prime culprit. A textile laborer told me, "The corruption of past governments and the business sectors is the reason. Workers work their heads off for a few miserable pennies so that they can come back the next day and start all over again."[43] A phone employee said that the explanation was "graft and corruption that came from foreign loans [under the *proceso*] that have never been accounted for."[44] A bank employee argued,

> The government doesn't give security to national and foreign investors. There is no stimulus for new investments. Also the deindustrialization heritage of Martínez de Hoz [the *proceso* economics minister] where people sold homes to buy artificially cheap dollars. Industries simply closed since people spent their time buying cheap dollars rather than producing. Later the dollar found its real level and people went into bankruptcy.[45]

Interestingly, only 9 percent among workers saw the debt problem as the fault of U.S. imperialism or as meddling by the IMF or international banks in Argentine affairs.[46] Here laborers were much less prone (3.3 percent) than employees (16 percent) to blame foreign actors for present Argentine conditions. Significantly, only 4.5 percent of all workers blamed the CGT and/or Peronist policies for their economic situation. None of the laborers and only 10 percent of the employees focused on the CGT or Peronism. As indicated in interviews, workers felt that although current conditions were caused by a combination of national and international circumstances, they could be redressed by effective government leadership.

As to the solutions for Argentina's economic crisis of the mid-1980s, reactions to Alfonsín's Austral Plan—the stabilization plan launched in mid-June 1985 that included a major currency reform—were varied. When I questioned the workers about these fiscal reforms, they were split in their opinion: 46.4 percent supported the plan, and 53.6 percent opposed it. Laborers were more supportive (by 55 percent), whereas 64 percent of the white-collar service employees were negative.

Laborers were much more inclined to give Alfonsín good marks for launching the Austral Plan, seeing it as a positive attempt to control wages and prices and to stop what had become hyperinflation by early June 1985.[47] Partly this response was due to their generally better pay when the Austral Plan was inaugurated. Equally important was the greater skepticism of employees concerning the true motivations behind Alfonsín's economic measures. The most prevalent criticism from all workers (32.7 percent) was that, while the plan had good intentions, it had been weakened considerably since its initiation, and that price rises had far outstripped wages, with a debilitating impact on workers' income. Moreover, 20 percent of the employees saw the Austral Plan as merely measures to administer the debt and not geared to economic growth as such.

What was very popular among all workers was Alfonsín's complementary plan to reactivate the Argentine economy. In this case 84.3 percent of the workers thought it positive as projected; however, of those who were supportive (51.9 percent), most saw it mainly as "all talk . . . so far nothing in practice."[48] Only slightly more than one in ten workers saw the economic reactivization plans in a negative light, claiming they were antisocial in impact or that productive governmental investment was insufficient. As one bank employee made the case: "I don't see any real plan. If they don't give workers a dignified salary, there can't be any reactivization."[49]

As popular as the concept of "reactivization" of the Argentine economy was among workers, they were almost as enthusiastic about Alfonsín's proposals to privatize areas of the state-controlled economy.[50] To the question, "What do you think of the plan to privatize various state enterprises?" 71 percent of the working class agreed that it was a good thing, while only 24.5 percent disagreed. A textile worker told me, "It is a good idea. If there are any losses in profits, the people don't have to pay more in taxes or rates [electricity, gas, telephone] to bail them out."[51] An autoworker said, "That would be very good, the best thing that could happen; the day they get rid of the state employees, there will be such a development explosion, you can't imagine."[52] A metalworker, though expressing some reservations, agreed. "I would like what is ours to be ours. But when one knows something is not going well, you have to do something. If private enterprise will provide employment, I welcome it. I don't like to see the public sector shrink, but one has to be realistic."[53] Despite their jobs in the state-sector electrical industry, two light and power workers had this to say: "It is a good idea. The state can't subsidize so many industries. Reserving electrical energy and other vital energy for the state [gas, petroleum, nuclear energy], all the rest should be sold, for example, the telephones, railways, airlines, etcetera,"[54] while a fellow worker said, "It doesn't scare me; it might be better, more efficient, better pay. Its not a question of national security whether SEGBA, SOMISA [the nationalized iron and steel company], or whatever are privatized."[55]

One of the first targets talked about during the Alfonsín administration was the privatization of parts of the ENTEL state telephone enterprise. Though even a majority of its organized employees supported privatization, some had reservations. This was reflected in the comments of a telephone employee who said, "In theory, it is a good idea, but two-thirds of the personnel would be fired. It is unlikely to happen because, politically, it is too unpalatable."[56] On the other hand, a bank employee working for the private Banco Galícia y Buenos Aires said, "I absolutely agree in all areas. Government should handle public administration. Businessmen should run all other businesses."[57] A teacher said, in favor of privatization: "Yes, as long as [the privatized industries] are not crucial, such as metallurgy [SOMISA], petroleum [YPF], and mining. On the other hand, utilities [ENTEL, GAS de ESTADO, and SEGBA], yes."[58]

Despite reservations among a minority of employees, 74 percent of employees generally favored the privatization schemes launched under Alfonsín, and the figure among laborers was a similar 68.3 percent. The most common justifications for positive responses were that the private sector was more efficient than the public sector, that national firms should be privatized if they were deficitary and that only *critical* state enterprises should remain in government hands. Thus there was major working-class agreement on this issue, even among public-sector employees.[59]

The media and the level of information

On a more personal level, I asked the workers, "In the last several years, have you read anything in the newspapers that really made you angry?" Workers spoke of violent crimes, assaults, and murders in their neighborhoods, as well as violent outbreaks at soccer stadiums. Here laborers (by 38.3 percent) were far more focused on questions of law and order than were employees (10.6 percent). Among employees, the *proceso* state terror and the Malvinas War revelations of military incompetence and corruption were the major provocation (34 percent), while 23.3 percent of laborers spoke of those problems. Thus laborers more than employees focused on questions of immediate and direct concern to them — that is, visible community issues — rather than on larger issues of national import that had a greater hold on the employee sector.

Inversely, workers were asked what they had read in the newspapers over the last years that "really gave them satisfaction." The results, given in table 29, offer further evidence that employees had a larger, more global

TABLE 29. Issues Reported in Newspapers That Gave Workers Satisfaction (in percent)

Issue	Laborers	Employees	Total
Return to democracy with Alfonsín victory; end of *proceso* dictatorship	20.0	38.0	28.2
Medical and scientific advances	16.7	18.0	17.3
Argentina's world soccer championship victories (1978 & 1986)	20.0	14.0	17.3
	(N = 60)	(N = 50)	(N = 110)

Note: Percentage responses do not add up to 100 because of multiple responses. The table includes only the highest three responses.

vision of society and were more prone to select issues with broader ramifications and that their sensitivity to the meaning of democracy was apparently more sharply honed than that among laborers. Of course, differences in the variable of education is a leading explanation for these divergences.

Though on the whole workers seemed generally well informed on the issues of the day, their print media diet concentrated heavily on daily newspapers, to the general exclusion of magazines. (See tables 30 and 31.) Many workers noted the prohibitive cost of magazines in Buenos Aires and said that if they purchased them at all, it was on a rotating basis with their fellow workers. *Clarín*, a readable, tabloid, "middle-class" newspaper, a favorite of civil service administrators and professionals, was far and away also the favorite newspaper among both blue-collar and white-collar workers. But other publications had very different levels of appeal to the two groups. *La Crónica*, a popular tabloid geared to sensational crime and sports

TABLE 30. Workers' Favorite Newspapers (in percent)

Favorite Newspaper	Laborers	Employees	Total
Clarín	63.3	76.0	69.1
La Crónica	18.3	2.0	10.9
La Razón	1.7	16.0	8.2
Oligarchic, financial press, newspapers such as La Prensa, La Nación, Ambito Financiero, Cronista Comercial	1.7	26.0	12.7
Other	15.0	8.0	11.8
None	13.3	2.0	8.2
	(N=60)	(N=50)	(N=110)

Note: Percentage responses do not add up to 100 because of multiple responses.

TABLE 31. Workers' Favorite Magazines (in percent)

Favorite Magazines	Laborers	Employees	Total
None	60.0	48.0	54.5
Various technical, scientific, crafts magazines	6.7	16.0	10.9
Gente	11.7	8.0	10.0
Various sports magazines	10.0	2.0	6.4
Humor	1.7	10.0	5.5
El Periodista, El Porteño	0.0	8.0	3.6
Other	10.0	16.0	12.7
	(N=60)	(N=50)	(N=110)

Note: Percentage responses do not add up to 100 because of multiple responses.

news, was practically unread by employees and came in a distant second with laborers. As their second choice, employees favored *La Razón*, at that time a popular evening newspaper with the second largest circulation in Argentina. Employees also read various examples of the so-called oligarchic-financial press.[60]

Views of institutional actors

In attempting to ascertain workers' views regarding Argentina's leading institutional actors, I began by querying, "What do you think of the role of Argentine trade unions?" Laborers were more impressed with the role of unions, with 61.7 percent giving positive assessments while even 52 percent of employees had a favorable opinion. Some of the more representative comments from blue-collar laborers follow. "Without unions," said a textile laborer, "the country would lack direction, like a ship without a rudder."[61] An automobile worker explained, "There are too many internal union struggles. The CGT is used to achieving political power by catapulting their leaders, rather than their ideas,"[62] while a metalworker said of unions, "They're important and necessary. If it wasn't for the unions we would be in the situation of the times when you went to the harvest and slept with the animals."[63]

Representing white-collar employees, a telephone worker told me, "As institutions, unions are fine, but they are poorly run by the leadership; . . . the rank-and-file organizations [shop committees] are made up of good people but the union delegates are not good interpreters of our needs."[64] Another telephone employee said, "The unions have to defend workers, but they are not there to jump into politics. The union shouldn't be used for politics, nor should politics be used to win within the union—each in his own area without mixing them."[65] A bank employee observed, "The unions in Argentina are essentially boss-controlled; . . . no one elects the leadership democratically; they choose among themselves. There has to be a reform of the union law of 1946 which allows the majority list full control of each union."[66] Another bank employee said, "[Unions] have been a political force to contend with but sadly they are not well led; . . . unions, nevertheless, are an arm that defends the working class. Without them we would be slaves."[67] Finally, a teacher told me, "[Unions are] important when they are led by labor questions not when their motivations are political. The CGT wants to reactivate the country but constantly brings it to a stop [through work stoppages]."[68]

The single most reiterated reaction to unions (51.7 percent among laborers and 44 percent of employees) was that they were "crucial representatives of the workers."[69] Employees were substantially more critical of unions than were laborers, faulting them most often for corruption and for being more political than is appropriate for trade union organizations.[70]

On the other hand, workers reacted to Argentine businessmen with hostility. This was the attitude of 61.8 percent of workers. Among laborers the rate of negative response was 55 percent and among employees a very high 70 percent. Workers who felt most exploited had the most negative feelings about the role of the Argentine business class in the nation's economy. (See table 32.)

A light and power worker told me, "They want to have big profits, invest little, and produce even less."[71] A bank employee said, "The businessmen ought to try as hard as the workers do. There is a law that has never been respected [Article 14b of the Argentine Constitution]: that workers participate directly in the profits of the firm, which would increase its efficiency and productivity."[72] A teacher replied to the question, "Mostly, [businessmen] are speculators not producers."[73]

Among laborers, the biggest complaint against Argentine businessmen was their poor treatment of workers (26.7 percent) while they admitted (by 21.8 percent) that they were important as sources of investment and employment. Even more employees, on the other hand, were extremely negative concerning Argentine businessmen, with 38 percent labeling them as a selfish, antinational group. For them, especially employees in the public sector, private-sector employment considerations were far less important to their own livelihood. On the other hand, laborers appeared to focus more than employees on personal issues in their assessment of Argentine businessmen, such as how they were treated and under what conditions they happened to work.[74]

Quite in contrast, foreign companies received the most positive responses from workers among all major institutions in Argentina: 62.7 percent of the sample saw them in a favorable light (which breaks down to 81.7 percent among laborers and 40 percent among employees). In addition,

TABLE 32. Workers' Opinions of Businessmen by Feelings of Exploitation

	"Do you feel exploited?"		
Opinion of Businessmen	Yes	No, but pay and working conditions are poor	No
Negative	90.6	61.3	48.8
Positive	9.4	38.7	51.2
Total	100.0	100.0	100.0
	(N = 32)	(N = 31)	(N = 41)

$X^2 = 14.231$, 2 df, $p < .001$

27.3 percent of the workers thought foreign investments were very necessary as long as they are under state supervision. Thus, among multiple responses, 90 percent of all workers gave a generally favorable opinion of foreign companies' role in Argentine society. On the negative side, 18.2 percent of the sample saw foreign firms as having a deleterious effect (a very small 8.3 percent among laborers and 25 percent among employees). A metalworker responded, "They're fine with me. Hopefully, more foreign firms will come to raise production and decrease unemployment."[75]

Interestingly, telephone employees, who work for a state enterprise, were among the most complimentary to foreign firms. One telephone employee said, "They are important. They ask more of their employees, but they pay better."[76] Another telephone employee said, "I don't think they are so bad. They bring in modern technology. And with more firms there is more work and Argentina develops. They also bring another concept of work. They provide better services. What is modern in Argentina is thanks to the foreign firms or their merger with an Argentine company."[77] Still a third telephone employee told me, "We owe much to them, but there are hidden things that one doesn't know; from what I see they've brought progress to the country, but I don't know at what price."[78] A bank employee spoke of his own past experiences when he said,

> I worked for twenty years for Fiat and I have a very good opinion of the company. I was well paid and treated with consideration and respect for my capacity. The firm paid for me to learn new techniques and thanks to Fiat I got to see half the country [as a sales representative]. They are very different from Argentine companies.[79]

There were some reservations, however, particularly among workers in the service sector, about the role of foreign firms in Argentina. A bank employee replied, "It has various aspects; it can help the country a lot through development or it can control a country. Foreign firms are a double-edged sword. The government has to regulate the situation. The first goal is to develop that which is authentically national."[80] Still another bank employee had this comment: "There has to be a balance between the needs of the country and the profits of the corporations. At the moment, they ask for too many advantages in return for their investments."[81] A teacher was even more adamant. He said, "[Foreign firms] have to be more controlled, although they have an important role. You have to prevent the massive flight of capital. Some has to stay to serve the country. The fault is not in the pig, but who feeds him."[82]

The most common response among laborers (by 55 percent) was that foreign enterprises created jobs, treated the workers more fairly than

Argentine companies, paid better, and paid on time.[83] A significant minority of the total (27.3 percent) saw foreign investments as crucial, but only under state supervision. Laborers again saw foreign investments more in terms of bread-and-butter gains and employment, whereas employees (particularly in the state sector) took a more generalized, ideological stance vis-à-vis foreign companies. Textile, auto, metal, and even light and power workers and telephone employees were all heavily supportive of foreign investment in Argentina. Bank employees and teachers were the most skeptical among rank-and-file unionists concerning the role of foreign enterprise.

Argentina's large landowners were widely regarded with suspicion among workers. Overall, 55.5 percent took a negative view, with no significant differences between laborers and employees.[84] Only 32.7 percent of workers responded positively to the question about landowners' contribution to the economy. An autoworker told me, "The landowner in the past was different from now; before he was an immigrant who knew the land and developed relationships with the peons. Now he could be an industrialist who becomes a landowner without knowing the first thing about the land."[85] A telephone employee said, "They are manipulators and selfish. They are the brake to national development,"[86] while a bank employee added, "They have a negative impact because instead of seeding the land intensively, they let cattle roam indiscriminately."[87] Another bank employee saw them as a typical oligarchy. "They always believed they owned Argentina. They worked only for themselves as a class. Within their 'ghetto' everything, outside the 'ghetto' nothing. It's as if they've never wanted to integrate with the rest of society."[88] Finally, a teacher told me, "[They are] feudal lords who should have long ago disappeared from the scene."[89] On the other side of the coin, a bank employee typified a minority opinion when she said, "The landowners are practically the only thing that moves the country ahead."[90]

Though a minority of workers (19.1 percent) believed the large landowners to be the key to Argentine productivity, the majority saw them as insufficiently productive. However, only among employees did a significant number (20 percent) speak about land reform as a solution to the problem.

The Argentine military received even lower ratings than businessmen and landowners, with 64.5 percent of the sample expressing negative reactions (55 percent of laborers and 77.6 percent of employees). Only 14.5 percent of the total (21.7 percent of laborers and and only 6.1 percent of employees) saw the military as playing a positive role in Argentina.[91] One textile worker told me, "They should stay in the barracks. They aren't equipped to govern. It would be like workers running the government."[92] An autoworker said, "If we get rid of the military we would get rid of half the country. . . . We were born with the military. We have lived very little without them."[93] A metalworker concurred. "The only thing that I reproach them for is that they try to govern."[94] A light and power worker told me, "[The military] are horrible, full of stripes, bars, and decorations — nothing else; we have more generals than the United States has."[95] Another light and power worker had this to say: "[They] are no good at governing, nor fighting wars; they are only good for secret services and keeping the country in the dark about their misdeeds and crimes."[96]

Among employees, whose responses to this question were overwhelmingly negative, a telephone employee said, "The role of the military has been unfortunate in recent years. They are as corrupt as other groups, plus they have a poor educational level which allows them to be manipulated by capitalist interests."[97] A bank employee said, "It's all our fault as Argentines. In our desire to have power we use whatever means, even if we leave the logical and natural area of our competence. This is the situation with the military or whatever other profession. As a bank employee, I can't presume to operate on a sick patient."[98]

Finally, a teacher added, "They have filled a vacuum of power left by civilian political parties. Now it's the thing to do to criticize them. The middle class has always, in time of troubles, knocked on the barrack's door."[99]

Though the major attacks on the Argentine military cited their inept and nefarious interference in political life (32.7 percent), workers' answers demonstrated some recognition of collusion on the part of other economic sectors. Except on the question of the landowners, where all workers shared comparable negative opinions, employees generally were much more critical than laborers regarding the major institutional actors in the Argentine economy. In particular, they were wary of the Argentine military and businessmen. (See table 33.)

TABLE 33. Workers' Ratings of Institutional Actors (in percent)

Groups	Laborers pos./neg.	Employees pos./neg.	Total pos./neg.
Foreign companies	81.7/8.3	40.0/25.0	62.7/18.2
Labor unions	61.7/40.0	52.0/64.0	57.8/51.0
Landowners	31.7/56.7	34.0/54.0	32.7/55.5
Argentine business	38.3/55.0	26.0/70.0	32.7/61.8
Military	21.7/55.0	6.1/77.6[a]	14.5/64.5[a]
	(N=60)	(N=50)	(N=110)

Note: Percentage responses do not add up to 100 because of multiple responses.
a. In responses about the military, employees' N=49 makes total N=109.

On the "dirty war," human rights, and the Malvinas War

The military's unpopularity among Argentine workers stemmed from the very severe repression that they and society as a whole had suffered under the recent armed forces' dictatorship,[100] coupled with the military's incompetence and ineffectiveness in prosecuting the Malvinas War against Great Britain. When I asked the workers, "What is your opinion of the 'war against subversion'?" 50 percent reacted negatively, while 43.6 percent spoke of it in positive terms. Here there were dramatic differences between blue-collar and white-collar workers: 51.7 percent of the laborers supported the "war against subversion" and 38.3 percent opposed it, while 64 percent of the employees opposed it and 34 percent supported it. The figures show an inverse ratio between the two sectors of the working class.[101]

This split in opinion highlights a complicated set of opposing values in various aspects of the workers' lives. Those who supported the "war against subversion" questioned its effectiveness; those who opposed it did so on the grounds of its indiscriminate attacks and its hidden agenda. An autoworker told me, "It was a mistake; the war should have been against all the social problems. Then subversion would have been unnecessary. We can kill all the guerrillas, but if the social problems remain, more guerrillas will reappear."[102] A light and power worker said, "It was a war against workers, not soldiers."[103] A metalworker said,

> It was O.K., but poorly handled. It should have been a war with more openness, without hiding things. . . . It should have been done as in Italy where a group was eliminated in the light of day [tactics used against the Red Brigade]. The way in which the military exterminated the subversives made the military look bad and made the terrorists look good."[104]

A telephone employee explained, "The innocents paid along with the sinners. There were excesses, abuses, and personal questions. Whoever dissented was a subversive."[105] On the other hand, a bank employee reached this conclusion:

> It was the law of the jungle, an eye for an eye, a tooth for a tooth; but also there were other interests at stake and that was why so many people disappeared. I doubt that the majority of the young people who were involved in the struggle and died in attacks on the military regiments understood what they were doing. They were like cannon fodder for interests they didn't understand and were brainwashed. The military, defending special interests, shot first and asked questions later, fall whoever falls (*caiga quien caiga*)."[106]

Similarly, a fellow bank employee said, "It was a smoke screen to cover up the repression which had other ends in mind, like moving ahead with the

Martínez de Hoz economic plan."[107] Last, I heard these very typical opinions from two bank employees: "While [the military] were aiming exclusively at people who were armed it was correct, but later it was pure genocide."[108] Another said, "It was necessary, but with obvious excesses on both sides. It is difficult to say who began the terror."[109]

Employees seem to have had a clearer idea of the question of "due process" in the war's prosecution than had laborers. Blue-collar workers were more likely to see subversion as tantamount to criminal behavior that undermined social values and social stability. The major criticisms of the "war against subversion" focused on the junta's indiscriminate violence and the extralegal character of its methods. The major argument workers used to defend the war (by 22.7 percent) was that it was necessary to regain stability and order. In summary, half of the workers thought the military junta's war of repression was an evil and the other half, a necessary evil.

As critical as the workers were of the excesses of the military regime that preceded the restoration of Argentine democracy, their opinion of the Montoneros' violent guerrilla struggle was unanimously condemnatory.[110] Among all workers, 89.1 percent attacked either their means, ends, or both means and ends — although 22.7 percent of the total admitted that while the Montoneros might have been idealists, that their methods were ill-conceived. A textile worker told me, "By attacking social institutions like theaters, movies, and schools — this hurt their image, dirtied their name, and made them into terrorists."[111] Another textile worker considered them "well-off people with nothing better to do with their time; middle-class kids, that's all — governors' kids, kids of wealthy families. . . . They weren't workers."[112] Further, an autoworker told me, "I didn't understand their motives. I didn't agree with their methods. If they take justice into their own hands, who is safe?"[113] Another autoworker wondered, "I don't know whether they were subversives or liberators, but I was against the violent methods they used."[114]

White-collar employees had similarly censorious opinions. A telephone employee said, "They should have participated in political activity. I don't agree with their military methods, nor with arms as an emblem or path to right social wrongs."[115] A bank employee added, "I didn't agree with their methods. It didn't matter who got in the way of their bombs. Whoever died, died."[116] Finally, a teacher remarked, "I feel negative about the Montoneros in general. They destroyed a peaceful march to national progress. They started a chain reaction of violence."[117]

The Montonero experience was very traumatic for the Argentine working class. The workers felt largely victimized by the consequences of the military reactions that fell largely on them rather than on the young and rather more privileged revolutionaries, who could more easily leave the country or go underground. The *Nunca Más* report made it clear that the majority of the military government's victims were the working class.[118] Historically, the Argentine working class has not been "inclined towards these dramatic displays of 'revolutionary gymnastics,' each of which left a heavy toll of militants jailed, deported, or simply dismissed from work."[119] In a large, well-organized trade union movement, Argentine workers were much more predisposed to a Polish "solidarity" model of union behavior than a *Tupamara* urban or *Guevarista* rural struggle, even against the military regime as ferocious as the *proceso*.[120] And in the last analysis, indeed, it was the CGT that brought down the junta, and not the Montoneros.

Then, too, on the question of the "disappeared" (*los desaparecidos*), while a majority of workers expressed a negative reaction to the *proceso* (60 percent), a bare majority of laborers (51.7 percent) versus a large majority of employees (70 percent) questioned the methods that involved summary kidnapping (and often murder) of targeted victims. A significant 30 percent of the laborers and 18 percent of employees condoned the practices that resulted in "disappearances." Again laborers, more often than employees, were apt to explain the phenomenon in terms of their suspicions that the disappeared must have been, in most cases, violent guerrillas or that "they must have done something" (*algo lo habian hecho*) to deserve "disappearing." Employees were more likely to see the phenomenon as a violation of human rights, an illegal trampling of "due process."[121]

For example, an autoworker said, "I didn't spend the military period so badly; those who disappeared must have done something."[122] A teacher conjectured, "Not all who have supposedly disappeared have [truly] disappeared. Some are alive and out of the country. There were excesses on both sides. The fault is not only with those who repressed people but also with those who made the repression necessary."[123] On the other hand, a telephone employee explained that the disappearances were "a cover to eliminate all opposition. The issue must be kept alive until all people are accounted for."[124] A bank employee said, "It was terribly sad. It hurts me deeply. It didn't hit my family, but had it, I would never rest for a moment."[125]

The years of a "dirty war" of repression and the resulting "disappeared" have left a complex residue. Beyond the passivity ingrained in young workers described earlier, there were also multiple feelings of guilt, denial, and sometimes an ambivalent identification with the message of the military. Their own repression caused workers to distance themselves from both their oppressors and those who, in their opinion, made the oppression in some sense necessary.[126]

However, only 8.2 percent of the workers defended the junta command-ers' claims of innocence during their trials under the Alfonsín administra-tion. Given the overwhelming evidence of criminality marshaled against the military in late 1985, 85.5 percent of the workers felt the convictions were either just (35.5 percent) or too lenient and should have gone deeper into the ranks of the military command (50 percent).[127] A textile worker told me, "[The trials showed that] sadism was in evidence. . . . They were like Nazis really; peoples' homes and identities disappeared as if they were not born and did not live. . . . It was not only a war but a sacking, a pillage, a plunder."[128] A telephone employee agreed. "No, [the trials] were an arranged justice. The Nuremberg Trials in post-Hitler Germany is what I would like to see — something that goes deeper into the ranks of the war criminals,"[129] and a bank employee said, "I don't believe in 'due obedience'; . . . they should have judged more people. You can't ever justify torture."[130] A fellow bank employee put it this way:

> No, they give life imprisonment to a common murderer; yet they give some military men who killed hundreds of persons no more than ten years. The trials of the military were also aimed to pacify the people in terms of what the UCR promised the electorate. The junta should have been treated like common criminals.[131]

Again, laborers showed greater indulgence toward the military than employ-ees; 45 percent expressed satisfaction with the trials, whereas 64 percent of white-collar employees felt the sentences were too lenient and the trials should have gone deeper into the military establishment.

Laborers and employees agreed in overwhelmingly condemning the Argentine military's role in the disastrous Malvinas War against Great Britain, which universally undermined the military government in 1982. The workers were eloquent in their thorough disapproval. Among textile workers we heard these two typical responses: "Thousands of recruits died and three captains died! Before the war, the military had reached rock bottom";[132] "It was an adventure . . . just to put a flag on an island."[133] An autoworker answered, "To have sent kids to their death; the manner in which it was prepared and organized and the lack of matériel and support services was a disaster,"[134] and another said, "As a war it was bad, but as an intention to lay claim to something which is supposedly ours, it seemed correct."[135] A metalworker said:

> That morning when I first heard the communiqué that we had taken the is-lands I felt so happy I cried. After, I felt very hurt when I realized it had been a political maneuver fooling so many people and so many youngsters dying. I guess they had no idea how the British would react.[136]

A light and power worker agreed. "The cause was just, but the military used the war as a screen to hide what was happening in the country."[137]

Among white-collar employees, opinions were similar. A telephone worker said, "They should have conducted it with capable leadership. It was a hurriedly organized war without planning and thought. It was only good in that it defended an Argentine right."[138] From three bank employees came strong condemnations. One said, "If with the support of the United Nations we haven't been able to achieve anything concrete in the last 100 years [sic], how are we to think that, as an underdeveloped country, we can confront militarily the second most powerful country in the West?"[139] Another answered, "It was a drowning man grasping a straw. Luckily they didn't win because we would still have the military in power."[140] Finally,

> It was an absurd war. When it began there were very few British on the Malvinas Islands. One could have believed that with this democratic government the islands could have been ours without violence. But as always in our history someone convinced the military to undertake this stupidity and now the islands are an armed fortress.[141]

In summary, 74.5 percent of all workers condemned the Malvinas War effort as illogical, unnecessary, and politically motivated, while 21.8 percent, even though defending Argentine sovereignty over the islands, faulted the military for its poor preparation, timing, and methods.

Summary

Argentine workers, particularly blue-collar laborers, have maintained their Peronist affiliation and ties, especially in times of troubles when their material bases have been challenged. Employees, on the whole, are more issue-oriented and have a wider world view, and hence tend to be more politically volatile. Like Peronism, unions are partially a way of life for workers; they maintain them in a centrist mode of political behavior that eschews, at the same time, right and left alternatives while organizing them to battle the perennial scourge—inflation. The military was roundly censured as not only repressive and venal in its disregard for human rights but also, along with its oligarchic allies, corrupt and incapable of managing the economy. At the same time, workers fear the sectarian and revolutionary left as precipitating the unleashing of the fanatical right, both military and civilian.

The role of the Argentine state as entrepreneur is under increasing attack by the working class, which more and more sees production and management as the responsibility of the business sector, and which desires to restrict the state's role to one of maintaining equity, order, justice, and a decent level of social welfare—that is to say, to limit it to regulatory, police, judicial, legal, social, educational, and fiscal responsibilities. Workers generally viewed the privatization of inefficient state sectors with equanimity and welcomed foreign investment as a viable and improved alternative to state enterprises, but particularly as a replacement for distrusted local Argentine capital.

7 *Class and Ideology Among Argentine Workers*

> >

The Values of Class

THE QUOTATION from Saúl Ubaldini that opens this book demonstrates the contradictions in workers' conceptions of class identification and the significance of class. The attractions of so-called middle-class pleasures and culture — fundamental ingredients of the Peronist ideology and predisposition — were strongly felt by the Argentine workers I interviewed. The tenets of historical Peronism continue to be principal ingredients in workers' conceptions of themselves. As a light and power worker told me in no uncertain terms, "I'm neither of the left, the right, or the center; I'm a Peronist."[1]

Indeed, as I discovered, a Peronist outlook among Argentine workers was translated into a series of ideological convictions that did not conform to the typical left-right political spectrum. Rather, workers displayed a more complicated and seemingly contradictory orientation — social-democratic on questions of income and social policy, liberal on questions of politics, and even conservative on questions of social structure. Argentine workers, thoughlargely predisposed to Peronist options, did not see this loyalty as a commitment to the left. The traditional association between Peronism and welfare capitalism and social justice for the working class did not presuppose a radical restructuring of society or revolutionary political upheaval to attain these ends.

When asked to classify their political position along a left-right continuum, the Argentine workers I interviewed placed themselves largely in the

center. (See table 34.) Almost two-thirds chose a generally centrist orientation, with laborers tilting slightly to the right and employees slightly to the
left. (The overall average position was somewhat right of center.) Answers to
my questions, however, made it clear that many workers who saw themselves
as center, center-right, and rightist in outlook predominantly sympathized
with Peronism and Radicalism and did not in the least consider themselves
members of the traditional conservative right.[2]

The tendency to the left was generally less common than that to the
right; 23 percent of the laborers judged themselves to be on the right or
center-right, whereas 20 percent of employees saw themselves as on the left
or center-left. There was very little support among laborers for the left or
even center-left when compared to employees, among whom support for the
left (16 percent) was twice that for the right (8 percent).[3] Textile, automobile, and metalworkers predominantly described themselves as center-
right; state light and power workers were in the center; and telephone
workers, bank employees, and teachers, center-left. Again, as revealed by
workers' opinions on a number of major issues, a discernible ideological
dichotomy could be seen between laborers and employees.

Age, gender, and education clearly affected workers' responses about
ideology and class. Younger workers, for example, more often described
themselves as on the center-left of the ideological spectrum and older
workers on the center-right. (See table 35.) Similarly, as shown in table 36,
better-educated workers tended toward the center-left, and those who had
not completed secondary school were often at the center and on the center-
right.

When asked what class they belonged to (see table 37), laborers'
responses were split evenly between the middle and the lower class. (I did
not use the term "working class.")[4] On the other hand, almost four out of
five employees saw themselves as middle-class. (A surprising two out of three

TABLE 34. Workers' Ideological Self-Placement (in percent)

Political Position	Laborers	Employees	Total
Left	3.3	16.0	9.1
Left-center	8.3	14.0	10.9
Center	41.7	42.0	41.8
Center-right	11.7	16.0	13.6
Right	16.7	8.0	12.7
Other	1.6	0.0	1.0
Don't know/no answer	16.7	4.0	10.9
Total	100.0	100.0	100.0
	(N=60)	(N=50)	(N=110)

TABLE 35. Workers' Ideological Self-Placement by Age (in percent)

Ideological Orientation	Under 40	40 and Over
Right, Center-Right	18.5	44.2
Center	55.6	37.2
Left, Center-Left	25.9	18.6
Total	100.0	100.0
	(N=54)	(N=43)

X^2 = 7.540, 2 df, p < .03

TABLE 36. Workers' Ideological Self-Placement by Educational Level (in percent)

Ideological Orientation	Did Not Complete Secondary	Completed Secondary	Some University
Right, Center-Right	41.8	6.7	18.5
Center	45.5	66.7	40.7
Left, Center-Left	12.7	26.7	40.7
Total	100.0	100.1	99.9
	(N=55)	(N=15)	(N=27)

X^2 = 14.352, 4 df, p < .01

Note: Figures do not always total to 100.0 because of rounding.

TABLE 37. Workers' Class Identification (in percent)

Class Identification	Laborers	Employees	Total
Middle class	48.3	77.6	61.5
Lower class	48.3	20.4	35.8
Other	3.3	2.0	2.7
Total	99.9	100.0	100.0
	(N=60)	(N=49)	(N=109)

Note: Figures do not always total to 100.0 because of rounding.

blue-collar textile workers saw themselves as middle-class. However, almost half of the textile workers were married women, so they may have chosen the perceived social class of their husbands.) Women employees in particular saw themselves as more middle-class than males, partially because they tended to be younger and to have more education. (See tables 38 and 39.)

Workers gave multiple reasons for their choice of class position. (See table 40.) Over half focused on levels of *material comfort* as the deciding factor in their reasoning, although (as could be expected) employees differed

TABLE 38. Workers' Class Identification by Gender (in percent)

Class Identification	Male	Female
Middle Class	53.8	89.3
Lower Class	46.2	10.7
Total	100.0	100.0
	(N = 78)	(N = 28)

$X^2 = 9.656$, 1 df, $p < .002$

TABLE 39. Workers' Class Identification by Educational Level (in percent)

Class Identification	Did Not Complete Secondary	Completed Secondary	Some University
Middle Class	54.0	64.7	84.6
Lower Class	46.0	35.3	15.4
Total	100.0	100.0	100.0
	(N = 63)	(N = 17)	(N = 26)

$X^2 = 7.453$, 2 df, $p < .03$

TABLE 40. Workers' Reasons for Class Identification (in percent)

Reasons	Laborers	Employees	Total
Level of material comfort (owning house, car, standard of living, salary level)	67.8	47.8	56.2
Combined material and cultural level	23.7	34.8	28.6
Cultural level, education, outlook, mentality	6.8	45.7	23.8
Other	1.7	0.0	1.0
	(N = 59)	(N = 46)	(N = 105)

Note: Percentage responses do not add up to 100 because of multiple responses.

substantially from laborers in that almost as many employees chose *cultural* factors as material ones.[5] Among laborers, a textile worker told me, "I am in the middle class because the poor barely survive. I can dress, always have enough to eat, and send my children to school."[6] Meanwhile, a metalworker explained, "I'm middle-class because I have a job, a nice family. I can't complain; I have most of what I need. There are others much worse off than me — those would be the lower class."[7] A light and power worker said, "I'm middle-class because of my work and status in society. With sacrifice I have certain comforts that the lower class doesn't have."[8] A telephone employee explained it this way: "I'm middle-class because I continue to enjoy the prerogatives of the middle class—a house, an education, meals, heat, clothing, etcetera. The other day a friend of mine, a union delegate of FOETRA, approached me and said, 'These days we're dying of hunger,' and I said, 'Come on, now, we lunch together every day.'"[9] As a bank employee put it, "I belong to a falling middle class because my resources don't allow me to be in a really middle-class position, but my educational and cultural level and my future prospects put me there."[10]

On the other hand, a metalworker said, "I'm lower-class. I've done nothing yet to classify myself as in the middle class."[11] A bank employee commented: "I belong to the lower class because of the things I don't have and the limitations on my wants such as going to movies and eating out with my three children. Nor have I been able to afford a color television yet,"[12] while a teacher told me, "I am with the lower class because I get up early, take buses to work, work many hours, and am a renter."[13]

In general, laborers tended to associate class position with their level of material consumption, though a sizable minority (almost one in four) saw the definition of class as consisting of *both* material and cultural/educational attainments. On the other hand, employees experience class in terms of their general values and questions of culture and education. For example, two-thirds of laborers mentioned only material consumption as a test of class status, whereas less than half of the employees defined class purely in those terms. Less than 7 percent of the laborers defined class solely in cultural terms, whereas 45.7 percent of employees did so. Thus though a majority of all workers focused on material factors, employees were far more likely than laborers to include culture, education, and a way of looking at the world that was concerned with more than one's immediate standard of living.

The observable difference between laborers and employees concerning class perceptions also emerged in responses to the question, "What changes would you like to see in this country?" Here the most frequent answer among laborers (43.3 percent) spoke of the need for better income distribution, fair wages, retirement benefits, and full employment. On the other hand, 48.3 percent of employees decried the egotism and selfishness among Argentines, their divisiveness, and their lack of civic spirit.[14] Again, laborers focused on the daily struggle for bread-and-butter gains, while employees, despite lower salaries, were more likely to focus on overall issues of culture and society.

Similarly, when asked about the causes of poverty, laborers most often responded that there was not enough employment and work to go around, or they blamed the problem on Argentines' laziness, lack of ambition, or individual shortcomings. (See table 41.) On the other hand, more employees attributed poverty to the lack of a national social policy on income distribution and wages, or to lack of education and cultural opportunities.

A metalworker said that the causes of poverty were "the people themselves. They're too comfortable, not willing to work hard to escape from poverty. They come from the provinces and move into a slum, find some services they didn't have in the provinces, and there they stay."[15] Another metalworker said, "There is a lack of education. For lack of information people lose the opportunity to educate their children. Its a cycle of events that hopefully we'll break with the democracy."[16]

Meanwhile, a bank employee said, "There is not enough work. It's a vicious cycle. There are people who want to work but they aren't given the opportunity to escape from poverty and they are kept marginalized. Also there is a lack of education. It's not the people's fault."[17] On the other hand, a telephone employee answered the question in this way:

At the root of poverty there is always the influence of historic factors that keep our country poor. First it was Spain, then England, and now the United States. Dependency is the reason. Being a colony and especially the destruction and deterioration of industry and the indebtedness contracted during the last military government.[18]

TABLE 41. Workers' Opinions on the Causes of Poverty (in percent)

Causes of Poverty?	Laborers	Employees	Total
Lack of national social policy, poor income distribution, low salaries	26.7	38.0	31.8
Not enough work, jobs, employment opportunities	30.0	16.0	23.6
Lack of educational and cultural opportunities	23.3	24.0	23.6
Laziness, lack of ambition, individual shortcomings	28.3	16.0	22.7
Imperialist foreign policy, dependency, foreign debt	8.3	20.0	13.6
Lack of national economic development	8.3	16.0	11.8
	(N = 60)	(N = 50)	(N = 110)

Note: Percentage responses do not add up to 100 because of multiple responses.

Laborers seemed to focus more on the manifestations of poverty rather than the deeper underlying causes for it. Moreover, more than employees, they saw poverty in terms of individual shortcomings than as an outcome of social policy or economic circumstances. This was associated closely with their personal aspirations and the model of behavior of friends they admired. A respect for strong individualism was still an important value among Argentine laborers. Laborers said, as it were, allow us to find a good job and we will make a go of it and improve ourselves and the prospects for our children. Employees, on the other hand, tended to see opportunities as more problematic and saw economic and social policies less amenable to rapid solution. Again, it was clear that employees, more than laborers, tended to attribute responsibility to faulty leadership and erroneous policies, and consequently were more predisposed to broad and diffuse leftist approaches to social change.

This apparent differentiation between laborers and employees appeared again, though to a lesser degree, on the question of class mobility. The workers were asked, "In your opinion, is it easy or difficult to move from one social class to another?" (See table 42.) This question was widely understood to mean moving not into the middle class, where the great majority of workers already felt they belonged, but into the more exalted ranks of the employers or the landowning classes.[19] Virtually all workers felt that it was impossible to move into the upper class: 90 percent of the laborers thought it "difficult," or "very difficult," to make the transition, whereas 95.9 percent of the employees made that judgment. Only one in ten laborers thought it "easy" to move from one class to another, while only 2 percent of employees held out such hope. Not a single worker thought it would be "very easy" to make the move.

Laborers, curiously, appeared slightly more sanguine about upward mobility than employees, who, having achieved "middle-class worker"

TABLE 42. Workers' Perceptions of Opportunities for Class Mobility (in percent)

Degree of Difficulty	Laborer	Employee	Total
Very difficult	23.3	14.3	19.3
Difficult	66.7	81.6	73.4
Easy	10.0	2.0	6.4
Very easy	0.0	0.0	0.0
Other	0.0	2.0	0.9
Total	100.0	99.9	100.0
	(N = 60)	(N = 49)	(N = 109)

Note: Figures do not always total to 100.0 because of rounding.

status, saw more clearly the barriers to further upward mobility—although in general over nine workers in ten saw it as difficult at best

As to why upward mobility was improbable, a metalworker said, "It's difficult, because as much as I work, a worker can't move from one class to another; that goes for the lower and middle classes."[20] A light and power worker said, "Class divisions are very abstract. Social measures are one thing, economic measures are another. Divisions are fluid. Money is the only divider. There is no social barrier against money. There are economic reasons for educational and cultural advantages."[21] A telephone employee told me, "To move from one social class to another you need pure luck. Into the upper class, no one enters, no matter how hard you work,"[22] while a fellow employee explained it thus: "You just don't pass from one class to another."[23] As a bank employee explained it, "It's easy if you have the means, but the difficulty is having the means."[24] Another said, "To pass from the middle class to the lower class is easy, but to pass from the middle class to the upper class is difficult."[25] Finally, another bank employee answered the question by saying, "By studying or working it is impossible. It is only possible by way of the lottery, luck, corruption, or robbery."[26]

Over three-quarters of the workers saw a rigidity in the class structure separating the *working* class (whether middle-class or lower-class worker) from the *upper* class. This was the view of 71.4 percent of the laborers and 82.5 percent of employees. The single most common answer (25 percent) was that making a class transition was virtually impossible in Argentina simply through a change in wages or salaries. Again, employees were more realistic about the possibilities of upward mobility and saw fewer opportunities than did laborers vis-à-vis entry into the upper sectors of Argentine society.

Unionized workers were also asked this question about class conflict: "Some say that different social classes want different things and enter into conflict with each other. In your opinion, how important is this class conflict in Argentina?" The answers revealed the very complicated conceptualizations of class in Argentina. On the one hand, there was a recognition of the porous boundaries between the lower and middle strata of the working class; on the other hand, workers acknowledged the impregnable wall separating both laborers and employees from the bourgeoisie.

Specific responses followed patterns observed before. Laborers were more likely to describe class differences in individual terms or to ascribe to people generally the same wants and aspirations in life.[27] Employees were more prone to recognize the reality and, in many ways, the inevitability and insurmountability of class differences. However, the idea of class conflict as a mobilizing prelude to class struggle was almost totally absent from all responses. Rather, workers recognized the existence of class conflict, but saw it as a natural phenomenon in all societies and that it was useless to attempt to contravene. Anyway, they felt, it was just a case of those who had made it and those who would like to be in their shoes if given the chance—hardly ammunition for class warfare.

On the extent of class conflict in Argentina, one textile worker commented, "Really, [there is] none; every class can improve their situation without conflict,"[28] while an autoworker explained, "No real class conflict exists; it depends on one's worth and will power."[29] (See table 43.) As a light and power worker said,

> I see it in different resorts. The poor go to Mar del Plata, San Bernardo, Mar de Ajo, Santa Clemente de Tujo, and Santa Teresita; the rich go to Pinamar, Villa Gessell, and Punta del Este [Uruguay]. The boss sees his worker at some beach resort and says, "How did he get here?" and next summer he goes to a more exclusive resort.[30]

A similar awareness of class distancing, but from a different perspective, came from a metalworker. "It shocks me that in the upper social levels with their inheritance, that they get involved in drugs. The rich don't appreciate what sacrifice is. They live an easy life and they lose control. You have to protect your children from that influence."[31]

To the same question, a bank employee said, "[All] classes want the same thing. The upper class wants to keep its level and the lower class wants to attain it."[32] A teacher agreed: "No, there is no class conflict. There are simply those above and those who would like to get there."[33] Finally, another bank employee said, "There have always been class problems. The upper class has always sold out to foreign interests while the lower class has always defended the country."[34]

TABLE 43. Workers' Opinions on the Importance of Class Conflict in Argentina (in percent)

Reasons	Laborers	Employees	Total
Conflict doesn't exist; we all want the same things	38.3	26.0	32.7
Conflict exists between upper class and workers	33.3	34.0	33.6
Conflict exists, but it is a natural phenomenon	21.7	36.0	28.2
Other	6.7	4.0	5.5
Total	100.0	100.0	100.0
	(N = 60)	(N = 50)	(N = 110)

Thus although more than three of five Argentine workers acknowledged the existence of class conflict, only a little over one-third framed the problem in terms of a divergence of class interests.[35] Even so, the overwhelming preponderance of these did not extend this conflict into class struggle beyond the action of various interests pulling and pushing in different directions. Rather, they viewed class differences not as a collective matter but as barriers to individual upward social mobility. The privileges of the bourgeoisie were accepted, if not always without resentment. Argentine workers viewed class conflict as a competition in which they were at some disadvantage — but, nevertheless, one in which the rules of the game allowed room for political and trade union measures aimed at a more equitable and just situation.

Comparing the Values of Liberty and Equality

When workers were asked, "What kind of government do you prefer: populist, military, democratic, conservative, or socialist?" most powerfully endorsed democracy. (See table 44.) Democratic government was the overwhelming favorite among all workers, with populism (the traditional term that often implies Peronism) a distant second, and socialism third. More and more workers (laborers as well as employees) saw no mutual exclusion between the Peronist movement and democratic government, and only a minority of self-described Peronist workers saw Peronism as necessarily incompatible with democracy. Peronists were more likely to be populists than those who identified with the Radical party, who rarely preferred populism; nevertheless, a significant majority of Peronists chose democracy. (See table 45.)

TABLE 44. Workers' Preferred Type of Government (in percent)

Preference	Laborers	Employees	Total
Democratic	68.3	68.0	68.2
Populist	16.7	10.0	13.6
Socialist	5.0	16.0	10.0
Conservative	0.0	4.0	1.8
Military	3.3	0.0	1.8
No preference	6.6	0.0	3.6
Other	0.0	2.0	0.9
Total	99.9	100.0	99.9
	(N = 60)	(N = 50)	(N = 110)

Note: Figures do not always total to 100.0 because of rounding.

TABLE 45. Workers' Preferred Form of Government by Party Identification (in percent)

Government Preference	Party Identification		
	Peronist	Radical	Other
Democratic	68.4	84.2	50.0
Populist	26.3	2.6	11.8
Other	5.3	13.2	38.2
Total	100.0	100.0	100.0
	(N = 38)	(N = 38)	(N = 34)

$X^2 = 22.559$, 4 df, $p < .001$

Again, these responses reaffirmed other results of the survey: Peronist workers who saw themselves as in the center or even to the center-right did not necessarily support a conservative or a military government, but rather a social-democratic government that would maintain a distance from left-revolutionary solutions that implied government intervention into the society and economy.[36] (See table 46.)

When asked to explain their choice, workers overwhelmingly cited traditional Western definitions of democracy: namely, representative government, majority rule, and the safeguarding of civil liberties.[37] This typical response was exemplified by the teacher who said, "Democracy is a means of reaching a majoritarian understanding within a context that allows for dissent."[38] On the other hand, populist responses were represented by the textile worker who said, "Democracy without a good meal is useless,"[39] and the metalworker who said, "Yes, [under democracy] one has more freedom to speak as one feels, do what you want, have a little more liberty, but I don't see its benefits and advantages for a worker."[40]

In general, 57.3 percent of the sample explained their choice in terms of

TABLE 46. Workers' Preferred Type of Government by Ideology (in percent)

Government Preference	Ideological Identification		
	Right	Center	Left
Democratic	69.0	80.4	36.4
Populist	6.9	15.2	22.7
Other	24.1	4.3	40.9
Total	100.0	99.9	100.0
	(N = 29)	(N = 46)	(N = 22)

$X^2 = 17.962$, 4 df, $p < .002$

Note: Figures do not always total to 100.0 because of rounding.

what kind of government would be most representative, would preserve basic civil liberties and freedoms, and would allow for majority rule. More laborers than employees (61.7 to 52 percent) chose this thoroughly democratic option. The second most common explanation (23.3 percent of laborers and 32 percent of employees) evaluated governments as to which was the best for workers and/or the most humane or just (27.2 percent). Only 7.3 percent of workers preferred a government that provided peace and stability and defended society against license—a traditionally conservative response. At the other end, only 4.5 percent of workers opted for a government that was antielitist, assured income equality, and publicly controlled the means of production, a response traditionally associated with the left.

Nor was there any good evidence for so-called working-class authoritarianism, even among the least educated strata of Argentine workers, who are usually said to have this propensity. (See table 47.) Among all workers, regardless of their level of education, democracy was the preferred choice.

Workers were asked to explain how they understood democracy and to explain its advantages, if any. Workers powerfully and eloquently defended democracy and its traditional meaning. Ninety percent mentioned either constitutional guarantees of civil rights and liberties, or full political representation and participation, as the cornerstones of democracy.[41] Two-thirds of laborers focused on these rights, whereas every employee mentioned either one or the other. The few attacks on democracy were focused on (1) its inability to protect society against license and delinquency (11.7 percent of the laborers but no employees said this) and (2) its often regressive socioeconomic policies (mentioned by 6.7 percent of the laborers and 10.0 percent of the employees).

TABLE 47. Workers' Preferred Form of Government by Educational Level (in percent)

Government Preference	Did Not Complete Secondary	Completed Secondary	Some University
Democratic	67.7	76.5	64.3
Populist	15.4	11.8	10.7
Other	16.9	11.8	25.0
Total	100.0	100.1	100.0
	(N = 64)	(N = 27)	(N = 28)

X^2 = 1.758, 4 df, n.s.

Note: Figures do not always total to 100.0 because of rounding.

Thus, though there is a minority view that democracy is too permissive and antilabor, the majority of workers give it solid marks as the best possible political system. Explaining the advantages of democracy, a textile worker said, "The right to your opinion, the participation of people in their government . . . like a home where the children also are allowed to express their opinion."[42] Another textile worker found democracy "where issues are resolved publicly in Congress and where the people are informed — not in isolation or secretly . . . public disclosure above all."[43] A metalworker told me, "[Under democracy] you can go around freely and say what you think; with the military government you had to be so careful — like putting eye drops in your eye."[44] A light and power worker said, "I walk where I want. I speak what I feel and I feel good about things, even though economically life is difficult. Compared to the repression, which is the only other system I really know, it is worlds apart."[45] Several days earlier a fellow light and power worker had said to me, "I have experienced other systems of repression. Now we can walk about freely in the streets, speak freely, even against the government. Hopefully, this will go on for many years and last forever."[46] Another light and power worker agreed: "Compared to other times in my life, the freedom under Alfonsín is greatest. Under Perón you couldn't say what you thought. You could lose your job. If I said I don't like Perón, I'd have had a lot of trouble. Even though I don't like Alfonsín's policies, I can express myself really freely."[47]

On the other hand, a telephone employee put it this way: "Democracy permits you to say everything, but it still limits you in any case. There are still limitations and controls. People believe democracy is full and total liberty, and it's not like that, you know."[48] A teacher argued, "There are no advantages unless it is real social democracy not political democracy."[49] Another teacher agreed: "Formal democracy is basically theater without content."[50]

All in all, the democracy established under Alfonsín was given very high marks among the workers. Asked about the future of the Alfonsín government, more than four of five workers hoped and expected that Alfonsín would finish his constitutional term of office and transfer power to a civilian successor. Less than 5 percent of the workers had any question or doubt about the democratic survivability of Alfonsín's Radical government. Employees were somewhat more cognizant of the importance of preserving a constitutional system (88 percent), although over three-fourths of laborers were also so aware.[51]

Thus the workers' commitment to political democracy was strongly felt and eloquently expressed. However, on questions of social egalitarianism there was much less consensus. To the question, "Do you believe that in this society everyone is equal?" over half the workers said no, that there were recognizable socioeconomic and class differences, even though people were equal in the human and legal sense. On the other hand, 39.1 percent of the workers gave an unequivocal no, saying that people had different capacities, aptitudes, intellects, and personalities, so that full equality was an unattainable myth. Only 8.2 percent of those interviewed emphasized the basic equality of all people in the moral and ethical sense.

A light and power worker put it this way: "Yes; before God and the law, we should all have the same rights and obligations. That doesn't mean a Communist-forced equality. Each person should be judged on his merits."[52] A telephone employee said, "By birth we are all equal, but we become differentiated by social things, money, ideology, etcetera,"[53] while a fellow employee reiterated, "We are equal in terms of rights and duties but economics draws the distinctions."[54] A bank employee said, "Relatively, in terms of citizens' rights, yes, but some are more equal than others."[55] Another bank employee told me, "People are equal, but within the context of Argentina, people aren't equal. There is social and class discrimination."[56]

Employees showed themselves more egalitarian in their views than laborers, 70 percent saying that there were differences but that there should not be—at least not in moral, ethical, and legal terms. Only 40 percent of laborers took this position. On the other hand, 48.3 percent of laborers spoke of the many personal differences among people that make equality impossible, whereas only 28 percent of employees took this position. The laborers were more likely to accept individual human differences, even if these were translated into social advantages. These responses made it clear that in most cases employees had a stronger sense of moral outrage and could be more susceptible to political appeals to redress political and legal inequities through public policies. Laborers, on the other hand, appeared more fatalistic as to the inevitability of individual differences as a source of inequality.

However, there was an overwhelming acceptance of the existence of *social* inequality, whether based in individual, social, or economic differences. To the question, "Are there some people in society who are not equal to you?" 88.2 percent of all workers answered yes. Only 14 percent of employees gave an unequivocal and fundamentally egalitarian answer: no. Among laborers there was an even more minuscule 6.7 percent negative response. Again, this indicates that among this minority of workers, twice as many employees as laborers might favor fundamental changes in social conditions to alleviate inequalities in class structures and relationships.

Workers pointed to many kinds of inequality in Argentina. (See table 48.) A typical reply came from a telephone employee: "Yes, [inequality] is a

TABLE 48. Workers' Explanations for Social Inequality (in percent)

Reasons	Laborers	Employees	Total
Values, personality, and different capacities	50.0	45.8	48.1
Socioeconomic class and cultural inequalities	18.3	33.3	25.0
Membership in privileged groups (the military, the church, landowners, etc.) mark differences	13.3	22.9	17.6
Other	16.7	2.1	10.2
	(N = 60)	(N = 48)	(N = 108)

Note: Percentage responses to not add up to 100 because of multiple responses.

necessary and normal situation. Politics, religion, and other factors differentiate people."[57] And, as a bank employee said, "There is no such society in which everybody is equal in terms of how they think, their opinion, interests, and aspirations."[58] Another bank employee put it this way: "There is a great difference between a person born in a slum and a person born in Barrio Norte [a wealthy residential area of Buenos Aires]; what makes them different is their educational and cultural levels,"[59] And a teacher told me, "Yes, people are different by ambition, chances, and opportunities to study."[60]

Thus laborers were more likely to see inequalities in terms of individual strengths and weaknesses, while employees saw them more as the result of social factors (domination by privileged groups) and larger policy outcomes (unequal educational opportunities). Specifically, textile, automobile, and metallurgical workers were least likely to cite class and cultural conditions as explanations for inequality, focusing instead on differences of personality, while light and power workers and telephone employees represented mixed opinions. On the other side, bank employees and teachers demonstrated the greatest awareness of social barriers.[61]

On the theoretical question of income equality, the overwhelming preponderance of workers (88.2 percent) felt that guaranteeing the same income to all people who work had negative ramifications. The question was framed, "What do you think of the idea that would allow all persons who work to receive the same income?" The most common response (60 percent) was that people should earn different wages and salaries depending on their level of education, expertise, experience, and talent. Only 22.7 percent of all workers thought equal income for all those who work a good idea: 38.3 percent of laborers, and a minuscule 4 percent of employees, supported income equality.[62] Departing from their usual responses to previous questions, employees were much more supportive of income differentials than laborers, of whom a substantial minority saw the whole question in terms of social justice. The employees' propensity to less egalitarianism in wages and salaries was associated with their better education and professional training, which they no doubt felt ought to be materially rewarded.

By and large, there was strong majoritarian endorsement of existing economic differences. In fact, even among laborers, there was strong support for awarding superior income to those who had studied and worked hard.[63] For example, a textile worker told me, "There must be differences in salaries. After all, professionals have burned the midnight oil to get where they are!"[64] A metalworker made a similar point, saying, "No, it can't be like that [equalized income]. Because if one has different talents . . . for example, a machine operator can't earn the same as an engineer who has built a career and whose sacrifice has to result in a reward."[65] A light and power worker agreed; "No, we can't all earn the same. We would lose incentives. But the base salary should be a dignified one."[66]

Among employees, a similar majority consensus on income differences emerged. A bank employee said, "There should be a minimal but just basic wage [that would enable one] to live a normal life, and from that point on there should be steps, but always giving everyone the same opportunities."[67] Another bank employee made a similar point. He said, "No, [equalizing incomes] wouldn't be fair. The wage floor should be fixed at a decent level, but after that, one should be rewarded for studies, ability, and aptitude."[68] Meanwhile, a teacher said, "No, there has to be a social pyramid. A worker can't earn what a manager earns. I as a worker cannot expect to earn what President Alfonsín earns."[69] A colleague agreed, "Certain differences are necessary based on responsibilities and contributions [to society]."[70]

Although workers acknowledged income differentials as a reward for industry and education, their overall commitment to democracy and liberty, and their opposition to an elitist society with advantages reserved for a minority of well-placed groups, was incontestable. To the question, "In your opinion, are there any groups in Argentina that have too little power?" there was strong sentiment that the working class (primarily) and the poor (secondarily) had too little power relative to other groups in Argentina. (See table 49.)

When we combine responses naming the working and lower classes as having too little power with those naming the poor and indigenous groups (i.e., Indians), we see that over four out of five workers perceived of themselves and those below them on the social scale as having too little power in Argentine society.[71] Even the middle class was cited by 2.7 percent

TABLE 49. Workers' Opinions as to Which Groups Have Too Little Power in Argentina (in percent)

Groups	Laborers	Employees	Total
Working class, lower class, certain unions	48.3	50.0	49.1
Poor and marginal people, slum dwellers, the unemployed	30.0	24.0	27.3
Indigenous people (Indians)	5.0	6.0	5.5
Other	6.7	26.0	15.5
Don't know or no answer	18.3	6.0	12.7
	(N = 60)	(N = 50)	(N = 110)

Note: Percentage responses do not add up to 100 because of multiple responses.

as not having adequate power, grouping them with such obviously disadvantaged social groups as the handicapped, and retired persons (all classed as "Other" on table 49). Who, then, has power in Argentina? Responses to the question, "In your opinion, are there any groups in Argentina that have too much power?" are given in table 50.

Workers had a clear idea of which groups in Argentina had too much power — adding to the traditional "feudal" estates (the large landowners, the military, and the church) a fourth group: powerful industrialists. However, laborers differed from employees as to the relative power of the church and the industrial hierarchy. Blue-collar workers cited wealthy landowners, the military, and Argentine industrialists — but not the Catholic church — as

TABLE 50. Workers' Opinions as to Which Groups Have Too Much Power in Argentina

Group	Laborers	Employees	Total
Large landowners, the wealthy class, the oligarchy	40.0	50.0	44.5
The military	31.7	34.0	32.7
Catholic church	8.3	34.0	20.0
Large industrialists	15.0	16.0	15.5
Government officials	6.7	10.0	8.2
Foreign capitalists	3.3	12.0	7.3
CGT	3.3	10.0	6.4
Other	3.3	2.0	2.7
Don't know or no answer	20.0	6.0	13.6
	(N = 60)	(N = 50)	(N = 110)

Note: Percentage responses do not add up to 100 because of multiple responses.

having too much power. Even higher numbers of white-collar employees mentioned landowners, the military, and domestic industrialists, and 34 percent of employees also saw the church as too powerful. Interestingly, laborers took an extremely benign view of foreign industrialists, particularly as compared to the homegrown variety.[72]

A strong antagonism toward the Catholic church on the part of employees was an outstanding difference between them and laborers. This correlated with workers' religious identification; 80 percent of the laborers, but only 62 percent of the employees, considered themselves practicing Catholics. A sizable 34 percent of employees did not consider themselves religious, whereas only 11.7 percent of laborers put themselves in that category.[73]

On the other hand, employees were three times more likely than laborers to single out foreign capitalists and their own trade union confederation, the CGT, as having too much power. And as we saw earlier, foreign capitalists and the Argentine trade union movement received good marks among workers generally. Moreover, workers did not see the government itself as a major power center group when compared to social groups with power to manipulate the government: large landowners, the military, Argentine industrialists, and the Catholic church.

These perceptions about who had too much power conformed generally to the workers' answers to the question, "Who runs Argentina?" (See table 51.) Again, the Argentine working class saw the landowning upper class as the dominant political power in the nation. Argentine industrialists were

TABLE 51. Workers' Opinions as to Who Runs Argentina (in percent)

Groups	Laborers	Employees	Total
Large landowners, the upper class, the oligarchy	36.7	44.0	40.0
Large industrialists	20.0	14.0	17.3
Leading government officials	18.3	8.0	13.6
Foreign interests, the IMF, international banks	3.3	22.0	11.8
The military	8.3	10.0	9.1
Catholic church	6.6	8.0	7.3
Political parties	1.7	4.0	2.7
CGT	0.0	2.0	1.0
Other	1.7	6.0	3.6
Don't know or no answer	18.3	0.0	10.0
	(N=60)	(N=50)	(N=110)

Note: Percentage responses do not add up to 100 because of multiple responses.

singled out as the second major wielder of power. The government came in third because, obviously, a share of the workers believed that it did "run" the country or that it made key political decisions in Argentina. (It is important to remember that this question was not framed as to who had too much power but what group was the dominant *center* of decision making.) This accounts for the lower ranking of the military in answers to this question relative to previous questions, and obviously also reflects the fact that the military had been recently ousted from power and replaced by a civilian democratic government. The wording of the question also accounts for the low rating of the Catholic church, which, again, does not overtly make policy decisions.

What remains clear was the workers' perception that the power to make decisions was in the hands of the landowning oligarchy. (They also possibly saw the military as a surrogate of these landowning interests.) Similarly, by a ratio of almost 7:1 over laborers, a substantial minority of employees perceived that the IMF and international banking circles exercised political power over government decisions. And in the last analysis there was overwhelming recognition by workers that the CGT did not run Argentine society but merely reacted to other power centers' policy initiatives.

On questions of civil liberties and freedom, Argentine working-class attitudes were essentially marked by tolerance and respect for others. Over 99 percent of the workers saw no problem in people of all races, nationalities, and religions living together in Argentina. Although racial differences are few in Greater Buenos Aires, some ethnic, nationality, and (to an extent) religious differences may be discerned. Nevertheless, throughout my interviews, with a couple of rare exceptions, I heard no religious or ethnic slurs. As a means of soliciting any ethnic-religious aspersions or latent fear or suspicion of one or another minority group, I asked the workers, "Is there any group that should be prevented from occupying important positions in society?" With no appreciable difference between laborers and employees, 69.1 percent responded that no one should be denied that right. The only prominent groups to be singled out as potentially dangerous were criminals, delinquents, and antisocial elements, mentioned by 5.5 percent of the workers.

Continuing to mine this vein, I asked, "Is there some group in Argentina that would take advantage if they enjoyed too much freedom? [If so,] who?" (See table 52.) One metalworker looked with suspicion on "the shameless ones (*los sinvergüenzas*) and those who don't want to work. To prevent license, one's rights end where another's rights begin."[74] For a phone employee, "The deviants, rapists, violators would take advantage,"[75] while a bank employee commented, "That's our sickness—always some group trying to

TABLE 52. Workers' Opinions as to What Social Groups Might Take Advantage of Too Much Freedom (in percent)

Groups	Laborers	Employees	Total
Antisocial delinquents, drug addicts, pornographers, sex offenders	53.3	28.0	41.8
No group	11.7	24.0	17.4
The military	8.3	18.0	12.7
Left-wing guerrillas	16.7	4.0	10.9
The oligarchy, large landowners	8.3	12.0	10.0
Right-wing paramilitary groups	8.3	10.0	9.1
Other	15.0	24.0	19.1
Don't know or no answer	13.3	2.0	7.3
	(N = 60)	(N = 50)	(N = 110)

Note: Responses do not total to 100 because of multiple responses.

occupy greater space of action if they can. The military, especially, and the large landowners are examples of this."[76]

On the other hand, an autoworker replied, "Either all or none; none more or less than the other; none would take particular advantage. That's the roots and nature of liberty to allow all to mobilize and act freely."[77] A bank employee said, "No, there are always excesses. Democracy is a very difficult equilibrium to reach. You have to keep trying, no matter what,"[78] and a teacher added, "None, that's liberty; debate will regulate the excesses. Extremism is usually caused by absence of true liberty."[79]

A respect for fair play and civil liberties seemed strongly rooted among workers. They cited as "dangerous" only groups they associated with transgressions against duly constituted law. The sole exception was the landowning oligarchy — but even then, hostility toward landowners seemed to be associated with their violations of the constitution in their propensity to welcome military intervention as a means to have their way when civil procedures fail them. As indicated by previous responses to the questionnaire, laborers had stronger fears than employees about the stability of their neighborhoods and society in general, fears that came across in their greater focus on threats from antisocial elements and left-wing guerrillas.[80] Employees appeared to have greater respect for the absolute practice of civil liberties in all areas of society.

In the final question about class and ideology, I asked the workers, "Some people say that there should be more freedom than there is now; others think that there should be less. What do you think?" (See table 53.) A textile worker responded, "Liberty is fine; license, no; . . . for me Argentina is still in diapers because of the years of de facto military governments."[81] A

**TABLE 53. Workers' Opinions as to Whether Argentines Should Have More
or Less Freedom (in percent)**

Desired Degree of Freedom	Laborers	Employees	Total
Neither: fine as it is now	68.3	66.0	67.3
Less: too much freedom causes crime	25.0	14.0	20.0
More: there is never enough freedom	5.0	20.0	11.8
Other	1.7	0.0	0.9
Total	100.0	100.0	100.0
	(N = 60)	(N = 50)	(N = 110)

metalworker said, meanwhile, "We aren't prepared for much liberty. One
has to be careful with liberty. Because of that you have all the violence at the
soccer stadiums. Liberty has to be well controlled."[82]

On the other hand, a light and power worker told me, "Liberty is special;
one must defend it, but not abuse it either; one has a great appreciation of
liberty after the *proceso*,"[83] while a fellow worker said, in a fashion
reminiscent of John Stuart Mill, "Liberty is very important for experimenta-
tion of ideas, for example sex education, but not for selling drugs at a kiosk.
Liberty is always at risk. It depends on what issue and in what area."[84] A
bank employee told me, "The equilibrium at the moment is fine. After the
dictatorship there was first an explosion of freedom, but now it's finding a
good medium."[85] Finally, a teacher explained, "Liberty is always wonderful.
It cannot be limited in any way."[86]

Almost four of five workers supported the levels of freedom maintained
under the Alfonsín government or sought even greater freedom, while only
one in five felt there was too much freedom and that license threatened
social conventions and authority. Employees were particularly more em-
phatic in wanting even more freedom—one of five took that position—
whereas one of four laborers supported less freedom, focusing on "law and
order," as it were.[87]

Workers' educational level was very significantly correlated with values
that were truly concerned with infringements on liberty in Argentine
society. (See table 54.) This came across very clearly in workers' support for
freedom, which rose in proportion to the workers' years of schooling. It was
interesting that workers who were libertarian were consistently those who
expressed antimilitary views, as well as a general antagonism to the "dirty
war" and the "disappearances." (See table 55.) Also, it was significant that
those workers who said they were not religious also were most libertarian on
any number of questions.[88] (See table 56.)

TABLE 54. Workers' Opinions as to Whether Argentines Should Have More or Less Freedom, by Educational Level (in percent)

Desired Degree of Freedom	Did Not Complete Secondary	Completed Secondary	Some University
Neither: fine as it is now	65.6	70.6	71.4
Less: too much freedom causes crime	29.7	17.6	0.0
More: there is never enough freedom	4.7	11.8	28.6
Total	100.0	100.0	100.0
	(N=64)	(N=17)	(N=28)

$X^2 = 18.005$, 4 df, $p < .001$

TABLE 55. Workers' Opinions about Those Who "Disappeared" Under the Military Regime, by Views on Desired Degree of Freedom (in percent)

Question of "Disappeared"	"Should Argentines Have More or Less Freedom?"		
	Neither; Fine as It Is	Less	More
Negative	77.0	55.0	92.3
Positive	23.0	45.0	7.7
	(N=74)	(N=20)	(N=13)

$X^2 = 6.463$, 2 df, $p < .04$

Summary

Class consciousness among the Argentine working class was largely expressed in survey responses as demands for improving the lot of laborers and employees under more benign forms of welfare capitalism. It was channeled heavily into working within the political process through institutionally organized labor union pressures. Employees more than laborers expressed diffuse ideological grievances against the social system and therefore were potentially far more likely to endorse systemic challenges to the status quo. By the same token, white-collar employees were ideologically further to the left than laborers and showed a stronger sense of political pluralism and all it entailed. Yet blue-collar laborers' views were not conservative by any means and were very cognizant of the state's obligations toward social justice and better working conditions. Thus there were substantial areas of overlap between the two groups that united all elements of the Argentine working class.

TABLE 56. Workers' Libertarianism by Religosity (in percent)

Desired Degree of Freedom	"Are You Religious?"	
	Yes	No
Neither more nor less; fine as it is	68.3	68.0
Less	25.6	0.0
More	6.1	32.0
Total	100.0	100.0
	(N=82)	(N=25)

X^2 = 16.983, 2 df, p < .001

Further, the Argentine working class seemed very amenable to a rational coalition based on solid technological agreements between the Argentine government and foreign capital. They objected strongly to the speculative practices of Argentine businessmen and their inhumane treatment of workers on salary and wages. They were dubious about the productive potential of state enterprises.

Peronism in 1985–1986 continued to be the ideological anchor of many workers who considered themselves centrist, left, or right. Workers were centrist in their adherence to a mix of privately fueled capital development and state-administered social programs; leftist in endorsing a social-democratic vision of giving the working class a better share of national wealth; and rightist in advocating controls on destabilizing forces that might threaten their homes and communities. Whatever their political predispositions, however, pluralism and democracy have taken hold of Argentine workers like no other ideological beliefs—beliefs intensified by almost a decade of violence and repression prior to 1983.

IV

Theoretical Retrospective

8 *Argentine Workers and the Question of Class Consciousness*

The Meanings and Boundaries of Class

MARX IS STILL our best source for defining the essential economic difference between capitalists and workers as they are embedded in the social fabric. He wrote of the dramatically different place of each in the productive process. On the one hand, workers sell their labor as a form of commodity for a specific exchange value conceded to them by the capitalist as money. In return, capitalists obtain value-producing labor which enhances the productive and, importantly, the reproductive powers of capital.[1]

Marx's admirable depiction of class differences is less useful, however, as an explanation of the formation of class consciousness. His writings are replete with theoretical conceptions of workers as a class having overlapping rational, cohesive, and fraternal bonds that will inevitably lead them to attack and collectively triumph over capitalist control of the means of production.[2] In fact, at one point in *The 18th Brumaire of Louis Bonaparte*, Marx restricts the concept of class itself to those who can act collectively and coherently in their own common interests through organizational ties; at the same time, he describes the individualist peasants as so "many potatoes in a sack." He goes on to say, "In so far as a purely local connection only exists among the smallholder [peasants] and the identity of their interests fosters no community spirit, no national bond and no political organization among them, they do not form a class."[3]

Lenin perceptively reinterpreted Marx's concept of an objectified and collectivized historical class consciousness by positing more solid and specific socioeconomic and political conditions that would precede its awakening. Lenin revised Marx's predictions on the basis of his immersion in the actual conditions facing the Russian work force. Lenin understood very well the mélange of working-class wants that only from a great distance could be seen as comprising an overriding ethical sense of class justice or a humanitarian form of collectivism.

Aware of these contradictions, Lenin wrote that the working-class struggle is often fought against state corruption, landlord brutality, police repression, intellectual and religious persecution, the humiliation of soldiers, and so on. All of these grievances, including many that are not necessarily economic ones, nevertheless provide the real common ground on which workers may come together to pursue mutual goals.[4] It is important to remember that both the Cordobazo insurrection of 1969 and the post-Malvinas street demonstrations in 1982–1983 were expressions of a combination of antibureaucratic, antimilitary, and broadly conceived social grievances sparked by student outrage in the Cordobazo and by popular revulsion at the military's cynicism and corruption in the latter uprising.

In another place, Marx's insight into the nostalgic desire of the nineteenth-century working class to recapture the spirit of artisan life of early capitalism seems to catch the essence of the working class in general, and contemporary Argentine workers in particular, better than any effort to see this class lurching forward to create new social structures. And again, distinct from Marx's other characterizations of the proletariat,[5] Argentine workers, especially laborers, share with the bourgeois class a respect for nationhood, law, morality, religion, family life, private property, high culture, citizenship, civil liberties, and freedom.

These apparently contradictory departures of actual workers from their theoretical counterparts make it necessary to rethink the very idea of class in existing country contexts. E. P. Thompson understood the complexity of working-class consciousness when he wrote,

> The class experience is largely determined by the productive relations into which men are born—or enter involuntarily. Class consciousness is the way in which these experiences are handled in cultural terms: embodied in traditions, value systems, ideas and institutional forms. If the experience appears as determined, class consciousness does not.[6]

There are of course struggles in which workers participate. But it is doubtful that they participate strictly as a class or that class interests are paramount or even identifiable by them. Przeworski writes, "Individuals occupy places within the system of production; collective actors appear in struggles at concrete moments of history. Neither of these, occupants of places or participants in collective actions, are classes. Class is the relation between them, and in this sense class struggles concern the social organization of such relations."[7] As we have seen among Argentine workers, class differences are not automatically translated into class consciousness. Consciousness is derived from actual political struggle.[8]

Marx's understanding of precapitalist class structures included a multitude of shaded distinctions. He and Engels wrote in the *Communist Manifesto*, "In earlier epochs of history we find almost everywhere a complicated arrangement of society into various orders, a manifold gradation of social rank. In Ancient Rome we have patricians, knights, plebeians, slaves; in the Middle Ages, feudal lords, vassals, guild-masters, journeymen, apprentices, serfs; in almost all of these classes, again, subordinate gradations."[9] Though Marx had reason to emphasize "two great hostile" classes facing each other, he was aware of the subtleties of class divisions even under capitalism. In his critique of David Ricardo, he wrote about the "continual increase in numbers of the middle classes . . . situated midway between the workers on one side and the capitalists and landowners on the other . . . [who] rest with all their weight upon the working basis and at the same time increase the social security and power of the upper ten thousand [the bourgeoisie]."[10]

Marx was also conscious of the internal differences within the working class, such as between laborers and state employees and commercial workers. Though all were exploited under the capitalist system, he observed, only laborers were directly tied to the source of the physical production of surplus value and thus were strategically very critical. In *The Civil War in France*, Marx wrote of the "state parasites, richly paid sycophants and sinecurists in the higher posts, who absorb the educated members of the masses and turn them against themselves in the lower places of the hierarchy."[11]

However, to incite workers to change, Marx abandoned his more sociological reading of earlier historical periods. Marx recognized that eventually serfs raised themselves into membership in the feudal community, that during late feudalism members of the petty bourgeoisie rose to the bourgeois level. Yet workers under capitalism were denied these aspirations and possibilities.[12]

Revolution or Reform?

One's perception of the revolutionary imperatives of the condition of the working class apparently depends on one's form of analysis. The more ethical and philosophical one's interpretation, the more likely it will be to have revolutionary implications; a sociological or anthropological interpretation could more readily imply a need for reform.

To posit the inevitability of revolution, one must depict a crisis of profound dimensions — as Marx did in his early writings. In *The Economic and Philosophical Manuscripts*, Marx described a worker misshapen by capitalism, confined to a feeble and slavish existence.[13] These conditions cried out for sweeping changes. A notable assessment of the necessity of revolution is found in Marx's *Contribution to the Critique of Hegel's Philosophy of Right*, in which he wrote that a class must be formed that has radical chains — that it is subject to universally shared suffering.[14] Thus workers were predestined to revolt and throw off their shackles, Marx concluded. As he argued in *The Holy Family*, they need not even fully understand the historical role they will have to play:

> It is not a matter of what this or that proletarian or even the proletariat as a whole *pictures* at present as its goal. It is a matter of *what the proletariat is in actuality* and what, in accordance with this *being*, it will historically be compelled to do.[15]

The proletariat is alone and isolated, wrote Marx. It must reshape society in its own image.[16] Thus inevitably the old order must and will be replaced by a new society, with workers in the lead. This scenario is prescribed in *The German Ideology*.[17]

A belief in the separateness and self-sufficiency of the proletariat was best exemplified in the early twentieth century by Rosa Luxemburg. Time and again she wrote of the heroic capability of a revolutionary working class to take control of bourgeois society's vast means of production: industry, business, and land. Mere reformism and democracy, according to Luxemburg, only strengthened and consolidated the power of capitalism. The day-to-day struggles of the working class in themselves cannot result in social transformation.[18]

With the failure of democratic forms of socialism in the West, among them the Rosa Luxemburg-led Spartacus uprising of 1918, Marxist critiques of society were directed more and more toward capitalism's successful attempts to coopt and channel workers' authentic needs and wants — by manipulation and the imposition of cultural norms, by encouraging consumerism, and by providing certain material rewards. This was the message of important social philosophers such as Georg Lukács, Antonio Gramsci, Wilhelm Reich, and Herbert Marcuse, among many others.[19] Lukács depicted the particular way in which this subjugation occurs; Gramsci described the penetration of bourgeois culture into other levels of society;

and Marcuse spelled out the losing struggle of the working class to become a revolutionary agent in the West.

Lukács was particularly strident in depicting workers as still subjugated by immediate and momentary interests, as opposed to developing the more consequential mediated and long-term interests of class that were eventually bound to emerge. He was particularly impressed by the reification of everyday commodity relations, which he said had the power of "subjugating men's consciousness." But he thought that workers would eventually shake off the virus of consumerism to achieve the emancipation predicted by history.[20]

Gramsci,[21] Reich, and Marcuse predicted the suspension and postponement of proletarian socialist revolution in the West because of the panoply of agencies of cooptation available to modern bourgeois culture. Gramsci described the complexity of values among even the humblest of citizens and the need for revolutionary ideologues to address these seemingly contradictory mass sentiments.[22] Gramsci's contemporary Wilhelm Reich, in a similar vein, wrote that socialism would be achieved only by satisfying the immediate needs of the masses.[23]

Marcuse forcibly makes the point that after the development of post–World War II capitalism, technology provided certain creature comforts that essentially obscured the evidence of capitalist domination, while democratic processes allowed people to "move up" and help consolidate the social system.[24] Marcuse thus shifted his hopes away from the West's industrial proletariat to that of the underclass and lumpen elements and, possibly, to the Third World work force. Finally, Michael Burawoy best exemplifies the "waiting for Godot" school of predictions of working-class revolution. Burawoy contends that within imperialist structures workers will eventually revolt against the oppression of the international capitalist production process, as well as against overall social exploitation, which he calls "hegemonic despotism."[25]

Yet within socialist theory there is another strand that has always approached revolutionary upheavals with caution and skepticism. Marx himself was sometimes wary of the inevitable repercussions of attempted proletarian uprisings. In *Class Struggles in France*, he wrote with sadness and regret of the June 1848 massacre of 3,000 workers[26] and again in *The 18th Brumaire of Louis Bonaparte* he wrote of the social isolation of the defeated proletariat.[27]

Moreover, Friedrich Engels wrote to a friend in 1886, "One or two million votes . . . in favor of a workers' party acting in good faith, are actually infinitely more valuable than a hundred thousand votes obtained by a platform representing a perfect doctrine."[28] But it was Engels's friend Eduard Bernstein whose *Evolutionary Socialism* best epitomized this strand of democratic socialism. His analysis of the Germany of the last decades of the nineteenth century led him to question the necessity for working-class revolution. He observed that the growth of the German Social Democratic party and its electoral successes had been translated into parliamentary representation. These developments occurred alongside the increasing strength of trade unions and what he perceived to be the workers' rising share of income, greater working-class ownership of land and stocks, and workers' gradual integration into respectable bourgeois society.

Bernstein believed that although the forms of capitalist production remained essentially the same, the distribution of wealth and the legal protection of the laboring classes had been substantially enhanced through social legislation—a direct consequence of trade union and socialist party pressure.[29] These gains had been made without revolution. In Bernstein's words:

> No one has questioned the necessity for the working classes to gain the control of government. The point at issue is between the theory of social cataclysm and the question whether, with the given social development in Germany and the present advanced state of its working classes in the towns and country, a sudden catastrophe would be desirable in the interest of social democracy. I have denied it and deny it again, because in my judgement a greater security for lasting success lies in a steady advance than in the possibilities offered by a catastrophic crash. . . . The conquest of political power by the working classes, the expropriation of capitalists, are no ends in themselves but only means for the accomplishment of certain aims and endeavors. . . . And as I am firmly convinced that important periods in the development of nations cannot be leapt over I lay the greatest value on the next tasks of social democracy, on the struggle for the political rights of the working man, on the political activity of working men in town and country for the interests of their class, as well as on the work of the industrial organization of the workers.[30]

Bernstein had to defend himself against charges that he had disavowed socialism entirely and that he had opted for a revisionist opportunism. To these accusations he replied:

> I have extraordinarily little interest or taste for what is generally called the final goal of socialism. This aim whatever it be, is nothing to me, *the movement everything*. And by movement I understand not only the general movement of society, that is, social progress, but political and economic agitation and organization for effecting this progress.[31]

The goal for Bernstein and his democratic socialist followers became social and economic justice without a blueprint. Several decades later, under the shadow of German Nazism, Wilhelm Reich wrote, "The ultimate aim of socialism can only be achieved by fulfilling the immediate aims of mass individuals, by ensuring a much greater degree of satisfaction of their needs. Only then can revolutionary heroism occur in the *broad masses*."[32]

In the contemporary period, Alec Nove most adequately summarizes this belief in incremental socialism. He writes, "By aiming for an unattainable 'workers' power,' by indulging . . . in 'dreams of general emancipation,' one fails to devise means by which workers can in fact exercise their power as consumers and as producers, means which are inevitably limited by practical possibility."[33]

Beyond Class

The Argentine case, I think, shows that it is inappropriate to view a certain alienation on the job complemented by indulgence in forms of consumerism as evidence of a lack of social consciousness on the part of workers. Though it may indicate the absence of *class* consciousness as a prelude to revolution, it by no means rules out awareness of class differences. Labor conflicts in Argentina are most successful and most appealing when they oppose erosion of consumer power, a rising cost of living, and a relative decline in wages. These economic downturns imply a decline in workers' ability to appropriate social and individual needs.

The working-class need for higher wages is as self-evident as a desire for better education, which is linked to economic advancement. Consumerism on the other hand is a controversial question in socialist theory. The evidence from my interviews with Argentine workers seems to support the notion that consumption (beyond a subsistence level) is a means for attaining human satisfaction. For example, a worker's purchase of a home can be viewed as overconsumption, or it can be seen as furthering a worker's independence and autonomy from the landlord. Automobiles might be seen as superfluous consumption, or they can be seen as strengthening the Argentine worker's ability for new experiences through greater mobility, individualized travel, and wider opportunities for recreation. The desire to equip one's home with electronic equipment can be viewed as slavish conformity and conspicuous consumption, but such products can also be seen positively (and more accurately, I think) because of the educational and cultural emancipation they represent, not to mention their capacity to give pleasure. In these ways the Argentine working class can translate consumption into autonomy, recreation, and the pursuit of what it is to be human.[34]

Lenin, depicting workers' spontaneous demands under the czar in *What is to be Done?* wrote, "[The] 'spontaneous element' in essence, represents nothing more or less than consciousness in an embryonic form."[35] Possibly the gratification of specific personal, economic, and educational needs are all workers ever seek as individuals. Yet pressure to fulfill such personal demands forms the basis of collective measures taken against injustice and unfairness, whatever the sustaining ideological fabric of the social system. Going beyond these desires to participating in organized and widespread upheaval to achieve social change is usually a decision of a revolutionary sect, the intelligentsia, or party bureaucrats.

Are such extensions of basic human needs ever explicitly desired by the supposed beneficiaries of that upheaval? In the only case of Marxist-led democratic socialism in Latin America — Chile before 1973 — Peter Winn writes, the militant revolutionaries who took over the Yarur textile plant under Allende tended to be better-educated student-workers with a visionary outlook.[36] The dichotomy between student intellectuals and workers was demonstrated before and after the Tiananmen Square massacre in Beijing in June 1989. As one worker made clear, he was hesitant about taking part in the demonstrations because he feared losing his job. "If there are going to be arrests, he said, the police will arrest citizens [read *workers*] before students."[37]

Further, events under both capitalist and socialist systems in the late 1980s indicated that, for workers, moral and material needs are closely linked and cannot be rigorously separated. A Cuban dissident, speaking of the absence of material incentives to worker productivity in Cuba, wrote, "Benefits that can only be perceived through a social consciousness that has not yet been created cannot serve as stimuli for production; rather, the worker requires individual incentives even if part of the surplus value is to be reinvested in the common good [health, education and social services]."[38] An East German who escaped to West Germany via Hungary and Austria explained, "I can't explain all the thoughts that were behind the decision to leave. The situation where I came from had reached a point where there seemed to be no reason for remaining, no hope for improvement in my life. Now, I'm going to stay with relatives and get a job, I'll work, save some money, get a car and an apartment. For now, that's all I want."[39] Another example comes from Neil Kinnock, head of the British Labour party. Arguing with a firebrand socialist colleague, he said, "What are we to say to a docker who has a house, a microwave and vacation in Marbella? Let us take you out of your misery, brother?"[40]

Beyond the issue of consumerism, however, the Argentine case also calls into question Marx's denial of supraclass sentiments like nationalism and ethnic pride among the working class. Marx was originally responsible for separating the concepts of *class* and *nation*. He and Engels wrote in the

Manifesto, "The Communists are further reproached with desiring to abolish countries and nationality. The working men have no country. We cannot take from them what they have not got."[41] Again, in the *18th Brumaire*, Marx attempted to argue that the proletariat are not bound by ties of "property, family, religion and order," as if these values were alien to the working class.[42] Marx minimized the countless ties and values that the proletariat shared with the bourgeoisie even a century and a half ago,[43] and there are even more innumerable interclass connections today.

At the very least, it has been readily apparent (since the monumental failure of the Second International to resolve this question during World War I) that working-class struggles are often expressed politically as nationalism. Lenin's success in carrying off the Bolshevik Revolution was due precisely to the fact that he understood and used the national question in the pursuit of peace and the defense of the Russian workers' immediate interest in employment and the basic necessities of life—food, land, and liberation from oppression.[44] For his part, Lenin was supremely conscious of nationalism and ethnicity as supplementing class as inspirations to struggle against state power. Central to an understanding of Lenin's idea of revolution is his attack on those who called the Irish national rebellion against Great Britain something less than a revolt.[45]

Historically, the abstract concept of *class*, in and of itself, has not been enough to identify a social group without the addition of other, no less important, concerns and frustrations that bind people together. In this Gramscian tradition, Przeworski writes,

> Classes are not a datum prior to political and ideological practice. Any defi-
> nition of people as workers—or individuals, Catholics, French speakers,
> Southerners, and the like—is necessarily immanent to the practice of politi-
> cal forces engaged in struggles to maintain or in various ways alter the exist-
> ing social relations.[46]

When workers have thrown in their support during a revolutionary upheaval, their motive has usually been to compensate for material deficiencies. "The triumph of the extreme left is associated in most workers' minds not with 'abolition of the wage system,'. . . but with the material income allegedly denied them by capitalism and capitalists."[47]

As I discovered in my survey, the enemy is not capitalism as such but those who employ its rewards in selfish and extravagant ways that appear irresponsible to workers on salaries and wages. Although the Argentine working class recognizes class differences (mainly those between the upper class and the rest of society), this does not translate automatically into an "us" and "them" situation. Workers merely want some of the things that are denied them under present capitalist arrangements. This type of belief concerning the manifestations of capitalism rather than its structural underpinning remains the complicated reality for most Argentine workers. And it does no good to attribute these views to "false consciousness" (thus eventually redeemable), as have doctrinaire Marxists. As Raphael Samuel writes, Communists generally "allowed no space for contradictory class locations or status discontents. [They] pathologized social mobility."[48] Antielitism is a much more anchored view for Argentine workers than the sense of an ongoing class struggle.

Conflicts over Distribution

Historically, there is accumulating evidence that Argentine working-class agitation has been antielitist and antiestablishment rather than anticapitalist. Charles Bergquist writes, "Argentine economic nationalism focused its critique not on the social basis of ruling-class power, but rather on the legitimacy of the cosmopolitan liberal oligarchy that exercised political domination over Argentine society."[49] This was nowhere more evident than in the makeup of the street demonstrations in support of Perón in the city of La Plata in 1945. As Daniel James indicates, the laborers attacked the symbols of elite society — the university in La Plata, *La Prensa* (the newspaper that was recognized as representing the interests of the agrarian upper class), the elite Jockey Club and other exclusive sports clubs such as Gimnásia y Esgrima, as well as other opulent cultural and commercial institutions. "[The marchers] . . . deliberately crossed the university campus, chanting slogans like 'alpargatas si, libros no!' and 'less culture and more work!'"[50] As I have said, the organized left was patronizing toward this kind of sponta-neity that emerged during early Peronism. Even though these masses, the lumpen of 1945, became the cannon fodder for anti-Peronist demagoguery after Perón's fall, and also the "victims" of union bureaucracies since the 1960s, their impulse remained antielitist not anticapitalist. As Alvaro Abós puts it, they were always workers of one kind or another,[51] and as such part of the system.

Because the target was elitism not capitalism, the intermediary that channeled worker discontent by organizing workers into a party and into unions was Peronism, not the left. Peronism was the workers' means of economic redress, social status, and access to political power. Perón's political emancipa-tion of the Argentine worker (he also extended voting rights to Argentine women in 1949) was in a way anticipated a century ago by Friedrich Engels as he discussed Bismarck's extension of the German voting franchise:

The irony of world history turns everything upside down. We the "revolutionaries," the "rebels"—we are thriving far better on legal methods than
on illegal methods and revolt. The parties of order, as they call themselves,
are perishing under the legal conditions created by themselves. They cry de-
spairingly, . . . "legality is the death of us"; whereas we, under legality, get
firm muscles and rosy cheeks and look like eternal life. And if we are not so
crazy as to let ourselves be driven into street fighting in order to please
them, then nothing else is finally left for them but themselves to break
through this legality so fatal to them.[52]

Eduard Bernstein took Engels's view a step further toward democratic
socialism by affirming that the compromises that democratic capitalism
allowed could bring progress. In fact, he called democracy the "high school
of compromise." Certainly, he admitted, in early stages of capitalist development workers would be freely choosing their own "butcher," but over time,
with the increase in educational and cultural opportunities, the electoral
process would serve them well. It has indisputedly done so in Argentina, at
least when electoral mandates have been respected. By their force of
numbers alone, Bernstein felt, workers could transform governments into
responsible representatives of the people.[53]

Even Bernstein's longstanding political enemy Rosa Luxemburg admitted that the close connection between a democratic socialist party and an
aggressive trade union base among workers could be positive. She believed
further that the trade union movement must be the economic arm of the
socialist party, even as the party was the political arm of the trade union
movement. Thus, forging a union-party nexus was an essential first step in
creating a revolutionary climate.

Rather than her revolutionary prognoses, it is Luxemburg's appraisal of
the situation under democratic forms of capitalism that sheds light on the
historical Peronist party–trade union connection in Argentina. Of course,
Luxemburg, like Lenin, worried about the unions accepting the bourgeois
rules of the game and continuing to be satisfied with piecemeal handouts. Yet
in the case of the German unions (repeated in the Argentine case),
Luxemburg saw that the antiregime ideology had to come from the
interaction between political socialism and the necessarily economist needs
of trade union organizations.[54] In this the Peronist connection has served to
politicize Argentine unions at the same time that the party's dependence on
working-class votes has forced political leaders to respond to workers'
desires and needs.

Because of this relationship, Argentine workers have managed to make
real gains by joining the electoral process; at the same time, they have
continued to hang on dearly to their labor organizations—a loyalty that has

been especially important when the government's executive powers have been seized by undemocratic and unfriendly regimes. The post-1984 Ubaldini leadership within the CGT has understood these situations very well, and has successfully blended political shrewdness with labor activism to achieve results. The historical connection between the "62" and the Peronist party and the impact of the "25" on the Peronist political platform and nomination procedures have been combined with the use of general strikes to fortify the image of militancy that stirs the imagination of the rank and file. Though not always successful, as my survey indicates, the combination of negotiation, politicking, and confrontation seems appropriate in the Argentine context. Ubaldini did not cultivate, under the democratic administration of Alfonsín, simple trade union consciousness (against which Lenin himself railed), nor did he try to implant the revolutionary consciousness that Rosa Luxemburg aspired for workers. Rather he furthered a political consciousness that combined workers' day-to-day interests with fundamental interests of the working class.

Marx made it clear that absolute misery and poverty among workers were not necessarily the prerequisites of socialist revolution. In fact, he had only words of support for the concrete gains that workers' organizations had accomplished by the 1870s. He spoke of the constant historical struggle between laborers as a collectivity and the capitalist class concerning the extension and limits of the workday and the conditions under which work is carried out.[55] He joined workers in celebrating their interim and incremental gains. (Of course, his revolutionary prognosis was that in the inevitable future struggle over state power, workers would emerge victorious.)

Even Bernstein believed that the laborer's instinctual struggle for fairness was aimed at the core of capitalism itself. He wrote, "The fight regarding hours of labor is similarly a fight over the profit-rate. If the shorter day of labor does not directly cause a diminution in the amount of work done for the wage given hitherto . . . yet it leads by a side way to an increase in the workers' demands for better conditions of life, and so makes a rise in wages necessary."[56] While Rosa Luxemburg argued that class struggle required two essential ingredients — first, to put limitations on the levels of capitalist exploitation within bourgeois society, then to abolish the bourgeois system of exploitation altogether[57] — it is the former strategy that has universally stood the test of circumstances and time. Harry Braverman, though critical, observed this trend decades later when he wrote that increasingly the working philosophy of Marxism had shifted from a critique of the mode of production to a critique of the mode of distribution.[58]

Peronism has been the major antiestablishment force in Argentina, though the movement has remained wary of revolution. Workers in Argentina have seemed to understand their role in society as crucial without believing that they are capable of fomenting alternative visions of society. On a daily basis, they view the labor movement as the appropriate agency for resistance and struggle. For the majority of the working class, the trade union structure is *political* because it has survived even when Peronism was outlawed and the CGT was their primary means of expressing opposition to repressive civil and military governments. The historical Peronist coalition made up of workers, the church, entrepreneurial sectors, and the armed forces shows a continuing propensity that is more ecumenical than exclusionary. These multiclass lessons of early Peronism are still part and parcel of contemporary working-class values.

Proletarians without Marx

With Engels, Marx wrote in the *Manifesto*,

> The proletarians cannot become masters of the productive forces of society, except by abolishing their own previous mode of appropriation, and thereby also every other previous mode of appropriation. They have nothing of their own to secure and to fortify; their mission is to destroy all previous securities for, and insurances of, individual property.[59]

Argentine workers often see themselves in class terms but not as a special class, a destined class, a class above all classes, nor as the *only* class with *unique* problems, needs, and aspirations. Thus this Marxian recipe does not acknowledge the inherent contradiction in their feeling that they belong within a social system they are supposed to destroy.

As the survey has shown, the workers of Argentina do not see themselves in homogeneous or monolithic terms but rather as heterodox among themselves and conciliatory toward other social sectors of society. They don't feel they have the answers, and therefore they expect to share power, not to monopolize it. Built into their notion of society is the inevitability of conflict and competition, with conciliation as the operative force. The Argentine working class sees elements of conflict between classes, expressed as competing class interests; however, they do not translate it into class warfare. Nor does it necessitate a violent change of class differences or obliterating the rungs of the ladder that society has provided and offered to them as individuals.

They believe that what is needed in order to "make it" is better opportunities rather than a revolutionary overhaul of society, which they perceive as perhaps jeopardizing their own interests. They do not share

Marx's sentiments in his address to the Communist League in 1850: "For us it cannot be a question of changing private property but only of destroying it, not of smothering class antagonisms but only of wiping out classes, not of improving society but of founding a new one."[60] The Argentine working class does not believe that socialism is necessarily in their interest, nor that capitalism is necessarily not in their interest. Rather, Argentine workers seem to understand innately what Joseph Schumpeter once wrote: "The labor movement is not essentially socialist, just as socialism is not necessarily laborite or proletarian."[61]

Historically, social change has always been very slow and complicated. And it is critical to remember — though Marx never emphasized this fact in terms of explicit time spans — that the so-called capitalist revolution was not a rebellion or a revolution in the sense that we use the term today, but an evolving political process of bourgeois empowerment that paralleled the changing economic configuration of European societies. In that sense it was an evolving transformation that had no finite beginning and appears to have no foreseeable end. In fact, there is increasing evidence that twentieth-century socialist experiments are essentially powerful regime penetrations into society in order to speed up national economic development in an overall capitalist world culture.

In many instances during early capitalism, fractions of the bourgeoisie allied themselves with extrabourgeois forces, to one degree or another, from time to time. These types of class alliances often could not have been predicted.[62] It should come as no surprise that the working class today also demonstrates little social homogeneity or ideological consistency or that extraclass alliances for workers are possible. More important, neither the bourgeoisie nor the proletariat ever acted as a definable, concrete class entity, collectively giving birth to a new social system. The belief in such monolithic action seems to be a social science abstraction that is not rooted in the complexities of historical social reality.

When there have been violent ruptures of social institutions and processes (mainly during the twentieth century), they have usually been fomented by organized minorities of professionals and intellectuals with the support of armed cadres and militias — exactly the types of individuals that Lenin believed were essential for carrying off any revolution in Russia. For twentieth-century revolutionaries, quite distinct from Marx, seizing and controlling the means of production has been a strictly political question and not one of historical economic materialism. Because, according to theorists, the socialization of the means of production requires a radical break with the capitalist political structure — liberalism, fascism, or whatever — it has always implied a series of voluntarist and political blows that would rip away the means of production from the capitalist owners. There is little evidence that the working class as a whole has wanted to do this. The majority have *demonstrated* but not revolted. That they have been amenable to social and political change is clear, but that they have been willing *active agents* of revolution is much less clear.

One of the problems of Marxist interpretations of history and culture is the assumption that only bourgeois revolutionary changes are predicated on some interested material base, whereas a socialist transformation is predicated on a the existence of a (mythical) overwhelming majority of people who are united by no particular material interests. It is as if the metaphor of the full circle of socialist unanimity is taken literally so as not to allow any irregularities or divisions. Thus, this type of Marxist interpretation represents powerful circular reasoning. For example, although in *The German Ideology* Marx understands perfectly the mixed nature of presocialist capitalist development, he nevertheless suspends his analysis in order to predict a final, unanimous, and decisive struggle—a struggle that will be more radical because it is supposedly the negation of all previous societal classes and conditions.[63]

In 1895, shortly before his death, Engels accepted the notion (with some skepticism) that it is continuously activist minorities rather than *classes per se* that create radical changes over and above the norms and dispositions of the workers involved. Whether he was beginning to perceive *socialist* minorities within the same historical process is still open to conjecture.

> All revolutions up to the present day have resulted in the displacement of one definite class rule by another; all ruling classes up till now have been only minorities as against the ruled mass of people. A ruling minority was thus overthrown; another minority seized the helm of state and remodeled the state apparatus in accordance with its own interests. This was on every occasion the minority group, able and called to rule by the degree of economic development, and just for that reason, and only for that reason, it happened that the ruled majority either participated in the revolution on the side of the former or else passively acquiesced in it. But if we disregard the concrete content of each occasion, the common form of all these revolutions was that they were minority revolutions. Even where the majority took part, it did so—whether wittingly or not—only in the service of a minority; but because of this, or simply because of the passive, unresisting attitude of the majority, this minority acquired the appearance of being the representative of the whole people.[64]

Compounding the problem are the Marxian assumptions that social stratification, exploitation, and the alienation of working people, present since biblical times, can, with the onset of socialism, be suddenly superseded.[65] This was not the case in feudal or capitalist patterns, nor is there any evidence that it is happening under modern social experiments, even if we consider various existing forms of socialism as radical departures from capitalism. Schumpeter, a half a century ago, detected that the belief that it could was a leap of faith among Marxists: "In fact it was a bold stroke of analytic strategy which linked the fate of the class phenomenon with the fate of capitalism in such a way that socialism, which in reality has nothing to do with the presence or absence of social classes, became by definition, the only possible kind of classless society, excepting primitive groups."[66]

Marx had actually little to say about the political mechanisms that would guide the evolution of the disappearing classes and state. Other than his eulogy to the Paris Commune, there is no full-fledged treatment of that question.[67] In other words, there is no assessment of the *politics* of socialism. What we have rather are two predictions that the final social upheaval — namely, the communist revolution — would unalterably abolish previous modes of production and state patterns of authority. In one of Marx's most categorical writings on the subject, *The German Ideology*, he said,

> The proletarians, if they are to assert themselves as individuals, will have to abolish the very condition of their existence hitherto (which has, moreover, been that of all society up to the present), namely labor. Thus they find themselves directly opposed to the form in which, hitherto, the individuals of which society consists, have given themselves collective expression, that is, the State. In order, therefore, to assert themselves as individuals, they must overthrow the State.[68]

In this piece there is an explicit commingling of the necessary connections between wage labor, classes, social structure, and the state — all of which are condemned to abandonment.

On the other hand, in analyzing existing forms of socialism, Nove points to the powerful persistence of productive specialization among economic units, specialization among people, horizontal division of labor, and vertical hierarchies in the organizational chain of command.[69] Not even a small socialist society like Cuba, where moral incentives are more finely honed and where full political participation is apparently openly required, has found that it could manage without capitalist social structures. Recent decades have made it plain that Cuban labor unions are not authentic working-class institutions. Their leaders tend to see their function as more mobilizational than representational, more emulative of elite workers than helpful to the average laborer, more directed to enhance efficiency and productivity at all levels than to protect workers' rights, more interested in promoting workers' cultural and technical capabilities than acting for their material demands, more ready to collaborate with management than to take a combative or adversarial stance.[70] A 1987 study by Linda Fuller found that the unions' major role in Cuba is perceived as not promoting worker power but instead stimulating worker productivity in ways very reminiscent of capitalism.[71]

Gramsci saw clearly that the ultimate oppression even under relatively politically free democratic bourgeois societies was to be found in the work setting. Here the relationships are "those of oppressor to oppressed, of exploiter to exploited, where freedom for the worker does not exist, where democracy does not exist."[72] This has changed in the last fifty years, but not as fundamentally as one would have thought. The tyranny of the factory and office is still a reality. Power holders in both the West and Eastern bloc countries exploit working people through their control of the means of production. At the moment an apparently irreversible trend allows surplus value to continue to be funnelled for corporate and/or state interests and social responsibilities. If anything, there was considerably more cynicism on the part of the working class in Eastern Europe because of the elements of official ideology that belie worker exploitation and also because of the dearth of political options, commodity choices, consumer outlets, and the limited sphere of the private world.

Workers' alienation from their labor and what they produce also remains with us as an inevitable feature of modern society, whether capitalist or socialist. We recall from chapter 5 Marx's stirring words from *The German Ideology* that under communism a person will hunt in the morning, fish in the afternoon, rear cattle in the evening and criticize after dinner, without ever becoming a hunter, a fisherman, a herdsman or critic.[73] This romanticized notion of a life that probably never was and is unlikely to ever be sets standards and beliefs about the nature of work that cannot survive scrutiny. Nove perceptively commented that Marx's utopian sketch more accurately describes the pursuit of hobbies than work. Rewriting this picture in the modern context, Nove says, would be like saying, "Men will freely decide to repair aero-engines in the morning, fill teeth in the early afternoon, drive a heavy lorry in the early evening and then go to cook dinners in a restaurant, without being an aero-engine maintenance artificer, dentist, lorry driver or cook. Then it looks a trifle nonsensical, does it not?"[74]

As we saw in my Argentine survey, feelings of alienation that come from routinization, repetition, boredom, and lack of autonomy on the job are part and parcel of most people's working experience. Thoughtful procedural changes and task assessments that could alleviate these problems, ranging from time sharing to job rotation, still would not abolish lingering feelings of subordination and lack of control over one's labor or the workplace.

Marx himself described these feelings in the days before public and union policies ended some of the most onerous physical burdens of factory labor. His is still the best description we have of the psychological dimensions of alienation.[75]

The Anatomy of Class Conflict

Historians have never recorded a massive, direct, dialectically clear class conflict. Rather, we have seen and experienced many smaller conflicts representing competing interests that over time have brought certain reforms and evolutionary change. Often class questions are disputes over income needs translated into material and cultural pursuits based on conflicts over small-scale productivist questions in the factory and on the land. Rarely are these conflicts concerned with questions that penetrate the consciousness or capture the imagination of masses of people. Yet these inevitable material conflicts and grievances can form the basis of the larger struggles that encompass ethnic and national questions. As Wilhelm Reich stated in the 1930s and Adam Przeworski echoed fifty years later, since ideology and politics have an autonomous impact on class formation and struggles, simply focusing on individuals' positions in the relations of production is not a sufficient basis of analysis.

The Argentine working class is naturally reformist, but its latent hostility toward elitism is always ready to be sparked into confrontation. While predicting a proletarian revolution, Lukács accepted that "the deed of the proletariat can never be more than to take the *next step* in the process. Whether it is 'decisive' or 'episodic' depends on the concrete circumstances, but in this context, where we are concerned with our knowledge of the structure, it does not much matter as we are talking about an unbroken process of such disruptions."[76] Hobsbawm resolves the apparent paradox in calling a labor movement (such as Argentina's) "reformist" despite its militancy against injustice in this way:

> To identify the labor aristocracy in its period of glory with a moderate and reformist labor movement remains correct. Such strata could be politically or socially radicalized when their position was threatened or undermined. This is what has happened in the 20th century, which is why the classic Marxist analysis of the labor aristocracy, whatever its relevance for the 19th century, plainly ceases to be useful after 1914 except, paradoxically, for the opposite purpose to the one for which it was originally devised.[77]

Thus one often sees labor mobilized on behalf of lost gains, or a decline in the standard of living, or a reduction of political influence. The Argentine case in point is the Cordobazo uprising of 1969. Daniel James writes of the Córdoba workers:

> They were able to mobilize their membership and adopt a political role which challenged the regime and advocated a socialist revolution. Yet, this mobilization was based largely on a loyalty toward the combativity and honesty of the leaders rather than on specifically ideological factors [read *socialism*]. The consciousness-raising function of the union was, in these circumstances, of very limited success. For most of this period the discrepancy between the political pretensions of the militant leadership and the political loyalties of the rank and file remained muted.[78]

As I have noted before, the militancy that fostered the Cordobazo uprising, did not come from the verticalist sectors of the Peronist movement but instead from prestigious, charismatic union leaders who happened to represent revolutionary and leftist political parties. It was their moral and ethical standing as incorruptible labor leaders and not their political affiliation on the left that was critical to these events.[79]

Conclusion

So work we must, as Argentine workers understand. The challenge is to protect one's dignity and one's environment on the job. The nature of work has changed, and so has the Argentine working class, which is more complex and varied than ever before. Despite their overarching agreement on the larger question of their place in the social structure, Argentina's workers as a class may be divided by party loyalties, union affiliation, region, gender, age, and other sociological factors. Though Argentine workers share many aspects of life, still a common denominator is that they must work to live and they have little control over the important means of production in society.

As Bernstein said almost a century ago, even though the working class have more in common among themselves than the "people" of 1789, nevertheless their individual needs and interests are multiple, and would be so even if the propertied and governing classes were thrown out of power.[80] Bernstein was the first to predict that no society would be able to abolish the ensuing conflicts. And with the continuing existence of such conflict, adversarial politics will continue to rear its head. Marxism has placed too much faith in a future symmetry. As Donald MacRae wrote,

> One of the ambitions of the political left is always that after the necessary change, the transformation of society by enlightenment, or reform, or revolution and catastrophe, all ancient opposition will be healed. Law and Will,

Male and Female, Town and Country, shall be at best, made one — at worst, be reconciled. The romantic exile will return home. Antique evil and injustice will cease. The oppositions of class will be ended. Nature and Art (or artifice or science) will be united; and the noble savage will also be the natural sage.[81]

As we have seen, many of the principal tenets of communist theory, going back to the *Manifesto* itself, are incompatible with Argentine workers' view of themselves and their world. The communists' traditional calls for the abolition of private property and inheritance, the centralization of credit, the collective ownership of agricultural lands, the equal obligation of all to work at comparable tasks and to receive like remuneration, the abolition of all social distinctions — none of these theoretical goals sits well with the Argentine working class. None seems compatible with the more ephemeral, short-range needs and aspirations of their daily lives.

In words reminiscent of Wilhelm Reich, Erik O. Wright analyzes the obstacles to building socialism:

The difficulty of such a task is that immediate interests are real; they are not merely mystifications, false consciousness. A viable socialist movement cannot deny the importance of immediate interests, but must adopt strategies which attempt to join immediate and fundamental interests in such a way that the organizational capacities of the working class are strengthened rather than weakened in the process.[82]

Echoing Lenin, he continues,

Revolutions occur not when the masses of the people are willing to abandon all immediate interests for the prospect of realizing fundamental interests, but when the struggle for immediate interests begin to coincide with the struggle for fundamental interests.[83]

Thus revolutionary socialists in Argentina are left without an explicit historical agent — that is to say, *the* working class. There is no longer a manifest message, nor even an exact carrier of a message. Perhaps, as Bauman writes, the left must learn to accept "that the values promoted by the bourgeois revolution need to be defended only by exposing the mechanisms that prevent their fulfillment."[84] It is important to take Argentine workers as human beings. That is the best way to enshrine them as a class. They are neither devils nor angels. Bernstein wisely once wrote that he had come across socialist writings depicting workers as totally immature and in need of salvation, and then, further along, other passages that attributed all culture, all intelligence, and all virtue to the working class.[85] These attitudes derail the real work of democratic socialism — to achieve social justice and fairness.

This goal was well summarized recently by an Italian editor active in the Communist party. He said that he had suffered many political disappointments during his life. But having been a committed communist had given him "something no one will ever be able to take away from [him], something that . . . is important for any man: a capacity for indignation and rebellion."[86] The Argentine working class would applaud.

9 *Workers and Democratic Political Culture*

"Our life is more than our work"[1]

The Argentine Working-Class Context

ARGENTINA IS NOT beset, as many Third World and Latin American nations are, with racial, ethnic, and religious conflicts. Differences exist, but they have not caused the deep-seated divisions that sustain economic and political differences elsewhere. Wealthy industrialists and landowners, professionals, middle-class workers, and laborers are not clearly definable by factors other than income and schooling. Levels of culture and education have continued to outpace general social development, resulting in a large economically active sector that absorbs large elements of the work force. Indices of modernity—levels of consumption, sophistication of media communications (electronic and print), health care, school enrollments, and access to culture—have militated against the formation of strict class divisions. Cultural mechanisms, particularly in Greater Buenos Aires, have produced a broad social coherence that militates against deep chasms among middle-class workers and laborers.

As indicated by census figures, and confirmed in my survey, a high proportion of Argentine workers are homeowners (although some structures are rudimentary). Wide-scale home ownership further emphasizes the sense of interclass overlap that weakens social polarization. The proletarians without property that Marx described are in the minority in Argentina. Further, workers have much in common with the bourgeoisie in family relations; modern industrialization has not, as Marx wrote, "stripped [them] of every trace of national character." Nor is it true that "law, morality, religion are . . . so many bourgeois prejudices behind which lurk in ambush just as many bourgeois interests."[2] Rather, workers accept the principles of bourgeois liberal economics and the legal and ethical system that has grown with it. Marx would find among today's Argentine workers little support for "the abolition of bourgeois individuality, bourgeois independence and bourgeois freedom,"[3] even though those values have redounded disproportionately, since the writing of the *Manifesto* a century and a half ago, to the benefit of those who control money, property, and the means of production. Though it is clear that Marx perceived the ownership of private property to be the direct root cause of social alienation,[4] he misjudged its universal appeal among all classes.

Workers as Citizens

Marx, like de Toqueville, correctly understood that the strength of the bourgeois system lay in the creation of antifeudal, republican forms of society in which the bourgeois message could penetrate all corners of society without inhibition.[5] But what for Marx was a charade that rudely subjugated the worker was for de Toqueville a qualitatively different order of things that forever altered the life of the working classes:

> As opulence ceases to be hereditary, the distance, both in reality and in opinion, which heretofore separated the workman from the master is lessened every day. The workman conceives a more lofty opinion of his rights, of his future, of himself; he is filled with new ambition and new desires, he is harassed by new wants. Every instant he views with longing eyes the profits of his employer; and in order to share them he strives to dispose of his labor at a higher rate, and he generally succeeds at length in the attempt.[6]

Eduard Bernstein, at the end of the last century, indeed documented some of these sociological changes among the working classes of Western Europe. As absolute income rose and property ownership became more dispersed among the general population, so did political aspirations. Particularly acute was Bernstein's response to Marx's belief that the worker had no homeland with which to identify. To the contrary, he wrote,

> The worker, by the influences of socialism, moves from being a proletarian to a citizen. The workman who has equal rights as a voter for state and local councils, and who thereby is a fellow owner of the common property of the nation, whose children the community educates, whose health it protects, whom it secures against injury, has a fatherland.[7]

The material process of development under capitalism from proletarian to citizen was seen by Bernstein's Marxist detractors (among others, Plekhanov and Luxemburg) as indicating a capitulation to a "Philistine" position: the social integration of workers was seen to be an abandonment of strong moral and ethical concerns. Bernstein's defense against these charges focused on the ease with which such judgments were made by persons "born in the bourgeoisie," who could already enjoy the very things to which workers aspired.[8]

Rosa Luxemburg understood at the turn of the century that greater consumption and access to small-scale property on the part of workers did not significantly alter the means of production. Since that time, however, her alternative democratic visions, such as organizing the work process in some other way than allowing a minority to control production, investment, and state economic policy, have not emerged. Luxemburg minimized the basic democratic values that still survived under advanced capitalism and underestimated the system's attractiveness for the working class. And more to the point, she refused to accept that the very struggles of the working class are not incompatible with democratic capitalism, even though the means of production remains outside workers' control.[9]

As Habermas acknowledged, all members of modern capitalist society share the same civil law, the same basic rights to personal freedom, and the same essential political rights as citizens.[10] Moreover, in some ways, our very definition of what it is to be modern — our sense of social change, openness to new experiences, multiplicity of opinions, access to information, educational and occupational aspirations — are linked to social changes that occurred under capitalism.[11] The private realm of the worker is freer; there is greater room for the expression of dissident opinions; and in some spheres workers are viewed as citizens as much as producers. Outside of their jobs, writes David Halle, "Most workers contrast what they see as a certain fluidity in their lives outside the workplace with their considerably more restricted lives at work."[12]

Argentine Workers and the Democratic Capitalist Culture

Competition and individual initiative, which we have somehow attributed to the rise of capitalism even though these imperatives surely existed in modified forms before, is apparently universal — east and west, north and south. A Hungarian metalworker, Miklos Haraszti, tells us,

> Competition, in one form or another, is part of our lives. It follows us into our homes and makes us slaves. Look at the main interest of the majority:

football [soccer] a competitive sport. . . . By identifying with a particular
team each of us trains himself for competition . . . factory slang is dominated
by the language of competitive sport: "to deliver a knockout," to "run it
into the ground" and so on.[13]

After seventy years of Soviet socialism, a respect for personal initiative has
survived, apparently undiminished. Natalya Dyachenko, attempting to
organize a charity project in Moscow, discovered that "for so many years,
people here have been taught to believe that if a man is unlucky, if he is
homeless, if he falls on hard times, then it is his own fault. The public is not
quite ready to accept our work."[14] In Brazil, Lula (Luis Inácio da Silva), the
Workers' party's unsuccessful presidential candidate in 1989, analyzed his
previous defeat in the election for mayor of São Paulo in 1985:

> My initial slogan was "Lula, former laundryman, former lathe operator with
> a fourth-grade education." People like to do better than that. So our campaign
> was actually a step backward. Instead of being positive and upbeat, showing
> that a worker could run for office, we tried to paint a negative picture.[15]

For Argentine workers, socialism implies a dictatorial end to democracy,
not a communal solution to the problems of capitalism. They see the imposition of economic centralization by authoritarian political means as a greater
menace than the existing ills and inequities of capitalism. Rather, like
members of other social sectors, workers find gratification in many features
of capitalism. The political consciousness of the working class seems to
involve self-determined values that are not tied to the manner in which
people earn a living. In other words, social freedom and autonomy, competitiveness, consumerism, and love of leisure are not necessarily evidence of
bourgeois cultural penetration but rather of universal desires. The fulfillment of these desires, in most instances, is the real aim of working-class and
union struggles.

As history shows, working-class mobility and choice made greater gains
under capitalism than under earlier economic systems, as Marx himself
readily understood.[16] Modern capitalism is more receptive to democratic
challenges concerning workers' goals than are existing socialist experiments.
Moreover, capitalism—which began, according to Marx, as late as the
eighteenth century—is still maturing. It could continue to evolve for several
more centuries, with inevitable pluses and minuses. The Roman Empire
declined over the course of centuries, and feudalism survived a millennium.
Authentic socialism is likely then to come about through a long process of
many smaller and larger challenges to the fundamental inequities of capital
rather than through hammer blows aimed at state power that do not ensure a
better road to democratic socialism.

Worker as Entrepreneur

Marx in the *Manifesto* had explained that workers under capitalism "really wish to return to the vanished status of the workman of the middle ages."[17] Elsewhere in the *Manifesto*, Marx acknowledged the importance of private property to the happiness and well-being of the petty artisan and small peasant under early capitalism. Marx admitted a connection between personal property and independence, but predicted that these freedoms would fade under deepening capitalism.[18] Marx returns to this theme later in *The German Ideology*:

> Thus there is found with medieval craftsmen an interest in their special work and in proficiency in it, which was capable of rising to a narrow artistic sense. For this very reason, however, every medieval craftsman was completely absorbed in his work, to which he had a contented, slavish relationship, and to which he was subjected to a far greater extent than the modern worker, whose work is a matter of indifference to him.[19]

Working in totally different political and economic contexts, David Halle (speaking of North American chemical workers) and Miklos Haraszti (discussing Hungarian metalworkers) describe the same desires that often burst forth in the regimented factory setting. For example, Hungarian metalworkers steal free time during and after work to make "homers," objects made of scrap metal that they cut, grind, and mold into trinkets, gadgets, and tools for home use or as ornamental gifts for family and friends. Haraszti writes:

> The tiny gaps which the factory allows us become natural islands where, like free men, we can mine hidden riches, gather fruits, and pick up treasures at our feet. We transform what we find with a disinterested pleasure free from the compulsion to make a living. It brings us an intense joy, enough to let us forget the constant race: The joy of autonomous, uncontrolled activity, the joy of labor without rate-fixers, inspectors and foremen.[20]

The Argentine workers I interviewed also demonstrated desires for a more creative, autonomous, independent existence. Rather than being symbolic of a petty-bourgeois malignancy, their attitudes reiterated Marx's own notion of the venality and suffocation of regimented working life. Striving to own one's own business (common among Argentine workers),[21] seems to be more indicative of a drive for democratic autonomy than for capital accumulation. With hard work and long hours, the workers I talked to felt they could thrive with a small enterprise, developing and reinvesting in it. A willingness to sacrifice to get ahead was the personal trait they most admired in other people. While they were working purely for wages and salaries, their progress seemed blocked.

As previously indicated, a large minority of Argentina's economically active population are entirely or partially self-employed: many work in the informal, underground economy, while others hold a second job.[22] Thus Argentine workers combine self-interest with ascertainable values of autonomy and freedom.

Under East European socialist governments up to 1989, the same values were espoused. For example, Joseph Konrad and Ivan Szelenyi wrote in 1979,

> The workers, who thought that socialism meant the abolition of exploitation, do not understand why they cannot work as independent small producers, or in family productive units, or as members of cooperatives organized and run on a basis of free, voluntary association, in which no one is exploited and where they could still earn more than in the great state enterprises where they must produce four or five times their wages in order to support (among others) an overblown administrative apparatus which supervises them and disciplines them to achieve higher production.[23]

The Worker as Consumer and Property Owner

In *The 18th Brumaire of Louis Bonaparte*, Marx grudgingly acknowledged the political factors that led to Louis Bonaparte's populist reign—factors which involved values of order, peace and tranquility, family, and protection of property.[24] Liberal democracy in contemporary times has had a far better record of defending these areas of interest than has authoritarianism of either the right or left. These values, essentially outside the work experience, are crucial in assessing working-class lives. Marx, in both the *Manuscripts* and *Capital*, plainly felt that under capitalism the worker's vital functions are fulfilled outside of work and the production process. This seemingly contradicts his own notion that workers under capitalism have no way of realizing certain independent values or of enriching their lives by the appropriation of certain goods on a certain level. Thus, despite Marx's disclaimer,[25] workers appear to have much "to secure and to fortify" under capitalism.

The commodification of the worker as a factor of production is undeniable, but yet, at the same time, a fair remuneration for labor allows the worker a measure of control and well-being in personal life. The circulation of commodities develops an endless series of economic and commercial exchanges that can be monitored and modified under conditions that protect political freedom and civil liberties. Paradoxically, consumerism also inhibits some of the negative consequences of the commodification to which Marx refers by giving workers the basic means by which to carve out private areas of physical and psychological satisfaction. Only by romanticizing the potential creativity of work in modern times can one believe that life outside work is more routine than the work experience itself. The idealization of what labor *might* be led Marx to describe, in terms provocative to this day, the travail of working life. "The worker feels himself to be freely active only in his animal functions — eating, drinking and procreating, or at most also in his dwelling and in personal adornment — while in his human functions [working] he is reduced to an animal. The animal becomes human and the human becomes animal."[26]

In the twentieth century, as my survey of the Argentine working class highlighted, workers have increasingly staked out private existences that are far more palatable than their working lives. Though writing about different milieus, both André Gorz and Eli Zaretsky have found that contemporary workers are increasingly able to fulfill existential needs in private, autonomous pursuits not directly related to their work experience. For Gorz, authentic autonomy is relegated to what one does for oneself without undue outside pressure and compulsion. His commentary, though it focuses on the West European wage earner, is also appropriate for today's Argentine worker:

> Essentially, the "freedom" which the majority of the population of the over-developed nations seek to protect from "collectivism" and the "totalitarian" threat, is the freedom to create a private niche protecting one's personal life against all pressures and external social obligations. This niche may be represented by family life, a home of one's own, a rock garden, a do-it-yourself workshop, a boat, a country cottage, a collection of antiques, music, gastronomy, sport, love, etc. Its importance varies inversely with the degree of job satisfaction and in direct proportion with the intensity of social pressures. It represents a sphere of sovereignty wrested from a world governed by the principles of productivity, aggression, competition, hierarchical discipline, etc. Capitalism owes its political stability to the fact that, in return for the dispossession and growing constraints experienced at work, individuals enjoy the possibility of building an *apparently* growing sphere of individual autonomy outside of work.[27]

And, speaking from a North American context, Zaretsky confirms the assessment that personal life and human relationships, separated from the direct control of productive life, have become ends in themselves.

> Introspection intensified and deepened as people sought in themselves the only coherence, consistency, and unity capable of reconciling the fragmentation of social life. The romantic stress on the unique value of the individual

began to converge with the actual conditions of proletarian life, and a new form of personal identity developed among men and women, who no longer defined themselves through their jobs. Proletarianization generated new needs—for trust, intimacy, and self-knowledge, for example—which intensified the weight of meaning attached to the personal relations of the family. The organization of production around alienated labor encouraged the creation of a separate sphere of life in which personal relations were pursued as an end in themselves.[28]

Writers such as Miklos Haraszti, Robert Schrank, Barbara Garson, and David Halle, who have entered the workplace, either as workers or as observer-interviewers, confirm my Argentine survey experience. Their workers also speak most enthusiastically when the subject matter concerns their children and their children's education, family, friends, their houses, weddings, outings, sports, sex, and television programs.[29]

Even within the Israeli kibbutzim, among those who have undertaken to live and work cooperatively, there is a growing malaise regarding the lack of individual autonomy and material rewards. More and more kibbutz members are demanding their own television sets, no longer willing to conform to the taste of the majority. Nor are members satisfied with basic accommodations, for they increasingly seek more living space and greater amenities in their apartments.[30]

Whether one considers Bolivian peasants or U.S. workers, there seems to be a relationship (though certainly not always one-to-one) between property, whether a house or a piece of land, and the enhanced ability to pursue life, liberty, and happiness.[31] The reification of personal and home life has become a major means for softening the rigors of modern work life.[32] The pleasure of consumption has become a critical lubricant making capitalism acceptable, partially compensating for unequal ownership of the means of production. The classical left-right dichotomy in Argentina has been altered substantially by the infusion of questions that bear much more on consumption than on the methods of production. The capitalist class in Argentina—that is, owners of the major means of production—have managed, by providing economic growth, to circumvent any serious dialogue about the ethical justification of private control over the critical factors of production. As a result, Argentine workers (like workers elsewhere) see the key question in their lives much more in terms of the exchange they make between labor time paid and its value in commodity consumption than in the more impersonal question of the exchange values created by profits for their employers. Alienated labor, paradoxically, often leads workers to derive considerable satisfaction from consumption, leisure, and cultural pursuits.

Democracy and Authoritarianism

Despite economic hardships, the Alfonsín years, coming on the heels of an era of darkest repression, have served to consolidate the virtues of social peace and tranquility to which the Argentine working class largely aspires. Invariably, the workers I interviewed, whether staunch Radicals or fervent Peronist opponents of the Alfonsín government, warmly supported the same thing—namely, a peaceful political transition—whether this meant the confirmation or the ouster of the Radical administration at the polls. Workers were often extremely critical of the socioeconomic policies of the Radical government, but at the same time very appreciative of being given the right to give full voice to their opposition.

The workers' prime goal seemed to be to search out areas of autonomous activity over which they could have partial or full control to compensate for the lack of control in the workplace. In fact, this is how most workers interpreted democracy—*as guaranteeing a sphere of practical autonomy*. Workers attributed the personal freedom they enjoyed under the Alfonsín administration to democracy's support of individual autonomy, movement, and decision making. Laborers in particular often interpret legal, civil, and human rights in terms of these values on a personal level. Such attitudes explain why some workers often gave military regimes of the past (for example, those of Generals Onganía and Lanusse) good marks despite their assaults on legal, civilian governments. Past military regimes were favorably compared to the *proceso* military dictatorship because of their deference to democratic social norms, if not democratic political processes. The distinction workers made is that during the last military dictatorship, as distinct from previous military juntas, their sphere of autonomy was highly restricted and their daily freedom of movement and activity severely jeopardized.

Given all these positive attitudes toward democracy, post-Alfonsín Peronism has a major challenge to maintain the integrity of democratic institutions inherited from the previous Radical administration. Historically, Peronist governments have not assured the levels of civic democracy that were achieved under Alfonsín. In exchange for greater social equity and fairer income distribution, Peronist governments have often skirted the essential features of due process; the protection of civic freedoms has been subordinated to social and economic advances. But true democratic socialism requires a balance between political liberties and social/economic progress.

Nonetheless, many ostensibly authoritarian measures instituted under Perón substantially increased the overall freedom of Argentine workers and enabled them to pursue their collective interests without state or corporate interference. The various Peronist labor laws, the rights of association and collective bargaining, the rights of political involvement—all have strengthened Argentine democracy despite their problematic beginnings. But social and economic legislation must broaden the frontiers of human possibility and enhance working-class political access and social contentment; when it doesn't do this, it must be opposed—slavery once had to be abolished by fiat, fascism repressed by all means available.

Despite some of its early methods, Peronism was an authentic movement against a formally democratic liberalism that actually excluded large portions of the Argentine population from its beneficence. And in retrospect Perón deserves credit for preserving the basic liberal framework that espoused a division of government powers, spheres of private autonomy, the viability of political parties, and the separation of government from society. As Bernstein wrote, in the past, authoritarian measures may have had to be applied for democratic ends. The true test of a just society remains the ever greater extension of liberty and the commitment to the "development and the securing of the free personality."[33]

Genuine socialism cannot create new victims. Again Bernstein tells us,

> Socialism will create no new bondage of any kind whatever. The individual is to be free, not in the metaphysical sense, as the anarchists dreamed—i.e., free from all duties towards the community—but free from every economic compulsion in his action and choice of a calling. Such freedom is only possible for all by means of organization. In this sense one might call socialism "organizing liberalism," for when one examines more closely the organizations that socialism wants and how it wants them, he will find that what distinguishes them above all from the feudalistic organizations, outwardly like them, is just their liberalism, their democratic constitution, their accessibility.[34]

Bernstein welcomed the assimilation of whatever was progressive in historical liberalism as societies moved toward democratic socialism. Others were more jaundiced. Lenin, for example, acknowledged the dual cultural influences of bourgeois liberalism and socialism that were simultaneously imposed on working-class outlooks.[35] Though blaming bourgeois cultural manipulation for this dualism, Gramsci recognized the contradictory attachments among the masses that included both communist and maximalist as well as reformist and liberal democratic wills.[36]

Similarly, Peronist populism has historically combined two essential features of Argentine political culture: the concept of social justice and the concept of freedom. Notions of popular freedom are relatively old, coming down through liberal theories from the eighteenth and nineteenth centuries, but concepts of social justice for the entire population are more recent. They have emerged in the political pluralism, attached to developing twentieth-century capitalism, that seems responsive to mass needs. But workers arrived at these values independently; they were not patronizingly imposed by the elite, the bourgeois owners of the means of production. Liberal political culture has allowed workers effectively to demand social justice, which inherently implies a lessening of the burdens of severe exploitation.

Argentine liberalism allowed later Peronist governments to give Argentines greater social and economic equality and political participation, encapsulated by the word *dignidad* among rank-and-file workers. The exploitation that Marx referred to as dissolvable is unlikely to occur in contemporary society. What remains manageable is controlling the methods and levels of the relationship between capital and labor. Within that context, Perón accomplished much. Hernández Arregui has lucidly analyzed Peronism as Argentina's feasible yet authentic form of practical socialism.[37]

The Argentine CGT seems very aware of the possibilities and limitations of this political position. Labor leaders have understood their task as inhibiting the superexploitation of the labor force, as humanizing capital, and as controlling excess profits that result in mediocre salaries and working conditions. Argentine labor has been historically consistent about this. Since Peron's first fall from power in 1955, labor has attempted to maintain its share of income and political access. This continuing outlook is demonstrated by a speech made in 1960 by Eleuterio Cardoso, leader of a meatpackers' union:

> The executive committee has struggled for the respect of the rights acquired by the workers; . . . we were careful that the state organisms recognized and acted on whatever violations of these rights took place. This attitude of basing ourselves on legal resorts did not always bear fruit but it did allow us to keep intact the union structures which were constantly threatened; . . . no social class has shown greater effort in the defence of constitutional legality than the working class, because the rule of law is for the workers' organizations the same as oxygen for life; . . . as a citizen I am absolutely loyal to the Peronist movement and its leader; . . . as a workers' leader, however, I cannot lead my union by ways and tactics which experience has taught me are impractical and counterproductive.[38]

Thus, as Buchanan writes, neither the bourgeoisie nor the working class achieves all it would like. Regular elections and civil norms inhibit superexploitation and political authoritarianism while "in the economic sphere, a series of institutional arrangements similarly provide a framework in which the convergence of second-best choices occurs on materially calculated grounds of self-interest. The risks inherent in adopting best choice strategies encourage mutual adoption of second-best options."[39]

Authoritarianism in the East

Argentine workers, as we have discovered, oppose communist solutions for a variety of reasons, though principal among them is their sense that it would close their options as laborers and employees and produce a system that would be injurious to historical gains and their achieved level of formal rights. The pre-1989 socialist experiments represented, in many ways, the antithesis of systems that protected working-class rights: unions lacked basic autonomy from the state, union policies were seen as adjuncts of central planning commissions, workers were restricted in the occupations they chose, and private property and entrepreneurial rights were tenuous at best.

Twentieth-century socialist systems have advocated above all else the nationalization of industry, something the Argentine workers have seen quite enough of already. Democratic capitalism — despite its obvious shortcomings — when compared to feudal systems, socialist systems since 1917, fascism, and various Third World forms of bureaucratic authoritarianism has protected individual rights, social autonomy, and pluralist politics. For the Argentine working class, the Argentine Communist party (with its historical ties to the Soviet Union) does not authentically speak against foreign dependency, nor champion effective militant unionism, nor provide a model of support for human and civil rights in society.[40] The authoritarian bent visible in pre-1989 East European and Soviet systems may have had its birth in portions of Marx's and Engels's own writings. What I particularly have in mind are remarks like the following, from Engels's "Socialism, Utopian and Scientific":

> The first act in which the state really constitutes itself as the representative of the whole society — the taking possession of the means of production — is at the same time its last independent act as a state. The interference of the state power in social relations becomes superfluous in one sphere after another, and then ceases of itself. The government of persons is replaced by the administration of things and the direction of the process of production. The state is not "abolished," it withers away.[41]

This says too much and at the same time too little. It depicts a society bereft of politics and value conflicts, and yet insists on the continuing need for centralized resolution of mundane questions. By separating administration from politics and conflict, it deprives society of a way to debate the larger social and political questions so crucial to gadflies ever since Socrates raised questions about seemingly established truths. Engels would have the state collapsing only because society has achieved some homogeneous closure on questions of social needs. The public and private merge. This leaves open the question of what kind of dialectic relationship, if any, is left under these conditions. When the bourgeois state that mediates conflicting social interests (admittedly, not fairly on behalf of workers) is replaced by organs that theoretically represent unanimity, the way is open to an imposed Rousseauean "general will" that precludes opposition and dissent.

It is better, perhaps, to accept the inevitability of continuing forms of public law and order as inevitable and to carry on the struggles concerning their moral and ethical status. Elected political leaders need power and visibility so that they can be observed and evaluated by those whom they govern. To pretend to dissolve the differences between state and society is to perpetuate a myth of unending social conformity.

Marx's and Engels's thinking has also led to the idea that under socialism universal human happiness will only be a question of technical social engineering, since the larger questions of authority and control will have been resolved. This was Lenin's interpretation, when describing Taylor's motion-study research designed to enhance worker productivity:

> The Taylor system like all capitalist progress, is a combination of refined brutality of bourgeois exploitation and a number of the greatest scientific achievements in the field of analyzing mechanical motions during work, the elimination of superfluous and awkward motions and the elaboration of correct methods of work, the introduction of the best system of accounting and control, etc. The Soviet Republic must at all costs adopt all that is valuable in the achievement of science and technology in this field. The possibility of building socialism depends exactly upon our success in combining the Soviet power and Soviet organization of administration with the up-to-date achievements of capitalism. We must organize in Russia the study and teaching of the Taylor system and systematically try it out and adapt it to our ends.[42]

Thus the "administration of things" deteriorates into the "dictatorship of the proletariat," which historically appears as a step backward in the development of democratic socialism. Socialism as an idea in itself is still worthwhile, even as it continues to elude our grasp. It is a valuable goal if it means the decentralization of the power of the owners of the means of production, whether state or private, and a greater pluralist distribution of decision making in society at large and in the workplace. But in the light of my conversations with Argentine workers, one must reaffirm Bernstein's belief that though socialism is the end, what is more important is that democracy should be the means. As Kolakowski writes,

> If, instead of private ownership, the power to control the means of production and distribution is confined to a small ruling group uncontrolled by any measure of representative democracy, there will be not less exploitation but

a great deal more. The important thing is not the material privileges; . . .
what matters is that the mass of society is excluded from decisions as to the
use of the means of production and the distribution of income. Exploitation,
in short, depends on whether there is or is not effective machinery to enable
the workers to share in decisions concerning the product of their labor, and
hence it is a question of political freedom and representative institutions.[43]

Prior to 1989, twentieth-century socialist regimes have not entailed
increased democracy; instead, they have established dictatorial one-party
states in the name of "the people." Max Weber forecast just such a
development when he predicted that socialism would be more likely to lead
to a "dictatorship of the official" than to a "dictatorship of the proletariat."[44] In these circumstances, a new ruling elite that is unequivocally
dominant not only in the political sphere but also in the economic sphere
takes control. In the Argentine capitalist system, however, the dominance of
the industrial bourgeoisie in the economic sphere is not translated so neatly
into the political sphere. There is more what Ralph Miliband has called the
"relative autonomy of the state,"[45] compared with a relative lack of
autonomy in the East European and Soviet economies. In a word, the owners
of the means of production in state socialism also have a monopoly over
distribution. There was no public dialogue over these questions. Konrad and
Szelenyi, writing basically of Hungary in the 1970s, state,

> The workers' interests are fundamentally different from those of the redis-
> tributors. It is the most elemental interest of the workers to raise the price
> of labor, removing the determination of surplus product from the sphere of
> politics and changing the ratio of wages to surplus, to the advantage of
> wages. In order to achieve that, the purely administrative "sale" of labor
> must be turned into a transaction; the sale of labor-power under govern-
> ment compulsion must be done away with, so that the workers gain the
> right to decide for themselves whether or not to sell their labor or some
> product which they have made, and the right to make the price of their
> labor the subject of collective bargaining in a real labor market."[46]

As Haraszti makes clear in *A Worker in a Workers' State*, the party
apparatus, the state administrators, the foreman, and the union representatives are all in collusion against the worker.[47] On the other hand, in
Argentina, as well as elsewhere under various forms of liberal capitalism,
union contestation is present and the bargaining process (though alternately
weak and refortified) is nevertheless alive. This relationship between
management and labor has been typified by Bowles and Gintis as a dynamic
tension between the equal pulls of property and democracy,[48] while
Kesselman and Krieger have called this political compromise the "post-war
settlement."[49]

Private entrepreneurial methods and ends may have been a part of antiquity as well as modern times, whether in ancient Greece of the city-states, or during the Roman Empire, the medieval period, or the Renaissance. Only advanced technology and wage labor has made capitalism seem distinct from the past. Pre-1989 socialism has featured an inefficient, centralized form of capital accumulation, and thus the move toward political democratization is a necessary prelude to the establishment of "market socialism." Socialist systems, while pretending to ignore, minimize, and undermine human self-interest, ego-assertion, and self-maximization, have only managed to intensify hypocrisy and cynicism. The desire for private self-fulfillment is probably a human trait that cannot be transcended. The Argentine workers' values bear witness to this phenomenon.

Conclusion

Since the long anticipated emancipation of the working class — the Marxists' predicted social revolution — now seems unlikely to occur as a specific historical event, we should discuss other ways of protecting political and civil freedoms and assuring distributive justice. The Alfonsín years opened the way for an unprecedented climate for democratic development in Argentina. Carlos Menem's Peronist government, which followed, has focused on traditional liberal freedoms, but it has deviated from the heretofore economic focus of democratic socialism. After the Radicals' emphasis on consolidating liberal political institutions in Argentina, a less distributionist-minded Peronist government has come to power.

Though the working class seems no longer to be the agent of revolution, it continues to have a major stake in increasing democratization in Argentina. As my survey showed, Argentine workers value democracy as a political good in and of itself, without any direct manifestation in specific social policies. Obviously, formal and abstract democracy cannot satisfy all workers' economic needs, but it creates a social environment that leads to progress in resolving them. When liberty is assured, Argentines can pursue greater equality and fraternity.

In retrospect, although the Mensheviks lost out to the Bolsheviks in 1917, the vision of the former has better stood the test of time. In their historical conception of capitalist development and maturation, they more clearly understood the uneven course of European social development. The Leninist vision of a unified working class beholden to a totalistic ideology and an omnipotent state has been increasingly discredited. Working-class frustrations are not necessarily the product of bourgeois society and culture, whose values workers share. Imagining a total emancipation from that culture implies a serious faith in authoritarianism not shared by most workers. What the Argentine workers are after is the protection of democratically inspired arenas of personal autonomy and control. Such protection has not been high on the agendas of monopoly capitalism or state socialism. Much of what workers aspire to is not the product of the capitalist economy but of the democratic liberalism that developed alongside the power of capital.

Who owns the means of production is of secondary concern to Argentine workers. More primal is personal independence and the material satisfaction that constitute the real politics of everyday living. Despite the decline of purchasing power among the working class under Alfonsín, despite the deterioration of public services, poor retirement benefits, the lack of improvement in educational and medical services, and the stagnation of social welfare coverage, the workers strongly endorsed the democracy that Alfonsín's government restored.

Though workers acknowledge the need to privatize areas of governmental industrial units in order to make society more productive, they also see the need for a judicious, mediating state that intervenes on their behalf when necessary. For that to happen, a large administrative state is certainly needed. The direction and content of that regulatory state is the subject of politics in welfare-capitalist and democratic socialist societies. Joseph Schumpeter predicted that in future socialist regimes many of the great issues of national life, such as the role of immediate enjoyment versus the welfare of future generations, debates between labor and capital "will be as open as ever and there is little reason to expect that men will cease to fight over them."[50] Socialist governments up to 1989 badly miscalculated the need for this continuing debate and thus ceased to represent a model for Third World workers, such as those described in this study.

De Toqueville, on the other hand, understood the internal logic of democratic-capitalist society that gives it its seductive qualities and achieves a collective self-interest that promotes social stability.

> The principle of self-interest rightly understood produces no great acts of self-sacrifice, but it suggests daily small acts of self-denial. By itself it cannot suffice to make a man virtuous; but it disciplines a number of persons in habits of regularity, temperance, moderation, foresight, self-command; and if it does not lead men straight to virtue by the will, it gradually draws them in that direction by their habits.[51]

This certainly comes close to the Argentine workers' perceptions of life under the aegis of welfare capitalism.

V

The Contemporary Overview

10 *Post-Alfonsín Peronism*

> >o

Assault on the State

THE PERONIST administration of Carlos Menem that succeeded the Alfonsín government in 1989 has approached workers in a way that emphasizes what I have tried to bring forth in this study: namely, as citizens, parents of schoolchildren, consumers, taxpayers, homeowners, and even commuters. The last few years have shown that Argentine workers are not unalterably opposed to the privatization of inefficient governmental enterprises if the change promises improved services, since they are also consumers and citizens. Nor are workers opposed to a reexamination of the system that maintains Argentina's domestic industries as highly subsidized, noncompetitive, "hothouse" enterprises if a more competitive system would open up new markets and thereby offer new sources of employment. By the same token, union leaders need not oppose the modernization of poorly managed industries if, in the long run, it would mean higher productivity and hence better wages.

In other instances, Menem's policies of encouraging early retirement for public service employees, freezing government hiring, limiting public-sector strikes, and advocating flexible, nonunion work contracts have brought out existing inconsistencies within Peronism, particularly its alliance with the Ubaldini-Azopardo wing of the CGT. Peronism has always been a majority party, and when Peronists are in power, internal policy contradictions are likely to arise, as they did in 1952–1955, 1973–1975, and have emerged again since mid-1989. But while some of Menem's initiatives have caused considerable debate within the Peronist coalition, they have received generally

209

favorable support in mass public opinion polls — arguably a fair indicator of fundamental rank-and-file union views.

Menem's 1990 privatization of state-run firms such as the telephone enterprise (ENTEL) and the airline (Aerolíneas Argentinas)[1] has intensified certain persistent contradictions within the CGT, although the union rank and file, as I surveyed, has been predisposed to welcome these innovations for several years. The differences among Peronist officials, party factions, and labor and political alignments have all been magnified in this third phase of Peronism. What makes the controversies appear wider and deeper is the worldwide frontal assault on populism and a strong state sector — two standards traditionally defended by Peronism.

But as the survey showed, only a minority of the working-class sample I interviewed were convinced populists, and fewer still gave credence to statist forms of government intervention in the economy. Thus in large measure Antonio Cafiero's democratization of the Peronist party apparatus since 1985 and Carlos Menem's initiatives to privatize outmoded government enterprises since 1989 closely reflect the values and attitudes that Argentine laborers and employees expressed to me during the Alfonsín years. Menem's views closely reflect the sentiments that many workers espoused in interviews. Particularly noteworthy is Menem's comment: "The state as a political organization and historical category continues to have validity. What are no longer viable are its activities as a business, as producer, as industrialist, and as merchant."[2]

Menem's major break with traditional Peronism, however, was brought on by contemporary Argentina's weakened economic viability, which has been intensified by the foreign debt. This combination forced Menem to reevaluate the traditional Peronist compromise that gave a substantial share of national income to the working class while public- and private-sector enterprises enjoyed a protected domestic market. Far more than Perón did during the 1950s or 1970s, Menem has focused almost exclusively on generating new sources of productivity and national income rather than on distributing the income earned by a shrinking domestic economy. The Peronist balance between the need to capitalize and the desire to continue populist income policies has been reexamined; as a result, the Menem administration's "productive revolution" has replaced traditional populism not only by politically embracing representative democracy but also by distancing itself from Keynesian-based public policies. Menem has divorced Peronism from a demand-driven economy, focusing rather on supply-side economics that in the short run will necessarily hurt labor's traditional incomes policy. But, as Menem himself put it, "If Peronism doesn't change, it will disappear the way Communism has disappeared."[3]

Menem's view of Argentine capitalism is that it has been unprepared for risk, closed to world competition, and insufficiently integrated into the major world markets.[4] To pursue the goals of dynamic capitalism, Menem chose a clearly consistent neoliberal rationalization of the Argentine economic structure. To effect his policies, in mid-1989 the Peronist government instituted two important pieces of emergency legislation: the Reform of the State Law and the Law of Economic Emergency. These laws, enacted within several weeks of each other, gave the Menem administration the right to subject public-sector enterprises to outright privatization or specific concessionary arrangements. The first measure covered the much discussed privatization of not only the telephone, airline, and railway systems, but also the state petroleum corporation (YPF), the state coal corporation, the highway network, the state electrical enterprise (SEGBA), sanitation services, water resources, the post office, the ports, the Buenos Aires subway, a naval foundry and shipyard, the national mint, a state sugar company, the leading grain terminal, recreational and ecological zones, and various cultural entities, including government radio stations and television channels.[5]

The Law of Economic Emergency inhibited further deficit financing of government enterprises and put limits on their recourse to subsidies from the central treasury. Moreover, it stipulated that foreign capital and local private enterprises shall be treated equally. The last important features were designed to increase state employee productivity and reduce employee rolls by attrition and early retirement.[6] Within eighteen months, approximately 50,000 temporary employees had been fired, voluntarily retired through early retirement inducements, or "excessed" (with severance pay) through the collapse of agencies.[7]

In October 1990, Menem instituted an emergency decree measure limiting the right to strike in the public service sector, which included utilities, transportation, communications, health, and education — enterprises "that could jeopardize life, health, or the security of the community."[8] The decree provided for obligatory conciliation and arbitration and allowed for possible sanctions if strikes were explicitly declared illegal.

The last piece of major legislation to be proposed in the neoliberal vein was the National Law of Employment, which Menem had threatened several times to implement by decree if Congress did not act expeditiously to pass it. Although the Menem administration proposed the legislation as long ago as November 1989, it had not been approved by Congress a year later. The projected law is a very complex piece of legislation that attempts to "flexibilize" the labor contract. The proposal is aimed at the rigidity of Argentine union contracts that supposedly inhibit employers from hiring workers on a trial basis and keep manufacturers and other entrepreneurs from experimenting with and expanding into new enterprises or productive branches and outlets, proximate to their existing interests.

A second function of this law is ostensibly to stimulate employment and provide necessary experience for otherwise unemployed young workers. Specifically, the measure allows for a minority of workers to be hired by renewable, short-run contracts that usually run from six months to two years. However, employers must open their books to the respective unions to demonstrate the conditions that require such actions. They cannot use temporary workers to fill permanent positions that have been vacant for six months, cannot substitute them for striking workers, and cannot use them to replace fired permanent workers. These stipulations are designed to prevent employers from purposely avoiding hiring under established union contracts.

Under these flexible contracts, employers pay only 50 percent of the normal pension, social welfare, and family contributions, and in most cases (for young people under twenty-four years of age) no severance pay is required if workers are fired during the life of the contract. It is envisioned that a good portion of these short-term contracts should go to youth apprenticeship programs in which all who finish will be awarded "certificates of completion" testifying to their experience, and the best might conceivably be hired later under normal, permanent union contracts.[9]

These de facto subcontracting measures could conceivably be welcomed by Argentine workers, who (as we have seen) seek good income and growth opportunities every bit as much as job security with poor pay — the situation of unionized employees since 1975. Clearly, even before Menem, many workers thrived in the insecure underground economy, often doubling their income thereby. This was particularly true for those working in the public sector (for example, light and power workers, bank and telephone employees, and teachers).

I returned to Buenos Aires in mid-1990 to interview eight of the workers with whom I had spoken four years earlier. There had been few dramatic shifts in values and attitudes in the interim. For the most part, workers again made it clear that they opposed the government's role in most areas of productivity such as heavy industry, utilities, transportation, and hotels. However, they saw the government's rightful function as administering education, justice, social welfare, and public policy making—conducting foreign affairs and formulating Argentina's defense, fiscal, and monetary policies. As a light and power worker explained, "If [state enterprises] are not efficient, sell them."[10] A textile worker told me, "We all pay the debt for the inefficient public sector,"[11] while another SEGBA light and power worker said, "If the state can't do it, it's time to let someone else do it. We need it all — technology, machinery, you name it."[12]

Certainly the mounting evidence of the difficulties of Argentina's public enterprises substantiates the workers' perceptions — views that are further corroborated by public opinion polls taken after the announcement of Menem's privatization initiatives. For example, in mid-1990 the leading deficitary state enterprises were the state telephone company (ENTEL), the state electrical enterprise (SEGBA), and the Argentine railways.[13] The privatization of ENTEL and Aerolíneas Argentinas in 1990 were applauded in public opinion polls by 73 percent and 56 percent, respectively. (The latter was probably less roundly endorsed because of its much smaller deficit of $34 million.) Public opinion throughout 1990 and early 1991 approved the moves toward privatization being undertaken and contemplated. In August 1990 a poll supported the privatization of Argentine railways (83 percent), the post office (82 percent), SEGBA (78 percent), sanitation and sewage (75 percent), the gas company (75 percent), the highway network (70 percent), the coal enterprise (YCF, 66 percent), the petroleum corporation (YPF, 66 percent), the merchant marine fleet (58 percent), and military factories (56 percent).[14]

Another important measure of the lack of public confidence in the state's ability to manage the economy came on August 5, 1990, when a referendum was held on reforming the constitution of the Province of Buenos Aires. Although both major parties — the Radicals and the Peronists — endorsed the referendum, it was overwhelmingly defeated by two-thirds of the voters in a province traditionally associated with populist, interventionist public policies. Apparently, the key amendments that led to the overwhelming rejection of the reform were provisos giving the provincial government the right to expropriate private property for public use, and language implying that economic activity must be harmonized with overall collective and community concerns.[15]

The Residue of Opposition

The rush to circumscribe and reduce the Argentine state's (admittedly ineffectual) productive role, the attempt to insert the nation's economy into competitive international markets and to make it more attractive to foreign capital, have also fostered certain countervailing tendencies. Albeit still a minority, a loose coalition has emerged linking the Ubaldini-Azopardo sector of the labor leadership and the opposition Alfonsín wing of the Radical party. This developing coalition reflects concern about the neoliberal, triumphal approach that seemingly has abandoned all faith in the traditionally paternalist functions of the Argentine state. This fear was expressed by a bank employee who told me, "By destroying the Argentine state, we are diminishing its role of protecting all its citizens. The state will no longer be mediating and softening class conflicts."[16]

The Menem administration ostensibly has made more profound changes in and had greater impact upon Argentine society than did the Alfonsín government of the late 1980s. An important difference, of course, lies in the Menem administration's greater political legitimacy because of Peronism's longstanding defense of the interests of the Argentine working class. Thus the abrupt shift by the Menem government away from traditional Peronist populism, though it surprised many of its followers, was absorbed with far more equanimity than if this fundamental reorientation had been implemented by Alfonsín, who would immediately have been accused by trade unionists of making a frontal assault on the working class.

Nevertheless, there were some early repercussions from these new economic realities: Argentina's shrinking state sector and a drive for fiscal austerity and privatization. These have aggravated the existing social malaise and signal what could be a prolonged and frustrating period of economic transition. There are signs of significant social change afoot: as of mid-1990, unemployment had reached 8.5 percent, while the underground economy continued to grow at the expense of formal employment of private and public salaried workers.[17] In addition, certain indices of poverty had risen.[18] Workers paid proportionally more for utilities and transportation and were pressured to produce more on the job, as the discipline of the marketplace began to deepen under Menem.[19]

Though Argentine labor unions remain strong, the continuing growth of the informal, second economy leads us to speculate about the impact of contemporary capitalist development on the political influence of the CGT. Certainly the deindustrialization of the military *proceso* years, followed by Alfonsín's and Menem's focus on restricting the state sector in favor of private-sector employment, has strengthened the petty-bourgeois sector, both formal and informal. What is more, as I have indicated, this sector also represents an attractive alternative for workers displaced from the formal wage sector.[20]

The Menem government has received substantial support from the Peronist CGT. There are several reasons for this alliance, which is suprisingly firm in the wake of moves toward privatization and state rationalization that will diminish, at least in the early stages, the numerical strength of the trade unions. Of primary importance is the visible split in the CGT. In late September 1989, at a CGT congress held at the San Martín Theater in Buenos

Aires, a group of union delegates led by Güerino Andreoni of the Commercial Workers' Union defeated the Saúl Ubaldini–Azopardo faction by a vote of 719 to 644, with 92 abstentions. Ubaldini has never accepted the defeat as legitimate and has impugned the election because of "procedural" irregularities. However, the decline of his influence is evident in the shrinking organizational powers of the now minority, more militant wing of the trade union movement.

The Andreoni majority faction, more firmly supportive of Menem's policies, increasingly marginalized the Ubaldini wing of the labor movement. Since the mid-1989 split, for example, more and more important unions have accepted the necessity of Menem's privatization initiatives. Among the unions included in my survey, members of the textile, automobile, light and power, telephone, and bank employees all generally supported the Andreoni–San Martín faction, while only the teachers' union remained aligned with the Ubaldini-Azopardo faction.[21] The important industrial union — the metalworkers, under Lorenzo Miguel — maintained good relations with both leadership factions, though on policy matters it remained closer to the Andreoni–San Martín group. It has not broken with the Ubaldini-Azopardo group in the hopes of reconciling some of the differences and reestablishing a united position of critical support for President Menem.

The majority CGT faction's conciliation with Menemism was made evident by the fact that, through mid-1991, not a single general strike was launched against the Peronist government. (It is to be remembered that the CGT organized thirteen general strikes against the policies of the Alfonsín administration.) Since Menem took office in mid-1989, it has been the service unions — including teachers, bank and telephone workers, and public employees — that have shown the greatest militancy and propensity to strike. For example, taking a statistical measure in July 1990, La Nación found that these four service unions accounted for over 40 percent of all labor conflicts in that month.[22]

The support of the majority of CGT union leaders has been critical for Menem's key economic initiatives. It has been a period of watchful waiting. The rank and file have been even more sympathetic — which confirms what I discovered in my survey during the mid-1980s. The Ubaldini-Azopardo perspective is currently out of step with the views of most unionized workers and the people at large regarding what Argentina must do to modernize its economy. The Ubaldini model of unionism under Menem also deviates from the West European model of union behavior, which seeks conciliation and compromise between growth capital and labor. Support for Ubaldini will continue to deteriorate unless Argentina's capitalist reform becomes clearly rapacious — that is, unless it becomes a European-type capitalist resurgence *without* a European-type social net. This eventuality would give the Ubaldini CGT faction a legitimate political space.

Since the advent of "Menemism," the San Martín majority faction of the CGT leadership is closer to the rank-and-file view of Argentine society that I heard expressed in interviews. Several critical areas separate Ubaldini's views from those of rank-and-file CGT members. First, Ubaldini's emphasis on protecting and expanding the domestic market, which echoes the import-substitution industrialization policy of past Peronist regimes, would find only minority support among most Argentine workers. Instead, they recognize the necessity of internationalizing and expanding Argentina's economy. Second, the proposed Ubaldini labor alliance with the smaller, domestic-oriented Argentine employers is unlikely to find favor with the majority of workers who remain skeptical, as we have noted, about the productive will and instincts of homegrown industrialists. Workers showed greater confidence in foreign private capital investment as a fulcrum for revitalizing the economy. This view was reiterated in most cases when I reinterviewed Argentine workers in 1990. For example, one light and power worker told me pessimistically, "We need foreign capital to make it easier for Argentines to invest; too many Argentines sell factories and convert them to dollars; Argentine capitalists want to ride piggy-back on foreign capital. If Argentine capital doesn't invest, others will and we can't complain. If we wait for Argentine capital, we'll wait another hundred years."[23] Third, the Ubaldini faction's position on opposing privatization finds little resonance among workers, significantly even those entrenched in the public sector. Finally, Ubaldini's focus on unemployment as the major scourge of the Argentine economy is not echoed by the average worker, who sees runaway inflation as the much greater evil. In all these areas, the San Martín faction comes closer to representing the state of mind of the contemporary Argentine organized worker.

Ubaldini's convictions are most often reflected by public-sector employees (for example, certain teachers, civil servants, and bank employees) who worry about the long-run impact of mass layoffs, foreign domination of key Argentine public enterprises, and the unraveling of Argentina's control over its own economy. Mirroring the rank-and-file unionists, both CGT leadership factions agree on the need for government credits for all kinds of productive investments and a revamping of the tax structure to tap wealthy unproductive capitalists and landowners.

Certainly Menem's policies represent a watershed. As a bank employee told me, "This is a major change. It will mark an epoch. It will be remembered as before and after Menem. The Argentina that was is gone."[24] With the exception of Menem's positive assessment of the agrarian sector's productive role in Argentine modernization and his 1990 pardon of officers and generals who executed the *proceso*, his administration has moved in the direction that workers had been tending toward for some time. Speaking before the Buenos Aires Stock Exchange, where Perón initiated his populist coalition in 1944, Menem captured these values when he said, "Our policy will be popular, but not populist; national but not chauvinist, social and not Marxist. . . . Four decades ago we nationalized the companies; now privatization is necessary because of their deficits and disequilibrium."[25]

Certainly in the plebescite-like spirit of Argentine public rallies, first instituted by Perón on October 17, 1945, Menem's Plaza de Mayo crowds represent a broad-based outpouring of support that goes beyond union members to include many upper-class persons, professionals, and other elements of society usually absent from Peronist rallies. Menem has been given good marks in public opinion polls through 1990, often rated more highly than his own administration. Thus far, the Argentine populace is apparently giving him time to prove the validity of his economic policy.[26]

Though as of this writing Menem's Peronist reformulation has not been subjected to an electoral test, the opposition seems in disarray. The bulk of the Radical party, under Eduardo Angeloz, governor of Córdoba, has generally supported Menem. Indeed, during the campaign for the presidential election, which the Radicals lost, Angeloz's platform was largely adopted by the Menem administration. At the same time, Alfonsín in his 1983 presidential campaign emphasized the obsolescence of Peronist populist economics that only fostered inefficiency and bureaucratization.[27] Thus it was disconcerting in the post-1989 period to hear him criticize the very policies he had advocated and unsuccessfully tried to implement.

But far more impotent in the face of world events since 1989 has been the Communist left in Argentina. The bulk of the party has maintained its dogmatic rigidity even in the face of the political upheavals in Eastern Europe and the Soviet Union. Its emphasis on the class struggle and anti-imperialism as a basis for wooing the Peronist workers has not significantly changed in the last generation.[28]

At the Argentine Communists' twenty-seventh party congress in 1986, speakers called for the struggle of the world's people against "*yanqui* war and aggression" and eulogized Soviet industrial might—which, they asserted, would double in the next fifteen years, was "carried out without exploitation," and provided the populace with "basic necessities." Soviet society was declared to be "infinitely more democratic" and "more pluralistic than the bourgeois republics" because it is in the process of "perfecting a socialism based on the daily, active and conscious participation of the working class."[29]

Thus when the Gorbachev reforms of glasnost and perestroika began to be asserted and felt in the Soviet Union, the Argentine Communist party opposed the changes, much as the Cuban Communists have done under Fidel Castro. When a reformist faction attempted a revision of party policy in mid-1990, it was excluded from leadership circles.[30] Signficantly, the party's former leader, Fernando Nadra, resigned his affiliation in May 1990, saying that the party has no political future because of its "dogmatic, sectarian and opportunistic conceptions." He spoke of a "sinister apparatus that had begun to persecute dissidents" within the party. He said the party had adopted "an external mask and an interior fear, if not an indirect rejection, of the new perestroika thinking."[31]

The Menem government's attempt to invigorate a decrepit and paternalist economic structure by strengthening elements of the free market is strikingly similar to the productive revolutions currently occurring in Eastern Europe and the Soviet Union. However, Peronism shares with the Soviet Union's Communist party common antecedents of legitimacy not present in Eastern European party governments that had been externally imposed by Soviet troops: both the Peronist party and the Communist party of the Soviet Union are outgrowths of popular movements in each country's history. Indeed, Menem has in this regard a significant historical advantage over Mikhail Gorbachev in his efforts to administer perestroika. Contemporary Peronism represents not only a historically vindicated movement but also one that has been sanctioned time and again by popular support in contested elections. This reaffirmation of Peronism represents an important source of political capital and general goodwill that the Soviet Communist party cannot share.

The market-driven assertions of the Alfonsín administration have been deepened and more finely honed under Menem. The reversal of traditional Peronist income distribution, certain labor union givebacks, decreases in state employment, and the focus on revitalizing inefficient enterprises, were all goals of the previous Radical government, but only Menem's Peronist government has seriously begun to address these issues. In fact, there has been a virtual continuity, under two democratically elected civilian governments, on reactivation and privatization of unproductive sectors of the public economy. With no serious political competition from the traditional left, Menem has solidified his hold on the center and center-right to such a degree that the Alfonsinist faction of the Radical party has been forced to mount a critique of Menem's economic policies from a left-center position. All this indicates a quite normal adjustment, a recognizable strategy in a solidifying two-party system.

By this rightward shift, Peronism has managed both to strengthen and to institutionalize Argentine democracy by not threatening certain conservative industrial and agrarian interests that have traditionally looked to the military for vindication, particularly in the absence of a credible political alternative on the right.[32] And, as my survey indicated, the Peronist voter has become a more complicated citizen whose traditional populist attachments have been gradually overshadowed by democratic predispositions. Thus we observe three movements toward a stabilizing democracy: an affirmation of democratic political culture, a peaceful succession of two civil democratic governments, and internal democratization within the Peronist party. The "embourgeoisiement" of Peronism has served to normalize Argentine politics and to bring major economic and social issues to the center of the political arena rather than keeping them at the radical edges. Menem's victory over the Radicals' Eduardo Angeloz in 1989 was the first time in Argentine history that a change in the civil government entailed a change of party but not of regime (as, for example, a military intervention).

The historical nexus between Peronism and the CGT has allowed the Menem administration much more leeway in conducting public policy than the Alfonsín government achieved. Nevertheless, the Argentine trade union movement is being challenged as it has not been since World War II. The CGT is not suffering the benign neglect of prewar years, or rapacious military oppression, or the austerity policies of unfriendly civil governments. Rather, it faces the excruciating turmoil caused by the constraints and demands of modern capitalist development in a world which, for the moment, offers no other viable model.

Opposition to "Menemism" from the Ubaldini-Azopardo labor faction has thus emerged and will no doubt continue and possibly deepen. On the other hand, the CGT majoritarian San Martín union leadership will be forced to develop new responses to current challenges such as unemployment caused by advances in technology, job retraining, profit sharing, productivity incentives, worker redundancy, and other developments that are not part of its traditional defense of decent wage levels, good working conditions, and social benefits. The tensions will increase as the organized labor force expands to include more white-collar workers. My survey showed that the more ideologically critical values and attitudes were expressed by teachers, telephone, and bank employees. These "middle-class workers" and others (for example, civil servants, state enterprise workers in the utilities, health and hospital workers, transportation workers, postal workers, and so on) will mount the greatest resistance to changes necessitated by adapting to modern capitalism.

Workers will resist rapid forms of modernization if such development infringes directly on labor's historical gains such as rights in the workplace, job security, and health and vacation benefits. The CGT will need a holding action to defend labor's gains even while it supports the necessary overhaul of Argentina's productive structure. Workers will most likely demand consultation with state and capital interests, mechanisms for retraining the work force, and a national system of unemployment insurance to mitigate inevitable worker dislocations. Workers made their outlook on such matters evident in my survey in their concern for improving their own and their children's education and cultural opportunities, and acquiring the technical competence to meet the changing requirements of the marketplace.

Argentina's business and labor communities will have to work together to reach compromise solutions that balance the proportional worth of each. For example, for a period of time, workers may be willing to accept between 30 and 35 percent of national income, if in the future, as the national product increases, they can achieve levels above 50 percent. Clearly, most of the key decisions will likely be made by multinational capital and Argentine state interests. However, if the demands of labor are given more weight and influence in such decisions, then business and the state can rightfully expect greater labor productivity. This will likely democratize capital to a degree and make it more responsible to labor as it seeks to spread the risk.

High levels of unionization continue to be important for the maintenance of labor's credibility in Argentina. Efficiency in the capital sector need not mean the slow demise of the trade union movement, as the Swedish experience teaches us. In this regard, as this study has demonstrated, the Argentine organized working class has significant advantages over the work forces of most of the developing world. Cultural and economic influences in Argentina are multinational and do not derive from a single neocolonial relationship. Argentine class relationships are fluid within the vast middle sectors of the social structure. There are few of the linguistic, ethnic, cultural, religious, and racial differences that are typical of so many developing nations. There are no huge pockets of indigenous people living in extreme poverty. The self-employed sector is relatively stable and viable. Many workers own their own homes. All these sociological factors support the bargaining power of Argentine labor.

At the same time, the CGT is uniquely integrated into the Argentine political and economic structure. Since the first phase of Peronism, it has had enduring relationships with other key corporate interests such as the Catholic church, the military, and the key landowners' and industrial associations (such as the Sociedad Rural and the Unión Industrial). It has a long history of sharing power and influence. Despite the 1989 split in the ranks of CGT leadership, the absence of major sectional and demographic bifurcations allows the labor confederation to bargain from a position of relative unity and cohesion. Thus, in a transitional period of austerity-driven economic management, the CGT should be able to make its political weight felt, and dampen policies that unleash market forces in an unfettered manner. There can be no authentic capitalist democracy in Argentina — certainly no democratic socialism — without a strong and independent trade union movement watchfully allied to the Peronist party.

11   Conclusion

▶ ▶

THERE ARE INHERENT dangers in extrapolating from the Argentine case to more general questions of working-class values. Thus it is with more than a little trepidation that I project some tentative conclusions about unions and workers in the industrial and industrializing West beyond the confines of Argentina.

This study has used the approach of political sociology: defining the worker's sense of his or her place in contemporary society and relating that to the conflicts engendered by modern industrial development. In this study I have not neglected what I would call the third-third of workers' lives — that is, what they think about during those eight hours of each working day in which they are neither at their primary place of employment, nor asleep. Satisfaction can come in all kinds of psychic, material, or intellectual ways, or all in combination — whether it is promotion on the job, a scholarship for a child, reading a soccer magazine, buying an attractive overcoat, or taking a weekend outing in the country.

Workers are far more complex than they are assumed to be in much of the literature on class consciousness. Election returns, government upheavals, military coups, and general strikes are only partial manifestations of the complicated world in which the working class plays a significant role. A demand for political and personal liberty and autonomy is deeply ingrained among organized workers of all persuasions. On the question of social equality, on the other hand, there is much less consensus. Political theory has not come up with an accepted notion of the optimum relationship between liberty and equality, and equality remains a more ambivalent and conflicted concept. We do know, however, that equality without liberty is not satisfying for most people. On the other hand, liberty is valued in a more absolute sense and is seen to be jeopardized only if it is accompanied by the most extreme forms of inequality. The compromises between these two values requires a social system that allows for a freedom of inquiry that continually measures and evaluates the relationship between the two.

Modern industrial society, whether capitalist or socialist, has displaced formerly economically semi-independent and self-reliant people into collective niches in order to create the economic surplus that allows for integral political organization and social viability. Modernizing societies require the hierarchization and bureaucratization of groups into functional conglomerates that are more efficient and thus more controllable from the top down. This process seems inevitable, given the economies of scale necessary to achieve competitiveness both domestic and international. In turn, these economic relationships have usually spawned complex pluralist political cultures based on indirect political representation. The capitalist market has been sustained by democratic forms of government, while, at the same time, representative democracy has developed a comfortable relationship with large spheres of private market activity. But though advantaged economic groups have benefited most from private forms of property relationships, demands for democratic participation, greater social justice, and economic redistribution have also been heard.

Nevertheless, in such a society freedom is not absolute. Wage laborers, employees, bureaucrats, professionals, intellectuals—all are tied to the constraints of the market and the state. Their overall social responsibilities require daily conformity and compromise. Even doctors work for huge institutions, lawyers for large firms or corporations, priests for an international hierarchy, poets for universities, scientists for institutes and industries—and they too represent fractions of the contemporary middle-class worker on salary. Those on salaries officially make up close to three-quarters of the economically active people in Argentina; in most Western nations, this group comprises more than four-fifths of the total.

Laborers and middle-class workers do not control where, when, or how they work. They are directly or indirectly trained and supervised by others. They usually have a continuing relationship with their employer, abiding by certain accepted rules and regulations. Employers oversee the work, set the hours, and provide the place and equipment for producing a product or service. Further, workers are paid by the hour, week, or month. These conditions are common to all.

But this productivist side of workers' lives does not take account of a multitude of other needs and interests. Marx was among the first to call for the study of real workers in real situations so that knowledge of their conditions would form an integral part of human history. Marx complained that too much history excluded the study of the common man in favor of the political actions of rulers and special interests.[1] This study has attempted to flesh out in one country what workers value in their lives.

The evolution of workers into citizens, with multiple needs and wants, has had various consequences. For example, the maturation of the capitalist-property nexus to democratic forms of representation, and the hetero-geneity of the working class has decreased the possibility of major revolutionary upheavals in society. At the same time, modern democratic systems have offered worker-citizens the chance to bring about redistributive justice through representative channels, making cataclysmic change less necessary.

In Western nations, the campaign for social and economic reform has been linked to the vigorous policies of democratic socialist political parties and a large, unified trade union movement. Argentina has had both these ingredients ever since World War II. Though the Peronist party can hardly be described as a democratic socialist party, mainly because of its internal authoritarian tendencies and supraparty corporative alliances with other interest groups, its program links Peronism to the social democratic tradition. On the other hand, Argentine labor reformism has not embraced the optimistic, triumphalist Marxian notion of a working class "for themselves," seeing the need to collectively confront capitalism and thereby end the cycle of exploitation.

At the same time, Argentine bread-and-butter trade unionism has not led to labor's cooptation by capitalist interests or its incorporation into the state. The Argentine case most closely resembles the democratic socialism envisioned by Eduard Bernstein; militant reformism against unfair capitalist practices and procedures within a context of democratic political processes. "Democracy is at the same time means and end," Bernstein wrote. "It is the means of the struggle for Socialism and it is the form Socialism will take once it has been realized."[2]

In general, social democratic demands, when they represent the majority, have been at least partially satisfied in capitalist-dominated states by maintaining decent wages, working conditions, and benefits, by providing education, health care, consumer protection, family allowances, and housing. These gains in turn blunt the edge of rigid, formalistic class consciousness. Such incremental achievements must be taken as serious advances; to accept only more global theoretical working-class goals as "correct" is to reduce workers to pawns separate from the rest of society and their roles as citizens, voters, consumers, taxpayers and parents.

Class consciousness and even class struggle are better defined as unmet and unsatisfied political and economic demands of the majority of the population—that is, people on wages and salaries. In this way, Bernstein's reinterpretation of class broadens the definition of available classes that are opposed to the ills of the capitalist system and in favor of democratic socialism. Broad-based democratic socialist parties can act as a major vehicle, along with trade unions, for integrating oppositional forces confronting injustice. In the so-called revisionism of Eduard Bernstein there is a place for the great majority, though disparate and heterogenous, to unite behind programs that confront rapacious capital. But for this to happen, new popular needs, which will continually manifest themselves, must be acknowledged and satisfied as they arise, and not seen as part of a millennial struggle between evil and good, domination and revolution.

Democratic forms of capitalism have shown a historic ability to respond to basic demands from below even though the basic characteristics of the market remain unchanged. In the absence of institutional crisis and breakdown, in which workers will not remain idle observers, this remains a solid area of achievement for the working class. As long as the political system offers regular, democratic elections and legitimate legislatures, this system, though not perfect, will serve as an important institutional watchdog over the policies and activities of capitalists and capital. But because under contemporary liberal democratic capitalism of the Argentine variety the working classes will always be given less than their fair share of national income, there will always be a social dynamic demanding income redistribution as a goal of the working class. Workers will continue to push for greater parity up to the point of capital disinvestment on the part of the private sector.[3]

In representative democracies as currently constituted, the state measures which level of equilibrium is justifiable. Ideally, this is achieved by organized three-way mediation among capitalists, workers, and the state; whatever its problems, this system turns out to be better for workers than the collusion between capital and state managers against workers that existed under socialism in East Europe and the Soviet Union before 1989.

The traditional platform of the left—nationalizing industry and bank deposits, collectivizing land, and monopolizing foreign trade—have become largely irrelevant issues for democratic socialism. Rigid adherence to those goals probably further delays democratic socialism's accession to power largely because these ends do not necessarily raise productivity, which is what puts redistributive justice on the political agenda. Though this would lead one to believe that the working class has been absorbed into a capitalist hegemonic project, the workers themselves feel (as we have seen) that if capital grows, so do their life chances as individuals. Capitalism has thus been more successful than socialist alternatives because historically it has created a larger surplus value in good times to be distributed to the working class. Under recent socialist experiments, there have been few good times. Argentine workers made it clear to me that they would rather live under an inefficient capitalist system than an inefficient socialist system, since in the former there are far more outlets for protest and criticism. Moreover, capitalism offers workers greater choice and opportunity to rise or fall by their own abilities—a deeply felt value among Argentine laborers and employees.

In this regard, the Argentine CGT has played a critical role since the days of early Peronism. The centralization of Argentine unions, inspired by Perón, is an important ingredient of democratic socialism because the organized working class can confront in a united way the other major components of a corporate society—namely, the state and large capitalist enterprises. This is not too different from how the German trade union movement saw its role at the close of last century: central to their concerns were struggles over the state's role in "social and economic regulation and the struggle for basic civil rights . . . of and for the proletariat."[4]

During the Alfonsín democracy, the three major wings of the Argentine labor confederation—the Ubaldini faction, the "62" (under Lorenzo Miguel), and the *Renovador* "25"—concentrated in different but complementary ways on wage and welfare questions to focus on unifying socioeconomic grievances. The problem has been to give priority to economic issues while at the same time resolving potentially divisive issues among workers, such as social and foreign policy questions (crime, drug abuse, pornography, the right of divorce, environmental pollution, defense questions, the contra war in Nicaragua, the Soviet/Cuban path, etcetera). The CGT's traditional strong support for Peronism seems to have been the best course. Through the Alfonsín years, Peronism has been the most progressive political alternative for Argentine workers, even if now and again progressive individuals emerge in Congress representing the Radicals or smaller parties.

A business-unionism, economist and nonpolitical, however, would probably leave workers in the political wilderness. Rather, a strong left-center stand will at least foster conditions making *one* of several parties *responsible* to labor The best that could happen for workers would be for political parties to feel forced to compete for a wage and social welfare vote. The CGT, under Ubaldini's leadership in the 1980s, did not attempt to form a monolithic working-class party nor to assert a rigid class-based notion of seizing power. Again, it conformed to the workers' own skepticism about working-class rule, should that even have been a realistic option. The words of Bernstein echo here: "The different nature of their needs and interests would quickly become known to [workers] as soon as the propertied and governing classes are removed from, or deprived of, their position."[5]

Workers like everyone else participate in, enjoy, and value bourgeois-liberal ideology — that is, liberty and the right to a minimum standard of living. The choice of housing, jobs, travel and vacations, education, consumer goods (including automobiles and electronic equipment) are all prerequisites to a sense of well-being and freedom. The fact that freedom is not seen by workers as a totally abstract quality by no means compromises that freedom; social outlets and material satisfactions are the backbone of freedom's benefits. Workers' commitment to their own well-being does not necessarily blunt their sense of justice or *dignidad*.[6]

The Argentine CGT has continued to pursue working-class goals effectively. It has, for example, defended the legality of one union per industry in collective bargaining procedures and the automatic payroll dues collection system. It has maintained control over the administration of workers' social, vacation, and health benefits and has preserved its special role within the Peronist party apparatus. Although the labor confederation has at times appeared to be controlled from above, this has usually occurred under Peronist governments when the general condition of the working class improved. Though Argentine state regimes have continually sought to control unions, it is important to remember that this relationship to the state has given unions access to power, something the Argentine left sees only as simple "cooptation." When conditions for labor have worsened, the CGT has quickly moved into opposition, regardless of what type of government is in power. This was clearly seen during the last stages of the Isabel Perón government in 1975, and there was even increasing labor opposition to Perón himself and an increase in worker assemblies and strike activity between 1952 and 1954. Such confrontation cannot be excluded as a possibility under the Carlos Menem government, as suggested by the oppositional stance of the CGT-Azopardo group since 1989.

Though the CGT's natural tendency is to encourage a special connection to Peronism, this alignment has been tempered by the reality of state-labor relationships. In modern democracies, it is increasingly the state and not the capitalist class that mediates the basic compromise between capital and labor. The state's hitherto imposing role in economic decision making combined with its conflict-laden role as prime employer requires labor to maintain close relationships with both government and private capital. Thus the cooptation that organized labor in Argentina is often accused of by the left is a necessary means of earning a responsible place at the key bargaining table.

Since 1945, Argentina's unified, coherent, and massive labor confederation has assured organized workers a legitimate and recognizable role in society. The CGT has managed to preserve its place as the representative and champion of workers' needs (though its program does not cover *all* working-class values, as I learned in my survey) under all types of governments — populist, liberal-democratic, and military. The CGT has demonstrated the primacy of the political sphere by acting variously as pressure group, coalition builder, and organizer of public demonstrations. What has in the last analysis maintained the CGT's leverage as an important bargaining unit is its ability to maintain a modicum of autonomy and independent judgment while at the same time lending its substantial wealth and political influence to social democratic initiatives, which have traditionally sprung from the Peronist coalition.

Modern governments have not become the executive committee for managing "the affairs of the whole bourgeoisie" but rather managers of the affairs of the whole society, including the working classes. There is no absolute fusion between the interests of the state under capitalism and the capitalist class itself; the special responsibilities and functions of the modern state that encompass all sectors of society often conflict with the immediate interest of the capitalist sectors.[7] Workers, a majority in Argentina, as elsewhere, have been able to make a double claim on the state as the nation's largest popular as well as corporative group: first as citizens and consumers, then as producers.

My survey indicated that privatization and foreign investment have the critical support of the typical Argentine worker, who sees positive possibilities from responsible forms of capitalist development. The Argentine working class has not been impressed with the left's picture of marketplace exploitation. It has never indulged in idealizing revolutionary socialism. It has well understood Joseph Schumpeter's dictum, "We have to guard not only against the dangers that lurk in any attempt to compare a given reality with an *idea*, but also against the error or trick inherent in any comparison of a given reality with an *ideal*."[8] For many Argentine workers, the Eastern European forms of socialism stripped of rhetoric were but poorer varieties of capitalism with a political dictatorship to boot. To them, central ownership of the means of production seems more antithetical to workers' rights than the more dispersed forms of capitalist ownership.

I am beholden to Marx's view of the irrationality of capitalism, of the reality of exploitation, and the desirability of a harmonious, nonalienated culture, but am dubious about a revolutionary scenario as the way to achieve it. Revolutionary socialism would only lead, I believe, to other political forms that are not necessarily better than reforms undertaken by social democratic parties, even though the latter have not as yet successfully confronted monopoly capitalism. The socialist revolutions of the twentieth century did not prevent Stalinism, the Khmer Rouge, or Maoism — examples of what

Bernstein predicted would occur when millennialism was applied in dogmatic ways.

Left intellectuals speak of "reforms" and reforms. I agree on the
importance of seeking *fundamental*, structural "reforms" along with bread-
and-butter reforms. But we cannot postpone or defer the latter by thinking
they are exclusive of or less consequential than fundamental and immediate
changes in workers' lives. I don't know many intellectuals of the left who
would want to live in a slum or live without at least a stereo, or maybe a VCR,
coffee maker, and phone-answering machine. I don't know any professionals
who are political radicals who lack for any of these items by necessity, only by
choice. Bernstein felt this same contradiction at the turn of the century.

Revolutions, even those inspired by the most appalling social and
economic conditions, sometimes merely replace one kind of injustice for
another. Under revolutionary leadership, real workers tend eventually to be
shunted aside and resubordinated. At least gradual, democratic reformism
doesn't arouse expectations that, when not fulfilled, stimulate cynicism and
deep alienation, as we have seen in contemporary Eastern Europe and the
Soviet Union. The leftist propensity to "clean the slate" and begin history all
over again is something that Edmund Burke debunked — successfully, I
think. History cannot be ended by fiat, except by authoritarian measures.
Stalin emerged as a totalitarian of the left without any internal alternatives or
threats to his hegemony. It happened because of the paternalism and elitism
built into a reflexive and dogmatic Marxism.

I agree with Schumpeter's view of the necessity for democratic controls
over socialism. Leadership accountability and responsibility are essential to a
democracy. In a modern context these are the only forms of viable and
sustainable control over the heads of government. Democratic ways of
limiting governments have a much better record of success under welfare
capitalism than under revolutionary socialism in the twentieth century.
Trade unions must pursue independent and autonomously arrived at solutions to society's problems. However, working-class organizations cannot
have complete independence. They are part of society. Workers, whoever
they are supposed to be, do not see themselves as separate; intellectuals of
the left have largely created this characterization.

Apocalyptic politics is foreign to most Argentine workers. They do not
understand the accusation, made by writers from Marcuse to Burawoy, that
liberal-capitalist reforms are mere guises for enhanced repression and
therefore a qualitative leap to socialism is justified. Workers, like peasants,
are like everyone else; when they take extreme measures into their own
hands and join revolutionary movements, they do so for explicable human
reasons. When popular-class violence breaks out, it is not to bring in a

millennial utopia but to protect property and land (for example, Zapata and his peasant followers in Mexico); to return to their land, jobs, and families in peace (the Bolsheviks and their followers); to protect themselves against arbitrary landlord taxation (Mao Zedung and his followers); to defend themselves against a dictator's arbitrary undermining of a democratic constitution (Castro and his followers); to protest the reversal of previously won working-class benefits (the Cordobazo labor leaders and their followers); and to protect small entrepreneurs from repressive state monopoly capital (the Sandinistas and their followers).

The substantive goals of equality and liberty cannot be attained simultaneously. Therefore the best possible position for workers in Argentina and elsewhere is to accept everyday politics and a quantitative, cumulative view of progress. Argentine workers largely aspire to an improving life through better work opportunities, education for themselves and their children, and leisure to enjoy what they have earned. Though a minority of workers have left Argentina in frustration on these very accounts, most remain, critically optimistic and not despairing.[9]

In a play I saw in Buenos Aires in 1987 called *Made in Lanus*, a couple who had emigrated to California (Mabel and Oswaldo) return for a brief visit to friends (Yoli and Cacho) in their old neighborhood in Greater Buenos Aires. Yoli says to her husband, Cacho, who is tempted also to leave Argentina, "When your auto body shop was on fire, everybody helped save it; it was Cacho's shop . . . [in the United States you would be just another mechanic]." Yoli at another point takes pride in struggling *acá* and says, "*Cosas tiene que durar.*" If she doesn't make it, her daughter will; if not, her daughter's daughter. Autonomy and the willingness to struggle for a better future is paramount for Argentine workers. The struggle itself is not a problem if one is fairly compensated during the struggle; absence of hope is the problem, and the Argentine working class, despite their protestations, continues to have hope.

Notes
Bibliography
Index

Notes

Chapter 1. Putting Workers in Perspective

1. Interview with light and power (Luz y Fuerza) worker, January 3, 1986. This and all subsequent testimony from Argentine workers and quotations from Argentine writers are the author's translations.

2. Carl Boggs, *Gramsci's Marxism* (London: Pluto Press, 1976), p. 71.

3. Wilhelm Reich, *Sex-Pol Essays: 1929–1934* (New York: Random House, 1966), p. 358.

4. *New York Times*, March 7, 1987, p. 8.

5. For this backdrop I rely on the many historical accounts contained in the writings of Alvaro Abós, Torcuato Di Tella, Louise Doyon, Hugo del Campo, Ricardo Gaudio, Gino Germani, Julio Godio, Felix Luna, Walter Little, Miguel Murmis and Juan Carlos Portantiero, Peter Smith, Hobart Spalding, and others, as well as the testimony of former labor leaders on the early Peronist phenomenon as transcribed by the Oral History Project of the Instituto Torcuato Di Tella in Buenos Aires.

6. There are several exceptions, particularly in the British, North American, Italian, Chilean, Cuban, and Mexican settings. See the works of John Goldthorpe et al., *The Affluent Worker: Political Attitudes and Behavior* (Cambridge: Cambridge University Press, 1968); Studs Terkel, *Working* (New York: Pantheon Press, 1974); Barbara Garson, *All the Livelong Day* (New York: Penguin Books, 1974); Robert Schrank, *Ten Thousand Working Days* (Cambridge, Mass.: MIT Press, 1978); Robert Lane, *Political Ideology: Why the American Common Man Believes What He Does* (New York: Free Press, 1962); John Low-Beer, *Protest and Participation: The New Working Class in Italy* (Cambridge: Cambridge University Press, 1978); Peter Winn, *Weavers of the Revolution: The Yarur Workers and Chile's Road to Socialism* (New York: Oxford University Press, 1986); Maurice Zeitlin, *Revolutionary Politics and the Cuban Working Class* (Princeton, N.J.: Princeton University Press, 1967); Ian Roxborough, *Unions and Politics in Mexico: The Case of the Auto Industry* (New York: Cambridge University Press, 1984). On Argentina, two exceptions (though, like the Winn and Roxborough

studies on Chilean textile workers and Mexican autoworkers, they treat only one industrial or occupational sector) are José Nun's "Despidos en la indústria automotríz argentina," *Revista Mexicana de Sociología* 40 (1979), 55-106; Juan José Llovet, *Los lustrabotas de Buenos Aires* (Buenos Aires: CEDES, 1980).

7. As Peter Winn writes: "[Research on Latin American workers] . . . must become more fully the history of work and workers, studying not just structural and statistical parameters, national organizations and major strike movements, but also the concrete everyday experience of workers in the factory and community, their living standards and life styles, culture and consciousness, internal divisions and relations with other groups" "Oral History and the Factory Study: New Approaches to Labor History," *Latin American Research Review* 14 (1979), 130.

8. Among many others, see Edgardo Catterberg, "Las elecciones del 30 de Octubre de 1983, El surgimiento de una nueva convergencia electoral," *Desarrollo Económico* 25, no. 98 (July/September 1985), 260-67; Santiago Senén González, *Diez años de sindicalismo argentino: de Perón al proceso* (Buenos Aires; Ediciones Corregidor, 1984); Juan Carlos Torre, *Los sindicatos en el gobierno, 1973–1976* (Buenos Aires: Centro Editor de América Latina, 1983); Juan Villarreal's chapter in Eduardo Jozami's *Crisis de la dictadura argentina* (Buenos Aires: Siglo XXI, 1985), 245-81.

9. Winn, *Weavers of the Revolution,* p. 8. Robert Lane, over a quarter of a century ago, asked some of these questions in the North American context. I found many of Lane's queries very relevant in the formulation of my Argentine questionnaire. He wrote that his book was about "three aspects of political ideology. First, it undertakes to discover the latent political ideology of the American urban common man. Second, it attempts to explain the sources of this ideology in the culture and experiences this common man knows . . . and, third, it deals (more briefly) with the way in which the American common man's ideology — or any ideology — supports or weakens the institutions of democracy" (Lane, *Political Ideology: Why the American Common Man Believes What He Does*, p. 3, and Appendix A, pp. 481-93).

10. The major full-blown restatement of Marx's position for contemporary culture is Georg Lukács, *History and Class Consciousness* (Cambridge, Mass.: MIT Press, 1971).

11. For example, as Bauman suggests, for Marxists, workers were a particularly tempting agency of revolution since they also needed the supervision and direction of the intelligentsia. See Zygmunt Bauman, "The Left as the Counter-Culture of Modernity" *Telos* 70 (Winter 1986–1987), 81-93.

12. E. P. Thompson, *The Making of the English Working Class* (London: Pelican Books, 1968), p. 9.

13. Ibid.

14. Karl Marx and Friedrich Engels, *The Communist Manifesto* (New York: International Publishers, 1948), p. 11.

15. Eduard Bernstein, *Evolutionary Socialism* (New York: Schocken Books, 1961), p. 105.

16. E. P. Thompson, *The Making of the English Working Class*, p. 11.

17. Carlos Vilas, *Nationalism and Revolution in Nicaragua* (New York: Monthly Review Press, 198), p. 37.

18. Eric Hobsbawm, *Workers: Worlds of Labor* (New York: Pantheon Books, 1984) p. 280.

19. Bernstein, *Evolutionary Socialism*, p. 116.

20. John Booth and Mitchell Seligson, "The Political Culture of Authoritarianism in Mexico: A Reexamination," *Latin American Research Review* 19 (1984), 106-24; Susan Taino, "Authoritarianism and Political Culture in Argentina and Chile in the mid-1960s," *Latin American Research Review* 21 (1986), 73-98; David Halle, *America's Working Man: Work, Home and Politics Among Blue-Collar Property Owners* (Chicago: University of Chicago Press, 1984).

21. See for example the works of Theodore Adorno, Milton Rokeach, and S. M. Lipset.

22. Booth and Seligson, "The Political Culture of Authoritarianism in Mexico," pp. 117-18.

23. Taino, "Authoritarianism and Political Culture in Argentina and Chile," p. 81.

24. *Estructura sindical en la Argentina* (Buenos Aires: Ministerio de Trabajo, 1986), pp. 16-17.

25. See Héctor Palomino, "El movimiento obrero y sindical en una larga transición" *El Bimestre* 26 (1986), 12-20; and Alvaro Abós, *Los sindicatos argentinos: Cuadro de situación, 1984* (Buenos Aires: Centro de Estudios para el Proyecto Nacional, 1985).

26. The opening salvos of Bernstein, Luxemburg, and Lenin initiated a continuing twentieth-century debate. Among many other contributions by each, see Eduard Bernstein, *Evolutionary Socialism*; Rosa Luxemburg, *Reform and Revolution* (New York: Pathfinder Press, 1970); and V. I. Lenin, *What is to be Done?* (New York: International Publishers, 1969).

27. Hobsbawm, *Workers: Worlds of Labor*, p. 281.

28. For a comprehensive study of Argentina's changing social structure, see Hector Palomino, *Cambios ocupacionales y sociales en Argentina, 1947–1985* (Buenos Aires: CISEA, 1987).

29. See Juan Villarreal's chapter in Eduardo Jozami et al., eds., *Crisis de la dictadura argentina* (Buenos Aires: Siglo XXI, 1985), pp. 245-81.

30. Héctor Palomino, "El movimiento obrero y sindical en una larga transición," *El Bimestre* 26 (1986), 12-20.

31. Eduardo Lucita, "Elecciones sindicales y autoorganización obrera en Argentina," *Cuadernos del Sur*, no. 3 (July/September, 1985), 5-54.

32. See Jorge Schvarzer, *Martínez de Hoz: La lógica política de la política económica* (Buenos Aires: CISEA, 1983).

33. Erik O. Wright, *Class, Crisis and the State* (London: New Left Books, 1978), p. 97.

34. Alejandro Portes, "On the Interpretation of Class Consciousness," *American Journal of Sociology* 77, no. 2 (1971), 13.

35. Leaders of the Peronist party in Buenos Aires, after its defeat in the 1983 presidential elections and 1985 legislative elections, were concerned about clarifying its democratic principles to the population by distancing itself from the Herminio

Iglesias right-wing faction, while continuing to espouse trade union social and economic demands. See Peter Ranis, "The Dilemmas of Democratization in Argentina," *Current History* 85 (January 1986), 29ff.

36. UOM also includes a large minority of iron and steel workers, particularly SOMISA (state iron and steel enterprise) and ACINDAR (very large private iron and steel enterprise) located in the industrial cities of San Nicolás and Villa Constitución.

37. My research assistants were (1) a *licenciada* in sociology from the University of Buenos Aires, (2) a *licenciada* in international relations from the University of El Salvador in Buenos Aires, (3) a *licenciada* in political science from Catholic University in Buenos Aires, and (4) a third-year student of political science at the John Kennedy University in Buenos Aires.

38. The tapes also enabled me to clear up any uncertainties following the interviews. Each evening I would listen to the day's recordings and would telephone my assistants if any responses lacked clarity. I also taped my own interviews for the first eight months, or until I was absolutely sure of my ability to understand Spanish nuances and the Porteño slang occasionally contained in the workers' responses. This permitted me to listen to the interviews again to double check the accuracy of the answers I filled in during interviews.

39. The open-endedness of the structured interviews allowed for in-depth probing of individual answers. The interviews were meant to be free-flowing, casual, uninterrupted conversations that would not channel answers as multiple choice and restrictive questionnaires sometimes do, although this made the responses harder to collate and categorize into a survey data-book for computerization. My idea was to learn as much as possible about the world of the workers and not to place them in a procrustean bed so as to facilitate tabulation and quantification.

40. However, while I was interviewing UOM metalworkers in August 1986, the shop stewards' committee decided (after five interviews had been conducted) that, because of the detailed and personal nature of the questionnaire, they would prefer that we not tape the responses. Thus the balance of the interviews (ten) were conducted without being recorded. It is important to emphasize that this was the decision of the union shop delegates, not the wish of individual metalworkers. Interestingly, the metallurgical union is known as one of the most "verticalist" and least pluralist of the major Argentine trade unions.

41. This occurred during the first couple of weeks of my stay in Buenos Aires when I was conducting interviews at my residence. I realized that, given the length of the workday and workers' wages following the Austral reforms, requiring any kind of travel would be a major imposition on interviewees. From then on I went to the factories and the offices, usually receiving permission to interview during the workday itself.

42. Barbara Garson, *All the Livelong Day* (New York: Penguin Books, 1975), pp. xv-xvi.

43. See John Madge, *The Tools of Social Science* (New York: Doubleday, 1965), pp. xxvi-xxx.

Chapter 2. Labor and Peronism: The Historical Connection

1. See Gino Germani, *Política y sociedad en una época de transición* (Buenos Aires: Editorial Paidós, 1962); and Alfredo Galletti, *La realidad Argentina en el siglo XX: La política y los partidos* (Buenos Aires: Fondo de Cultura Económica, 1961).

2. Charles Bergquist, *Labor in Latin America: Comparative Essays on Chile, Argentina, Venezuela and Colombia* (Stanford: Stanford University Press, 1986), p. 105. I have some problems with his conception of "ownership of the means of production" by artisans who own a shoe repair store, have a bakery in their home, or do carpentry out of a small workshop. *Ownership* is very central to my own thesis in this book, but it is not the same thing as *ownership of the means of production*.

3. Ruth Thompson, "The Limitations of Ideology in the Early Argentine Labour Movements: Anarchism in the Trade Unions, 1890–1920," *Journal of Latin American Studies* 17 (May 1984), 98-99.

4. Ronaldo Munck, *Argentina: From Anarchism to Peronism* (London: Zed Books, 1987), p. 52.

5. Thompson, "The Limitations of Ideology in the Early Argentine Labour Movements," p. 83. One of the few parties that stood for structural reforms of society, the Socialist party of 1920 had a high infusion of artisans, small merchants, and independent professionals with but a bare majority of "workers" and employees. See Richard Walter, *The Socialist Party of Argentina, 1890–1930* (Austin: University of Texas Press, 1977).

6. See Miguel Murmis and Juan Carlos Portantiero, *Estudios sobre los orígines del Peronismo* (Buenos Aires: Siglo XXI, 1972).

7. Peter J. Van Hove, "Working-Class Crowds and Political Change in Buenos Aires, 1919–1945," Ph.D. diss., University of New Mexico, 1970; and Eduardo Jorge, *Indústria y concentración económica* (Buenos Aires: Siglo XXI, 1973), esp. pp. 151-52.

8. Juan José Llach, "Intereses económicos dominantes y orígenes del Peronismo," unpublished, 1973, pp. 25-26.

9. Murmis and Portantiero, *Estudios sobre los orígines del Peronismo*, p. 91. However, Monica Peralta Ramos writes that the trade union movement before Perón was divided into two important currents: one sought to maintain the independence of the unions as a working-class pressure group, while the other urged combination with the leftist parliamentary parties, subordinating the workers' purely domestic preoccupations to the international crusade against fascism. See *Etapas de acumulación y alianzas de clases en Argentina* (Buenos Aires: Siglo XXI, 1972), p. 94.

10. Luisa Montuschi, *El poder económico de los sindicatos* (Buenos Aires: Editorial de la Universidad de Buenos Aires, 1979). Between 1941 and 1945 there was a 20 percent rise in overall union membership. See Louis M. Doyon, "El crecimiento sindical bajo el Peronismo." *Desarrollo Económico* 15 (1975): 154.

11. Walter Little, "La organización obrera y el estado peronista, 1943–1955," *Desarrollo Económico* 18 (October/December 1979), 375; Doyon, "El crecimiento sindical bajo el Peronismo," 154.

238 Notes to Pages 18–20

12. Rodolfo Puiggros, *El Peronismo: Sus causas* (Buenos Aires: Ediciones Cepe, 1969), pp. 55-56; Ernesto González, *Qué fué y qué és el Peronismo* (Buenos Aires: Ediciones Pluma, 1974, p. 26; and Peter H. Smith, *Carne y política en la Argentina* (Buenos Aires: Paidós, 1968).

13. Ruben H. Zorrilla speaks of the widely held belief among union leaders that governmental statism can end the "anarchy" in society. See *El liderazgo síndical argentino desde sus orígines hasta 1975* (Buenos Aires: Siglo XX, 1983), pp. 29-32.

14. Arturo Jauretche, Instituto Torcuato Di Tella Oral History Project, interview conducted March–April 1971, pp. 165, 194.

15. See Felix Luna, *El 45: Crónica de un año decisivo* (Buenos Aires: Jorge Alvarez, 1969); Esteban Peicovich, *Hóla Perón* (Buenos Aires: Editorial Granica, 1973); and Enrique Pavon Pereyra, *Perón, el conductor de América* (Buenos Aires: Ediciones El Quijote, 1950).

16. These collective bargaining agreements would only be legitimate if approved by the secretary of labor. Perón used this provision to give official sanction to newly constituted friendly unions and to withhold recognition from rival existing unions. See Little, "La organización obrera y el estado peronista, 1943–1955," p. 338; and Van Hove, "Working-Class Crowds and Political Change in Buenos Aires, 1919–1945," pp. 229ff.

17. See Rodolfo Puiggros, *El Peronismo: Sus causas* (Buenos Aires: Ediciones Cepe, 1972), p. 140ff.; Enrique Silberstein, *Por qué Perón sigue siendo Perón: La economía Peronista* (Buenos Aires: Ediciones Corregidor, 1972), pp. 75-87; and Little, "La organización obrera y el estado peronista, 1943–1955." *passim*.

18. Juan Domingo Perón, *El pueblo ya sabe de que se trata* (Buenos Aires: Editorial Freeland, 1973), pp. 182-84.

19. Ibid., pp. 38-39.

20. Ibid., pp. 76, 93.

21. Ibid.

22. Ibid., pp. 166, 191.

23. Speaking in Junín, Buenos Aires, on October 15, 1944, Perón said: "The requirements of the nation cannot be exaggerated individualism, nor will there be state collectivization, which kills the individual and buries him in a prison." See Juan Domingo Perón, *El pueblo quiere saber de que se trata* (Buenos Aires: Editorial Freeland, 1973), p. 214. Interestingly, Perón likened his struggle in Argentina to Franklin Roosevelt's struggle in the United States. He praised Roosevelt often in 1945 and considered the New Deal similar to the kind of "national restoration" he envisioned for Argentina. Perón considered Roosevelt's struggle against the left and right parallel to his own position. See *El pueblo ya sabe de que se trata* (Buenos Aires: Editorial Freeland, 1973), p. 87.

24. Ibid. Perón, himself, as a member of the 1943 military junta, represented a departure from the leadership of the 1930s. As Feinman writes, "Their names shocked the oligarchy when they came to light: Perón, Ramírez, Farrell, González, Mercante. Where did they come from? They were the sons of the immigrant, hardworking Yrigoyen working class that had been introduced into military life as a

means of social ascent. . . . They were Catholics, nationalists, Axis sympathizers, more because of their professional and theoretical orientation than from any real political identification. They had been educated with the classic texts of the German military strategists, Clausewitz, Von der Goltz, and now had decided to get directly involved in politics." José Pablo Feinman, *El peronismo y la primacía de la política* (Buenos Aires: Editorial Cimarrón, 1974), p. 158.

25. Perón, *El pueblo quiere saber*, pp. 157-66.

26. Ibid., p. 167.

27. Felix Luna, *El 45* (Buenos Aires: Jorge Alvarez, 1969), p. 38ff.

28. See Enrique Díaz Araujo, *La conspiración del 43, el gou; Una experiéncia militarista en la Argentina* (Mendoza: Universidad Nacional de Cuyo, no. 19, 1970); and Peter Ranis, "Early Peronism and the Post-Liberal Argentine State," *Journal of Interamerican Studies and World Affairs* 21, no. 3 (August 1979), 320ff

29. On the development and implementation of the Peronist doctrines, see Rolando Concatti, *Peronismo* (Buenos Aires: Sacerdotes para el Tercer Mundo, 1972); Joseph Page, *Perón: A Biography* (New York: Random House, 1983); Robert Crassweller, *Perón and the Enigmas of Argentina* (New York: W.W. Norton, 1987); and Paul H. Lewis, *The Crisis of Argentine Capitalism* (Chapel Hill: University of North Carolina Press, 1990). An interesting footnote to history comes from an interview with Cipriano Reyes conducted by the Di Tella Oral History Project in January 1971. He said, "Everything that we call Peronist doctrine and principles is nothing more than the doctrine and principles of the Labor party program that Perón made his own and that we practically handed to him." According to Reyes, Perón even borrowed his famous greeting to the workers, "*Compañeros,*" without knowing the full historical meaning of the term. "When we explained its international context, he smiled and said, 'Ah, like we use 'buddies' in the army!'" (p. 19). For one of the key Peronist documents, see Juan D. Perón, *Doctrina Peronista* (Buenos Aires: Presidencia de la Nación, 1950).

30. Observers of Argentina often belittle Peronist ideology as a vapid and superficial attempt to contrive a pragmatic set of suppositions developed to fit the moment. In this context it is instructive to reread Barrington Moore's assessment of Italian fascism. He wrote, "During the summer of this year (1921) Mussolini made his famous observation that 'if Fascism does not wish to die or, worse still, to commit suicide, it must now provide itself with a doctrine. . . . I do wish, that during the two months which are still to elapse before our National Assembly meets, *the philosophy of Fascism could be created*' [my emphasis]." See Moore, *Social Origins of Dictatorship and Democracy* (Boston: Beacon Press, 1966), p. 451.

31. However, for the Argentine Communist leadership Perón felt only contempt. In an interview with Tomás Eloy Martínez, Perón said, "How are they going to make me believe that the Argentine Communists of Victório Codovilla [general secretary] were revolutionaries when I had seen them arm in arm with Antonio Santamarina [Conservative leader]. They weren't at all. They were a well-paid bureaucracy that didn't want to lose their allowances. We felt ourselves a thousand times more communist than they." Tomás Eloy Martínez, "Las memórias de Juan

Perón, 1895–1945," *Panorama* 7, no. 155 (April 1970), 25. This remains the popular view of Communists today among most workers.

32. See Mariano Grondona, "Justicialismo, Marxismo, Liberalismo," *Mercado*, July 26, 1973.

33. Monica Peralta Ramos, *Etapas de acumulación y alianzas de clases en Argentina* (Buenos Aires: Siglo XXI, 1972), p. 169.

34. Carlos Waisman writes, "The party itself was a small organization, with only a few thousand activists, and the growth of its influence in the early forties was due more to its participation as a liberal-democratic organization in the antifascist 'resistance,' whose social base was mostly middle class and whose very development, paradoxically, was a reaction to the pro-axis policies of the state than to its functioning as a revolutionary agent in the labor movement." See his *Reversal of Development in Argentina* (Princeton, N.J.: Princeton University Press, 1987), p. 195.

35. Marx wrote about these mid-nineteenth-century factions of society with undisguised venom: "There were tramps, discharged soldiers, discharged convicts, fugitive galley slaves, swindlers, charlatans, *lazzaroni*, pickpockets, conjurors, gamblers, pimps, brothel-keepers, porters, literary drudges, organ grinders, ragpickers, knife grinders, tinkers, beggars, in short the whole haphazard, dissolute battered mass which the French call *la bohème*; of these kindred elements Bonaparte formed the main body of the Society of 10 December. A "benevolent association"—to the extent that all members, like Bonaparte himself, felt the necessity of benefitting themselves at the expense of the workers. This Bonaparte, who constitutes himself *leader of the Lumpenproletariat*, who only here can find again in the mass those interests which he personally pursues, who recognizes in this scum, refuse, waste of all classes the only class on which he can unconditionally depend; this is the true Bonaparte, the Bonaparte *sans* phrase." Karl Marx, *The 18th Brumaire of Louis Bonaparte* (New York: International Publishers, 1963), p. 75.

36. Daniel James, "October 17th, 1945: Mass Protest, Peronism and the Argentine Working Class," presented at the annual meeting of the Latin American Studies Association, Boston, October 1986. It is very clear that the Argentine Communists are not alone in these attitudes; they may be found among Communists from Bolivia to England to Egypt to Indonesia. The orientation of the British Communists was like the Argentine Communists' view of *cabezitas negras*. As Raphael Samuel writes in "Class Politics: The Lost World of British Communism," *New Left Review* 165 (September/October 1987), 72-73:

> It was the normal Communist explanation for the phenomenon of working class fascism—a feature in such East End boroughs as Shoreditch and Bethnal Green. . . . In Liverpool it freely denoted those Irish districts of the city where the Communists were liable to be mobbed. . . . Communists would use it for those who were too demoralized to resist, susceptible to the capitalist press or impervious to serious impressions. People who liked their beer too much were "lumpen" as were those, such as "Spivs," who lived by their wits. . . . It was also a term of physical contempt, being often allied to notions of fatness and sloth. "Lumpen," though Communists were not aware of it, had affinities to

Burkean notions of the "mob," as well as "dangerous classes" of 19th century society. It is a measure of communism's alienation from the popular that it could be used as an unproblematic term of abuse."

37. Andrés Oscar Avellaneda, "El tema del peronismo en la narrativa argentina," Ph.D. diss., University of Illinois, 1973, p. 77. Martínez Estrada's famous anti-Peronist work is entitled *Qué es esto?* (Buenos Aires: Editorial Lautaro, 1956).

38. See ibid., p. 108ff.; and Arturo Jauretche, *El medio pelo* (Buenos Aires: Pena Lillo, 1969), p. 248.

39. Cited in Avellaneda, "El tema del peronismo en la narrativa argentina," pp. 129-30, cited from Alfredo Moffatt, *Estratégias para sobrevivir en Buenos Aires* (Buenos Aires: Jorge Alvarez, 1967), pp. 62-63. For some, the personal veneration of Perón became unbearable. See the Di Tella Oral History interview with the well-known nationalist, founder of the Liga Republicana and early supporter of Perón, Carlos Ibarguren, July 1971, p. 46.

40. Note that the Argentine Communists' collaboration with the right began at a time when international Communism subordinated its revolutionary aims to a popular front "class collaborationist" strategy against fascism, whereas the Cuban Communists' alliance with Castro came at the height of the cold war and coincided with rampant anti-imperialism in Cuba.

41. The concept of Bonapartism is derived from Marx's analysis in *The 18th Brumaire of Louis Bonaparte*. Gramsci later typified this autonomous rule above classes as Caesarism. See Antonio Gramsci, *Selections from Prison Notebooks* (New York: International Publishers, 1971). There is extensive theoretical literature on Argentine populism. See esp. Ernesto LaClau, *Politics and Ideology in Marxist Theory* (London: Verso Press, 1979); Fernando H. Cardoso and Enzo Faletto, *Dependencia y desarrollo en América Latina* (Buenos Aires: Siglo XXI, 1969); Miguel Murmis and Juan Carlos Portantiero, *Estudios sobre los orígines del Peronismo* (Buenos Aires: Siglo XXI, 1972); Guillermo O'Donnell and D. Linck, *Dependencia y autonomia* (Buenos Aires: Amorrortu, 1973); Torcuato Di Tella et al., *Argentina: Sociedad de masas* (Buenos Aires: Eudeba, 1965), chap. 8; and Carlos M. Vilas, "El populismo latinoamericano: un enfoque estructural" *Desarrollo Económico* 28, no. 111 (October/December 1988), 323-51.

42. See Jorge Abelardo Ramos, *La era del Bonapartismo*, vol. 5 of *Revolución y contrarevolución en la Argentina* (Buenos Aires: Editorial Plus Ultra, 1973), p. 185ff.

43. Cardoso and Faletto, *Dependencia y desarrollo en América Latina*, p. 116.

44. Various Argentine analysts have written, from widely disparate perspectives, on the Peronist regime's slow move away from populist policies and its more typical insertion into the international capitalist system. See, for example, Monica Peralta Ramos, *Etapas de acumulación y alianzas de clases en Argentina* (Buenos Aires: Siglo XXI, 1972); Milciades Peña, *Masas, caudillos y elites: La dependencia argentina de Irigoyen a Perón* (Buenos Aires: Ediciones Fichas, 1971); Alberto Belloni, *Del anarquismo al peronismo* (Buenos Aires: Peña Lillo, 1960); and José Luis Romero, *El pensamiento político de la derecha latinoamericana* (Buenos Aires: Paidós, 1970).

45. According to a close associate of Perón, Oscar Albrieu, after 1951, Perón would have the president of the party, Admiral Tessaire meet with the congressional delegation on important governmental legislative proposals. "The only thing he wanted from Congress was that they pass governmental initiatives. . . . Even as they were discussing a jurisdictional or legal question, if it occurred to the legislative block leader to mention that the bill in question was 'ordered by Perón,' the labor and female sectors (forty each) would get up and shout, 'Perón, Perón, Perón!'" and the unanimity would make debate and dialogue appear quite useless. . . . It came down to just mentioning Perón's name and the measure was law." Torcuato Di Tella Oral History project interview (August 1972), pp. 43-59.

46. See Peralta Ramos, *Etapas de acumulación y alianzas de clases en Argentina*, p. 118; and Hobart A. Spalding, *Organized Labor in Latin America* (New York: Harper Torchbooks, 1977), p. 175.

47. As Little indicates, union workers themselves became trade union leaders and some participated directly in the government of Perón. Workers became ministerial bureaucrats, gubernatorial assistants, legislators and representatives on the executive committees of newly nationalized industries. The CGT had acquired unquestionable influence in Perón's government. See Little, "La organización obrera y el estado peronista, 1943–1955," p. 345.

48. The Peronist Ministry of Labor also provided meeting halls for the smaller unions that had none, provided advisers for technical questions concerning collective bargaining agreements, and generally acted as a supportive intermediary during difficult negotiations. See Enrique Silberstein, *Por que Perón sigue siendo Perón: La economía peronista* (Buenos Aires: Ediciones Corregidor, 1972), p. 58.

49. See Doyon, "El crecimiento sindical bajo el Peronismo," 158-60.

50. Little, "La organización obrera y el estado peronista, 1943–1955, p. 370. We assume his figures encompass only the major, nationally organized union federations. Otherwise, the figure of 83 seems much too small. At the same time, apparently, more than half of all national unions in Argentina were established during the Peronist years. See Ruben H. Zorilla, *Estructura y dinámica del sindicalismo argentino* (Buenos Aires: Editorial La Pleyao, 1974), pp. 101-02.

51. See Louise M. Doyon, "Conflictos obreros durante el régimen peronista (1946–1955)," *Desarrollo Económico* 17 (1977): 442, 469.

52. See Bertram Silverman, "Labor Ideology and Economic Development in the Peronist Epoch," *Studies in Comparative International Development* 4, no. 11 (1968-69), 245-47; and Peralta Ramos, *Etapas de acumulación y alianzas de clases en Argentina*, p. 60. On the question of salary increases outrunning labor productivity under early Peronism, see Liliana de Riz, *Retorno y derrumbe: el último gobierno peronista* (Mexico City: Folios Ediciones, 1981), p. 95.

53. Llach reports workers' share of national income as averaging 46.1 percent in 1935–1943, 51.5 percent in 1944–1954, and 55.6 percent in 1949–1954. See Juan José Llach, "Intereses económicos dominantes y orígines del peronismo," unpublished, 1972, p. 14. Peralta Ramos reports that those on wages and salaries, as a percentage of national income in the industrial sector, reached a high of 57.7 percent in

1954 (*Etapas de acumulación y alianzas de clases en Argentina*), pp. 34, 150. Enrique Silberstein, in *Por que Perón sigue siendo Perón: La economía peronista* (Buenos Aires: Ediciones Corregidor, 1972), p. 13, puts the highest income distribution figures for workers at 56.9 percent in 1952 and the lowest at 45.2 percent in 1946. Antonio Cafiero cites workers earning 46.8 percent in 1946 and 61 percent in 1952, falling only to approximately 58 percent in 1955. See his *Cinco años después* (Buenos Aires, 1961), p. 128.

On the other hand, the Economic Commission For Latin America (ECLA), UN figures give workers' wages and salaries under Perón as a low of 37.3 percent in 1947 to a high of almost 47 percent in 1952. See ECLA, *Economic Development and Income Distribution in Argentina* (New York: United Nations, 1969), p. 169. According to another analysis, the workers' share of national income under Perón went from a low of 41 percent in 1946–1948 to over 48 percent in 1949–1951 to a high of just over 49 percent in 1952–1955. See Scott Mainwaring, "El movimiento obrero y el Peronismo, 1952–1955," *Desarrollo Económico* 21, no. 84 (January/March 1982), 519. Finally, Bertram Silverman puts the figures for wages and salaries in industry as percent of national income at a low of 45.2 percent in 1946 and a high of 56.7 percent in 1950 ("Labor Ideology and Economic Development in the Peronist Epoch," pp. 243-45). (Discrepancies in these figures are likely caused by sometimes including workers' social welfare and pension funds as part of their cumulative salary or wage.)

54. Among the best accounts of Perón's fall, see Joseph Page, *Perón: A Biography*; and Arthur P. Whitaker, *Argentine Upheaval* (New York: Praeger, 1956). Perón's second administration compounded the fervor of his enemies with evidence of corruption and scandal. See the uncompromising exposé of Perón's government in *El libro negro de la segunda tiranía* (Buenos Aires: Presidencia de la Nación, Comisión Nacional de Investigaciones, 1958).

55. Bruno C. Jacovella, "Los ingredientes de la história argentina," *Dinámica Social* 117 (June 1960), 13.

56. Juan J. Hernández Arregui, *Peronismo y socialismo* (Buenos Aires: Editorial Corregidor, 1973), p. 71.

57. Regime–labor union relationships during this period have been dealt with extensively in William C. Smith, *Authoritarianism, Democracy and the Crisis of the Argentine Political Economy* (Stanford, Calif.: Stanford University Press, 1989), esp. chap. 4; and Daniel James, *Resistance and Integration: Peronism and the Argentine Working Class* (New York: Cambridge University Press, 1988).

58. Carlos Waisman shows that toward the end of the Peronist regime, 52 percent of the industrial workers were employed by firms with up to 100 workers, in other words, firms representing the small and medium national bourgeoisie essentially producing for the domestic market. *Reversal of Development in Argentina* (Princeton, N.J.: Princeton University Press, 1987), p. 189.

59. Perón's increasingly radical rhetoric from exile is most clearly seen in two of his books: *La fuerza es el derecho de las béstias* (Madrid, 1957) and *La hora de los pueblos* (Buenos Aires: Editorial Norte, 1968).

60. When juxtaposed to the utter brutality of the *proceso* dictatorship, the Aramburu military regime pales in contrast. Nevertheless, it is easy to forget the

attempts under the first post-Perón military dictatorship to simply *abolish* Peronism. Rodolfo Terragno recounts how the regime prohibited "images, symbols, signs, significant expressions, doctrines, articles and artistic works that were or could be interpreted as being associated with Peronist ideology." Perón's name could not be written, nor could his picture be shown. Citizens were forbidden to use the words "third position" or Perón's initials (that is, JDP), nor could the date of Perón's rise to power, October 17, be publicized in any fashion. See Rodolfo Terragno, *Los 400 dias de Perón* (Buenos Aires: Ediciones de la Flor, 1974), p. 22. An attempted pro-Peronist uprising in June 1956 was met by firing squads and massive reprisals then unique in twentieth-century Argentine history. See Peter Ranis, "Parties, Politics and Peronism: A Study of Post-Perón Political Development," Ph.D. diss., New York University, 1965); and Ernesto González, *Qué fue y qué es el peronismo* (Buenos Aires: Ediciones Pluma, 1974), p. 71ff.

61. Gerardo Duejo, *El capital monopolista y las contradicciones secundárias en la sociedad argentina* (Buenos Aires: Siglo XXI, 1973), p. 48.

62. Under President Frondizi, new foreign investment laws, passed in 1959 and 1961, revised a rather more restrictive law in operation under Perón. It allowed foreign capital to enter Argentina unimpeded with almost no controls over profit repatriation after the initial investment arrangement and loosened restrictions on the importation of foreign capital goods. See Elsa Cimillo, et al., *Acumulación y centralización en la indústria Argentina* (Buenos Aires, Tiempo Contemporáneo, 1973), p. 76ff.; Carlos Vilas, "On the Crisis of Bourgeois Democracy in Argentina," *Latin American Perspectives* 9, no. 4 (Fall 1982), pp. 14ff.; and Juan Carlos Torre, "Workers' Struggle and Consciousness," *Latin American Perspectives* 1, no. 3 (Fall 1974), 80-81.

63. Peralta Ramos, *Etapas de acumulación y alianzas de clases en Argentina*, p. 144.

64. See Jorge Sábato and Jorge Schwarzer, "Funcionamiento de la economía y poder político en la Argentina," *Ibero-Americana* 13, no. 2 (1983), 11-38. Peralta Ramos, *Etapas de acumulación y alianzas de clases en Argentina*, p. 141, puts industrial growth rates in the decade of the 1960s as 38.4 percent, as against (for example) an 8.3 percent agricultural growth rate and a 13.6 percent growth rate in commerce.

65. It is clear that these heavy industries are capital-intensive, as we see a slow decrease in employment in manufacturing even while it is the most dynamic sector of the 1960s. See Héctor Palomino, *Efectos políticos y sociales de los cambios en el mercado de trabajo: Argentina 1950–1983* (Buenos Aires: CISEA, 1985), p. 9.

66. Gerardo Duejo, *El capital monopolista y las contradicciones secundárias en la sociedad Argentina* (Buenos Aires: Siglo XXI, 1973). Duejo writes (p. 65) that U.S. firms controlled 28.3 percent of total Argentine sales and Western European companies 31.7 percent. The balance was made up of the Argentine state sector (17.5 percent) and the Argentine domestic private sector (22.5 percent). Francisco Sercovich corroborates the figure of 60 percent foreign control over Argentine industrial enterprises in his "Dependencia tecnológica en la indústria argentina," *Desarrollo Económico* 14, no. 53 (April/June 1974), 40-41.

Also see Pablo Gerchunoff's and Juan Llach's findings regarding the increasing role of foreign companies in Argentina's most monopolized industries in "Capital industrial, desarrollo asociado y distribución del ingreso entre los dos gobiernos peronistas: 1950–1972," *Desarrollo Económico* 15, no. 57 (April/June 1975), 20ff.

Among the ten largest enterprises in Argentina by the end of the 1960s, eight were subsidiaries of multinational corporations and the other two were state companies. None represented private Argentine capital (Peralta Ramos, *Etapas de acumulación y alianzas de clases en Argentina*, pp. 160-61). Moreover, under Krieger Vasena, Onganía's economics minister, new banking legislation allowed foreign banking subsidiaries to buy up nineteen local banks between 1967 and 1969, which gave them control of 17.5 percent of deposits, 24 percent of industrial loans, and 18 percent of commercial loans. See "Argentina: In the Hour of the Furnaces," *NACLA*, 1975, p. 24.

67. See Karl Marx, *Capital* (New York: International Publishers, 1967), vol. 1.

68. Elsa Cimillo et al. *Acumulación y centralización en la indústria Argentina* (Buenos Aires: Tiempo Contemporáneo, 1973), p. 73.

69. On the Cordobazo of May 1969, see Juan C. Agulla, *Diagnóstico social de una crisis: Córdoba, Mayo de 1969* (Córdoba: Editel, 1969); Francisco J. Delich, *Crisis y protesta social; Córdoba, Mayo 1969* (Buenos Aires: Ediciones Signos, 1970); Daniel Villar, *El cordobazo* (Buenos Aires: Centro Editor de América Latina, 1971); and Ernesto González, *Qué fue y qué es el Peronismo* (Buenos Aires: Ediciones Pluma, 1974), p. 112ff.

70. These workers were represented by three very strong industrial unions with major impact on collective bargaining procedures, namely the metalworkers' union (UOM), the autoworkers' union (SMATA), and its affiliates SIDRAC (Sindicato de Trabajadores de Concord) and SIDRAM (Sindicato de Trabajadores de Materfer) and the Luz y Fuerza light and power workers.

71. Delich, *Crisis y protesta social*, p. 24.

72. Agulla, *Diagnóstico social de una crisis*, p.33.

73. Delich, *Crisis y protesta social*, p. 50.

74. Agulla, *Diagnóstico social de una crisis*, pp. 23, 81.

75. Ibid., p. 23. It is significant that salaries and wages constituted a higher percentage of national income than any other period dating back to 1951. See Pablo Gerchunoff and Juan J. Llach, "Capital industrial, desarrollo asociado y distribución del ingreso entre los dos gobiernos peronistas," pp. 27, 34. This is corroborated even for unskilled workers. See Adriana Marshall, "La composición del consumo de los obreros industriales de Buenos Aires, 1930–1980," *Desarrollo Económico* 21, no. 83 (October/December 1981), 372.

76. Peter Waldman has emphasized the latent antipathy toward the central government in Buenos Aires. This was fueled during the Cordobazo when troops from the East and the federal police were sent to help put down the uprising. See his "Anomía social y violencia," in *Argentina, hoy*, ed. Alain Rouquié (Mexico City: Siglo XXI, 1982), p. 247.

77. The slow decline of military options is exhaustively treated in William C. Smith, *Authoritarianism, Democracy and the Crisis of the Argentine Political Economy* (Stanford, Calif.: Stanford University Press, 1989).

78. Perón's most influential tracts were written while in exile between 1957 and 1968. One, *La fuerza es el derecho de las béstias*, was apparently written from his

initial exile stays in Paraguay and Venezuela. Two others, *Tres revoluciones militares* and *La hora de los pueblos*, were written in Spain. It is instructive to see the evolution of Perón's thinking during the decade of three post-Perón military governments, each more authoritarian than its predecessor.

79. Juan D. Perón, *La fuerza es el derecho de las béstias* (Madrid, 1957), pp. 11, 18-19, 59.

80. The letters exchanged between June 1956 and February 1966 represented a continuing dialogue between the left-Peronist orientation of Cooke and Perón's more pragmatic attempts to preserve and consolidate his role at the center of Argentine politics. Symbolically, Cooke's exile took him from Santiago, Chile, to São Paulo, Brazil, then to Montevideo, Uruguay, to Paris, and finally to Havana, whereas Perón moved from Paraguay and Venezuela, to Panama, to the Dominican Republic and finally to Madrid. See *Perón-Cooke: Correspondencia* (Buenos Aires: Granica Editor, 1971); and Juan D. Perón, *Tres revolucione militares* (Buenos Aires: Editorial Escorpión, 1963), pp. 131, 160-63.

81. Juan D. Perón, *La hora de los pueblos* (Madrid: Ediciones Norte, 1968), esp. see pp. 19, 11-12, 32-33, 40, 128.

82. See the impact of Cooke on Perón in *Perón/Cooke: Correspondencia*. Also James's comments on Cooke's role in *Resistance and Integration*, pp. 150-51.

83. True, the Montonero's strategic allies in guerrilla warfare, the Trotskyite ERP, never trusted Perón's conversion to any form of socialism.

84. Guillermo O'Donnell and D. Linck, *Dependencia y autonomía* (Buenos Aires: Amorrortu, 1973), p. 270.

85. Lanusse had set up residence requirements for presidential candidates that made it impossible for Perón to compete in the initial national elections of March 11, 1973. With the election of Cámpora, Perón returned to Argentina. With the forced withdrawal of Cámpora in June 1973, Perón became the candidate in new presidential elections on September 23, 1973. His margin of victory was the highest in modern Argentine history, with 62 percent of the total vote. See *La Opinión*, September 25, 1973.

Also for an account of the role of organized labor in the shift from left-Peronism to Perón in the presidency, see Juan Carlos Torre, *Los sindicatos en el gobierno, 1973–1976* (Buenos Aires: Centro Editor de América Latina, 1983).

86. Julio Godio, *El último año de Perón* (Bogotá: Ediciones Tercer Mundo, 1981).

87. These developments are treated in great detail by Julio Godio, *El último año de Perón* (Bogota: Ediciones Tercer Mundo, 1981), Liliana de Riz, *Retorno y Derrumbe: El último gobierno peronista* (Mexico: Folios Ediciones, 1981) and Guido Di Tella, *Argentina Under Perón, 1973–1976: The Nation's Experience With a Labor-Based Government* (New York: St. Martin's Press, 1983). In addition, see Peter Ranis, "Deadly Tango: Populism and Military Authoritarianism in Argentina," *Latin American Research Review* 21, no. 2 (1986), 149-65.

88. On Montonero strategy, see Richard Gillespie, *Soldiers of Perón: Argentina's Montoneros* (Oxford: Clarendon Press, 1982); Pablo Giussani, *Montoneros: La sobérbia armada* (Buenos Aires: Editorial Sudamericana Planeta, 1984); and Donald C. Hodges,

Argentina, 1943–1987: The National Revolution and Resistance (Albuquerque: University of New Mexico Press, 1988).

89. Juan Carlos Torre, *Los sindicatos en el gobierno, 1973–1976* (Buenos Aires: Centro Editor de América Latina, 1983), pp. 81, 118.

90. Apparently in only a little over fifteen months of the combined Cámpora/Perón administrations, workers' proportion of national income improved from 33 to 43 percent. See Rodolfo Terragno, *Los 400 dias de Perón* (Buenos Aires: Ediciones de la Flor, 1974), p. 94. For the impact of Peronism on industrial employment, see Héctor Palomino, *Efectos políticos y sociales de los cambios en el mercado de trabajo: Argentina 1950–1983* (Buenos Aires: CISEA, 1985), p. 13.

91. Torre, *Los sindicatos en el gobierno, 1973–1976*, pp. 63-64.

92. The impact of the *proceso* military on Argentine culture was devastating. For example, magazine circulation fell from over 135 million in Perón's last year to about 92 million by 1979; edited books in all categories (fiction, nonfiction, anthologies, reference works, children's books, social science, and history, etcetera) dropped from over 21 million copies in 1975 to under 3 million in 1980. The sale of phonograph records and audio tapes dropped from almost 31 million in 1975 to under 14 million by 1981. Argentine domestic film production also severely declined from thirty movies in 1975 to eight produced in 1982. See Oscar Landi, "Cultura y política en la transición a la democracia," *Crítica y Utopía* 10/11 (1983), 78-80.

93. Daniel Frontalini and Cristina Caiati, *El míto de la guerra súcia* (Buenos Aires: CELS, 1985).

94. The military claimed that 15,000 armed guerrillas and an equal number of active supporters were operating in Argentina. The Argentine Center for Legal and Social Studies (CELS) put the number of guerrillas at 2,000, of whom only about 500 were trained for warfare. Against these insurgents the military junta fielded a well-equipped force of 200,000 military and police combatants.

95. These statistics are derived from the testimony compiled by Argentina's National Commission on Disappeared Persons (CONADEP). By early 1986 *Nunca más*, as the report is titled, was already into its tenth printing (Buenos Aires: Eudeba, 1984).

96. Jorge Sábato and Jorge Schwarzer, "Funcionamiento de la economía y poder político en la Argentina," *Ibero-Americana* 13, no. 2 (1983), 30.

97. Edward Schumacher, "Argentina and Democracy," *Foreign Affairs* 62, no. 5 (Summer 1984), 1077.

98. *Statistical Bulletin of the OAS* (Washington, D.C., 1985), p. 24.

99. Jorge Schwarzer, *Martínez de Hoz: La lógica política de la política económica* (Buenos Aires: CISEA, 1983), p. 130. One labor observer sees 1978 as the nadir of workers' share of national income. He cites the figure of 29 percent. See Santiago Senén González, *Diez años de sindicalismo argentino: de Perón al Proceso* (Buenos Aires: Ediciones Corregidor, 1984), p. 93.

100. *El Bimestre* (July/August, 1984), 4–5.

101. Juan Villarreal, "Los hilos socialse de poder," in *Crisis de la dictadura argentina*, ed. Eduardo Jozami et al. (Buenos Aires: Siglo XXI, 1985), p. 251.

102. Vilas, "On the Crisis of Bourgeois Democracy in Argentina," p. 20. And Fernández has the salaried percentage of national income decreasing from 49 percent in 1975 to 33 percent in 1981. See Arturo Fernández, *Las prácticas sociales del sindicalismo* (Buenos Aires: Centro Editor de América Latina, 1985), p. 109.

103. Luis Beccaria and Alvaro Orsatti, *La evolución del empleo y los salarios en el corto plazo: el caso argentino, 1970–1983* (Buenos Aires: CEPAL, 1985), p. 45.

104. Ibid., p. 114. Further, both Villarreal and Candia show that there was a fall in basic wages and overtime and, inversely, an increase in bonuses and wages for piece work. Candia describes the evolution of the pay structure of industrial workers between the Perón and military governments. See Villarreal, "Los hilos sociales de poder," p. 250; and José Miguel Candia, "Argentina: proceso militar y clase obrera," *Cuadernos del Sur* 2 (1985), 35-45.

Compensation	1975	1981
Basic salary, normal hours	69%	58%
Overtime pay	8%	9%
Bonuses and piece work wages	8%	15%
Other (includes accident and vacation benefits)	15%	18%
Total	100%	100%

Source: Candia, "Argentina: Proceso militar y clase obrera," p. 41.

105. Francisco Delich, "Desmovilización sindical, reestructuración obrera y cambio sindical," *Crítica y Utopía* 6 (1981), 88.

106. Senén González, *Diez Años*, pp. 58-67, 138.

107. Ronaldo Munck writes, "In 1976 80% of all labor disputes occurred in the manufacturing sector and this declined sharply to 44% . . . in 1977." *Argentina: From Anarchism to Peronism* (London: Zed Books, 1987), p. 213.

108. Senén González, *Diez Años*, p. 73.

109. For a comprehensive breakdown of various union leadership splits under the military, including discussions of which unions where intervened and which were not and the extent of collaboration and opposition within the CGT to the military between 1976 and 1982, see Senén González, *Diez años*. For a more recent typology of union divisions, see Pablo Pozzi, "Argentina 1976–1982: Labour Leadership and Military Government," *Journal of Latin American Studies* 20 (May 1988), 111-38.

110. See the universally enthusiastic statements of all elements of the CGT leadership hours after the initial Argentine landing on the Malvinas Islands was announced. See Senén González, *Diez años*, pp. 165-67.

111. Héctor Palomino, "El movimiento de democratización sindical," in *Los nuevos movimientos sociales*, ed. Elizabeth Jelin (Buenos Aires: Centro Editor de América Latina, 1985), p. 39.

112. Oscar Oszlak, "Privatización autoritária y recreación de la escena pública" *Crítica y Utopía* 10/11 (1984), 40.

113. Quoted in Senén González, *Diez años*, p. 150.

Chapter 3. The Contexts and Conditions of Labor Under Alfonsín

1. See Carlos Waisman's discussion of labor's prime role in forging a corporatist Argentine state of Bonapartist dimensions in *Reversal of Development in Argentina* (Princeton, N.J.: Princeton University Press, 1987).

2. The laws were: Ministerio de Trabajo y Seguridad Social, Asociaciones Profesionales de Trabajadores, law 23.852 (October 2, 1945), law 14.455 (August 8, 1958), law 20.615 (November 20, 1973), law 22.105 (November 15, 1979); and Ministerio de Trabajo y Seguridad Social, Asociaciones de Uniones de Trabajadores, law 23.551 (March 3, 1988).

3. Ministerio de Trabajo, Régimen de Elecciones– Asociaciones Profesionales de Trabajadores, law 23.071 (1984).

4. Ministerio de Trabajo y Seguridad Social, Convenciones Colectivas de Trabajo, law 14.250 (October 1953).

5. Javier Slodky, *La negociación colectiva en la Argentina* (Buenos Aires: Puntosur, 1988), p. 25ff.

6. Ministerio de Trabajo y Seguridad Social, Convenciones Colectivas de Trabajo, law 23.545 (January 11, 1988).

7. Julio Godio and Javier Slodky, *El regreso de la negociación colectiva* (Buenos Aires: Fundación Friedrich Ebert, 1988), p. 16.

8. Ibid., p. 49; and Slodky, *La negociación colectiva en la Argentina*, p. 44.

9. Godio and Slodky, *El regreso de la negociación colectiva*, p. 50.

10. Juan Carlos D'Abate, "Trade Unions and Peronism," in *Juan Perón and the Reshaping of Argentina*, ed. Frederick Turner and José Miguens (Pittsburgh, Pa.: University of Pittsburgh Press, 1983), p. 69; and *Documentación e información laboral (DIL)*, no. 216 (August 1984). Another estimate puts the figure at 55 percent of the population and 68 percent of those economically active. Comparative figures for the total population in Brazil are 40 percent, in Mexico 36 percent, and in Venezuela 26 percent. See Arturo Fernández, *Las prácticas sociales del sindicalismo/1* (Buenos Aires: Centro Editor de América Latina, 1986), p. 66.

11. Among the unions I studied, *obras sociales* also often implied special loans for workers, school supplies for children, and legal aid in employer disputes.

12. *DIL*, no. 221 (January 1985), p. 11.

13. Juan Carlos Torre, *Los sindicatos en el gobierno, 1973–1976* (Buenos Aires: Centro Editor de América Latina, 1983).

14. Alejandro Portes, "Latin American Class Structures: Their Composition and Change During the Last Decades," *Latin American Research Review* 20, no. 3 (1985).

15. Instituto Nacional de Estatística y Censos (Buenos Aires, 1986), pp. 125-28 [hereafter INDEC]).

16. INDEC (1985) and *DIL* no. 228 (August 1985).

17. Organization of American States (OAS) *Bulletin* (1986), pp. 21-24.

18. *Argentina: Social Sectors in Crisis* (Washington, D.C., World Bank, 1988), pp. viii, 1.

19. The GNP by sector growth rates in 1985–1986 was as follows:

Sector	1985	1986
Manufacturing	−10.3	12.9
Construction	−6.6	8.9
Electricity, water, and gas	1.4	7.4
Commerce and services	−8.3	8.9
Banking	−1.2	6.8
Transportation and communication	−2.9	3.4

Source: World Bank Mission to Argentina, 1988.

20. Ibid, pp. 47-49.

21. Ibid, pp. 65-66.

22. These statistics have been compiled from *Argentina: Social Sectors in Crisis* (Washington, D.C., World Bank, 1988) p. viii and p. 40; and *Anuário Estadístic, 1981–1982* (Buenos Aires: INDEC, 1984), pp. 685-86.

23. These figures do not take into consideration the 62 percent of the Argentine population that are not reported as economically active. See *Anuário Estadístico, 1981–1982*, p. 125. José Nun has estimated that the underground economy which had encompassed 25 percent of economically active persons numbered as many as 40 percent by 1986. He believes that where the legal economy fell −.4 percent annually between 1970 and 1986, the underground economy, during the same period, grew by 3 percent annually. Further, his judgment is that three of five employed persons earns at least a part of their income in the underground economy. See José Nun, "Los Sindicatos y el sistema político," round table talk for the Centro Latinoamericano para el Análisis de la Democracia (CLADE), sponsored by Fundación Friedrich Ebert, Buenos Aires, August 1988, unpublished, pp. 35-36.

24. These figures are drawn from the 1980 INDEC census and published in English by the World Bank Mission report, p. 90.

25. Héctor Palomino, "Efectos políticos y sociales de los cambios en el mercado de trabajo: 1950–1983," *CISEA* 4 (1985), 26. Palomino relates high levels of stable self-employment to countries (such as Argentina) where urbanization and commercialization preceded industrialization [p.12]. Even as early as the turn of the century, Charles Bergquist had found self-employment as an important ingredient in the urban work force of Argentina.

26. Hector Palomino, *El Bimestre* 23, no. 16 (July/August 1984), 4-5. The self-employed went from 17 percent of economically active persons in 1970 to 19 percent in 1980. See Palomino, "Efectos políticos y sociales de los cambios en el mercado de trabajo: 1950–1983," p. 19. In Greater Buenos Aires it had reached 24 percent. See Héctor Palomino, "El movimiento de democratización sindical," in *Los nuevos movimientos sociales*, ed. Elizabeth Jelin (Buenos Aires: Centro Editor de América Latina, 1985), p. 37.

27. Luis Beccaria y Alvaro Orsatti, *La evolución del empleo y los salarios en el corto plazo: El caso argentino, 1970–1983* (Buenos Aires: CEPAL, 1985), p. 34.

28. Ibid., pp. 111, 117.

29. Ibid., p. 114.

30. Ibid., p. 120.

31. Juan Villarreal's chapter in Eduardo Jozami, et al.; *Crisis de la dictadura argentina* (Buenos Aires: Siglo XXI, 1985), p. 252.

32. Ibid., p. 130.

33. *Estadística mensual*, no. 161 (Buenos Aires: INDEC), p. 23.

34. Nicolas Iñigo Carrera and Jorge Potesta, "La situación del proletariado en la Argentina actual (1960–1987)" (Buenos Aires: Centro de Investigaciones en Ciencias Sociales [CICSO], September 1988, p. 12.

35. The United States (69 percent), Sweden (68 percent), and Finland (66 percent) are among those with the highest portion of national income going to wages and salaries. Among countries that make these statistics available, Mali has the lowest amount, with 24 percent going to workers. See the national accounts statistics in *The Europa Yearbook: A World Survey* (London: Europa Publications, 1988).

36. Peter Ranis, "The Dilemmas of Democratization in Argentina," *Current History* 85 (January 1986), 29-32, 42.

37. *La Nación*, September 18, 1985, p. 7.

38. *La Razón*, October 9, 1985, p. 14.

39. For the results of 438 labor union elections, see *Sindicatos: Elecciones, 1984–1986* (Buenos Aires: Ministerio de Trabajo y Seguridad Social, 1988).

40. *Estructura sindical en la Argentina* (Buenos Aires: Ministerio de Trabajo y Seguridad Social, 1987), pp. 20-39.

41. If one were just to count workers who participated in recent union elections, the figures for organized workers drops appreciably to 40 percent of those on wages and salaries. See ibid., p. 16. A leading Argentine labor expert estimates unionization among workers to be somewhere between 41 and 48 percent. See Alvaro Abós, *Los sindicatos argentinos: Cuadro de situación, 1984* (Buenos Aires: Centro de Estudios para el Proyecto Nacional, 1985), p. 69. With an official figure of close to 10 million economically active people in Argentina, approximately 34 percent of them are unionized—again, a comparatively high figure worldwide. See *The Europa Yearbook*, p. 350.

42. Ibid., pp. 16-19. Yet these figures on union affiliation still represent a drop from the reportedly almost 5 million members in 1950. See Héctor R. Roudil, *Reflexiones sobre los estatutos de la Confederación General de Trabajo* (Buenos Aires: Fundación Friedrich Ebert, 1988), p. 14. During the very antilabor climate of the military *proceso*, all former union members had to actively reaffiliate with their respective unions. In other words, doing nothing meant their membership ceased. Despite these unfriendly conditions, 90 percent of the rank and file rejoined.

43. *Creación* 1, no. 2 (July 1986), 35ff. The comparable U.S. figure, for example, has fallen below 18 percent.

44. Héctor Palomino, "Argentina: Dilemas y perspectivas del movimiento sindical," *Nueva Sociedad* 83 (May/June 1986), 92.

45. *Creación*, 1, no. 2 (July 1986), 39.

46. See Peter Ranis, "Parties, Politics and Peronism: A Study of Post-Perón Political Development," Ph.D. diss., New York University, 1965, p. 364ff.

47. Peter Ranis, "Peronism Without Perón: Ten Years After the Fall," *Journal of Inter-American Studies and World Affairs* 8 (January 1966), 118ff.

48. Roudil, *Reflexiones sobre los estatutos de la Confederación General de Trabajo*, p. 18.

49. Arturo Fernández, *Las prácticas sociales del sindicalismo, 1976–1982* (Buenos Aires: Centro Editor de América Latina, 1985), pp. 79-80.

50. Santiago Senén González, *Diez años de sindicalismo argentino: de Perón al Proceso* (Buenos Aires: Ediciones Corregidor, 1984), p. 142.

51. In 1984 the CGT had had four secretary generals representing the two earlier divisions. Representing the CGT-RA were Saúl Ubaldini of the brewery workers and Osvaldo Borda of the rubber workers. Representing the old CGT-Azopardo were Jorge Triaca of the plastics workers and Roman Baldassini of the postal workers.

52. Gustavo Miedzin et al., "Los agrupamientos político-sindicales: un intento de caracterización," *Cuadernos del FISyP* 8 (Fundación de Investigaciones Sociales y Políticas, September 1988), p. 7.

53. See *Sindicatos: Elecciones, 1984–1986* for more explicit details about union elections.

54. Ricardo Gaudio and Héctor Domeniconi, "Las primeras elecciones sindicales en la transición democrática," *Desarrollo Económico* 26, no. 103 (October/December 1986), 427.

55. Gaudio and Domeniconi, "Las primeras elecciones sindicales en la transición democrática," p. 432ff.

56. Ibid., p. 440.

57. Ibid., p. 441.

58. Gaudio and Domeniconi show that among the nonintervened unions only 14.3 percent had a recognizable opposition, whereas 31.2 percent of the formerly intervened had such alternative lists (ibid., p. 445).

59. Ricardo Gaudio and Héctor Domeniconi, "El proceso de normalización sindical bajo el gobierno radical," unpublished, 1986, p. 219.

60. Ibid., p. 12ff.

61. Eduardo Lucita, "Breve consideraciones sobre la reforma laboral," *Cuadernos del Sur* 5 (March/May 1987), 56ff.; Liliana de Riz et al., "El movimiento sindical y la concertación en la Argentina actual," in *El sindicalismo latinoamericano en los ochenta* (Santiago de Chile: CLACSO, 1985), p. 50ff.

62. Voting trends in the Alfonsín years were as follows (in percent):

Parties	1983	1985	1987	1989
Radicals-UCR	52	43	37	37
Peronists	40	36	41	47
Right	4	10	14	6
Left	3	6	4	2

Source: various periodicals and newspapers from these periods.

63. *Argentina: Social Sectors in Crisis* (Washington D.C.: World Bank, 1988), pp. 1-2, 87.

64. Ibid., p. 79.

65. Alvaro Orsatti, *La canasta obrera de consumo y su relación con el índice de costo de vida y los salarios* (Buenos Aires: Centro de Estudios Laborales (CEDEL), 1986), pp. 23-36.

66. Héctor Palomino, "Las huelgas de cuello blanco," *El Bimestre* 30 (November/December 1986), 24.

67. See Arturo Fernández's recapitulation of the CGT's eight points of June 1984 in "Sindicalismo y concertación social," *Justicia Social* 3, nos. 4/5 (September 1986/April 1987, 36-37; and *DIL*, nos. 219/220 (December 1984).

68. *DIL*, no. 233 (January 1986).

69. Paul G. Buchanan, "Reflections on Institutionalizing Democratic Class Compromise in the Southern Cone," presented at the annual meeting of the Latin American Studies Association, New Orleans, March 1988, p. 37.

70. For details, see "Los 26 puntos de la Unidad Nacional. Programa de la CGT," *Justicia Social* 2, no. 2 (1986), 126-30.

71. See various issues of *El Periodista*, nos. 130-34 (1987).

72. Abós, *Los sindicatos argentinos: Cuadro de situación*, p. 11.

Chapter 4. A Portrait of Seven Union Contracts

1. *Estructura sindical en la Argentina* (Buenos Aires: Ministério de Trabajo y Seguridad Social, 1987), p. 115.

2. *Documentación e Información Laboral* (hereafter *DIL*) no. 233 (January 1986).

3. In 1985–1986, the currency stabilization plan kept the Austral on a par value with the dollar. For that reason I will cite the dollar figure with its equivalent value in Argentina's then new currency initiated in June 1985.

4. *Convenciones Colectivas de Trabajo: Obreros Textiles*, no. 2/75 (Buenos Aires, June 1975).

5. An accident on the job would be compensated by 100 percent indemnification for one month. Based on an early 1970s legislation bearing on all unions (law 18.338), workers were entitled to approximately $3-6 a month for wife or husband and for each dependent child. (This would mean an additional 15 percent income for a typical married textile laborer with two children.) A laborer receives twelve consecutive paid days for marriage and three consecutive days for the death of a family member, and $20 to defray funeral costs.

6. A worker may be exempted from perfect attendance for the three days after a death in the immediate family, twelve days for marriage, two days (for the father) upon the birth of a child, and up to ten days days each year for documented absences dedicated to high school or university examinations. In addition, all workers receive the last Sunday in October as a paid holiday, the "Day of the Textile Laborer."

7. The Ford plant complex includes a well-equipped automotive high school whose graduates entered the intermediate levels of the assembly work force.

8. Once when I found no quiet place available, the interviewee (a road tester) drove me out to a Ford testing track where I conducted the interview in a pickup truck, occasionally diverted by a test car zooming by at eighty miles an hour.

9. *Clarín*, May 10, 1986. Moreover, into the early 1980s Ford was exporting approximately 6,000 units to Cuba.

10. Conversations with Ford management and corroborated by laborers, May 1986.

11. Alvaro Abós, *Los sindicatos argentinos: Cuadro de situación* (Buenos Aires: Centro de Estudios para el Proyecto Nacional, 1985), p. 74; and *Estructura sindical en la Argentina*, p. 127.

12. *DIL*, no. 219 (December 1984), p. 22.

13. *Convención Colectiva de Trabajo: SMATA*, no. 13/75 (Buenos Aires, July 1975).

14. The contract goes into elaborate detail. Cold water fountains must be made available for summer work and, if possible, cold drink and ice cream machines. Sanitary changing rooms and bathroom facilities with warm and cold showers must be maintained. Each laborer is issued a cake of soap, bathroom tissue, two towels, and one facecloth at regular intervals. Workclothes are provided annually; autoworkers get two sets of work overalls and a pair of work shoes.

15. Automobile workers receive three paid days off for the death of a spouse, child, or parent, and five days if the funeral is held over 300 miles away. They are also awarded three paid days for the death of a sibling or parent-in-law. Like textile workers, autoworkers receive paid days to attend high school or university examinations. They are also given a paid day when donating to a blood bank or taking a prenuptial blood test and a maximum of three days for a preinduction military medical examination. Laborers also receive one paid day for home moving. Last, each worker received a paid day on the "Day of the Autoworker" (February 24).

16. In addition, the factory shop committee must abide by the following norms and procedures: (1) the committee's activities shall not constitute a disruptive agitation nor interfere with the establishment's work procedures; (2) meetings will take place during normal working hours, agreed to between labor and management; (3) the union delegates cannot undertake union activities without expressly advising management through their on-the-job superiors; (4) the committee may raise questions with management; (5) these questions must be responded to within three working days, or—if questions are complicated—the time may be extended by three days; (6) on questions relating to accidents, absenteeism, changes in work rules, schedules, pay, and general working conditions and norms, the committee will first attempt to resolve these issues through immediate supervisors before bringing them before management.

17. *DIL*, no. 227 (July 1985), p. 3.

18. The early retirement plan was a successful money-saver for Ford because it largely appealed to the older, better paid workers—those, for example, in categories

#6 to #9 or those earning $1.58 an hour (about $250 a month) to those earning $2.80 an hour (about $450 a month).

19. *Estructura sindical en la Argentina*, p. 128. Also see *Creación* 1, no. 2 (July 1986), 40; Abós, *Los sindicatos argentinos: Cuadro de situación*, p. 74; and Héctor Palomino, "Elecciones en la UOM; un espejo de la normalización sindical" *El Bimestre* 24, no. 9 (January–February 1985), 3.

20. Palomino, "Elecciones en la UOM," p. 3.

21. For example, the largest eight sectionals of UOM have 60 percent of the total membership but only 39 percent of the 282 electoral votes at the national congress. As Palomino indicates, with 142 votes necessary to win national leadership, 138 of these come from single-list union sectionals (ibid., p. 5).

22. *Convenio Colectivo de Trabajo — Unión Obrera Metalúrgica*, no. 260/75 (July 1975).

23. As among other laborers, there is a "Day of the Metalworker," a paid holiday each September 7. An unusual provision is article 48, which prohibits a superior from reprimanding a laborer in a loud voice in the presence of his fellow workers.

24. Abós, *Los sindicatos argentinos: Cuadro de situación*, p. 73.

25. *Estructura sindical en la Argentina*, p. 191.

26. Ibid., pp. 130-32.

27. *Convenio Colectivo de Trabajo — Luz y Fuerza y SEGBA* (Buenos Aires, June 1975).

28. See the following works by Juan D. Perón: *El pueblo quiere saber de que se trata* (Buenos Aires: Editorial Freeland, 1973), *El pueblo ya sabe de que se trata* (Buenos Aires: Editorial Freeland, 1973), and *La comunidad organizada* (Buenos Aires: Presidencia de la Nación, 1950).

29. Conversation with director of personnel, Puerto Nuevo, February 1986.

30. Light and power workers normally work a seven-hour day with a twelve-minute refreshment break. In intemperate weather, if working outside on cable repairs or emergency connections, for example, they must be shielded by a tent or other protection. On an emergency job, workers shall not carry equipment and tools weighing more than twenty-six pounds and measuring more than 12 × 16 × 20 inches. Again, following a complicated scale, light and power workers who leave the firm to do particular jobs receive varying forms of bonuses, usually 5–10 percent of their wage. Those who must travel more than seven blocks by their own means are reimbursed in the amount of the cost of available transportation. Workers receive meal subsidies of about 1.5 percent of their wages if they have to work more than two hours beyond the end of the normal workday in order to finish a particular job, and workers may have a half hour of rest before beginning overtime work.

31. Preference is given to those who register for the last year of either secondary or higher education. Scholarships may be renewed for up to three years, and workers are expected to return to SEGBA for at least the same number of years as the scholarship.

32. *Convenio Colectivo de Trabajo* (Luz y Fuerza), p. 115.

33. Arriving to work more than five minutes after the hour is considered late. Workers who arrive late five times in one month, or thirteen times in a year, are given a warning. Those who receive three warnings in one year are suspended after the next warning.

34. After having worked for SEGBA for five to ten years, workers may receive a three-month leave of absence without pay. Those with more than ten years of service receive a six-month leave, which may be extended to one year. These leaves do not interrupt the accumulation of seniority and benefits, and workers' jobs are protected while they are on leave.

Regarding leaves with pay: light and power workers receive fifteen days for marriage, two days (for the father) upon the birth of a child, and one day for a child's marriage; six days for death of a spouse, parent, or child; three days for death of in-laws, siblings, or grandchildren; two days for death of grandparents (of either the worker or his/her spouse), uncles, cousins, nieces, nephews, sisters- and brothers-in-law, sons- and daughters-in-law; and one day for non–blood related uncles, nieces, nephews, and cousins of either of the spouses' in-laws!

35. In case of grave illness of an incapacitated parent where there are no other adults in the home, workers may receive a maximum of three weeks' leave a year. In the case of serious illness of a spouse or child where there is not another adult in the home, workers may receive up to three weeks' leave with pay each year. If the husband or wife of a worker is housebound and there are no other adults in the home, a worker again may request three weeks with pay in any one year. Maternity leave is covered by national legislation (law 18.338) and covers six months before birth and three months after. Light and power workers are also given two paid days for home moving. Also during the Argentine vacation period (October 1 to April 30), laborers can ask for a 20 percent advance on vacation pay. For health treatments or study obligations, workers may (case by case) ask for the required days off. Workers get two paid leave days to take secondary school or university examinations.

Light and power workers with less than five years on the job who suffer sickness or accident receive up to three months' paid sick leave. Those with more than five years' service receive up to six months of paid sick leave, which may be extended by another six months. Those with less than five years who care for dependent families receive an additional three months' paid leave.

36. Under the SEGBA contract, the management is committed to cleaning and disinfecting the workplace, providing sinks, hot and cold water, changing rooms, and individual lockers. Workers are given ten minutes for hygiene if they are about to begin an overtime period. In particularly warm areas of the workplace, the company must provide water fountains, soft drink machines, and dextrose- and salt-dispensing machines. In the power plant, there must be a sink, a toilet, potable water, and first aid cabinet for every twelve workers.

37. Many forms of electrical work are considered dangerous, including standing on beams, outdoor ladders, parapets, and scaffolding. It is also considered dangerous to work more than thirteen feet above the ground (measured as the distance from the worker's feet to the ground). Work on skylights and in manholes,

tents, and cabins near high electrical tensions is also considered dangerous. Finally, changing fuses and electrical plates, repairing fuse boxes, and repairing or splicing underground cables is also defined as dangerous. Workers engaged in these tasks receive 30 percent over their base pay.

38. *Estructura Sindical en la Argentina*, p. 194; Alvaro Abós, *Los sindicatos argentinos: Cuadro de situación*. p. 74.

39. *DIL*, no. 226 (June 1985), pp. 10–11.

40. *Convenio Colectivo de Trabajo: FOETRA*, no. 165/75 (June 1975).

41. Abós, *Los sindicatos argentinos: Cuadro de situación*. p. 73. The Ministry of Labor puts the membership as 125,000 in 1979, which increased to 162,000 by 1983.

42. For diversity, I expanded the sample to twenty interviews among the three banking sectors. Based on the relative weight of membership rolls, I interviewed ten union members from the state sector, five from the private foreign sector, and five from the private domestic banking sector. I chose the Central Bank of the Argentine Republic (BCRA) because of its critical orienting role among Argentine banks and because of its sizable public-sector affiliation (2,189). I chose the Banco de la Nación, as Argentina's largest state-sector bank, with 7,527 affiliates (among 20,000 employees). From the foreign private sector, I chose two: the powerful and influential First National Bank of Boston (Banco de Boston), with 1,169 affiliates, and Banco de Galícia y Buenos Aires (BGBA), one of the top two private banks in union affiliates (2,374) and the one with the largest number of customer accounts.

43. *Convención Colectiva de Trabajo: Bancários*, no. 18/75 (June 1975).

44. *Estructura sindical en la Argentina*, p. 199.

45. The interviews with teachers were conducted from late March to early May 1986. To get a meaningful sample among teachers, I contacted several of CTERA's key constituent groupings — the CTERA, UDA, and UMP unions on Rivadávia and Córdoba streets. After various orientations concerning the vast network of teachers' associations in Argentina, I chose samples from these unions as well as the AMET union. Particularly helpful were my contacts with the vice-president of UMP and two organizational secretaries of UDA. I divided the sample into ten from the national secondary school program and five from various primary schools in the capital. From high schools, there were five teachers from the Otto Krause Industrial School near the shipyards of downtown Buenos Aires (Paseo de Colón Street) and five from the middle-class Caballito section of Buenos Aires, represented by the Mariano Moreno preparatory school. Five interviews from three primary schools concluded the sample: from the upper-class residential area of Recoleta, the Juan José Castelli elementary school; from the middle-class sector of Belgrano, the Casto Munita elementary school; and from the poorer working-class northwest section of Buenos Aires, the José Anaindia elementary school. Again, lists were drawn up of union members in which I proportionally set aside seven interviews with UDA affiliates, five with UMP, and three with AMET technical teachers.

46. *Estatuto del Docente* (Buenos Aires: Sainte Claire Editora, 1985).

47. These figures were given to me during an interview with the undersecretaries to the general secretary of the UDA union in Buenos Aires, Domingo

Solimano, March 26, 1986.

48. Interview with UMP district delegate from the capital, April 17, 1986.

Chapter 5. The Rank-and-File Worker

1. Almost 87 percent of the union federations have central offices in Buenos Aires. See Daniel James, *Resistance and Integration: Peronism and the Argentine Working Class* (New York: Cambridge University Press, 1988), p. 167.

2. In a survey of ninety-seven important unions, Abós found that 80 percent of industrial unions were founded during early Peronism (1943–1955). Among tertiary sector service unions, only 20 percent had early Peronist auspices. See Alvaro Abós, *Los sindicatos argentinos: Cuadro de situación, 1984* (Buenos Aires: Centro de Estudios para el Proyecto Nacional, 1985), p. 66.

3. In another study, Alvaro Abós claims that UOM had up to 500,000 members through 1975. See his *La columna vertebral: sindicatos y peronismo* (Buenos Aires: Legasa, 1983), pp. 59-60.

Based on this seemingly exaggerated figure, UOM would have *lost* 76 percent of its membership in that decade.

4. There is no reliable comparative data for teachers, although scattered newspaper data suggests that CTERA has had substantial growth since the end of the military era in 1983. Abós's figures for the other unions are sometimes contradictory. Starting with his absolute union figures, I have done my own calculations which have altered his percentages slightly.

5. Abós, *Los sindicatos argentinos*, pp. 76-77.

6. Using the Portes or Coleman/Davis typology, for example, three of the union samples (namely, metalworkers, autoworkers and half of the bank employees) would be placed in the strategic, autonomous, private sector based on their significance and impact on economic life. Again, the balance of the bank employees' sample are in the strategic, government sector along with the light and power and telephone workers. In the nonstrategic, autonomous, private sector, our sample included the textile laborers, while the teachers represented the nonstrategic, governmental union sector.

Sphere	Strategic Sector	Nonstrategic Sector
Government	AB,FOETRA,LyF	CTERA
Autonomous, private	AB,SMATA,UOM	AOT

See Alejandro Portes, "Latin American Class Structures: Their Composition and Change During the Last Decades," *Latin American Research Review* 20, no. 3 (1985), 33; and Kenneth M. Coleman and Charles L. Davis, "How Workers Evaluate Their Unions: Exploring Determinants of Union Satisfaction in Venezuela and Mexico," presented at the annual meeting of the Latin American Studies Association, Boston, 1986, p. 3.

7. In August and September 1986, a labor study group associated with the Centro de Estudios para el Proyecto Nacional (CEPNA), under the direction of Alejandro F. Lamadrid, conducted a mail survey of union leaders and delegates on internal labor and broader political questions. It was published as *El nuevo sindicalismo: Opiniones y actitudes de su dirigéncia média* (Buenos Aires: CEPNA, 1987). A year later, Lamadrid came out with a more detailed breakdown of intraunion leadership tendencies published as *Política y alineamientos sindicales: Opiniones del nuevo cuadro gremial* (Buenos Aires: Puntosur, 1988). Several of its key findings were also referred to in Julio Godio, "La ideología de los cuadros sindicales intermedios," *La Ciudad Futura* 5 (June 1987), 8-11. Several of the questions lend themselves to comparisons with my study on the rank-and-file Argentine worker, particularly since it was undertaken toward the end of my own survey period.

The CEPNA-Lamadrid studies included the same data base of 441 middle-level union leaders and delegates drawn mainly from Greater Buenos Aires and the capital, but with half the remaining sample coming from Córdoba and Rosario. Fifty-five percent of the sample came from industrial unions and 45 percent from service unions. Of those responding to the questionnaires, 58 percent were delegates and 42 percent middle level union leaders. The great majority (85 percent) were under 40 years of age and with less than five years as union leaders, since Lamadrid wanted to tap the new union leadership that had arisen since the beginnings of the military dictatorship.

The CEPNA-Lamadrid studies were heavily drawn from Peronist delegates and union leaders (60 percent) and overly represented leftist leadership in the CGT (16 percent) and underrepresented UCR delegates (7 percent). On the other hand, it also attempted to distinguish attitudes among the Ubaldinista, "62," "25," and other factions of the CGT leadership. All told, forty-three unions comprised the survey but approximately one-third appeared to be small service unions with limited membership rolls.

8. The 1980 national census indicated that foreign-born Argentines had dropped to 7 percent, though in the Province of Buenos Aires it was 9 percent and in the capital 13 percent. See "Total de la República," *Censo Nacional de Población y Vivienda, 1980* (Buenos Aires: INDEC, 1982), pp. xxxi-xxxii. As in my sample, the leading foreign groups were Italians and Spaniards. See *Anuário Estadístico, 1981–1982* (Buenos Aires: INDEC, 1984), p. 175.

9. $X^2 = 8.411$, 1 df, $p < .004$.

10. See Silvia Sigal, *Attitudes Ouvrières en Argentine* (Paris: Centre D'Etude de Mouvements Sociaux, December 1974), Appendix 1, pp. 4-7. In 1967, Sigal organized a comparative Latin American study of working-class attitudes. The sample used was largely urban and metropolitan, tapping workers from, for example, Gran Buenos Aires and the capital, Rosario, and Córdoba. A completed questionnaire was received from 1,047 Argentine, Chilean and Colombian skilled and unskilled workers representing 90 manufacturing enterprises from the public service, modern foreign and private (large and small, modern and traditional) sectors in the three countries. Sigal's findings, based on a structured, non-open-

ended mailing, corroborate much of the demographic, occupational, and sociological data gathered in this survey.

11. This parallels the Argentine census that gives a figure of 1,346,000 people over five years of age out of an eligible population of 24,707,000 who did not attend school. The percentage comes to 5.4 percent. See *Anuário Estadístico*, p. 169.

12. In the CEPNA study (*El nuevo sindicalismo*, pp. 18-19), 55 percent of union delegates had completed primary and but not secondary education. In my survey, the figures were almost the same, with 53.6 percent falling into those categories. Workers' spouses' education followed a similar profile (in percent):

Workers' Spouses	Laborers	Employees	Total
Completed primary school	88.7	96.7	92.7
Completed secondary school	11.3	60.0	29.3
Completed university	0.0	10.0	7.3
	(N=51)	(N=22)	(N=73)

13. *Argentina: Social Sectors in Crisis* (Washington, D.C: World Bank, 1988), pp. 93-94. Argentina's school enrollment figures have risen over the last generation. Comparing the last two censuses, the following improvement is seen (in percent):

School Enrollment	1970	1980
Without schooling	6.8	4.9
Primary incomplete	39.6	29.5
Primary complete	29.8	32.1
Secondary incomplete	12.3	16.6
Secondary complete	7.3	9.9
University incomplete	2.4	3.8
University complete	1.8	3.2
Total	100.0	100.0

Source: Censo Nacional de Poblacion y, Vivienda, 1980 (Buenos Aires: INDEC, 1982), p. xxxviii.

14. $X^2 = 15.594$, 2 df, $p < .001$.

15. Interview with textile worker, October 1, 1985.

16. $X^2 = 8.905$, 2 df, $p < .01$.

17. Laborers were much more likely to be married than employees ($X^2 = 20.456$, 2 df, $p < .001$).

18. Single workers tended to have the highest levels of education, many having completed some university semesters. $X^2 = 19.593$, 4 df, $p < .001$.

19. Sigal (*Attitudes Ouvrières en Argentine*, Appendix 1, p. 8) similarly found Argentine workers to be generally content with their jobs, compared to Chileans and Colombians in the mid-1960s.

20. This phenomenon is corroborated by three studies of the U.S. working class. Barbara Garson (*All the Livelong Day* [New York: Penguin Books, 1975], p. 72ff.) writes that mechanics felt less confined to the same routine than did other workers

in a Helena Rubenstein factory; Robert Schrank (*Ten Thousand Working Days* [Cambridge, Mass.: MIT Press, 1978], pp. 14, 70ff., 232) speaks of being a "troubleshooter" roaming around the Gaines dog food factory without the direct supervision of foremen and supervisors: "I can stop and talk to people. The day goes like that." Schrank calls this "schmooze time" (Yiddish slang for small talk, chitchat). David Halle says of chemical workers, "With the exception of the mechanics, few Imperium [mythical name] workers find their jobs interesting or satisfying. . . . It is only when the machinery is not running smoothly that work connected with it becomes interesting" (*America's Working Man: Work, Home and Politics Among Blue-Collar Property Owners* [Chicago: University of Chicago Press, 1984], pp. 125-45).

21. Sigal (*Attitudes Ouvrières en Argentine*, Appendix 1, p. 9) found that what most satisfied Argentine workers in their work in the mid-1960s was job stability, interesting work, and good salaries, above such considerations as social benefits and promotional opportunities.

22. U.S. chemical workers have similar complaints. See Halle, *America's Working Man*, p. 125.

23. Interview with telephone employee, July 8, 1986.

24. Interview with bank employee, April 7, 1986.

25. Interview with bank employee, April 14, 1986.

26. Interview with bank employee, April 26, 1986.

27. See Garson, *All the Livelong Day*, p. 19ff. Haraszti writes of the heavier servitude of laborers compared to the "lighter" work of employees who have the ability to take coffee breaks, smoke a cigarette, or munch on something. See Miklos Haraszti, *A Worker in a Worker's State* (New York: Universe Books, 1978), p. 76ff. Paoli writes of the Brazilian textile factory being a private world of silence, where the deafening noise and thick cotton dust make it impossible to hear or see one's fellow laborers. Though prolonged use is prohibited, the toilet becomes the only refuge. The U.S. film *Norma Rae* depicts similar contemporary conditions. See Maria Celia Paoli, "Working-Class Sao Paulo and Its Representations, 1900–1940," *Latin American Perspectives* 14, no. 2 (Spring 1987), 209-12.

28. Interview with textile worker, October 4, 1985.

29. A textile worker told me he was earning about 45 cents an hour. His four bus trips cost 62 cents a day, or almost one and a half hours of work to cover his transportation costs (interview with textile worker, December 13, 1985).

30. Sergio Britos, "Las canastas de alimentos," *Boletín CESNI* (Centro de Estudios sobre la Nutrición) 1, no. 1 (June 1987).

31. For example, in the capital the top salary for a teacher with two children and twenty years of service was about $400 a month. Interview with elementary school teacher, April 17, 1986.

32. Using an index number of 100 for 1974, by 1985 primary schoolteachers throughout Argentina were earning an average of 69.4 and secondary school-teachers 65.8. See *Argentina: Social Sectors in Crisis*, p. 96. Bank employees, in my experience, also were a highly qualified, capable, cheap labor source. Often these

were young people interested in professional careers in other fields but forced in the interim to earn a living.

33. Interview with metalworker, August 27, 1986.

34. Interview with bank employee, January 13, 1986.

35. José Nun, in a talk given as part of a round table on "Los sindicatos y el sistema político" for the Centro Latinoamericano para el Análisis de la Democracia (CLADE), sponsored by the Fundación Friedrich Ebert, Buenos Aires, August 1988, unpublished, p. 36. Often Argentine workers' view of their formal job mirrored Szelenyi's depiction of the Hungarian state worker. "The Hungarian petty bourgeoisie dream suggests that one can create a good life if one works hard in the second economy. One should not worry much about unions, or what happens in the state sector and in the state job. Life begins after working hours anyway!" See Ivan Szelenyi, *Socialist Entrepreneurs: Embourgeoisement in Rural Hungary* (Madison: University of Wisconsin Press, 1988), p. 217.

36. It appears that occupational advancement, responsibility on the job, variety, and so on are sometimes more important than wages. This also seems to be true of the British worker as depicted by J. H. Goldthorpe in *The Affluent Worker in the Class Structure* (Cambridge: Cambridge University Press, 1969).

37. Halle, *America's Working Man*, p. 169.

38. This has not significantly changed since Sigal's survey of 1967 when 94 percent of her sample hoped that their children would have at least a completed secondary education if not higher education. *Attitudes Ouvrières en Argentine*, Appendix 1, p. 11.

39. Interview with textile laborer, November 1, 1985.

40. Robert Schrank writes (*Ten Thousand Working Days*, p. 103) that when the North American laborer rejects factory life for his children it is the "ultimate projection of himself." There is in the Argentine laborer something of the notion that *quién trabaja és estúpido* — somewhat the same idea that Schrank found expressed among U.S. workers that they work in factories "because we are stupid and this is all we can do."

41. Interview with metalworker, August 8, 1986.

42. Out of 4,893,000 autos registered in Argentina, three-quarters are in the capital and Greater Buenos Aires. (Figures extrapolated from *Anuario Estadístico*, p. 550). Argentines love their cars almost as much as their houses. Representative Barney Frank of Massachussetts put his finger on the phenomenon when he said (*New York Times*, December 22, 1988): "I told liberals that a lot of this was cultural, that for many people a car was as important as a book or a movie was to them. It was a source of relaxation and intellectual excitement. People tinker with their cars; they make their cars their hobby. A lot of people, including me, think of cars as simply a way of getting from here to there. But not everybody thinks like that and we have to understand that." (A car also gives the worker the independence to take the family out of the city without bureaucratic delay and inconvenience.)

43. There was no explicit question in my survey regarding home ownership. I only became interested in this trend during the course of my research. The question intrigued me and in most cases we appended the question at some point in the

interviews or it came out indirectly through the workers' responses to other questions. My quantification was made by explicit references made by workers during interviews, thus the high number of "No answer" responses.

44. *Anuário Estadístico, 1981–1982*, pp. 366-67. Figures were derived from my calculations of absolute figures for the capital and GBA.

45. Apparently similar phenomena are common to the working class of Lima, Peru. See Hernando De Soto, *The Other Path: The Invisible Revolution in the Third World* (New York: Harper and Row, 1989).

46. See Goldthorpe, *The Affluent Worker in the Class Structure*, *passim*.

47. André Gorz, *Farewell to the Working Class* (Boston: South End Press, 1982).

48. Haraszti, *A Worker in a Worker's State*, p. 65; Garson, *All the Livelong Day*, p. 64.

49. Paoli, "Working-Class São Paulo and Its Representations, 1900–1940," p. 213.

50. Daniel James, *Resistance and Integration: Peronism and the Argentine Working Class* (New York: Cambridge University Press, 1988), p. 125. James also makes an interesting connection as he shows that the *dia peronista* (Peronist day celebrated annually on October 17 to commemorate Perón's release from prison in 1945) is marked by social harmony and family togetherness as opposed to what James depicts as the bitterness and heaviness of the left-sponsored May Day. See James, "17 y 18 de Octubre de 1945: El Peronismo, la protesta de masas y la clase obrera argentina" *Desarrollo Económico* 27, no. 107 (October/December 1987), p. 454. One might add that Perón in his last speech as minister of labor, after being forced to resign in 1945, counseled the workers *de la casa al trabajo y del trabajo a la casa* ("from home to work and from work to home").

51. Karl Marx, *The Economic and Philosophical Manuscripts*, edited by Erich Fromm (New York: Frederick Ungar Publications, 1961), pp. 98-99.

52. Karl Marx, "The German Ideology," in *The Marx-Engels Reader*, ed. Robert C. Tucker (New York: Norton, 1978), p. 160. In a study of socialist economies, Nove has referred to this passage of Marx as referring to human hobbies and not work. See Alec Nove, *The Economics of Feasible Socialism* (London: George Allen and Unwin, 1983), p. 46.

53. Eduard Bernstein, *Evolutionary Socialism* (New York: Schocken Books, 1961), *passim*.

54. Interview with telephone employee, July 10, 1986.

55. In the 1967 survey, Argentine workers' most frequently mentioned extrawork activities were with family (Sigal, *Attitudes Ouvrières en Argentine*, Appendix 1, p. 8).

56. This reaffirms the 1967 survey in which Argentine workers felt that "personal effort" was the most important determinant of success in life (ibid., p. 12).

57. $X^2 = 9.879$, 3 df, $p < .02$.

58. Interview with automobile worker, May 20, 1986.

59. Interview with metalworker, August 19, 1986.

60. Interview with telephone employee, July 1, 1986. Just the day before, another telephone operator gave a similar complaint: "ENTEL doesnt't treat its employees properly and there is much injustice. There are 300 employees in this building without a doctor or nurse. Because of the old equipment, many telephone operators are experiencing hearing difficulties. The company is supposed to give us a

hearing test once a year but does not. Because of the volume of traffic and the overworked staff, we all experience nervous tension that is exhausting and unhealthy" (interview with telephone employee, June 30, 1986).

61. Interview with bank employee, January 13, 1986.

62. Interview with elementary schoolteacher, April 16, 1986.

63. $X^2 = 7.663$, 3 df, $p < .05$.

64. The Argentine state rightly bulks large in the thinking of Argentine workers, who are generally very cognizant of its large employment, investment, and orienting role in the economy. Even in the context of a nonrepressive state apparatus in the Alfonsín years, many economic decisions are conflated with political criteria for their implementation. As Erik Wright writes (*Class, Crisis and the State* [London: New Left Books, 1978], p. 236), "The very fact that such allocations pass through the state opens the door for their political contestation in ways which are impossible so long as accumulation is directed entirely within 'private' corporate boardrooms." Rubén Zorilla has seen the gradual growth of distrust of the state among the working class since the days of its close relationships during early Peronism (*El liderazgo síndical argentino desde sus orígines hasta 1975* [Buenos Aires: Siglo XX, 1983], p. 30ff.).

65. For example, in 1967 it was clear that workers looked principally to the government to improve their standard of living. See Sigal, *Attitudes Ouvrières en Argentine*, Appendix 1, p. 16.

66. If exploitation has any objective measure at all, it would be worker productivity and, at the same time, the cost to the capitalist per unit of labor. Both of these indices indicate that the level of worker exploitation has risen in Argentina during the last generation. A 1985 study by the UN Economic Commission for Latin America gives the following data:

Argentine Worker Productivity (1970 = 100)

	Total	Industry	
		Textiles	Metals
1975	99.7	100.6	97.3
1983	141.1	148.2	154.5

Cost per Unit of Labor

	Total	Textiles	Metals
1974	107.3	99.6	111.1
1982	48.5	40.7	49.7

Source: Luis Beccaria and Alvaro Orsatti, *La evolución del empleo y los salarios en el corto plazo: El caso argentino, 1970–1983* (Buenos Aires: CEPAL, 1985), pp. 120–24.

67. $X^2 = 11.929$, 2 df, $p < .003$.

68. Interview with textile laborer, September 18, 1985.

69. Interview with autoworker, May 20, 1986.

70. Interview with autoworker, May 21, 1986.

71. Interview with metalworker, August 7, 1986.

72. Interview with metalworker, August 8, 1986.

73. Interview with metalworker, August 21, 1986.

74. Interview with telephone employee, July 2, 1986.

75. Interview with telephone employee, July 3, 1986.

76. Interview with elementary schoolteacher, May 8, 1986.

77. Laborers were associated with far more union longevity than employees ($X^2 = 10.033$, 1 df, p < .002).

78. Interview with textile worker, October 7, 1985.

79. Interview with textile worker, October 30, 1985.

80. Interview with autoworker, May 20, 1986.

81. Interview with light and power worker, January 3, 1986.

82. Interview with elementary schoolteacher, April 17, 1986.

83. Like workers, industrial as well as service union leaders also focused principally on salaries (59 percent) or working conditions (40.4 percent) as the CGT's principal problems to confront. See CEPNA, *El nuevo sindicalismo*, pp. 33-34; and Lamadrid, *Política y alineamientos sindicales*, pp. 32, 71. As among service employees vis-à-vis industrial laborers, service union leaders also proportionally focused more on the problems of wages than did industrial union leaders.

84. This appears to be a pattern in most Latin American unions. See, among others, Ronaldo Munck, *Argentina: From Anarchism to Peronism* (London: Zed Books, 1987), p. 52ff.; and Henry A. Landsberger, "The Labor Elite: Is it Revolutionary?" in *Elites in Latin America*, ed. S. M. Lipset and Aldo Solari (New York: Free Press, 1968), p. 272ff.

85. Interestingly, workers who were satisfied with their employers were usually also satisfied with their union leaders ($X^2 = 3.931$, 1 df, p < .05).

86. Interview with autoworker, May 21, 1986.

87. Interview with metalworker, August 19, 1986.

88. Interview with light and power worker, January 7, 1986.

89. Interview with National Bank of Argentina employee, March 24, 1986.

90. Interview with secondary schoolteacher, March 6, 1986.

91. This was apparently equally true during the Onganía years when workers joined strikes mainly to improve their livelihood. Sigal, *Attitudes Ouvrières en Argentine*, Appendix 1, p. 15.

92. $X^2 = 4.140$, 1 df, p < .05.

93. Hobsbawm has said that the power of a union, particularly a public-sector service union, is measured by how much they can make life difficult for the nonstriking public, since what is at stake is not purely a private market or profits question. See Eric Hobsbawm, *Workers: Worlds of Labor* (New York: Pantheon Books, 1984), p. 280.

94. Those dissatisfied with wages, skewed toward the employee sector, were the most likely to want more participation in union decisions ($X^2 = 12.706$, 1 df, p < .001).

95. Likewise, in the CEPNA study (*El nuevo sindicalismo*, pp. 42-43) three-quarters of union delegates supported more frequent assemblies and greater power of worker assemblies to revoke leadership mandates.

96. Over 90 percent of CEPNA study delegates felt workers should be able to participate in decision making within their respective enterprises. Delegates from service unions were even more adamant (94.5 percent) than those from industrial unions (86.4 percent). [Note: My service union calculations of the CEPNA figures are based on a weighted average between the public and private service union delegates sampled, leaving out the public administration union delegates, since they were not included in my own study and thus their inclusion (though a minority of the total of service union delegates) would vitiate the comparisons between our studies.] However, by "participation in decision making," two-thirds of the delegates who answered yes were referring to the workers' ability to better observe the implementation of the union contract, and only 11.5 percent because it was their right as the working class (see ibid., p. 29; Lamadrid, *Política y alineamientos sindicales*, p. 66; and Godio, "La ideología de los cuadros sindicales intermedios," p. 8).

97. A good predictor for nurturing a participatory attitude among workers in their place of employment were their urban origins ($X^2 = 5.293$, 1 df, p $<$ .02).

98. $X^2 = 5.184$, 1 df, p $<$ .03.

99. $X^2 = 6.615$, 1 df, p $<$ .01.

100. $X^2 = 10.061$, 1 df, p $<$ .002.

Chapter 6. Workers as Citizens

1. In the CEPNA-Lamadrid studies, delegates were 60 percent Peronist and the rest distributed among left, independent and Radical leadership factions. Again, because of the many very small unions chosen in the study, the number of non-Peronist union leaders seem overrepresented. See *El Nuevo sindicalismo: Opiniones y actitudes de su dirigencia média* (Buenos Aires: CEPNA, 1987), p. 21; and Alejandro F. Lamadrid, *Política y alineamientos sindicales: Opiniones del nuevo cuadro gremial* (Buenos Aires: Puntosur, 1988).

2. In her 1967 mailing to Argentine workers, Silvia Sigal also found that only 24 percent of the sample dedicated some time to their union and only 12 percent had time for their political party of choice (*Attitudes Ouvrières en Argentine* [Paris: Centre D'Etude des Mouvements Sociaux, December 1974], Appendix 1, p. 16).

3. There are two very good voter studies for 1983, discussing the growing complexity of the Argentine electorate with its laborers, employees, self-employed, professionals and employers. See Jorge R. Jorrat, "Las elecciones de 1983: 'desviación' o 'realineamiento,'" *Desarrollo Económico* 26, no. 101 (April/June 1986), 89-120; and Edgardo Catterberg, "Las elecciones del 30 de Octubre de 1983, El surgimiento de una nueva convergencia electoral," *Desarrollo Económico* 25, no. 98 (July/September 1985), 260-67.

4. Not suprisingly, workers who were satisfied with their union leadership were most likely to identify with Peronism as opposed to the Radicals or third parties ($X^2 = 6.452$, 2 df, p $<$ .04).

5. Interview with metalworker, August 21, 1986.

6. *Qué Pasa* [Argentine Communist party newspaper], February 26, 1986; section 2 discusses party congress.

7. Peter Winn writes of the negative impact of failed strikes on Chilean worker solidarity with the Communists in *Weavers of the Revolutio: The Yarur Workers and Chile's Road to Socialism* (New York: Oxford University Press, 1986), p. 51.

8. Interview with secondary schoolteacher, March 6, 1986.

9. Interview with metalworker, August 14, 1986.

10. Interview with light and power worker, December 26, 1985.

11. Interview with bank employee, March 14, 1986.

12. Interview with bank employee, April 7, 1986.

13. Interview with secondary schoolteacher, April 9, 1986.

14. Interview with primary schoolteacher, April 14, 1986.

15. Interview with light and power worker, February 19, 1986.

16. Interview with telephone employee, July 7, 1986.

17. Interview with bank employee, January 10, 1986.

18. Interview with bank employee, January 15, 1986.

19. It is noteworthy to see the higher "intellectual" bent among employees in their much greater propensity to name scientific and literary figures. Laborers were twice as likely to name a sports figure than employees. Women make up 44 percent of the employee sample and are traditionally much less likely to be sports fans.

20. Daniel James writes of this nostalgia becoming a critical part of Peronist literature beginning in 1956 (*Resistance and Integration: Peronism and the Argentine Working Class* [New York: Cambridge University Press, 1988], p. 98). Two Argentine sociologists have focused on Perón's constant messages from exile that maintained an aura of mystery and suspense about him which made it possible to attach himself to the hearts and minds of Argentines through those many years. See Silvia Sigal and Eliseo Veron, *Perón o Muerte: Los fundamentos discursivos del fenómeno peronista* (Buenos Aires: Editorial Legasa, 1986), esp. 107ff.

21. In the CEPNA study (*El Nuevo sindicalismo*, p. 31), 75 percent of the delegates and union leaders felt that the majority of the working class were Peronists. Like the workers, they felt generally confident in the future viability of Peronism, particularly if it was able to put forward good leadership, continue to be unified and to reevaluate its historical doctrines to meet present conditions (ibid., p. 75).

22. Interview with metalworker, August 14, 1986.

23. Interview with light and power worker, February 19, 1986.

24. Interview with telephone employee, July 10, 1986.

25. Interview with bank employee, January 9, 1986.

26. CGT delegates also perceived Peronist disunity and poor contemporary leadership as having negative consequences for the trade union movement. See Lamadrid, *Política y alineamientos sindicales*, p. 49.

27. Interview with textile laborer, September 28, 1985.

28. Interview with textile laborer, November 1, 1985.

29. Interview with light and power worker, December 26, 1985.

30. Interview with light and power worker, February 11, 1986.

31. Interview with bank employee, January 15, 1986.

32. Interview with elementary schoolteacher, April 3, 1986.

33. Almost identical with workers, union delegates' opinions were equally at loggerheads with Communism: 80 percent felt that Marxism-Leninism was the ideology furthest from the aspirations of the Argentine working class (see CEPNA, *El Nuevo sindicalismo*, pp. 30-31). It is clear from reading the Communist press in Argentina that the party did not recognize its profound isolation from the working class, in that it maintains it has shared a "common struggle" with workers for over forty years.

34. Interview with metalworker, August 14, 1986.

35. Interview with metalworker, August 19, 1986.

36. Interview with light and power worker, December 26, 1985.

37. Interview with light and power worker, February 12, 1986.

38. Interview with bank employee, January 9, 1986.

39. Interview with secondary schoolteacher, March 6, 1986.

40. Interview with secondary schoolteacher, April 1, 1986.

41. The Argentine Communist party accepted, virtually without criticism, all aspects of Soviet domestic and foreign policies. The language of the party newspaper used rigid cold war terminology and its rhetoric appeared largely unchanged since the post–World War II period. For example, in the February 19 and 26, 1986, issues of *Qué Pasa* there was only obsequious coverage of the Twenty-Seventh Party Congress resolutions in Moscow. Moreover, there were no criticisms of existing Eastern European brands of socialism to be found in its pages.

42. Interview with telephone employee, July 7, 1986.

43. Interview with textile laborer, December 13, 1985.

44. Interview with telephone employee, July 2, 1986.

45. Interview with bank employee, April 26, 1986.

46. On the other hand, easily three-quarters of the editorials of the Argentine Communist party newspaper *Qué Pasa* between 1985 and 1986 wrote of the unswerving struggle between the forces of national liberation and imperialist-based dependency, demonstrating little awareness of the much more complicated national focus of both the CGT delegates as well as the union rank and file surveyed in this study.

47. The Austral Plan was at first generally popular with the population as a whole, given that inflation was a critical issue, with even a more universal impact than unemployment, since it affects all socioeconomic strata across the board. In Argentina, because of the huge underground economy, there is some protection from unemployment. But from inflation no one can hide.

48. Among union delegates, industrial reactivization was the most crucial step the Alfonsín government could take (40.6 percent) to revitalize the Argentine economy, with another important number mentioning the importance of a debt moratorium (40.4 percent). See CEPNA, *El Nuevo sindicalismo*, p. 81. Union leaders seemed to oppose the foreign debt for the economic reasons that it drained necessary capital investments rather than for reasons of imperialism or dependency.

49. Interview with bank employee, April 4, 1986.

50. Remarkably, there was an almost identical support for privatization among both laborers and employees ($X^2 = .000$, 1 df, n.s.).

51. Interview with textile worker, December 12, 1985.

52. Interview with automobile worker, May 21, 1986.

53. Interview with metalworker, August 21, 1986. In fact, the Alfonsín administration had pushed an "early retirement" program for civil servants aimed at over 100,000 public employees. About 15,000 had accepted by mid-1987. See *Página 12* (August 1987), various issues.

54. Interview with light and power worker, December 30, 1985.

55. Interview with light and power worker, February 11, 1986.

56. Interview with telephone employee, July 7, 1986.

57. Interview with bank employee, April 24, 1986.

58. Interview with secondary schoolteacher, April 9, 1986.

59. It was also clear that by 1985 the CGT itself was beginning to show its amenability to some sort of rationalization of governmental deficitary enterprises whether in the form of better management techniques or in some sort of mixed public/private form of production. See Héctor Palomino, "El movimiento de democratización sindical," in *Los nuevos movimientos sociales*, ed. Elizabeth Jelin (Buenos Aires: Centro Editor de América Latina, 1985), p. 56ff. This is supported by evidence from the CEPNA study of union delegates. Over half of the union leaders felt that either some state enterprises should be privatized (42 percent) or as many as feasible (9.1 percent). See CEPNA, *El Nuevo sindicalismo*, pp. 33, 83.

On the other hand, the Argentine Communist party appears noticeably out of tune with the majority of the Argentine working class by its staunch opposition to any privatization whatsoever.

See for example the June 25, 1986, issue of *Qué Pasa*, where the party reiterates again its uncompromising defense of all state enterprises.

60. According to the Argentine census, *Clarín* with 485,000; *La Razón*, with 273,000; and *La Nación* with 211,000 circulation were the leading Argentine daily newspapers. See *Anuário Estadístico*, 1981–1982 (Buenos Aires: INDEC, 1984), p. 277.

61. Interview with textile laborer, October 4, 1986.

62. Interview with autoworker, May 21, 1986.

63. Interview with metalworker, August 22, 1986.

64. Interview with telephone employee, July 3, 1986.

65. Interview with telephone employee, July 4, 1986.

66. Interview with bank employee, January 14, 1986.

67. Interview with bank employee, April 14, 1986.

68. Interview with secondary school industrial teacher, March 5, 1986.

69. The Argentine Communists in their publication *Qué Pasa* saw a major breach between the CGT leadership and the rank and file unionists that was not at all apparent in this survey. See for example *Qué Pasa*, April 30, 1986, p. 2.

70. Understandably, union leaders and delegates (68 percent) favored union active participation in politics, though industrial delegates (59.2 percent) were more lukewarm, compared to the enthusiastic endorsement by service union delegates

(73.5 percent). See CEPNA, *El Nuevo sindicalismo*, p. 59; Lamadrid, *Política y alineamientos sindicales*, p. 20; and Godio, "La ideología de los cuadros sindicales intermedios," p. 9.

On the other hand, an overwhelming 94.3 percent of union delegates wanted CGT's issue orientations developed by the unions either without interference from political parties (83.4 percent) or in collaboration with political parties (10.9 percent). Less than 1 percent of the union leaders felt that a political party should take the initiative in developing union positions (see CEPNA, *El Nuevo sindicalismo*, p. 63; and Lamadrid, *Política y alineamientos sindicales*, p. 47).

In terms of who should lead in opposing the government, 52.8 percent of the delegates favored either Peronist collaboration with the CGT (34.2 percent) or sole CGT leadership (18.6 percent). A large number of delegates (39.5 percent) favored the Peronist party as leader of the opposition (see CEPNA, *El Nuevo sindicalismo*, p. 32).

It is clear that middle-level union leaders want the CGT to develop its political positions but then are divided as to how to pursue these measures, though by and large the Peronist connection is seen as crucial.

71. Interview with light and power worker, February 14, 1986.

72. Interview with bank employee, January 14, 1986.

73. Interview with secondary schoolteacher, April 1, 1986.

74. Unsurprisingly, workers with negative experiences with their own employer translated that into a general distrust of Argentine businessmen ($X^2 = 7.885$, 1 df, $p < .005$). Interestingly, the original 1940s Peronist alliance between the national bourgeoisie and the working class seems to be an increasingly uneasy alliance, given the suspicion and distrust that contemporary workers hold for their Argentine employers.

75. Interview with metalworker, August 18, 1986.

76. Interview with telephone employee, June 30, 1986.

77. Interview with telephone employee, July 3, 1986.

78. Interview with telephone employee, July 8, 1986.

79. Interview with bank employee, March 14, 1986.

80. Interview with bank employee, April 28, 1986.

81. Interview with bank employee, April 30, 1986.

82. Interview with industrial secondary schoolteacher, March 5, 1986.

83. This was already the reputation that modern foreign firms had among the Argentine working class twenty years earlier. 75 percent of the Argentine workers who responded to Sigal's mailing believed that foreign enterprise helped the country's development, while only 19 percent thought it restricted development. It is also important to note that Sigal found that the state enterprises also had an equally good standing with workers. It was essentially, the traditional smaller Argentine private enterprise sector that received the most negative evaluations (*Attitudes Ouvrières en Argentine*, 1:24, and Appendix 1, p. 19).

84. $X^2 = .146$, 2 df, n.s.

85. Interview with automobile worker, May 22, 1986.

86. Interview with telephone employee, July 3, 1986.

87. Interview with bank employee, March 14, 1986.

88. Interview with bank employee, April 7, 1986.
89. Interview with secondary schoolteacher, April 9, 1986.
90. Interview with bank employee, March 16, 1986.
91. Employees were far more critical of the role of the military than laborers ($X^2 = 6.392$, 2 df, $p < .04$).
92. Interview with textile worker, October 28, 1985.
93. Interview with autoworker, May 21, 1986.
94. Interview with metalworker, August 15, 1986.
95. Interview with light and power worker, January 3, 1986.
96. Interview with light and power worker, February 21, 1986.
97. Interview with telephone employee, July 7, 1986.
98. Interview with bank employee, January 9, 1986.
99. Interview with secondary schoolteacher, April 7, 1986.
100. When the CEPNA study group asked union leaders and delegates to rate the relationship of the Argentine unions with leading institutional actors, the military also received the lowest "good" rating of 9.3 percent although the Alfonsín government closely followed with 14.3 percent. The Catholic church received, far and away, the highest rating with 56.7 percent reporting their relationship as good (see CEPNA, *El Nuevo sindicalismo*, p. 65; and Lamadrid, *Política y alineamientos sindicales*, p. 69). Further, 74.8 percent of the union delegates supported some kind of military reform, 27.4 percent explicitly advocating a change from the military doctrine of national security to one of national defense (CEPNA, *El Nuevo sindicalismo*, p. 34). This is obviously a reference to the out-of-control activities of the armed forces during the "dirty war" persecution of dissent.
101. Employees were significantly more critical of the "dirty war" against subversion than the laborers ($X^2 = 4.089$, 1 df, $p < .05$).
102. Interview with autoworker, May 22, 1986.
103. Interview with light and power worker, February 17, 1986.
104. Interview with metalworker, August 7, 1986.
105. Interview with telephone employee, July 8, 1986.
106. Interview with bank employee, January 9, 1986.
107. Interview with bank employee, April 4, 1986.
108. Interview with bank employee, April 14, 1986.
109. Interview with bank employee, April 24, 1986.
110. As Wilhelm Reich wrote in another historical context, "The broad non-political masses look upon Communists as 'men of violence.' Moreover, the view of the broad masses is *decisive*. The masses fear violence, want peace and quiet, and for that reason will have nothing to do with Communism" (*Sex-Pol Essays, 1929–1934* [New York; Random House, 1966], p. 346).
111. Interview with textile worker, October 4, 1985. The Montonero methods produced major public repudiation as well. See Peter Waldman, "Anomía social y violencia," in *Argentina, hoy*, ed. Alain Rouquié (Mexico City: Siglo XXI, 1982), pp. 246-47.
112. Interview with textile worker, December 13, 1985.
113. Interview with autoworker, May 16, 1986.

114. Interview with autoworker, May 21, 1986.
115. Interview with telephone employee, July 3, 1986.
116. Interview with bank employee, April 26, 1986.
117. Interview with primary schoolteacher, April 14, 1986.
118. Cited in CONADEP's *Nunca Más* (Buenos Aires: Editorial de la Universidad de Buenos Aires, 1984).
119. See Ronaldo Munck, *Argentina: From Anarchism to Peronism* (London: Zed Books, 1987), p.31.
120. Even in 1967, when violent revolutionary struggle could be assumed to have held out more appeal for Argentine workers, Sigal found in her survey that workers gave much higher credibility to the Onganía government and the trade union movement than to the revolutionaries (Sigal, *Attitudes Ouvrières en Argentine,* Appendix 1, p. 17).
121. Union delegates had a similar profile to rank-and-file union employees, 78.2 percent of them feeling that the defense of human rights forms a part of the task of trade union activities (CEPNA, *El Nuevo sindicalismo*, p. 95).
122. Interview with automobile worker, May 16, 1986.
123. Interview with secondary industrial schoolteacher, March 12, 1986.
124. Interview with telephone employee, July 10, 1986.
125. Interview with bank employee, April 4, 1986.
126. On the psychological dimensions of the political repression in Argentina, see Diana Kordon and Lucila Edelman, *Efectos psicológicos de la represión política* (Buenos Aires: Sudamerica Planeta, 1987), *passim*.
127. Among the CGT delegates, 82.8 percent also felt that the military trials should continue (CEPNA, *El Nuevo sindicalismo*, p. 35).
128. Interview with textile worker, October 7, 1985.
129. Interview with telephone employee, July 3, 1986.
130. Interview with bank employee, March 24, 1986.
131. Interview with bank employee, April 10, 1986.
132. Interview with textile worker, October 4, 1985.
133. Interview with textile worker, November 12, 1985.
134. Interview with autoworker, May 16, 1986.
135. Interview with autoworker, May 22, 1986.
136. Interview with metalworker, August 22, 1986.
137. Interview with light and power worker, February 12, 1986.
138. Interview with telephone employee, July 3, 1986.
139. Interview with bank employee, January 9, 1986.
140. Interview with bank employee, April 4, 1986.
141. Interview with bank employee, April 7, 1986.

Chapter 7. Class and Ideology Among Argentine Workers

1. Interview with light and power worker, February 12, 1986.
2. A voter survey conducted during the Alfonsín administration showed that

almost 60 percent of the population identified with corporatist, liberal, or tradition-al political values and only 40 percent with social democratic or left orientations. See Manuel Mora y Araujo, "The Nature of the Alfonsín Coalition," in *Elections and Democratization in Latin America, 1980–1985*, ed. Paul Drake and Eduardo Silva (San Diego: University of California Press, 1986), p. 186.

3. There was a strong association between workers' feelings of being exploited at the workplace and a leftist orientation ($X^2 = 18.895$, 4 df, $p < .001$).

4. Perón is largely responsible for the dignity attached to the term "working class." Thus I decided to use the terms "lower" and "middle class," not "working class," since most respondents would so identify themselves, making discrimination difficult. Harry Braverman came to similar conclusions about U.S. workers in *Labor and Monopoly Capital* (New York: Monthly Review Press, 1974), p. 28.

5. However, as explained in the next chapter, levels of material comfort were not traceable to a simple incomes test among workers. I found, for example, no association at all between level of wages and class perceptions ($X^2 = .334$, 1 df, n.s.).

6. Interview with textile worker, October 2, 1985.

7. Interview with metalworker, August 28, 1986. A U.S. laborer uses a similar reason for calling himself middle-class. "Am I middle-class? Yes, well . . . . It's if you have to work and you have a house and a car and a couple of bucks and every so often you blow $30 or $50 and take your family out to eat or to the movies and now and then you take a vacation." David Halle, *America's Working Man: Work, Home and Politics Among Blue-Collar Property Owners* (Chicago: University of Chicago Press, 1984), p. 222.

8. Interview with light and power worker, February 19, 1986.

9. Interview with telephone employee, July 10, 1986.

10. Interview with bank employee, April 10, 1986.

11. Interview with metalworker, August 28, 1986.

12. Interview with bank employee, April 7, 1986.

13. Interview with secondary schoolteacher, March 12, 1986.

14. With apparent sarcasm, the English-language newspaper, the *Buenos Aires Herald* (May 31, 1987, p. 2), catalogued some of these negative Argentine national characteristics. Among them were: "Always me first"; "Don't get involved, there's always the friend of a friend to fix any difficulty"; "Everyone else is an asshole"; It's better if it's imported—buy abroad and travel anywhere but within Argentina itself"; "Nice guys finish last; everyone else is a crook except me and my friends"; "It's someone else's problem"; "Work is for fools"; "The great outdoors is one big garbage can."

Similarly, Rodolfo Braceli writes ("Memoria y desmemoria. Examen de con-ciencia y de inconciencia," *Plural* 2, no. 6 [April 1987], 105) of the finely honed critical nature of Argentines: "[There is] someone sitting in a commuter train that doesn't leave on time and says, '*Esto no va más*' [a combination of 'We'll have to put a stop to this' and 'We can't take this anymore']. With difficulty among the ten or fifteen people who hear this will there be anyone who will say with equal firmness: '*Esto sí va mas.*' This is not the end of the world. The end of the world we've seen [reference to the *proceso* military dictatorship]."

15. Interview with metalworker, August 7, 1986.

16. Interview with metalworker, August 22, 1986.

17. Interview with bank employee, January 10, 1986.

18. Interview with telephone employee, July 8, 1986.

19. The Argentine Communists, judging by their newspaper, *Qué Pasa*, do not seem to accept the general working-class belief in the feasibility of upward social mobility in Argentina and the porousness of the middle sectors of the social strata.

20. Interview with metalworker, August 27, 1986.

21. Interview with light and power worker, February 11, 1986.

22. Interview with telephone employee, July 1, 1986.

23. Interview with telephone employee, July 10, 1986.

24. Interview with bank employee, January 9, 1986.

25. Interview with bank employee, January 14, 1986.

26. Interview with bank employee, April 21, 1986.

27. These attitudes among laborers have not appreciably changed in the last several generations. For example, Daniel James, (*Resistance and Integration: Peronism and the Argentine Working Class* (New York: Cambridge University Press, 1988), p. 90, quotes from a Peronist publication in 1957: "A textile workers' leader, Juan Carlos Loholaberry, voiced a common perception when asked his attitude to the socialist concept of the abolition of classes. He replied that Peronists could not be opposed to private enterprise but rather wanted to ensure that it contributed to the public good: 'As for the social classes, they conform to a natural order of things which is impossible to change. Thus we do not propose that they be abolished, but that they all aim for a single goal: social welfare.'"

28. Interview with textile worker, November 13, 1985.

29. Interview with automobile worker, May 20, 1986.

30. Interview with light and power worker, February 21, 1986.

31. Interview with metalworker, August 21, 1986.

32. Interview with bank employee, April 4, 1986.

33. Interview with industrial secondary schoolteacher, March 12, 1986.

34. Interview with bank employee, April 14, 1986.

35. We see a statistical association between workers who felt exploited and those who saw the existence of class conflict in Argentina ($X^2 = 8.819$, 2 df, $p < .02$). And again, workers with the most negative opinions of their employers were most likely to perceive this class conflict ($X^2 = 6.831$, 1 df, $p < .001$).

36. When CGT delegates were asked to describe the ideology closest to that of the Argentine working class, 80 percent gave the Western European model of either Christian socialism (49.2 percent) or democratic socialism (30.8 percent), both choices confirming the rank-and-file choice of democracy. See CEPNA, *El Nuevo sindicalismo*, pp. 30-31.

37. David Halle, in his study of New Jersey chemical workers, found similar evidence for laborers' classic visions of democratic government (*America's Working Man: Work, Home and Politics Among Blue-Collar Property Owners*, p. 198).

38. Interview with secondary schoolteacher, April 9, 1986.

39. Interview with textile worker, September 18, 1985.

40. Interview with metalworker, August 28, 1986.

41. The Argentine Communist party, as observed through its newspaper, *Qué Pasa*, does not seem to understand that Argentine workers have, for the most part, a serious commitment to formal democracy even in the absence of progressive social legislation. The Communist critique of so-called bourgeois democracy as being merely a legalistic facade appears to fall on deaf ears. See, for example, editorials and columns in *Qué Pasa*, January 1 and April 9, 1986.

42. Interview with textile worker, November 1, 1985.

43. Interview with textile worker, November 12, 1986.

44. Interview with metalworker, August 8, 1986.

45. Interview with light and power worker, January 3, 1986.

46. Interview with light and power worker, December 30, 1985.

47. Interview with light and power worker, February 19, 1986. Edgardo Catterberg found similar support for democracy among laborers in a survey taken with the ascension of Alfonsín ("Las elecciones del 30 de Octubre de 1983; El surgimiento de una nueva convergencia electoral," *Desarrollo Económico* 25, no. 98 [July–September 1985], 260-67).

48. Interview with telephone employee, July 3, 1986.

49. Interview with industrial secondary schoolteacher, March 6, 1986.

50. Interview with secondary schoolteacher, March 26, 1986.

51. CGT delegates were asked, "What was the importance of the 1983 elections?" Every delegate said that either it meant the return of democracy (70.4 percent) or the implementation of constitutional guarantees (32.8 percent). See Lamadrid, *Política y alineamientos sindicales*, p. 65.

52. Interview with light and power worker, January 7, 1986.

53. Interview with telephone employee, July 2, 1986.

54. Interview with telephone employee, July 8, 1986.

55. Interview with bank employee, April 21, 1986.

56. Interview with bank employee, April 28, 1986.

57. Interview with telephone employee, July 1, 1986.

58. Interview with bank employee, January 10, 1986.

59. Interview with bank employee, April 4, 1986.

60. Interview with primary schoolteacher, April 14, 1986.

61. It is quite startling to observe that between 1985 and 1986 the Argentine Communist publication, *Qué Pasa*, literally never distinguished between laborers and employees and almost always focused on material questions concerning the cost of living and salary levels, to the virtual exclusion of—for example—questions of social values.

62. Note: these percentages do not sum to 100 because of multiple responses.

63. As Alec Nove recalls, "I have seen the slogan 'abolish the wage system' somewhere on a wall in West Germany, but, of course, *not* a factory wall; it was in a

university." See *The Economics of Feasible Socialism* (London: George Allen and Unwin, 1983), p. 53.

64. Interview with textile worker, November 1, 1985.

65. Interview with metalworker, August 21, 1986.

66. Interview with light and power worker, February 17, 1986. In Nove's study of the viability of existing socialisms, he found that, whether in Western or Eastern Europe or the Soviet Union, workers don't foresee (or welcome, for that matter) the abolition of the wage system, as Marx had predicted (Nove, *The Economics of Feasible Socialism*, p. 56).

67. Interview with bank employee, April 4, 1986.

68. Interview with bank employee, April 21, 1986.

69. Interview with secondary industrial schoolteacher, March 5, 1986.

70. Interview with secondary industrial schoolteacher, March 6, 1986.

71. Argentine workers, though removed from the culture of the working poor in Buenos Aires, still show considerable sympathy for their plight. Such a degree of sympathy is not found in the United States (Halle, *America's Working Man*, p. 212). This could become more and more manifest in the post-Alfonsín period of falling expectations. It is very difficult to predict, but "lumpen" squatter demands for services, housing, and food could receive the active support of the Argentine working class. The food riots of the last months of Alfonsín's term combined such factors as the frustrations of Third World conditions with the organizational capacity of a First World trade union movement.

72. The Sigal study of 1967 found that Argentine workers employed by foreign firms were least likely to want to change jobs. See Silvia Sigal, *Attitudes Ouvrières en Argentine* (Paris: Centre D'Etude des Mouvements Sociaux, December 1974), Appendix 2, p. 1. The Communist newspaper, *Qué Pasa*, constantly reiterates the dependency theme of foreign domination, though this does not appear to be a prime concern among the Argentine working class, outside of their awareness that the foreign debt negatively affects their standard of living. See, for example, the commentary of Athos Fava, head of the Argentine Communist party, reprinted in *Qué Pasa*, August 1, 1986, p. 2.

73. However, nonbelievers or atheists made up only 1 percent of the survey; not one of these was a laborer. Less than 5 percent of the workers had a non-Catholic upbringing.

74. Interview with metalworker, August 15, 1986.

75. Interview with telephone employee, July 8, 1986.

76. Interview with bank employee, April 21, 1986.

77. Interview with automobile worker, May 21, 1986.

78. Interview with bank employee, April 4, 1986.

79. Interview with primary schoolteacher, May 8, 1986.

80. James holds that Argentine laborers' sense of class does not call for an autonomous working-class organization, but for an affirmation "of the values associated with home and family, *barrio* and workmates" (*Resistance and Integration*, pp. 97-98).

81. Interview with textile worker, November 1, 1985.

82. Interview with metalworker, August 14, 1986.

83. Interview with light and power worker, December 30, 1985.

84. Interview with light and power worker, February 21, 1986.

85. Interview with bank employee, April 26, 1986.

86. Interview with secondary schoolteacher, March 25, 1986.

87. Freedom was valued more highly among employees than among laborers (X^2 = 5.899, 2 df, p < .05).

88. For example, nonreligious workers were much more likely to condemn the "dirty war" (X^2 = 7.058, 1 df, p < .01) and the fate of the "disappeared" (X^2 = 3.730, 1 df, p < .05) than were religious workers.

Chapter 8. Argentine Workers and the Question of Class Consciousness

1. Karl Marx, *Grundrisse* (New York: Vintage Books, 1973), p. 274.

2. For example, see Marx's formulations in *The Communist Manifesto* (New York: International Publishers, 1948), pp. 9-18, and *The 18th Brumaire of Louis Bonaparte* (New York: International Publishers, 1963), pp. 124-25.

3. Marx, *The 18th Brumaire of Louis Bonaparte*, p. 124.

4. See Lenin's perceived anti-Czarist community of interests in *What is to be Done?* (New York: International Publishers, 1959), pp. 58-59. It is interesting that fifty years later Fidel Castro, in assessing the groups with grievances against Batista's dictatorship, compiled a similar list that included the unemployed, farmworkers, laborers, small farmers, teachers and professors, small businessmen, and young professionals. See *History Will Absolve Me* (New York: Lyle Stuart, 1961), p. 34.

5. See Karl Marx and Friedrich Engels, *The Communist Manifesto* (New York: International Publishers, 1948), p. 20; and "The German Ideology," in *The Marx-Engels Reader*, ed. Robert C. Tucker (New York: W.W. Norton, 1972), p. 245ff.

6. E. P. Thompson, *The Making of the English Working Class* (London: Pelican Books, 1968), p. 10.

7. Adam Przeworski, *Capitalism and Social Democracy* (Cambridge: Cambridge University Press, 1985), p. 388.

8. Inverting Marx, then, it is consciousness that gives rise to a particular sense of social being. As Raphael Samuel writes, significant class action for Lenin is "measured not by occupation or income but by allegiance" ("Class Politics: The Lost World of British Communism," *New Left Review* 165 [September/October 1987], 61).

9. Marx and Engels, *The Communist Manifesto*, p. 9.

10. Karl Marx's "Theories of Surplus Value," taken from Tom Bottomore, *Theories of Modern Capitalism* (London: George Allen and Unwin, 1985), p. 16. Marx also observes certain class boundary ambiguities in *Capital*, vol. 3, chap. 18.

11. *The Portable Karl Marx*, ed. Eugene Kamenka (New York: Penguin Books, 1983), p. 529.

12. Marx and Engels, *The Communist Manifesto*, p. 21.

13. Karl Marx, *The Economic and Philosophical Manuscripts* (New York: Frederick Ungar, 1961), p. 97.

14. *The Marx-Engel Reader*, ed. Tucker, p. 22.

15. Ibid, p. 105.

16. Marx depicts the isolation in *The 18th Brumaire of Louis Bonaparte* (New York: International Publishers, 1963), p. 25.

17. *The Marx-Engels Reader*, ed. Tucker, p. 157.

18. Rosa Luxemburg, *Reform or Revolution?* (New York: Pathfinder Press, 1970), pp. 29-31.

19. Their principal works on this subject are Georg Lukács, *History and Class Consciousness* (Cambridge, Mass.: MIT Press, 1971); Antonio Gramsci, *Selections from Prison Notebooks* (New York: International Publishers, 1971); Wilhelm Reich, *Sex-Pol Essays, 1929–1934*, ed. Lee Baxandall (New York; Random House, 1966); and Herbert Marcuse, *One-Dimensional Man* (Boston: Beacon Press, 1966).

20. Lukács, *History and Class Consciousness*, pp. 86, 185.

21. Gramsci, *Selections from the Prison Notebooks*. For many of Gramsci's dispersed insights on nonsocialist forms of Western cultural hegemony, see his section "Problems of Marxism," p. 381ff.

22. See Carl Boggs, *Gramsci's Marxism* (London: Pluto Press, 1976), p. 71.

23. Reich, *Sex-Pol Essays*, esp. the last two essays.

24. Marcuse, *One-Dimensional Man*, pp. 158-59, 256.

25. Michael Burawoy, *The Politics of Production* (London: Verso, 1985), p. 152.

26. Karl Marx, *Class Struggles in France* (New York: International Publishers, 1964), pp. 56-57.

27. Marx, *The 18th Brumaire of Louis Bonaparte*, p. 23. Kolakowski writes of a contemporary social theorist of Marx, Pierre Joseph Proudhon,

> For the translation of his dreams into reality Proudhon relied neither on political nor on economic action by the proletariat. He was opposed to revolutions and even strikes on the ground that violent action against the "haves" would lead to disorder and despotism and would only exacerbate class hostility. He believed that, as his ideals were rooted in human nature and their realization would be no more than the fulfillment of human destiny, he would reasonably appeal to all classes, without distinction.

See Leszek Kolakowski, *Main Currents of Marxism* (New York: Oxford University Press, 1981), 1:209.

28. Quoted in Przeworski, *Capitalism and Social Democracy*, p. 75.

29. Peter Gay, *The Dilemma of Democratic Socialism* (New York: Columbia University Press, 1952), p. 215ff.

30. Eduard Bernstein, *Evolutionary Socialism* (New York: Schocken Books, 1961), pp. xxviii-xxix.

31. Quoted in Gay, *The Dilemma of Democratic Socialism*, p. 62.

32. Reich, *Sex-Pol Essays, 1929–1934*, p. 294.

33. Alec Nove, *The Economics of Feasible Socialism* (London: George Allen and Unwin, 1983), p. 58.

34. Karl Marx himself was aware of these basic human needs of autonomy and leisure. This is clear when reading his *Economic and Philosophical Manuscripts*, written in 1844. We will return to this question in the following chapter.

35. Lenin, *What is to be Done?* p. 31.

36. Peter Winn, *Weavers of the Revolution: Yarur Workers and Chile's Road to Socialism* (New York: Oxford University Press, 1986), *passim*.

37. *New York Times*, May 30, 1989, p. 9.

38. Ariel Hidalgo, "Cuba: The Marxist State and the 'New Class,'" unpublished, 1986, p. 61.

39. *New York Times*, August 22, 1989, p. 14.

40. Ibid., October 16, 1987, p. 17.

41. Marx and Engels, *The Communist Manifesto*, p. 28. Schumpeter sardonically referring to national connections writes, "No such bonds existed for Marx. Having no country himself he readily convinced himself that the proletariat had none." Joseph Schumpeter, *Capitalism, Socialism and Democracy* (New York: Harper and Row, 1950), p. 312.

42. Marx, *The 18th Brumaire of Louis Bonaparte*, p. 25.

43. Marx argues, "In all these battles [the bourgeoisie] sees itself compelled to appeal to the proletariat, to ask for its help, and thus, to drag it into the political arena: the bourgeoisie itself, therefore, supplies the proletariat with its own elements of political and general education, in other words it furnishes the proletariat with weapons for fighting the bourgeoisie" (Marx and Engels, *The Communist Manifesto*, p. 19).

44. V. I. Lenin, *State and Revolution* (New York: International Publishers, 1943), p. 60ff. Also see the excellent sociological analyses of the Russian Revolution in D. H. Kaiser, ed., *The Workers Revolution in Russia, 1917* (New York: Cambridge University Press, 1987). Nationalism was also emphasized by Gramsci in *Selections from Prison Notebooks*, p. 242ff.

45. "To imagine that a social revolution is *conceivable* without revolts of small nations in the colonies and in Europe, without the revolutionary outbursts of a section of the petty bourgeoisie *with all its prejudices*, without the movement of non-class conscious proletarian and semi-proletarian masses against the oppression of the landlords, the church, the monarchy, the foreign yoke, etc — to imagine that, is tantamount to *repudiating social revolution*. Only those who imagine that in one place an army will line up and say 'we are for socialism' and in another place, another army will say 'we are for imperialism' and believe that this will be the social revolution, only those who hold such a ridiculously pedantic opinion could vilify the Irish rebellion by calling it a 'putsch.'" From Lenin's "Collected Works," quoted in Ronaldo Munck, *The Difficult Dialogue* (London: Zed Books, 1986), p. 62. More recently, Eric Hobsbawm has written of the Irish question, "Of course it is true that, in so far as any workers in late Victorian Britain were revolutionary, it was the overwhelmingly unskilled Irish. But they almost certainly sympathized with revolu-

tion not because they were laborers, but because they were Irish, and they were apt to think in terms of insurrection because a tradition of armed rebellion formed part of the political experience of their country." See Eric Hobsbawm, *Workers: Worlds of Labor* (New York: Pantheon Books, 1984), p. 222.

46. Adam Przeworski, "Proletariat into Class: The Process of Class Formation from Karl Kautsky's 'The Class Struggle' to Recent Controversies," *Politics and Society* 7, no. 4 (1977), 371.

47. Nove, *The Economics of Feasible Socialism*, pp. 60-61.

48. Samuel, "Class Politics: The Lost World of British Communism," p. 62.

49. Charles Bergquist, *Labor in Latin America: Comparative Essays on Chile, Argentina, Venezuela and Colombia* (Stanford, Calif.: Stanford University Press, 1986), p. 145. This is generally corroborated by Romero, though both forward the view about the special role of Chilean class expression in its history. See Luís Alberto Romero, *Los sectores populares en las ciudades latinoamericanos: La cuestión de la identidad* (Buenos Aires: CISEA, June 1987), pp. 1-33.

50. Daniel James, "17 y 18 de Octubre de 1945: El Peronismo, la protesta de masas y la clase obrera argentina," *Desarrollo Económico* 27, no. 107 (October/December 1987), 450, 457.

51. Alvaro Abós, *La columna vertebral: sindicatos y peronismo* (Buenos Aires: Editorial Legasa, 1983), p. 13.

52. Friedrich Engels, introduction to Karl Marx, *Class Struggles in France, 1848-1850* (New York: International Publishers, 1964), p. 27.

53. Eduard Bernstein, *Evolutionary Socialism* (New York: Schocken Books, 1961), pp. 144-45.

54. *Selected Political Writings of Rosa Luxemburg*, ed. Dick Howard (New York: Monthly Review Press, 1971), p. 255ff.; Stephen E. Bronner, *Rosa Luxemburg: A Revolutionary for Our times* (New York: Columbia University Press, 1987), p. 58ff. Lenin's view of trade unions are of course well known. See *What is to be Done?* (New York: International Publishers, 1969).

55. Karl Marx, *Capital*, vol. 1, chap. 10, sec. 5 (New York: International Publishers, 1967).

56. Bernstein, *Evolutionary Socialism*, p. 137.

57. *Selected Political Writings of Rosa Luxemburg*, ed. Howard, p. 252.

58. Harry Braverman, *Labor and Monopoly Capitalism* (New York: Monthly Review Press, 1974), p. 11. Also speaking of the U.S. context, Robert Schrank, a former laborer himself, writes, "The American labor movement has traditionally dealt with 'alienation' by seeking more for its members in pay and benefits while reducing the amount of time they have to spend at the job. Until we have found an alternative to our traditional way of organizing work, history may reveal that this has been the best response to a negative situation." Robert Schrank, *Ten Thousand Working Days* (Cambridge, Mass.: MIT Press, 1978), p. 236.

59. Marx and Engels, *The Communist Manifesto*, p. 20.

60. *The Portable Karl Marx*, p. 250.

61. Joseph Schumpeter, *Capitalism, Socialism and Democracy* (New York: Harper

and Row, 1950), p. 310.

62. Tom Bottomore, for example, argues, "The early capitalist entrepreneurs were not consciously attempting to bring into existence a capitalist society. They were pursuing their own economic interests in an environment shaped by many different circumstances — the advance of science and technology, the growth of towns and nation states, the expansion of trade, the spread of a 'calculating' attitude and a view of economic activity as a God-given 'calling' — which made possible the development of the capitalist mode of production" (*Theories of Modern Capitalism* [London: George Allen and Unwin, 1985], p. 83).

63. See *The Marx-Engels Reader*, ed. Tucker, p. 174.

64. Friedrich Engels, introduction to Karl Marx, *Class Struggles in France, 1848-1850* (New York: International Publishers, 1964), p. 14.

65. See Laclau's critique of André Gunder Frank's analysis of exploitation as the essence of capitalism. Laclau observes that if that were the case, capitalism would have to be placed in neolithic times. See Ernesto Laclau, "Feudalism and Capitalism in Latin America," *New Left Review* 67 (May–June 1971), 25ff.

66. Schumpeter, *Capitalism, Socialism and Democracy*, p. 19.

67. Karl Marx, "The Civil War in France," in *The Portable Karl Marx*, ed. Kamenka (New York: Penguin Books, 1983).

68. *The Marx-Engels Reader*, ed. Tucker, p. 200.

69. Nove, *The Economics of Feasible Socialism*, p. 46.

70. These conclusions are based on interviews conducted by the author during two month-long trips to Cuba in 1978 and 1982, as well as readings of *Granma* and *Bohemia*.

71. See Linda Fuller, "Power at the Workplace: The Resolution of Worker-Management Conflict in Cuba," in *Cuba's Socialist Economy: Toward the 1990s*, ed. Andrew Zimbalist (Boulder, Colo.: Lynne Rienner, 1987), p. 150. Further, Alexis Codina Jiménez has documented the failure of the initial Cuban experience with moral incentives. "In 1966, for each peso in wages paid, a production of 1.58 pesos was obtained; in 1970 this decreased to 1.38. In many labor centers worker absenteeism reached 20 percent and the use of the workday did not surpass 60 percent of efficient levels." Alexis Codina Jiménez, "Worker Incentives in Cuba," in *Cuba's Socialist Economy: Toward the 1990s*, ed. Zimbalist, p. 133.

72. Carl Boggs, *Gramsci's Marxism* (London: Pluto Press, 1976), p. 92.

73. *The Marx-Engels Reader*, ed. Tucker, p. 160.

74. Nove, *The Economics of Feasible Socialism*, pp. 46-47.

75. From Karl Marx, *Economic and Philosophical Manuscripts*, ed. Erich Fromm (New York: Frederick Ungar, 1961), pp. 98-99.

76. Lukács, *History and Class Consciousness*, p. 198.

77. Hobsbawm, *Workers: Worlds of Labor*, p. 223.

78. James, *Resistance and Integration*, p. 234.

79. For example, Agustín Tosco and René Salamanca.

80. Bernstein, *Evolutionary Socialism*, p. 103.

81. Donald G. MacRae, "Sinister Thoughts on the Left and Right," *Encounter*,

April 1977, p. 40.

82. Erik O. Wright, *Class, Crisis and the State* (London: New Left Books, 1978), pp. 109-10.

83. Ibid., p. 110.

84. Zygmunt Bauman, "The Left as the Counter-Culture of Modernity," *Telos* 70 (Winter 1986-87), 93.

85. Bernstein, *Evolutionary Socialism*, p. 216.

86. *New York Times*, January 23, 1989, p. 12.

Chapter 9. Workers and Democratic Political Culture

1. From a song title by the North American folk song group, Bright Morning Star.

2. Karl Marx and Friedrich Engels, *The Communist Manifesto* (New York: International Publishers, 1948), p. 20.

3. Ibid., p. 24.

4. See Marx's critique of private property as the alienation of man from his true nature and pursuits in the *Economic and Philosophical Manuscripts*, ed. Erich Fromm (New York: Frederick Ungar, 1961), p. 128ff.

5. Karl Marx, *Class Struggles in France* (New York: International Publishers, 1964), p. 67.

6. Alexis de Tocqueville, *Democracy in America* (New York: Alfred Knopf, 1958), 2:199.

7. Eduard Bernstein, *Evolutionary Socialism* (New York: Schocken Books, 1961), pp. 169-70.

8. Ibid., pp. 220-21.

9. Samuel Bowles and Herbert Gintis have written that the democratic process survives in a kind of troubled coexistence with capitalist economies. See their *Democracy and Capitalism* (New York: Basic Books, 1987), *passim*.

10. Jurgen Habermas, *Communication and Evolution of Society* (Boston: Beacon Press, 1979), p. 114.

11. See, for example, the definitions of what it is to be "modern" in Alex Inkeles and David Smith, *Becoming Modern: Individual Change in Six Developing Countries* (Cambridge, Mass.: Harvard University Press, 1974), p. 19ff.

12. David Halle, *America's Working Man: Work, Home and Politics Among Blue-Collar Property Owners* (Chicago: University of Chicago Press, 1984), pp. 76-77.

13. Miklos Haraszti, *A Worker in a Worker's State* (New York: Universe Books, 1978), p. 69.

14. *New York Times*, May 10, 1989, p. 6.

15. *Guardian*, May 17, 1989, p. 3.

16. See for example Marx's favorable comments about capitalist penetration of feudal vestiges in his articles on India for the *New York Daily Tribune* in *The Portable Karl Marx*, ed. Eugene Kamenka (New York: Penguin Books, 1983), p. 329ff.

17. Marx and Engels, *The Communist Manifesto*, p. 17.

18. Ibid., p. 23.

19. *The Marx-Engels Reader*, ed. Robert C. Tucker (New York: W.W. Norton, 1978), p. 178.

20. Haraszti, *A Worker in a Worker' State*, p. 142.

21. Already in 1967, in her survey mailing to Latin American workers, Sigal observed this propensity among Argentine workers. Over two-thirds of those that responded to the survey on working-class attitudes wanted to be self-employed and start their own business. See Silvia Sigal, *Attitudes Ouvrières en Argentine* (Paris: Centre D'Etude des Mouvements Sociaux, December 1974), Appendix 1, p. 10.

22. *El Periodista* 189 (April 1988); also see José Nun, "Los Sindicatos y el sistema político," round table talk for the Centro Latinoamericano para el Análisis de la Democracia (CLADE), sponsored by Fundación Friedrich Ebert, Buenos Aires, August 1988, unpublished, p. 36.

23. George Konrad and Ivan Szelenyi, *The Intellectuals on the Road to Class Power* (New York: Harcourt Brace Jovanovich, 1979), pp. 226-27.

24. Karl Marx, *The 18th Brumaire of Louis Bonaparte* (New York: International Publishers, 1963), *passim*.

25. Marx and Engels, *The Communist Manifesto*, p. 20.

26. Karl Marx, *The Economic and Philosophical Manuscripts* ed. by Erich Fromm (New York: Frederick Ungar, 1961), p. 99.

27. André Gorz, *Farewell to the Working Class* (Boston: South End Press, 1982), p. 80.

28. Eli Zaretsky, *Capitalism, the Family and Personal Life* (New York: Harper and Row, 1986), pp. 49-50.

29. See Haraszti, *A Worker in a Worker' State*, p. 65; Robert Schrank, *Ten Thousand Working Days* (Cambridge, Mass.: MIT Press, 1978), p. 208; Barbara Garson, *All The Livelong Day* (New York: Penguin Books, 1975), p. 176; and Halle, *America's Working Man*, p. 51. The same theoretical proposition was advanced four decades ago by Joseph Schumpeter in *Capitalism, Socialism and Democracy* (New York: Harper and Row, 1950), p. 258.

30. *New York Times*, March 5, 1989, p. 9.

31. On the question of Bolivian peasants, see, for example, José Havet, *The Diffusion of Power: Rural Elites in a Bolivian Province* (Ottawa: University of Ottawa Press, 1985), *passim*.

32. In the aftermath of Hurricane Hugo that struck Puerto Rico and South Carolina in September 1989 and the October 1989 earthquake in northern California, people responded to the loss of their homes and personal possessions as if they were extensions of themselves, mourning for their lost belongings as one would mourn for a departed friend. A month after Hurricane Hugo had devastated his precarious house trailer, a forlorn man was photographed seated amid the rubble that was his house still waiting for federal emergency assistance that he might apply toward a new trailer. He was quoted as saying, "My mind feels better when I'm here. It's home." A California woman standing amid the severe destruction of her house said, "I'd rather my throat be cut than move" (*New York Times*, October 22, 1989).

33. Bernstein, *Evolutionary Socialism*, p. 149.

34. Ibid., pp. 153-54.

35. V. I. Lenin, *What is to be Done?* (New York: International Publishers, 1969), p. 42.

36. Quoted in Carl Boggs, *Gramsci's Marxism* (London: Pluto Press, 1976), p. 71.

37. Juan J. Hernández Arregui, *Peronismo y Socialism* (Buenos Aires: Editorial Corregidor, 1973), *passim*, esp. pp. 117-19.

38. Daniel James, *Resistance and Integration: Peronism and the Argentine Working Class* (New York: Cambridge University Press, 1988), p. 131.

39. Paul G. Buchanan, "Reflections on Institutionalizing Democratic Class Compromise in the Southern Cone," presented at the annual meeting of the Latin American Studies Association, New Orleans, March 1988, p. 24.

40. For example, the Argentine Communist newspaper, *Qué Pasa*, in early 1986 eulogized the Soviet Union's twenty-seventh Communist party congress for its "support of peoples' world struggle against 'yanqui' war and aggression" and gave special importance to Soviet demilitarization and nonintervention in the affairs of other countries. Also emphasized in its pages was the greater mass democracy and pluralism in the Soviet Union and Eastern Europe than in the Western bourgeois republics and the fact that the peoples' republics of the east were "perfecting socialist co-decision making on the basis of the daily active and conscientious participation of the workers" (*Qué Pasa*, nos. 258 and 259, February 19 and 26, 1986).

41. Friedrich Engels, "Socialism, Utopian and Scientific," in *The Marx-Engels Reader*, ed. Tucker, p. 713.

42. From V. I. Lenin's collected works, quoted in Harry Braverman, *Labor and Monopoly Capital* (New York: Monthly Review Press, 1974), p. 12.

43. Leszek Kolakowski, *Main Currents of Marxism* (New York: Oxford University Press, 1981), 1:334.

44. See Tom Bottomore, *Theories of Modern Capitalism* (London: George Allen and Unwin, 1985), p. 26.

45. Ralph Miliband, *The State in Capitalist Society* (New York: Basic Books, 1969).

46. Konrad and Szelenyi, *The Intellectuals on the Road to Class Power*, p. 226.

47. Haraszti, *A Worker in a Worker' State*, *passim*.

48. Bowles and Gintis, *Democracy and Capitalism*, *passim*.

49. Mark Kesselman and Joel Krieger, eds., *European Politics in Transition* (Lexington, Mass.: D.C. Heath, 1987), *passim*.

50. Joseph Schumpeter, *Capitalism, Socialism and Democracy* (New York: Harper and Row, 1950), p. 213.

51. Alexis de Tocqueville, *Democracy in America* (New York: Knopf, 1958), 2:131.

Chapter 10. Post-Alfonsín Peronism

1. ENTEL was originally sold to a consortium made up principally of Telefonía de España, the Italian company STET, and France Cable and Radio, while Aerolíneas

Argentinas was bought by Spain's Iberia and the Argentine company, Cielos del Sur. In a poll sponsored by *La Nación*, 69 percent of those questioned supported the privatization of one, the other, or both, while 20 percent were opposed (*La Nación*, May 7, 1990, p. 6).

2. *Página 12*, August 2, 1990, p. 3.

3. "Argentina Tries to Sell Its Shaky Phone System," *New York Times*, April 23, 1990, p. D8.

4. *Clarín* (international edition), September 3-9, 1990, p. 4.

5. Ley de Reforma del Estado, no. 23.696 (August 1989).

6. Ley de Emergencia Económica, no. 23.697 (September 1989).

7. *Clarín: Supplemento Económico*, March 17, 1991, p. 5.

8. Ley de Derecho de Huelga, no. 2.148 (October 1990).

9. For more details about this projected law, see Ley Nacional de Empleo, in *El Cronista Comercial* (special supplement), November 11, 1989, pp. 1-8; and *La Nación*, July 26, 1990, p. 4.

10. Interview with light and power worker, July 17, 1990.

11. Interview with textile worker, July 20, 1990.

12. Interview with light and power worker, August 20, 1990.

13. *Clarín* (various issues, July-August, 1990).

14. *La Nación*, August 10, 1990, p. 2. A later, end-of-the-year survey corroborated this public support for various privatizations of state enterprises. Sponsored by Argentina's leading newspaper, the poll stated that 73.4 percent of the population was supportive of the policy of privatizations. See *Clarín* (international edition), December 24-30, 1990, p. 8. Also see another favorable survey published in *La Nación*, January 8, 1991, p. 1.

15. Various Buenos Aires newspapers, August 6, 1990.

16. Interview with bank employee, July 19, 1990.

17. *Clarín* (international edition), September 10-16, 1990, p. 3, and ibid., January 21-27, 1991, p. 5. Similar to de Soto's analysis of Peru, formal economic employment data hide significant numbers of workers active in the informal economy. See Hernando de Soto, *The Other Path: The Invisible Revolution in the Third World* (New York: Harper and Row, 1989). p. 177ff.

18. Particularly disturbing is a survey published by *Clarín* at the end of 1990 indicating that 30 percent of the Argentine population could be categorized as poor or marginally poor, that is those who earned less than $600 per capita per annum. See *Clarín* (international edition), November 26-December 2, 1990, p. 9.

19. Both William Smith and José Nun demonstrate that this pattern had already asserted itself in the last years of the Alfonsín administration. Smith describes the rise of labor productivity, the fall of real wages, and the decline of wages and salaries as a proportion of national income from 53.8 percent in 1975 to 30 percent in 1988. He also documents the increasingly skewed income distribution in favor of the wealthiest sectors of society. See William C. Smith, "Democracy, Distributional Conflicts and Macroeconomic Policymaking in Argentina, 1983–1989," *Journal of Interamerican Studies and World Affairs*, 32, no. 2 (Spring 1990), pp.

1-42. Meanwhile, José Nun depicts the continuous shift of the working class into the informal and/or service sectors as the industrial sector shrank during the Alfonsín administration. See José Nun, *Crisis económica y despidos en masa* (Buenos Aires: Editorial Legasa, 1989).

20. It is also important to remember how many employees work in both the formal and informal economies simultaneously. An Argentine economist, Juan Luís Bour, is quoted as saying (ironically) that state employment is "a form of unemployment insurance" for 35 percent of the urban work force. See Louis Uchitelle, "Argentina's Painful Path to Efficiency," *New York Times*, May 14, 1990, p. D4.

21. The light and power and bank employee unions remained "independent" until late 1990, when they accepted most of the Menem policies. By mid-1990, aside from the CTERA teachers' union, the only other major unions to support Ubaldini were the state employees' union, *ATE*, under Victor de Genaro, the transport workers' union, *UTA*, and unionized sanitation workers, under Rubén Pereyra.

22. *La Nación*, August 5, 1990, p. 10.

23. Interview with light and power worker, August 20, 1990.

24. Interview with bank employee, August 7, 1990.

25. *El Bimestre*, no. 46 (October 1989), p. 31.

26. See for example the poll published in *La Nación*, July 22, 1990, p. 6.

27. Gary W. Wynia, *Argentina: Illusions and Realities* (New York: Holmes and Meier, 1986), p. 134.

28. On the other hand, the Argentine workers take an altogether different view. A metalworker, for example, said, "This is not a country for communism. We are so rich we can produce everything. In Nicaragua it makes sense because it is poor and they have to ration out what little they produce." Interview with metalworker, August 7, 1990.

29. *Qué Pasa?* (No. 258) February 19, 1986, p. 10 and (no. 259) February 26, 1986, p. 2.

30. The secretary-general of the Argentine Communist party, reelected in December 1990, is Patricio Echegaray.

31. *La Nación*, May 21, 1990, p. 4. Significantly, elsewhere in Latin America leftist groups were adjusting differently to the post-1989 East European events. For example, sounding like Friedrich Engels in 1895, Alfonso Cano, Colombia's M-19 guerrilla leader, spoke of the validity of democratic socialism as opposed to violent revolutionary confrontation. Indeed, M-19, competing for the first time in elections, emerged as the third largest political force in Colombia (*New York Times*, September 2, 1990, p. 11). Meanwhile, in El Salvador, Joaquín Villalobos, the rebel commander, spoke of one-party rule as "absurd." He spoke of his coalition's goals as being achieved not through armed revolution but by way of pluralistic, competitive democracy. The guerrilla movement had moved "beyond Marxism," which he called "just one more political theory" (*New York Times*, March 7, 1991, p. 3).

32. In this regard, see Evelyn Huber Stephens, "Capitalist Development and Democracy in South America," *Politics and Society* 17 (September 1989).

Chapter 11. Conclusion

1. Karl Marx, "German Ideology," in *The Marx-Engels Reader*, ed. Robert C. Tucker (New York: Norton, 1978), p. 165.

2. Peter Gay, *The Dilemmas of Democratic Socialism* (New York: Columbia University Press, 1952), p. 301.

3. Workers in Argentina know instinctively that profits are inevitable. As Nove writes, "Imagine a situation in which, by powerful class struggle, the workers reduce net profits to zero. There is then in the model no net investment, therefore no growth because investment is assumed to be financed out of profits, directly or indirectly." Alec Nove, *The Economics of Feasible Socialism* (London: George Allen and Unwin, 1983), p. 4.

4. Giovanni Arrighi, "Marxist Century, American Century: The Making and Remaking of the World Labor Movement," *New Left Review* 179 (January/February 1990), 37.

5. Eduard Bernstein, *Evolutionary Socialism* (New York: Schocken Books, 1961), p. 103.

6. Saúl Ubaldini, himself, when speaking of his role as union leader, is quoted as saying, "I am a worker [like any other], and our only wish is to get to the end of the month with dignity." See *Esquiu*, February 25, 1990, p. 4.

7. This view was perhaps raised most clearly by Ralph Miliband in *The State in Capitalist Society* (New York: Basic Books, 1969).

8. Joseph Schumpeter, *Capitalism, Socialism and Democracy* (New York: Harper and Row, 1950), p. 200.

9. In an end-of-the-year survey, 64 percent of Argentines expected 1991 to be a better year for them personally than 1990. Moreover, while only 33 percent of them thought 1990 had been very good or good for the country, 59 percent expected 1991 to be a better year for Argentina. *Clarín* (international edition), December 24-30, 1990, pp. 8-9.

Bibliography

Abós, Alvaro. *La Columna vertebral: sindicatos y peronismo.* Buenos Aires: Editorial Legasa, 1983.

————. *Las organizaciones sindicales y el poder militar 1976–1983).* Buenos Aires: Centro Editor de América Latina, 1984.

————. "Sindicalismo, autonomía y política." In *Movimientos sociales y democracía emergente*, ed. Elizabeth Jelin. Buenos Aires: Centro Editor de América Latina, 1987.

————. *Los sindicatos argentinos argentinos: Cuadro de situación, 1984.* Buenos Aires: Centro de Estudios para el Proyecto Nacional, 1985.

Abrevaya, Carlos. "Por qué se embotella el tránsito hacia la democracía?" *Plural 2* (1987): 22-25.

Agulla, Juan C. *Diagnóstico social de una crisis: Córdoba, Mayo de 1969.* Córdoba: Editel, 1969.

Alberti, Blas Manuel, *Peronismo, burocracia y burguesía nacional.* Buenos Aires: Rancágua, 1974.

Albrieu, Oscar. Interview by Luís Romero, Buenos Aires: Instituto Torcuato de Tella Oral History Project, August, 1972.

Alexander, Robert J. *Juan Domingo Perón.* Boulder, Colo.: Westview Press, 1979.

Allub, Leopoldo. "Social Origins of Dictatorship and Democracy in Argentina." Ph.D. diss., University of North Carolina, 1973.

Altimir, Oscar. "Estimaciones de la distribución del ingreso en la Argentina, 1953–1980." *Desarrollo Económico* 25 (1986): 521-66.

Angeleri, Luis A. *Los sindicatos argentinos sin poder.* Buenos Aires: Editorial Pleamar, 1970.

Anteproyecto de Reforma de la Constitución. Buenos Aires, Partido Peronista, 1949.

Anthony, P. D. *The Ideology of Work.* London: Tavistock, 1977.

Anuário Estadístico, 1981-82. Buenos Aires: INDEC, 1984.

Anuário Sima (Servicio de Informaciones del Mercado). Buenos Aires: 1979.

Argentina: Social Sectors in Crisis. Washington, D.C.: World Bank, 1988.

Aronowitz, Stanley. "Why Work?" *Social Text* 12 (1985): 19-42.

Arrighi, Giovanni. "Marxist Century, American Century: The Making and Remaking of the World Labor Movement." *New Left Review* 179 (1990): 29-63.

Avellaneda, Oscar Andrés. "El tema del peronismo en la narrativa argentina." Ph.D. diss., University of Illinois, 1973.

Baily, Samuel L. *Labor, Nationalism and Politics in Argentina.* New Brunswick, N.J.: Rutgers University Press, 1967.

Balan, Jorge, and Elizabeth Jelin. *La estructura social en la biografía personal.* Buenos Aires: CEDES, 1979.

Balbus, Isaac. "The End of the Marxist Theory of Politics." Presented at the annual meeting of the American Political Science Association, New York, 1981.

Bauman, Zygmunt. "The Left as the Counter-Culture of Modernity." *Telos* 70 (1986-87): 81-93.

Beccaria, Luis, and Alvaro Orsatti. *La evolución del empleo y los salarios en el corto plazo: El caso argentino, 1977–1983.* Buenos Aires: CEPAL, 1985.

Belloni, Alberto. *Del anarquismo al peronismo.* Buenos Aires: Peña Lillo, 1960.

Bergquist, Charles. *Labor in Latin America: Comparative Essays on Chile, Argentina, Venezuela and Colombia.* Stanford, Calif.: Stanford University Press, 1986.

Bernstein, Eduard. *Evolutionary Socialism.* New York: Schocken, 1961.

Bissio, Raul, Floreal H. Forni, and Julio C. Neffa. "Estrategia y estructuras sindicales de los trabajadores industriales en el área metrópoli de Buenos Aires, 1955–1971." In *Movimiento obrero, sindicatos y poder en América Latina.* Buenos Aires: Editorial El Colóquio, 1974.

Blanco, Ruben V., *La clase media y el desarrollo de América Latina: Experiencia argentina.* Materiales de Estudios no. 44. San José, Costa Rica: CEDAL, 1972.

Blanksten, George I. *Perón's Argentina.* Chicago: University of Chicago Press, 1953.

Boggs, Carl. *Gramsci's Marxism.* London: Pluto Press, 1976.

Booth, John, and Mitchell Seligson. "The Political Culture of Authoritarianism in Mexico: A Reexamination." *Latin American Research Review* 19 (1984): 106-24.

Bottomore, Tom. *Theories of Modern Capitalism.* London: George Allen and Unwin, 1985.

Bowles, Samuel, and Herbert Gintis. *Democracy and Capitalism.* New York: Basic Books, 1987.

Braceli, Rodolfo. "Memória y desmemória: Exámen de conciencia y de inconciencia." *Plural* 2 (1987): 99-111.

Braun, Oscar. *El capitalismo argentino en crisis.* Buenos Aires: Siglo XXI, 1973.

Braverman, Harry. *Labor and Monopoly Capitalism.* New York: Monthly Review Press, 1974.

Britos, Sergio. "Las canastas de alimentos." *Bolitín CESNI* 1 (1987): 17-25.

Brodersohn, Mario S. "Sobre 'modernización y autoritarismo' y el estancamiento inflacionario argentino." *Desarrollo Económico* 13 (1973): 591-605.

Bronner, Stephen E. *Rosa Luxemburg: A Revolutionary for Our Times.* New York: Columbia University Press, 1987.

Buchanan, Paul G. "Reflections on Institutionalizing Democratic Class Compromise in the Southern Cone." Presented at the annual meeting of Latin American

Studies Association, New Orleans, 1988.

———. "State Corporatism in Argentina: Labor Administration under Perón and Onganía." *Latin American Research Review* 20 (1985): 61-95.

Burawoy, Michael. *Manufacturing Consent: Changes in the Labor Process under Monopoly Capitalism.* Chicago: University of Chicago Press, 1979.

———. *The Politics of Production.* London: Verso, 1985.

Cafiero, Antonio. *Cinco años después.* Buenos Aires: 1961.

———. Interview by Luis Gutiérrez, Buenos Aires: Instituto Torcuato Di Tella Oral History Project, May 1972.

Cámpora, Hector J. *La revolución peronista.* Buenos Aires: EUDEBA, 1973.

Candia, José Miguel. "Argentina: proceso militar y clase obrera." *Cuadernos del Sur* 2 (1985): 35-45.

Canitrot, Adolfo. "La experiencia populista de redistribución de ingresos." *Desarrollo Económico* 15 (1975): 331-51.

———. "La vialidad económica de la democracía: Un análisis de la experiencia peronista, 1973-76." *Estudios Sociales* no. 11. Buenos Aires: CEDES, 1978.

Canton, Dario. "Revolución Argentina" de 1966 y proyecto nacional." *Revista Latinoamericna de Sociología* 5 (1969): 520-43.

Cappelletti, Beatriz. *La concertación en la Argentina: antecedentes y experiencias.* Buenos Aires: CEPNA, 1985.

Cardoso, Oscar, and Rodolfo Audi. *Sindicalismo: el poder y la crisis.* Buenos Aires: Editorial de Belgrano, 1982.

Carri, Roberto. *Sindicatos y poder en la Argentina.* Buenos Aires: Editorial Sudestado, 1967.

Castro, Fidel. *History Will Absolve Me.* New York: Lyle Stuart, 1961.

Catterberg, Edgardo. "Las elecciones del 30 de Octubre de 1983, El surgimiento de una nueva convergencia electoral." *Desarrollo Económico* 25 (1985): 260-67.

———. "Political Attitudes, Social Background and Consensus Among Argentine Elites." Ph.D. diss., University of North Carolina, 1973.

Cavarozzi, Marcelo. *Autoritarismo y democrácia (1955–1983).* Buenos Aires: Centro Editor de América Latina, 1983.

———. "Sindicatos y política en Argentina, 1955-58." *Estudios CEDES* no. 1. Buenos Aires: CEDES, 1979.

Censo Nacional de Población y Vivienda, 1980. Buenos Aires: INDEC, 1982.

Cieza, Daniel. "El Frente del Pueblo: Una experiencia inédita en la Argentina." *Cuadernos del Sur* 5 (1987): 19-33.

Cimillo, Elsa, et al. *Acumulación y centralización en la industria argentina.* Buenos Aires: Tiempo Contemporáneo, 1973.

Ciria, Alberto. "Peronism Yesterday and Today." *Latin American Perspectives* 1 (1974): 21-41.

———. *Perón y el justicialismo.* Buenos Aires: Siglo XXI, 1971.

———. *Política y cultura popular: la argentina peronista, 1946–1955.* Buenos Aires: Editorial de la Flor, 1983.

La clase obrera argentina: Cambios y tendencias. Buenos Aires: Editorial Anteo, 1986.

Codina Jiménez, Alexis. "Worker Incentives in Cuba." In *Cuba's Socialist Economy: Toward the 1990s*, ed. Andrew Zimbalist. Boulder, Colo.: Lynne Rienner, 1987.

Coleman, Kenneth M., and Charles L. Davis. "How Workers Evaluate Their Unions: Exploring Determinants of Union Satisfaction in Venezuela and Mexico." Presented at the annual meeting of the Latin American Studies Association, Boston, 1986.

Concatti, Rolando. *Peronismo*. Mendoza: Sacerdotes para el Tercer Mundo, 1972.

Convenciones Colectivos de Trabajo. Buenos Aires: various contracts.

Cooke, John William. *Peronismo y revolución*. Buenos Aires: Editorial Granica, 1973.

————. El retorno de Perón: Un análysis revolucionario. Buenos Aires: Ediciones Segunda Etapa, 1964.

Corbiere, Emilio J. "Sindicatos, corporativismo y autogestión social." *Justicia Social* 2 (1986): 77-86.

Corradi, Juan E. "Argentina and Peronism: Fragments of the Puzzle." *Latin American Perspectives* 1 (1974): 3-20.

————. *The Fitful Republic: Economy, Society and Politics in Argentina*. Boulder, Colo.: Westview Press, 1985.

Crawley, Edward. *A House Divided: Argentina 1880–1980*. New York: St. Martin's Press, 1984.

D'Abate, Juan Carlos. "Trade Unions and Peronism." In *Juan Perón and the Reshaping of Argentina*, ed. Frederick C. Turner and José E. Miguens. Pittsburgh, Pa.: University of Pittsburgh Press, 1983.

Declaración de Tucumán del Movimiento Sindical Peronista Renovador. Tucumán, 1987.

De Imaz, José Luís. *Los hundidos: evaluación de la población marginal*. Buenos Aires: La Bastille, 1974.

De Pablo, Juan Carlos. *Economía política del peronismo*. Buenos Aires: El Cid, 1980.

De Riz, Liliana. *Retorno y derrumbe: el último gobierno peronista*. Mexico City: Folios Ediciones, 1981.

De Riz, Liliana, et al. "El movimiento sindical y la concertación en la Argentina actual." in *El sindicalismo latinoamericano en los ochenta*. Santiago de Chile: CLACSO, 1985.

De Riz, Liliana, Marcelo Cavarozzi, and Jorge Felman. "Concertación, estado y sindicatos en la Argentina contemporánea." Buenos Aires: CEDES, 1987.

De Soto, Hernando. *The Other Path: The Invisible Revolution in the Third World*. New York: Harper and Row, 1989.

De Tocqueville, Alexis. *Democracy in America*. 2 vols. New York: Knopf, 1958.

Del Campo, Hugo. "Continuidad y cambio en el movimeinto sindical argentino." *Cuadernos del Sur* 3 (1985): 55-66.

————. *Sindicalismo y Peronismo: los comienzos de un vínculo perdurable*. Buenos Aires: CLACSO, 1983.

Delich, Francisco J. *Crisis y protesta social; Córdoba, Mayo 1969*. Buenos Aires: Ediciones Signos, 1970.

————. "Después del dilúvio, la clase obrera." In *Argentina, hoy*, ed. Alain Rouquié. Mexico City: Siglo XXI, 1982.

Di Tella, Guido. *Argentina Under Perón, 1973–1976: The Nation's Experiment with a Labor-Based Government*. New York: St. Martin's Press, 1983.

Di Tella, Torcuato. "La búsqueda de la fórmula política argentina." *Desarrollo Económico* 11 (1972): 317-25

————. *Clases sociales y estructuras políticas*. Buenos Aires: Paidós, 1974.

————. "The October 1983 Elections in Argentina." *Government and Opposition* 19 (1984): 188-92.

————. *El sistema político argentino y la clase obrera*. Buenos Aires: EUDEBA, 1964.

Di Tella, Torcuato, et al. *Argentina: Sociedad de masas*. Buenos Aires: EUDEBA, 1965.

Díaz Araujo, Enrique. *La conspiración del 43: El gou; Una experiencia militarista en la Argentina*. Mendoza: Universidad Nacional de Cuyo, 1970.

Documentación e Información Laboral (monthly). Various issues, 1985-86.

Dorfman, Adolfo. "La industrialización: mito o realidad?" *Plural* 2 (1987): 65-68.

Doyon, Louise M. "Conflictos obreros durante el régimen peronista (1946–1955)." *Desarrollo Económico* 17 (1977): 437-74.

————. "El movimiento sindical bajo el peronismo." *Desarrollo Económico* 15 (1975): 151-63.

Duejo, Gerardo. *El capital monopolista y las contradicciones secundárias en la sociedad argentina*. Buenos Aires: Siglo XXI, 1973.

Economic Development and Income Distribution in Argentina. New York: United Nations Economic Commission for Latin America, 1969.

Edwards, Richard. *Contested Terrain: Transformation of the Work Place in the Twentieth Century*. New York: Basic Books, 1979.

Eloy Martínez, Tomás. "Perón: Un mundo nuevo se nos viene encima." *Panorama* 8 (1970): 66-67.

————. "Las memórias de Juan Perón (1895–1945)." *Panorama* 7 (1970): 20-25.

Engels, Friedrich. Introduction to Karl Marx, *Class Struggles in France, 1848-1850*. New York: International Publishers, 1964.

Epstein, Edward. "Control and Cooptation of the Argentine Labor Movement." *Economic Development and Cultural Change* 27 (1979).

————. "Labor Populism and Hegemonic Crisis in Argentina." In *Trade Unions and the State in Latin America*, ed. Edward Epstein. London: Allen and Unwin, 1989.

————. "Politicization and Income Distribution in Argentina: The Case of the Peronist Worker," *Economic Development and Cultural Change* 23 (1975): 615-31.

Erickson, Kenneth P. *The Brazilian Corporative State and Working Class Politics*. Berkeley and Los Angeles: University of California Press, 1977.

Erickson, Kenneth P., Patrick P. Peppe, and Hobart A. Spalding. "Research on the Urban Working Class in Argentina, Brazil and Chile: What Is Left to be Done?" *Latin American Research Review* 9 (1974): 115-42.

Estadística Mensual (monthly). Buenos Aires: INDEC.

Estatuto del Docente. Buenos Aires: Sainte Claire Editora, 1985.

Estructura sindical en la Argentina. Buenos Aires: Ministerio de Trabajo y Seguridad Social, 1987.

The Europa Yearbook: A World Survey, 1988. London: Europa Publishers, 1988.

Evans, Judith, and Daniel James. *The Political Economy of the Latin American Motor Vehicle Industry*. Cambridge: Cambridge University Press, 1984.

Falcoff, Mark. "Is Peronism Finished?" *Commentary* 77 (1984): 60-65.

Falcoff, Mark, and Ronald H. Dolkart, eds. *Prologue to Perón: Argentina in Depression and War, 1930–1943*. Berkeley and Los Angeles: University of California Press, 1976.

Fayt, Carlos S. *La naturaleza del peronismo*. Buenos Aires: Editorial Viracocha, 1967.

Feinman, José Pablo. *Estudios sobre peronismo: historia, metodo, proyecto*. Buenos Aires: Editorial Legasa, 1983.

———. *El peronismo y la primacía de la política*. Buenos Aires: Cimarrón, 1974.

Feldman, Ernesto. "La crisis financiera argentina: 1980-82." *Desarrollo Económico* 23 (1983): 449-55.

Fernández, Arturo. *Las prácticas sociales del sindicalismo, 1976–1982*. Buenos Aires: Centro Editor de América Latina, 1985.

———. *Las prácticas sociopolíticas del sindicalismo/1*. Buenos Aires: Centro Editor de América Latina, 1986.

———. "Sindicalismo y concertación social." *Justicia Social* 3 (1986-87): 27-46.

Frenkel, Roberto. "Salarios industriales e inflación. El periodo 1976–1982," *Desarrollo Económico* 23 (1983): 1-27.

Fuller, Linda. "Power at the Workplace: The Resolution of Worker-Management Conflict in Cuba." In *Cuba's Socialist Economy: Toward the 1990s*, ed. Andrew Zimbalist. Boulder, Colo.: Lynne Rienner, 1987.

Furci, Carmelo. *The Chilean Communist Party and the Road to Socialism*. London: Zed Books, 1984.

Gale, R. P. "Industrial Development and the Blue Collar Worker in Argentina." *International Journal of Comparative Sociology* 10 (1969): 117-50.

Galletti, Alfredo. *La realidad Argentina en el siglo XX: La política y los partidos*. Buenos Aires: Fondo de Cultura Económico, 1961.

Gambini, Hugo. *El 17 de Octubre*. Buenos Aires: Editorial Brujula, 1969.

———. *El primer gobierno peronista*. Buenos Aires: Centro Editor, 1971.

Garson, Barbara. *All the Livelong Day*. New York: Doubleday, 1975.

Gaudio, Ricardo, and Andrés Thompson. *Sindicalismo peronista/gobierno radical: Los años de Alfonsín*. Buenos Aires: Fundación Friedrich Ebert, 1990.

Gaudio, Ricardo, and Héctor Domeniconi. "Las primeras elecciones sindicales en la transición democrática." *Desarrollo Económico* 26 (1986): 423-53.

Gaudio, Ricardo, and Héctor Domeniconi. "El proceso de normalización sindical bajo el gobierno radical." Buenos Aires: unpublished, 1986.

Gay, Peter. *The Dilemma of Democratic Socialism*. New York: Columbia University Press, 1952.

Gazzera, Miguel. "La crisis de la negociación." In *Peronismo: De la reforma a la revolución*, ed. Norberto Ceresole. Buenos Aires: Peña Lillo, 1972.

Gerchunoff, Pablo, and Juan J. Llach. "Capital industrial, desarrollo asociado y distribución del ingreso entre los dos gobiernos peronistas: 1950–1972."

Desarrollo Económico 15 (1975): 3-34.

Germani, Gino. *Política y sociedad en una época de transición*. Buenos Aires: Editorial Paidós, 1962.

———. "El surgimiento del peronismo: el rol de los obreros y de los migrantes internos." *Desarrollo Económico* 13 (1973): 435-88.

Giddens, Anthony, and David Held, eds. *Classes, Power and Conflict*. Berkeley and Los Angeles: University of California Press, 1982.

Gillespie, Richard. *Soldiers of Perón: Argentina's Montoneros*. Oxford: Clarendon Press, 1982.

Giussani, Pablo. *Montoneros: La soberbia armada*. Buenos Aires: Sudamericana Planeta, 1984.

———. "El panorama cívico-militar en el segundo trienio de Alfonsín." *Plural* 2 (1987): 29-31.

Godio, Julio. "La ideología de los cuadros sindicales intermedios." *La Ciudad Futura* 5 (1987): 8-11.

———. "Los ocho retos del sindicalismo." *Nueva Sociedad* 70 (1984): 38-47.

———. *El último año de Perón*. Bogotá: Ediciones Tercer Mundo, 1981.

Godio, Julio, and Javier Slodky. *El regreso de la negociación colectiva*. Buenos Aires: Fundación Friedrich Ebert, 1988.

Godio, Julio, Héctor Palomino, and Achim Wachendorfer. *El movimiento sindical argentino (1880–1987)*. Buenos Aires: Puntosur, 1988.

Golden, Miriam A. "Historical Memory and Ideological Orientations in the Italian Workers' Movement." *Politics and Society* 16 (1988): 1-34.

Goldthorpe, John. *The Affluent Worker: Political Attitudes and Behavior*. Cambridge: Cambridge University Press, 1968.

———. *The Affluent Worker in the Class Structure*. Cambridge: Cambridge University Press, 1969.

Goldwert, Marvin. *Democracy, Militarism, and Nationalism in Argentina, 1930–1966*. Austin: University of Texas Press, 1972.

González, Ernesto. *Qué fue y qué es el peronismo*. Buenos Aires: Ediciones Pluma, 1974.

Gordon, David. *Segmented Work, Divided Workers: Historical Transformation of Labor in the United States*. Cambridge: Cambridge University Press, 1982.

Gorz, André. *Farewell to the Working Class*. Boston: South End Press, 1982.

———. *Paths to Paradise*. Boston: South End Press, 1985.

Gramsci, Antonio. *Selections from Prison Notebooks*. New York: International Publishers, 1971.

Grondona, Mariano. "Justicialismo, Marxismo, Liberalismo." *Mercado*, July 26, 1973.

Habermas, Jurgen. *Communication and Evolution of Society*. Boston: Beacon Press, 1979.

Halle, David. *America's Working Man: Work, Home and Politics Among Blue-Collar Property Owners*. Chicago: University of Chicago Press, 1984.

Haraszti, Miklos. *A Worker in a Worker's State*. New York: Universe Books, 1978.

Havet, José. *The Diffusion of Power: Rural Elites in a Bolivian Province*. Ottawa: University of Ottawa Press, 1985.

Heller, Amado. "Cambios en la estructura de la clase obrera." Presented at Jornadas de Actualización sobre la clase obrera, Buenos Aires, September, 1988.

Hernández Arregui, Juan J. *La formación de la conciencia nacional.* Buenos Aires: Hachea, 1960.

————. *Peronismo y socialismo.* Buenos Aires: Editorial Corregidor, 1973.

Hidalgo, Ariel. "Cuba: The Marxist State and the New Class." Unpublished, 1986.

Hobsbawm, Eric. *Workers: Worlds of Labor.* New York: Pantheon Books, 1984.

Hodges, Donald C. *Argentina, 1943–1987: The National Revolution and Resistance.* Albuquerque: University of New Mexico Press, 1988.

Hollander, Nancy C. "Si Evita Viviera." *Latin American Perspectives* 1 (1974): 42-57.

Horowitz, Joel. "Ideologías sindicales y políticas estatales en la Argentina, 1930-43." *Desarrollo Económico* 24 (1984).

Howard, Dick. *Selected Political Writings of Rosa Luxemburg.* New York: Monthly Review, 1971.

Howard, Robert. *Brave New Workplace.* New York: Penguin, 1985.

Huber Stephens, Evelyn. "Capitalist Development and Democracy in South America." *Politics and Society* 17 (1989):281–352.

Humphrey, J. *Capitalist Control and Workers' Struggle in the Brazilian Auto Industry.* Princeton, N.J.: Princeton University Press, 1982.

Ibarguren, Carlos. Interview. Buenos Aires: Instituto Torcuato Di Tella Oral History Project, 1971.

Iñigo Carrera, Nicholas, and Jorge Potesta. "La situación del proletariado en la Argentina actual (1960–1987)." Buenos Aires: CICSO, 1988.

Inkeles, Alex, and David Smith. *Becoming Modern: Individual Change in Six Developing Countries.* Cambridge, Mass.: Harvard University Press, 1974.

Instituto Nacional de Estadística y Censos (INDEC). Buenos Aires: various publications.

Instituto Torcuato Di Tella Oral History Project. Buenos Aires: various interviews.

James, Daniel. "17 y 18 de Octubre de 1945: El Peronismo, la protesta de masas y la clase obrera argentina." *Desarrollo Económico* 27 (1987): 445-61.

————. "The Peronist Left." *Journal of Latin American Studies* 8 (1976).

————. "Power and Politics in Peronist Trade Unions." *Journal of Interamerican Studies and World Affairs* 20 (1978): 3-36.

————. "Racionalización y respuesta de la clase obrera: contexto y limitaciones de la actividad gremial en la Argentina." *Desarrollo Económico* 21 (1981): 321-49.

————. *Resistance and Integration: Peronism and the Argentine Working Class.* New York: Cambridge University Press, 1988.

Jauretche, Arturo. Interview. Buenos Aires: Instituto Torcuato Di Tella Oral History Project, 1971.

Jelin, Elizabeth. "Conflictos laborales en la Argentina, 1973–1976." *Revista Mexicana de Sociología* 40 (1978): 421-63.

Jelin, Elizabeth, and Juan Carlos Torre. "Los nuevos trabajadores en América Latina: Una reflexión sobre la tesis de la aristocracia obrera." *Desarrollo Económico* 22 (1982): 3-24.

Jorge, Eduardo. *Industria y concentración económica.* Buenos Aires: Siglo XXI, 1973.

Jorrat, Jorge R. "Las elecciones de 1983: 'Desviación' o 'realineamiento.'" *Desarrollo Económico* 26 (1986): 89-120.

Jozami, Eduardo, Pedro Paz, and Juan Villarreal, eds. *Crisis de la dictadura argentina.* Buenos Aires: Siglo XXI, 1985.

Kaiser, D. H., ed. *The Workers' Revolution in Russia, 1917.* New York: Cambridge University Press, 1987.

Kamenka, Eugene, ed. *The Portable Marx.* New York: Penguin, 1983.

Kappner, Thomas. "The Political Economy of Populist-Nationalism in Argentina, 1943–1955: Peronism as a Transitional Stage in the Development of a Dependent Industrial Economy." Ph.D. diss., City University of New York, 1985.

Katz, Jorge. "Una interpretación a largo plazo del crecimiento industrial argentino." *Desarrollo Económico* 9 (1969): 511-42.

Katznelson, Ira, and Aristide Zolberg. *Working Class Formation: Nineteenth Century Pattern in Western Europe and the United States.* Princeton, N.J.: Princeton University Press, 1986.

Kenworthy, Eldon. "The Function of a Little-Known Case in Theory Formation, or What Peronism Wasn't." *Comparative Politics* 6 (1973): 1-35.

———. "Interpretaciones ortodoxas y revisionistas del apoyo inicial del peronismo." In *El voto peronista*, ed. Manuel Mora y Araujo and Ignacio Llorente. Buenos Aires: Sudamericana, 1980.

Kesselman, Mark, and Joel Krieger, eds. *European Politics in Transition.* Lexington, Mass.: D.C. Heath, 1987.

Klein, Emilio. "Los sindicatos y el sector informal." *Nueva Sociedad* 70 (1984): 95-101.

Kogan, Hilda, et al. "Articulaciones laborales en la crisis del sindicalismo argentino (1976–1981)." In *El sindicalismo latinoamericano en los ochenta.* Santiago: CLACSO, 1986.

Kolakowski, Leszek. *Main Currents of Marxism.* 3 vols. New York: Oxford University Press, 1981.

Konrad, George, and Ivan Szelényi. *The Intellectuals on the Road to Power.* New York: Harcourt Brace Jovanovich, 1979.

Kordon, Diana, and Lucila Edelman. *Efectos psicológicos de la represión política.* Buenos Aires: Sudamerica Planeta, 1987.

Korpi, Walter. *The Working Class in Welfare Capitalism: Work, Unions and Politic in Sweden.* London: Routledge and Kegan Paul, 1978.

Korzeniewicz, Roberto P. "The Labor Movement in Argentina, 1887–1973." Ph.D. diss., State University of New York, Binghamton, 1988.

Laclau, Ernesto. "Argentina: Peronism and Revolution." *Latin American Review of Books* 1 (1973): 117-30.

———. "Feudalism and Capitalism in Latin America." *New Left Review* 67 (1971): 19-38.

———. *Politics and Ideology in Marxist Theory.* London: Verso, 1979.

Laclau, Ernesto, and Chantalle Mouffe. *Hegemony and Class.* London: Verso, 1985.

———. "Post-Marxism without Apologies." *New Left Review* 166 (1987): 79-106.

Lamadrid, Alejandro Francisco. *El nuevo sindicalismo: Opiniones y actitudes de su dirigencia media*. Buenos Aires: CEPNA, 1987.

———. *Política y alineamientos sindicales: Opiniones del nuevo cuadro gremial*. Buenos Aires: Puntosur, 1988.

Landi, Oscar. "Cultura y política en la transición a la democracía." *Crítica y Utopía* 10/11 (1983): 7-91.

———. "La tercera presidencia de Perón: Gobierno de emergencia y crisis política." *Revista Mexicana de Sociología* 40 (1978): 1353-1410.

Landsberger, Henry A. "The Labor Elite: Is It Revolutionary?" In *Elites in Latin America*, ed. S. M. Lipset and Aldo Solari. New York: Free Press, 1968.

Lane, Robert. *Political Ideology: Why the American Common Man Believes What He Does*. New York: Free Press, 1962.

Lenin, V. I. *State and Revolution*. New York: International Publishers, 1943.

———. *What Is to Be Done?* New York: International Publishers, 1969.

Libro negro de la segunda tiranía. Buenos Aires: Presidencia de la Nación, Comisión Nacional de Investigaciones, 1958.

Licastro, Julian. "Peronismo y socialismo." *Política Internacional* 139 (1971): 4-13.

Lindenboim, Javier. *La terciarización del empleo en la Argentina*. Buenos Aires: Ministerio de Trabajo, 1985.

Lipset, S. M. "Comparing Canadian and American Unions." *Society* 24 (1987): 60-70.

———. *Political Man*. New York: Doubleday, 1960.

Little, Walter. "La organización obrera y el estado peronista, 1945–1955." *Desarrollo Económico* 19 (1979): 331-76.

———. "The Popular Origins of Peronism." In *Argentina in the Twentieth Century*, ed. David Rock. Pittsburgh, Pa.: University of Pittsburgh Press, 1975.

Llach, Juan J. "Estructura ocupacional y dinámica del empleo en la Argentina: Sus peculiaridades, 1947–1970." *Desarrollo Económico* 17 (1978): 539-93.

———. "Intereses económicos dominantes y los orígenes del peronismo." Unpublished, 1972.

———. "El Plan Pinedo de 1940, su significado histórico y los orígenes de la economía política del peronismo." *Desarrollo Económico* 23 (1984): 515-58.

Llovet, Juan J. *Los lustrabotas de Buenos Aires: Un estudio socio-antropológico*. Buenos Aires: CEDES, 1980.

Low-Beer, John. *Protest and Participation: The New Working Class in Italy*. Cambridge: Cambridge University Press, 1978.

Lucita, Eduardo. "Breve consideraciones sobre la reforma laboral." *Cuadernos del Sur* 5 (1987): 52-60.

———. "Elecciones sindicales y autoorganización obrera." *Cuadernos del Sur* 3 (1985): 5-54.

Lukács, Georg. *History and Class Consciousness*. Cambridge, Mass.: MIT Press, 1971.

Luna, Felix. *El 45: Crónica de un año decisivo*. Buenos Aires: Jorge Alvarez, 1969.

———. *Perón y su tiempo: La Argentina era una fiesta, 1946–1949*. Buenos Aires: Sudamericana, 1984.

Luxemburg, Rosa. *Reform or Revolution?* New York: Pathfinder Press, 1978.

MacRae, Donald G. "Sinister Thoughts on Left and Right." *Encounter* (April 1977): 40-44.

Madge, John. *The Tools of Social Science.* New York: Doubleday, 1965.

Mafud, Julio. *Sociología del peronismo.* Buenos Aires: Editorial America, 1972.

Mainwaring, Scott. "El movimiento obrero y el peronismo, 1952–1955." *Desarrollo Económico* 21 (1982): 515-30.

Mallon, Richard D., and Juan V. Sourrouille. *Economic Policy-Making in a Conflict Society: The Argentine Case.* Cambridge, Mass.: Harvard University Press, 1975.

Mannheim, Karl. *Ideology and Utopia.* New York: Harcourt, Brace and World, 1936.

Marconi, Elida. "Estudio sobre la división del trabajo en el proceso productivo, 1971-72." CICSO paper no. 9. Buenos Aires, 1973.

Marcuse, Herbert. *One-Dimensional Man.* Boston: Beacon Press, 1964.

Marin, Juan Carlos. "Acerca del estado del poder entre las clases: Argentina, 1973-76." CICSO paper no. 43. Buenos Aires, 1982.

Marshall, Adriana. "La composición del consumo de los obreros industriales de Buenos Aires, 1930–1980." *Desarrollo Económico* 21 (1981): 351-74.

———. "El salario social en la Argentina." *Desarrollo Económico* 24 (1984): 41-70.

———. *Políticas sociales: el modelo liberal.* Buenos Aires: Editorial Legasa, 1988.

Martínez Estrada, Ezequiel. *Qué és esto?* Buenos Aires: Editorial Lautaro, 1956.

Marx, Karl, and Friedrich Engels. *Capital.* Vol. 1. New York: International Publishers, 1967.

———. "Civil War in France." In *The Portable Marx,* ed. Eugene Kamenka. New York: Penguin, 1983.

———. *Class Struggles in France.* New York: International Publishers, 1984.

———. *The Communist Manifesto.* New York: International Publishers, 1948.

———. *Economic and Philosophical Manuscripts,* ed. Erich Fromm. New York: Frederick Unger, 1961.

———. *The 18th Brumaire of Louis Bonaparte.* New York: International Publishers, 1963.

———. *Grundrisse.* New York: Vintage Books, 1973.

Matsushita, Hiroschi. *Movimiento obrero argentino, 1930–1945: Sus proyecciones en la história del peronismo.* Buenos Aires: Siglo XX, 1983.

Miedzin, Gustavo, Amelia Peixoto, Alberto Fernandez, and Eduardo Lucita. "Las agrupamientos político-sindicales: un intento de caracterización." *Cuadernos del FISyP* 8 (1988).

Miguens, José E. "Las bases sociales del voto de la Izquierda." *Cambio* 1 (1975): 34-36.

———. "Estabilidad política o inmovilismo social." *Desarrollo Económico* 12 (1973): 923-30.

Miliband, Ralph. *The State in Capitalist Society.* New York: Basic Books, 1969.

Mills, C. Wright. *The Power Elite.* New York: Oxford University Press, 1959.

Ministerio de Trabajo y Seguridad Social, Asociaciones Profesionales de Trabajadores, various decrees and laws since 1945.

Montuschi, Luisa. *El poder económico de los sindicatos.* Buenos Aires: EUDEBA, 1979.

Moore, Barrington, Jr. *Social Origins of Dictatorship and Democracy.* Boston: Beacon, 1966.

Mora y Araujo, Manuel. " La estructura social del peronismo: un análysis electoral inter-provincial." Bariloche: Fundación Bariloche, 1974.

———. "The Nature of the Alfonsín Coalition." In *Elections and Democratization in Latin America, 1980–1985*, ed. Paul Drake and Eduardo Silva. San Diego: University of California Press, 1986.

Mora y Araujo, and Ignacio Llorente, eds. *El voto peronista.* Buenos Aires: Sudamericana, 1980.

Mouzelis, Nicos. "Marxism or Post-Marxism?" *New Left Review* 167 (1988): 107-23.

Munck, Ronaldo. *Argentina: From Anarchism to Peronism.* London: Zed Books, 1987.

———. "Capitalist Restructuring and Labour Recomposition Under a Military Regime: Argentina (1976–1983)." In *Trade Unions and the New Industrialization of the Third World*, ed. Roger Southall. Pittsburgh, Pa.: University of Pittsburgh Press, 1988.

———. "Cycles of Class Struggle and the Making of the Working Class in Argentina, 1890–1920." *Journal of Latin American Studies* 19 (1987): 19-39.

———. *The Difficult Dialogue.* London: Zed Books, 1986.

Murmis, Miguel, and Juan Carlos Portantiero. *Estudios sobre los orígines del Peronismo/1.* Buenos Aires: Siglo Veintiuno Editores, 1972.

Murmis, Miguel. "Tipos de capitalismo y estructura de clases." CICSO paper no. 1. Buenos Aires, 1975.

Navarro Gerassi, Marysa. *Los nacionalistas.* Buenos Aires: Jorge Alvarez, 1968.

North American Congress on Latin America. "Argentina: In the Hour of the Furnaces." New York: NACLA, 1975, pp. 1-105.

Nove, Alec. *The Economics of Feasible Socialism.* London: George Allen and Unwin, 1983.

Nun, José. *Crisis económica y despidos en masa.* Buenos Aires: Editorial Legasa, 1989.

———. "Despidos en la indústria automotriz argentina: estudio de un caso de superpoblación flotante." *Revista Mexicana de Sociología* 40 (1979): 55-106.

———. "Los Sindicatos y el sistema político," round table talk for the Centro Latinoamericano para el Análisis de la Democracia (CLADE), sponsored by Fundación Friedrich Ebert, Buenos Aires, August 1988, unpublished.

Nunca Mas: Informe de la Comisión Nacional sobre la Desaparición de Personas. Buenos Aires: EUDEBA, 1985.

Oddone, Jacinto. *Los socialistas y el movimiento obrero.* Buenos Aires: Ediciónes de la Fundación Juan B. Justo, 1982.

O'Donnell, Guillermo. "Corporatism and the Question of the State." In *Autoritarianism and Corporatism in Latin America*, ed. James Malloy. Pittsburgh, Pa.: University of Pittsburgh Press, 1977.

———. "Modernización y golpes militares: teoría, comparación y el caso argentino." *Desarrrollo Económico* 12 (1972): 519-66.

———. *Modernization and Bureaucratic-Authoritarianism: Studies in South American Politics.* Berkeley, Calif.: Institute of International Studies, 1973.

O'Donnell, Guillermo, and D. Linck. *Dependencia y autonomía.* Buenos Aires: Amorrortu, 1973.

Organization of American States (OAS) *Bulletin*. Various issues.

Orsatti, Alvaro. "La canasta obrera de consumo y su relación con el índice de costo de vida y los salarios." Buenos Aires: CEDEL, 1986.

———. "La nueva distribución funcional del ingreso en la Argentina." *Desarrollo Económico* 23 (1983): 314-37.

———. "Los salarios reales en el ciclo justicialista, 1973–1976." *Justicia Social* 3 (1987): 81-91.

Ortega Peña, R. *La doctrina peronista*. Buenos Aires: Centro Editor, 1971.

Oszlak, Oscar. "Privatización autoritária y recreación de la escena pública." *Crítica y Utopía* 10/11 (1984): 33-49.

Page, Joseph. *Perón: A Biography*. New York: Random House, 1983.

Palomino, Hector. "Argentina: dilemas y perspectivas del movimiento sindical." *Nueva Sociedad* 83 (1986): 89-103.

———. *Cambios ocupacionales y sociales en Argentina, 1947–1985*. Buenos Aires: CISEA, 1987.

———. "Los conflictos laborales: Las dos lógicas de la acción sindical." *El Bimestre* 28 (1986): 22-23.

———. "Los conflictos laborales: Tensión en el sector público." *El Bimestre* 29 (1986): 22-25.

———. "Democracía y autoritarismo en los sindicatos." *Revista de la Fundación Plural* 1 (1985): 38-43.

———. "Efectos políticos y sociales de los cambios en el mercado de trabajo: Argentina, 1950–1983." Buenos Aires: CISEA, 1985.

———. "Elecciones en la UOM, un espejo de la normalización sindical." *El Bimestre* 24 (1985): 2-6.

———. "Las huelgas de cuello blanco." *El Bimestre* 30 (1986): 23-25.

———. "Una imagen cualitativa de los conflictos laborales." *El Bimestre* 27 (1986): 18-21.

———. "El movimiento de democratización sindical." In *Los nuevos movimientos sociales*, ed. Elizabeth Jelin. Buenos Aires: Centro Editor de América Latina, 1985.

———. "El movimiento obrero y sindical en una larga transición." *El Bimestre* 26 (1986): 12-20.

———. "La normalización de la CGT." *El Bimestre* 31 (1987): 5-10.

———. "Normas nuevas y presiones antíguas." *El Bimestre* 38 (1988): 14-16.

Panaia, Marta. *Estudios sobre los orígenes del peronism/2*. Buenos Aires: Siglo XXI, 1973.

———. *Los trabajadores de la construcción*. Buenos Aires: Ediciones IDES, 1985.

Paoli, Maria Celia. "Working-Class São Paulo and its Representations, 1900–1940." *Latin American Perspectives* 14 (1987): 104-25.

Paul, Ellen Frankel. *Marxism and Liberalism*. Oxford: Basil Blackwell, 1986.

Pavón Pereyra, E. *Perón tal como es*. Buenos Aires: Macacha, 1973.

Peña, Milcíades. *Masas, caudillos y elites: La dependencia argentina de Irigoyen a Perón*. Buenos Aires: Ediciones Fichas, 1971.

———. *El peronismo: selección de documentos para la história*. Buenos Aires, Ediciones Fichas, 1973.

Penn, Roger. *Skilled Workers in the Class Structure*. Cambridge: Cambridge University Press, 1985.

Peralta Ramos, Monica. *Acumulación del capital y crisis política en Argentina (1930–1974)*. Mexico City: Siglo XXI, 1978.

———. *Etapas de acumulación y alianzas de clases en Argentina*. Buenos Aires: Siglo XXI, 1972.

———. "Liberation or Dependency?" *Latin American Perspectives* 1 (1974): 82-93.

Peralta Ramos, Monica, and Carlos H. Waisman, eds. *The Transition from Military Rule to Liberal Democracy: The Case of Argentina*. Boulder, Colo.: Westview Press, 1987.

Perelman, Angel. *Cómo hicimos el 17 de octubre*. Buenos Aires: Coyoacán, 1961.

Perón, Juan D. *Apuntes de história militar*. Buenos Aires: Ediciones de la Reconstrucción, 1969.

———. *La comunidad organizada*. Buenos Aires: Club de Lectores, 1949.

———. *La comunidad organizada, Con un apéndice de actualización doctrinaria*. Buenos Aires: Codex, 1974.

———. *La conducción política*. Buenos Aires, 1974.

———. *La fuerza es el derecho de las bestias*. Madrid, 1957.

———. *La hora de los pueblos*. Madrid: Editorial Norte, 1968.

———. *Doctrina peronista*. Buenos Aires: Presidencia de la Nación, 1950.

———. *Del poder al exílio*. Buenos Aires: Ediciones Distribuidora Baires, 1973.

———. *Política y estrategia*. Buenos Aires: Editorial Pleamar, 1973.

———. *El pueblo quiere saber de que se trata*. Buenos Aires: Editorial Freeland, 1973.

———. *El pueblo ya sabe de que se trata*. Buenos Aires: Editorial Freeland, 1973.

———. *Tres revoluciones militares*. Buenos Aires: Editorial Escorpión, 1963.

Perón-Cooke: Correspondencia. 2 vols. Buenos Aires: Granica Editor, 1971.

Piore, Michael J., and Charles F. Sabel. *The Second Industrial Divide*. New York: Basic Books, 1984.

Plan de gobierno, 1947–1951. Vol. 1. Buenos Aires: Presidencia de la Nación, 1946.

Plan trienal para la reconstrucción y la liberación nacional, 1974–1977. Buenos Aires: Poder Ejecutivo Nacional, 1973.

La pobreza en la Argentina: de necesidades básicas insatifechas a partir de los datos del censo nacional de población y vivienda, 1980. Buenos Aires, Estudios INDEC, 1984.

Portantiero, Juan Carlos. "Dominant Classes and Political Crisis." *Latin American Perspectives* 1 (1974): 95-120.

Portes, Alejandro. "Latin American Class Structures: Their Composition and Change during the Last Decades." *Latin American Research Review* 20 (1985): 7-40.

———. "On the Interpretation of Class Consciousness." *American Journal of Sociology* 77 (1971): 228-44.

Potash, Robert. *The Army and Politics in Argentina, 1928–1945: Yrigoyen to Perón*. Stanford, Calif.: Stanford University Press, 1969.

———. *The Army and Politics in Argentina, 1945–1962: Perón to Frondizi*. Stanford, Calif.: Stanford University Press, 1980.

Pozzi, Pablo. "Argentina, 1976–1982: Labour Leadership and Military Government." *Journal of Latin American Studies* 20 (1988): 111-38.

Proyectos del Ministerio de Hacienda. Buenos Aires: Consejo Nacional de Posguerra, 1945.

Przeworski, Adam. *Capitalism and Social Democracy.* Cambridge: Cambridge University Press, 1985.

————. "Proletariat into Class: The Process of Class Formation from Karl Kautsky's 'The Class Struggle' to Recent Controversies." *Politics and Society* 7 (1977): 343-401.

Puiggrós, Rodolfo. *El peronismo: Sus causas.* Buenos Aires: Carlos Pérez Editor, 1971.

————. *Pueblo y oligarquía.* Buenos Aires: Editorial Corregido, 1974.

Ramos, Jorge Abelardo. *La era del bonapartismo.* Vol. 5 of *Revolución y contrarevolución en la Argentina.* Buenos Aires: Editorial Plus Ultra, 1973.

Ranis, Peter. "The Argentine Working Class and Peronism under the New Democratic Regime: A Preliminary Assessment." New York: Bildner Center for Western Hemisphere Studies, 1987.

————. "The Dilemma of Democratization in Argentina." *Current History* 85 (1986): 29-33.

————. "Early Peronism and the Post-Liberal Argentine State." *Journal of Interamerican Studies and World Affairs* 21 (1979): 313-38.

————.. "Peronistas Without Perón." *Society* 10 (1973): 53-59.

————. "View from Below: Working Class Consciousness in Argentina." *Latin American Research Review* 26 (1991): 133-56.

Reich, Wilhelm. *Sex-Pol Essays, 1929–1934.* New York: Random House, 1966.

Reyes, Cipriano. Interview. Buenos Aires: Instituto Torcuato Di Tella Oral History Project, 1971.

Rock, David. *Argentina, 1516–1987: From Spanish Colonization to Alfonsín.* Berkeley and Los Angeles: University of California Press, 1987.

Rock, David, ed. *Argentina in the Twentieth Century.* Pittsburgh, Pa.: University of Pittsburgh Press, 1975.

Romero, José Luís. *El pensamiento político de la derecha latinoamericana.* Buenos Aires: Paidós, 1970.

Romero, Luís Alberto. "Los sectores populares en las ciudades latinoamericanos: La cuestión de la identidad." Buenos Aires: CISEA, 1987.

Roudil, Hector R. *Reflexiones sobre los estatutos de la Confederación General de Trabajo.* Buenos Aires: Fundación Friedrich Ebert, 1988.

Rouquié, Alain, ed. *Argentina, hoy.* Mexico City: Siglo XXI, 1982.

Roxborough, Ian. *Unions and Politics in Mexico: The Case of the Auto Industry.* New York: Cambridge University Press, 1984.

Roxborough, Ian, and Ilan Bizberg. "Union Locals in Mexico: The 'New Unionism' in Steel and Automobiles." *Journal of Latin American Studies* 15 (1983): 117-35.

Sábato, Jorge, and Jorge Schvarzer. "Funcionamiento de la economía y poder político en la Argentina." *Ibero-Americana* 13 (1983): 11-38.

Sabel, Charles. *Work and Politics.* Cambridge: Cambridge University Press, 1982.

Salaman, Graeme. *Working.* London: Tavistock Publishers, 1986.

Samuel, Raphael. "Class Politics; The Lost World of British Communism." *New Left Review* 165 (1987): 52-91.

Schmitter, Philippe C. "Still the Century of Corporatism?" *Review of Politics* 26 (1974): 85-131.

Schrank, Robert. *Ten Thousand Working Days*. Cambridge, Mass.: MIT Press, 1978.

Schumacher, Edward. "Argentina and Democracy." *Foreign Affairs* 62 (1984): 1070-95.

Schumpeter, Joseph A. *Capitalism, Socialism and Democracy*. New York: Harper and Row, 1942.

Schvarzer, Jorge. *Martínez de Hoz: La lógica política de la política económica*. Buenos Aires: CISEA, 1983.

Senén González, Santiago. *Diez años de sindicalismo argentino: de Perón al proceso*. Buenos Aires: Ediciones Corregidor, 1984.

————. *El sindicalismo después de Perón*. Buenos Aires: Editorial Galerna, 1971.

Sercovich, Francisco. "Dependencia tecnológica en la indústria argentina." *Desarrollo Económico* 14 (1974): 33-67.

Sigal, Silvia. *Attitudes Ouvrières en Argentine*. 2 Vols. Paris: Centre D'Etude des Mouvements Sociaux, 1974.

Sigal, Silvia, and Eliseo Verón. *Perón o Muerte: Los fundamentos discursivos del fenómeno peronista*. Buenos Aires: Ediciones Legasa, 1986.

Silberstein, Enrique. *Por qué Perón sigue siendo Perón: La economía peronista*. Buenos Aires: Ediciones Corregidor, 1972.

Silverman, Bertram. "Labor Ideology and Economic Development in the Peronist Epoch." *Studies in Comparative International Development* 4 (1968-69): 243-58.

Sindicatos: Elecciones, 1984–1986. Buenos Aires: Ministerio de Trabajo y Seguridad Social, 1988.

Slodky, Javier. *La negociación colectiva en la Argentina*. Buenos Aires: Puntosur, 1988.

Smith, Peter H. "La base social del peronismo." In *El voto peronista*, ed. Manuel Mora y Araujo and Ignacio Llorente. Buenos Aires: Sudamericana, 1980.

————. *Carne y política en la Argentina*. Buenos Aires: Paidós, 1968.

Smith, William C. *Authoritarianism and the Crisis of the Argentine Political Economy*. Stanford, Calif.: Stanford University Press, 1989.

————. "Democracy, Distributional Conflicts and Macroeconomic Policymaking in Argentina, 1983–1989." *Journal of Interamerican Studies and World Affairs* 32 (1990): 1-42.

Southall, Roger. *Trade Unions and the New Industrialization of the Third World*. Pittsburgh, Pa.: University of Pittsburgh Press, 1988.

Spalding, Hobart A. *Organized Labor in Latin America*. New York: Harper Torchbooks, 1977.

Szelenyi, Ivan. *Socialist Entrepreneurs: Embourgeoisement in Rural Hungary*. Madison: University of Wisconsin Press, 1988.

Taccone, Juan José. *Novecientos días de autogestión en SEGBA*. Buenos Aires, 1977.

Taino, Susan. "Authoritarianism and Political Culture in Argentina and Chile in the Mid-1960s." *Latin American Research Review* 21 (1986): 73-98.

Tamarin, David. *The Argentine Labor Movement, 1930–1945*. Albuquerque, University of New Mexico Press, 1985.

Terkel, Studs. *Hard Times*. New York: Pantheon, 1970.

———. *Working*. New York: Pantheon, 1974.

Terragno, Rodolfo. *Los 400 dias de Perón*. Buenos Aires: Ediciones de la Flor, 1974.

Thompson, E. P. *The Making of the English Working Class*. London: Pelican Books, 1968.

Thompson, Ruth. "The Limitations of Ideology in the Early Argentine Labour Movement: Anarchism in the Trade Unions, 1890–1920." *Journal of Latin American Studies* 16 (1984): 81-99.

Tieffenberg, David. *La legislación obrera en el régimen peronista*. Buenos Aires, 1955.

———. *Sindicatos: ideología y política, teoría y práctica*. Buenos Aires: Ediciones Teoría y Práctica, 1984.

Torrado, Susan. "La familia como unidad de análisis en censos y encuestas de hogares." Buenos Aires: CEUR, 1983.

Torre, Juan Carlos. "Un capítulo en la história del movimiento obrero argentino: la CGT y el 17 de octubre de 1945." New York: NYU Ibero-American Language and Area Center, 1976.

———. "El proceso político interno de los sindicatos argentinos." Buenos Aires: Instituto Torcuato di Tella, 1974.

———. *Los sindicatos en el gobierno, 1973–1976*. Buenos Aires: Centro Editor de América Latina, 1983.

———. "Sindicatos y clase obrera en la Argentina post-peronista." *Revista Latinoamericana de Sociología* 4 (1968): 108-14.

———. "La tasa de sindicalización en Argentina." *Ciencias Administrativas* 15 (1973): 209-21.

———. *La vieja guardia sindical y Perón: Sobre los orígenes del peronismo*. Buenos Aires: Editorial Sudamericana, 1990.

———. "Workers' Struggle and Consciousness." *Latin American Perspectives* 1 (1974): 73-81.

Tucker, Robert C., ed. *The Marx-Engels Reader*. New York: Norton, 1972, 1978.

Turner, Frederick C., and José E. Miguens, eds. *Juan Perón and the Reshaping of Argentina*. Pittsburgh, Pa.: University of Pittsburgh Press, 1983.

Valenzuela, Samuel. "Workers' Movements in Periods of Democratic Transition." *Comparative Politics* 21 (1989): 445-66.

Van Hove, Peter J. "Working Class Crowds and Political Change in Buenos Aires, 1919–1945." Ph.D. diss., University of New Mexico, 1970.

"Los 26 puntos de la unidad nacional: programa de la CGT." *Justicia Social* 2 (1986): 126-30.

Vilas, Carlos. "On the Crisis of Bourgeois Democracy in Argentina." *Latin American Perspectives* 9 (1982): 5-30.

———. "El populismo latinoamericano: un enfoque estructural." *Desarrollo Economico* 28, no. 111 (October–December 1988):323–51.

———. *The Sandinista Revolution: National Liberation and Social Transformation in Central America*. New York: Monthly Review, 1986.

Villar, Daniel. *El cordobazo*. Buenos Aires: Centro Editor de América Latina, 1971.

Villarreal, Juan. *El capitalismo dependiente*. Mexico City: Siglo XXI, 1978.

————. "Los hilos sociales de poder." In *Crisis de la dictadura argentina*, ed. Eduardo Jozami, Pedro Paz, and Juan Villarreal. Buenos Aires: Siglo XXI, 1985.

Waisman, Carlos H. *Modernization and the Working Class: The Politics of Legitimacy.* Austin: University of Texas Press, 1982.

————. *Reversal of Development in Argentina*.Princeton: Princeton University Press, 1987.

Waldman, Peter. "Anomía social y violencia." In *Argentina, hoy*, ed. Alain Rouquié. Mexico City: Siglo XXI, 1982.

Walter, Richard. *The Socialist Party of Argentina, 1890–1930.* Austin: University of Texas Press, 1977.

Wells, Miriam J. "What Is a Worker? The Role of Sharecroppers in Contemporary Class Structure." *Politics and Society* 13 (1984): 295-320.

Winn, Peter. "Oral History and the Factory Study: New Approaches to Labor History." *Latin American Research Review* 14 (1979): 130-40.

————. *Weavers of the Revolution: The Yarur Workers and Chile's Road to Socialism.* New York: Oxford University Press, 1986.

Wright, Erik O. *Class, Crisis and the State.* London: New Left Books, 1978.

————. "A General Framework for the Analysis of Class Studies." *Politics and Society* 13 (1984): 383-424.

Wynia, Gary W. *Argentina: Illusions and Realities.* New York: Holmes and Meier, 1986.

Zaretsky, Eli. *Capitalism, the Family and Personal Life.* New York: Harper and Row, 1986.

Zimbalist, Andrew, ed. *Cuba's Socialist Economy: Toward the 1990s.* Boulder, Colo.: Lynne Rienner, 1987.

Zorrilla, Rubén H. *Estructura y dinámica del sindicalismo argentino.* Buenos Aires: Editorial La Pleyad, 1974.

————. *Intelectuales y sindicatos.* Buenos Aires: Editorial de Belgrano, 1982.

Index

310

Index

Italy: economic system of, 23; immigration to Argentina from, 93, 94; and the Red Brigade, 137

James, Daniel, 24, 102, 178, 187
Justicialismo(Justicialism, "third position"), 23, 33, 64, 81, 82
Khmer Rouge, the, 228
Kinnock, Neil, 176
Konrad, Joseph, 195, 203
Koval y Blanck (metallurgical plant), 13, 78

Labor laws. *See* Law of Professional Associations
Labor movement: history of, 17–22
Labor party: and presidential candidacy of Perón, 20
Labor tribunals: establishment of, 19
Lamadrid, Alejandro F., 259n7
Lanusse, General Alejandro, 31, 198
Latin America: and democratic socialism in Chile, 176; and mass movements, 24; and reactions to events in Eastern Europe, 286n31; rural-to-urban migration in, 94
Law of Economic Emergency, 211
Law of Professional Associations (decree-law 23.852): centralizing tendencies of, 26; collective bargaining and provisions of, 44–45; and the military dictatorship, 38; modifications of, 45–48, 249n2; and unions, 19
Law of Union Restructuring, 60, 62
Lenin, V. I.: on cultural influences on working class, 199; and organized minorities in Russia, 182; revisions of Marx by, 170; and Russian nationalism, 177; and social engineering of Taylor, 202; *What is to be Done?*, 175–76
Light and Power workers. *See* Luz y Fuerza
Loholaberry, Juan Carlos, 274n27
López Rega, José, 35
Luder, Italo, 54, 118, 123
Lukács, Georg, 172–73
Lula (Luis Inácio da Silva), 193
Luxemburg, Rosa, 172, 179, 180, 192

Luz y Fuerza (Federación Argentina de Trabajadores de Luz y Fuerza, light and power workers union), 12; benefits of, 83, 255n30, 256nn34,35; and education, 82; and military interventions, 38; membership in, 80

Malvinas War, 38, 58, 130, 137, 140–41
Management: decision making of, 114–15; workers' complaints about, 104–05, 106
Maoism, 228
Marcuse, Herbert, 172–73, 229
Martínez de Hoz, José, 39
Martínez Estrada, Ezequiel, 24
Marx, Karl: *Capital*, 195; *The Civil War in France*, 171; *Class Struggles in France*, 173; the *Communist Manifesto*, 171, 177, 181, 191; *Contribution to the Critique of Hegel's Philosophy of Right*, 172; *The Economic and Philosophical Manuscripts*, 172, 195; *The 18th Brumaire of Louis Bonaparte*, 169, 173, 195; *The German Ideology* 103, 172, 183, 184, 185, 194; *The Holy Family*, 172; and the industrial laborer, 3, 4; and private property, 194; and study of real workers, 223–24; and support for workers' organizations, 180; and view of the home, 102–03
Marxism, critique of by Perón, 20
MAS (Movement Toward Socialism), 76
Menem, Carlos: 1989 victory of, 121; Peronist government of, 22, 204; popular support for, 217; and privatization of state-run firms, 210, 211, 213; and strike limitations, 211–12
Mensheviks, 204
Mercedes Benz, 71
Mexico, 6, 43, 54, 65
Miguel, Lorenzo: and "62" faction, 59, 60, 226; and 1984 election, 79, 112; and relations with CGT factions, 215
Miliband, Ralph, 203
Military, the: reform of, 271n100; workers' hostility toward, 135–36
Military dictatorship of 1976–83 (El proceso de reorganización nacional): brutality of, 28; as cause of debt crisis, 127–28; as compared to past military